PURCHASED WITH FUNDS FROM
LIBRARY RESOURCES GRANT
#OEG-0-74-4506

D1412432

PROPERTY OF
DEPARTMENT OF POLITICAL SCIENCE
WILKES COLLEGE
WILKES-BARRE, PA. 18703

Land and Population Movements in Kenya

WITHDRAWN

S. H. OMINDE
Professor of Geography
University College
Nairobi

Land and Population Movements in Kenya

EUGENE SHEDDEN FARLEY LIBRARY

1933

WILKES COLLEGE   WILKES-BARRE, PA.

NORTHWESTERN UNIVERSITY PRESS
EVANSTON

HB 2126
K4 O47

Copyright © 1968 by S. H. Ominde

Library of Congress Catalog Card Number 68-9820

Printed in the Republic of Ireland
by Hely Thom Limited Dublin

Employment and Rural Development University College Nairobi 1966

This piece of work is the outcome of invaluable assistance and co-operation by various institutions and individuals whose help I now have the pleasure to acknowledge. I am particularly indebted to the University College Nairobi for financial support in connection with the research and field work and for the use of facilities in the production of the book.

My special thanks are due to the Ministry of Economic Planning and Development for the use of statistics on which the work is based. I am particularly grateful to the former Chief Demographer, Dr. J. G. Blacker, for his inspiration and assistance and to his successor Mr. J. A. Mwaniki who continued the generous assistance.

I wish to offer thanks for the valuable help received from the Department of Geography, University College, Nairobi. My special thanks are due to Messrs. G. D'Souza, L. Rattos of the Cartographic Section, and to Mrs. Mangat and Miss V. Jcrath for their part in the production of the manuscript.

I am particularly indebted to my colleagues, Messrs. R. B. Ogendo, K. G. McVicar, F. F. Ojany, R. S. Odingo and R. A. Bullock for reading the manuscript and for the many helpful suggestions. Finally, my thanks are due to my wife for her constant encouragement in the preparation of the work.

It has been stated that the two principal impediments to a rapid realisation of improved living standards in Kenya are the limited nature of resource base and the inability of the people to utilise efficiently those resources that do exist. In the first instance we are concerned with the limited range that the environment offers as a challenge and in the second place we are concerned with sources of development capital and the requisite skilled manpower. It is well known that no major mineral resources for modern industrial activities have so far been discovered in the country. But in the basic resources of agricultural land, of wild life and of water, the country has an adequate basis which, through careful planning and wise use, can assure the people of the country a much higher standard of living. Through its social and economic policy the Government of Kenya is committed to higher living standards for the whole country.

However, although the wise use of existing resources is of paramount importance to the nation it is becoming increasingly evident that any improvement in the living standards whatsoever is dependent on the relationship between the rate of growth of the population and the rate of growth of the economy as a whole. Analysis of both the recent 1962 population census and the first national census of 1948 suggests a growth rate of 3 per cent per annum. The indications are that this growth rate will continue and may well increase. With an expected population growth rate of 3 per cent and a declining death rate, Kenya is faced with the prospect of about 15 million people by 1980 and about 30 million by the end of the present century. To assure the country of a continued higher standard of living, the economy must grow at a higher rate than the population.

But it is not merely the size of a country's population that is of interest to the student of geography. Perhaps the most critical problem in the present stage of the country's development is mounting unemployment. On the basis of the present rate of growth the Government must prepare policies to absorb an increase of about 965,000 men and women by 1970 together with the 150,000 who were unemployed in 1964[1]. It is hoped that

81-159007

[1]Ray R. S. *The Structure of Employment in Kenya Conference on Education, Employment and Rural Development* University College Nairobi 1966

many of these men will be absorbed on the land through a more intensive use of agricultural opportunities and that the rest will have to be provided for by developments in industry, commerce and the public sector. Such a policy will increasingly rely on a thorough study of population problem areas and in particular on a critical appraisal of the successes and failures of past economic policies on a national basis. Kenya and indeed most parts of Africa lack such detailed regional studies of the relationship between land, population and economic growth.

This work is essentially a study of the dynamic features of Kenya's population, an aspect which for lack of statistics has in the past received little attention. It is the outcome of an interest in the effect of the geography of the country and economic policies on the movement of population and the implications of the movement to planning.

This book falls into three main sections. An introductory chapter traces the evolution of Kenya's boundaries up to the time of the 1962 census. These boundaries and their changes represent an attempt at the organisation of the administrative units within which human movements and economic activities have taken place. For a country with a history such as that, the importance of boundaries in determining differences in the economic development of the country cannot be overlooked. But the study refers to a particular stage in the internal evolution of boundaries, which are still changing. The detailed treatment of the evolution of the boundaries here is intended to show the nature of difficulties that might arise if we attempt to make comparisons with earlier years.

The second section of the book discusses the land and the evolution of the economy of the areas which form the framework for population distribution and mobility. In this section the emphasis is intended to focus attention on the contrast that has developed between the former African areas and that part of the Republic formerly reserved for European settlement. This section covers the important development of urban centres and their industrial features.

The third section which constitutes the main part of the book deals with the general questions on population, its characteristics and distribution. This section falls into three distinct parts. The first part is concerned with the general characteristics of population, which must be understood in order to appreciate subsequent details of the population movements. The second part considers the elements of population movements, the volume, direction and the selective nature of these movements. In the final part a summary is made of the major types of migration as they appear in Kenya, together with their causes and consequences. The basic data for the study is derived from Volumes I and II of the Kenya Population Census 1962 and from post-enumeration 10 per cent Sample Surveys of the age-sex and birthplace data.

However, my primary objective in this detailed study of the dynamics of Kenya's population in relation to the land is to draw attention to the need for increased emphasis on population geography in relation to planning. Informed physical, economic and social planning requires more detailed studies of problem areas. The central role of population discipline provides the population geographer with a special opportunity to participate in an interdisciplinary approach to the study of such problem areas. It is my hope that this study will assist administrators and the public in the assessment and solutions to many of our development problems for which adequate information has hitherto been lacking.

Simeon H. Ominde

Nairobi
January 1968

Land and Population Movements in Kenya

Part One

1 Evolution of the Boundaries of Kenya

1. INTRODUCTION

The Republic of Kenya today covers an area of some 224,960 square miles of which 5,171 square miles is water surface and 219,789 square miles land surface. The shape of the Republic and its extent today is the culmination of a series of international boundary decisions involving the imperial powers of Britain, Germany, France, and Italy in the last decades of the nineteenth and the early part of the twentieth century. In the evolution of its boundaries and problems arising from these, Kenya is a striking example of similar states which developed directly from the expansionist activities of the imperial powers. Its pattern of economic development and population problems have been largely influenced by its geography and in particular its location on the diverse highland area and its projection into the arid corridor that separates the Ethiopian massifs and related East African highlands.

2. EVOLUTION OF INTERNATIONAL BOUNDARIES

The beginnings of the boundaries of modern Kenya can be traced back to the Anglo-German Agreement of October-November 1886 which first established the boundary that separates the mainland portion of Tanzania from the Republic of Kenya. The Agreement attempted to settle the question of the coastal limits of the spheres of influence, but also to a very large extent the direction of expansion into the interior. By this agreement, the territory between the Rivers Ruvuma and Tana was divided by a line running westwards from River Umba to Lake Victoria leaving the northern area under British and the southern portion under German influence.[1]

But the trend of the boundary into the interior suggests another major concern of the imperial powers. To both the British and the Germans the coastal foothold was meaningless unless it was conceived as a stage in the eventual control of interior and its trade potential. The British economic interests nursed by the British East Africa Association were consolidated in the area by the formation of the British East African Chartered Company in 1888. This interest was not confined merely to the control of the interior trade and its abundant manpower. The question of possible European permanent settlement in the central Highlands of Kenya was an early attraction. Further, it should be noted that the Anglo-German agreement of 1886 merely established the initial coast to interior division of interest in an area where the imperial powers were still trying to outbid one another. The western, northern, and eastern boundaries evolved gradually.

The second milestone in the organisation of the international boundaries of Kenya was in 1891 when the first of the Anglo-Italian Agreements gave recognition to the claims of Italy to protectorate status over Ethiopia and hence sealed off any possible expansion of the British sphere of interest beyond the desert wastelands of northern and north-eastern Kenya. This agreement however was no more than a statement of claim. The Gallas and some other pastoral groups continued to raid further south. It was only after a long negotiation that the northern boundary line between Lake Rudolf and River Juba was signed at Addis Ababa on 6 December 1907. The frontier delineation carried out by an Anglo-Abyssinian Commission assigned Lake Rudolf to the British and Lake Stefanie to Abyssinia[2]. A further adjustment was finalised in 1947.

In the meantime an agreement had been reached in August 1899 with the Royal Italian Government over the eastern boundary. On the basis of this, it was agreed to limit the Italian sphere of influence to the east and north of River Juba[3]. But the boundary imposed on one of the most sensitive parts of the country took its present form with the transfer of most of Jubaland Province east of the forty-first meridian to Somaliland in 1925. From these developments, it seems that the earliest of the international boundaries to be demarcated were those settling the specific areas of interest of the imperial powers. The early interest in these boundaries was primarily prompted by strategic consideration. In their demarcation they established the area within which the modern state of Kenya has evolved.

The late demarcation of the western boundary which marks the third stage is perhaps one of the most important changes in the evolution of international boundaries. A

[1]Oliver R. & Matthew G. *History of East Africa* Vol. I Clarendon Press, Oxford 1963

[2]Ward F. & Milligan J. W. *Handbook of East Africa* 1912

[3]McDermott P. J. *British East Africa* p. 97 Chapman and Hall, London 1893

number of factors both economic and strategic were important in these changes which covered the first three decades of the present century. The first and perhaps the most important of these was the early preoccupation of the British East Africa Company with the populous Lake shore areas and more particularly with Buganda[4]. At a time when apart from the knowledge of population and climate little was known of the real agricultural potential, the drive to Uganda would appear to have been based on hopes of securing markets and on the possibilities of development of the resources of the interior.

The declaration of a British Protectorate on 1 July 1895 and the subsequent definition of the boundaries of this protectorate by a proclamation on 31 August 1896 mark the first important step in the evolution of the present international boundary in the west[5]. The alignment of the first western boundary was definitely influenced by topographical details of central Kenya. It closely followed the trend of the eastern wall of the Rift Valley from just north of Lake Rudolf to the Anglo-German boundary in the south (Figure 1.1)[6]. As a result of this boundary definition the greater part of the area west of the new protectorate was included in the Eastern Province of Uganda Protectorate. In fact the area just to the west of Yala River and north of Kabras in western Kenya was part of the Central Province of Uganda of which Buganda formed a part[7]. Geographically it is important to note that the original nucleus of the present Republic was a much poorer country. Little was known of the interior islands of the better watered core and well populated country that now forms the base of Kiambu, Muranga, Kirinyaga, Embu and Meru.

The extension of the boundary of the Protectorate westwards to Lake Victoria basin thus greatly increased the potentials of the new protectorate. It was the outcome of the interplay of a complex set of forces. From the economic standpoint it marked the realisation of an objective which had for some time strengthened the Company's interest in controlling Uganda. But far more important, it provided the potential in land and human resources on which much of the development of modern Kenya has been based. It brought to the protectorate with its meagre population and limited agricultural area, the fertile highlands of the Nakuru-Naivasha area, the

west rift highlands and the well populated Lake Basin which Thompson (1883–4) had earlier visited. Little development had taken place in this unstable area before the transfer. The Entebbe administration which controlled the area was more preoccupied with Buganda and the area further west. The shortage of manpower and the undeveloped nature of the area accounted for much of the administrative neglect and greater interest in Buganda.

But quite apart from the problems of the Entebbe administration, the need for security of the rail construction and its early completion was causing concern. The construction of the railway line was threatened by frequent attacks arising from the growing fighting power of the Nandi. There were also frequent clashes between the Nandi and the surrounding ethnic groups[8].

Fearn[9] has suggested that the existence of the potential area of European settlement was an important factor in the transfer. This area was at the time sparsely occupied following a series of clashes and cattle plagues among the pastoral populations of the highlands. The transfer of the area to the East African Protectorate was formally approved by the Foreign Office on 5 March 1902 under the title 'Kisumu and Naivasha Provinces'. The final delineation was approved on 8 July 1902. However, unlike the first western boundary of the Protectorate there were no obvious landmarks to act as a guide. When it was eventually marked, it created the artificial division of homogeneous ethnic groups which has continued as a criticism to the present day. Further north, the last adjustment along the western portion of the Republic was in the Turkana area to the north-west. By transfer of Karasuk and the area further north-west to Kenya (Figure 1.2) the present shape of the Republic took its final form[10].

[4]Oliver R. & Matthew G. *History of East Africa* Vol. I Clarendon Press, Oxford 1963
[5]*Colonial Annual Report 1927: Colony and Protectorate of Kenya* pp. 4–15
[6]*Kenya: Report of the Regional Boundaries Commission* Appendix VI Map 1 Cmnd 1899 H.M.S.O., London 1962. Note that the full page maps in Figures 1.3 to 1.8 all come from this source where they are numbered Maps 1 to 7
[7]Johnston H. *Uganda Protectorate* Vol. I Hutchinson, London 1902
[8]Matson A. T. 'Uganda's Old Eastern Provinces and East Africa's Federal Capital' pp. 43–53 *Uganda Journal* Vol. 22 No. 1 March 1958
[9]Fearn H. *An African Economy* Oxford University Press, London 1961
[10]*Atlas of Uganda: Lands and Surveys* Uganda 1962

Figure 1.1

EVOLUTION OF THE BOUNDARIES OF KENYA/3

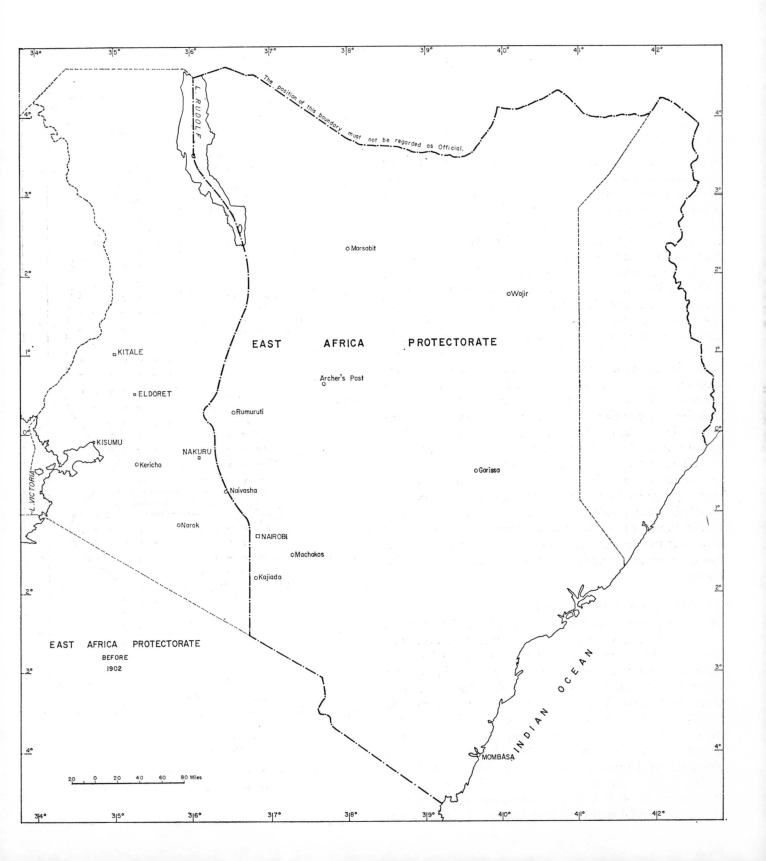

3. EVOLUTION OF INTERNAL BOUNDARIES UP TO 1962 (*Figures 1.3–1.8*)

With continuing pressure on the government for boundary alterations it is worthwhile giving a close attention to the principles that have influenced the organisation of the administrative boundaries within the country. However, a closer examination of the problem of internal boundaries has a much deeper relevance to the study of population movements. It is to serve as an introduction to the genesis of the units which form the framework of population mobility. We have considered the evolution of the international boundary of Kenya and noted the beginnings of the process in the scramble for the continent. We have also noted that the process was virtually completed in about two decades. However, it is necessary to stress that while the underlying forces in the evolution of the international boundaries were economic and strategic the evolution of internal boundaries appears to suggest an unstable compromise of a number of factors. The organisation of the internal boundaries required more than just the strategic interests and economic potentials.

Administrative boundaries are in essence just one aspect of spatial organisation. They may be influenced in varying degrees by a number of important factors such as ethnic homogeneity, economic organisation, political consideration or administrative convenience. We may now examine the influence of these factors in the internal evolution of the boundaries up to the time of the 1962 census.

The Old Protectorate 1895 (*Figure 1.1*)

We have referred to the fact that Kenya began as a coast-based interest and that its geographical evolution resembles that of many similar states established by the colonial powers during the scramble for Africa. This original coast-based nucleus consisted of the three provinces of Seyidie, Tanaland, Jubaland, and Ukambani. Seyidie, the best known at that time included the land between the Tana River delta and the Anglo-German boundary. The Tanaland Province embraced the land on either side of the river whose economic potential had been earlier realised. But the rest of the interior from Seyidie Province to the Rift Valley formed Ukambani Province. It may be argued that the ethnic factor had already been

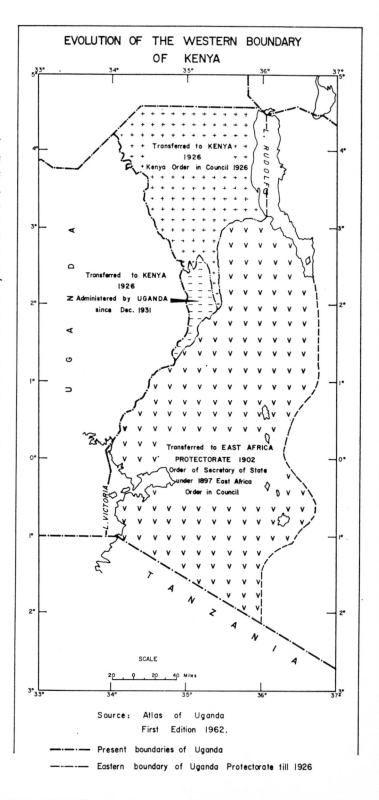

EVOLUTION OF THE WESTERN BOUNDARY OF KENYA

Source: Atlas of Uganda
First Edition 1962.

—·—·— Present boundaries of Uganda

—·—·— Eastern boundary of Uganda Protectorate till 1926

noted in the delimitation of Ukambani. However, it would appear that the inclusion of an area embracing more than three distinct ethnic elements is indicative of the arbitrary nature of the boundaries. Administrative convenience appears to have been more important.

In the district sub-division the units that emerged were named after the most important settlements. Thus Seyidie was sub-divided into Vanga, Malindi, and Mombasa, representing the important settlements along the coast from which the areas could be administered. River Tana formed a convenient geographical unit which gave name to Tanaland Province. It was divided into the districts of Tana River and the more northerly district of Lamu. The rest of the Province consisted of Witu Sultanate and the Kiunga sub-district in the north. Lamu then was not a coast-based district.

The New Protectorate 1909[11] (*Figure 1.3*)
With the transfer of part of Uganda to the East African Protectorate the territory took a new shape and at the same time presented fresh problems of administrative organisation. The rapidly expanding frontier had moved faster towards the west but remained relatively static in the semi-arid and arid northern half of the country. The important objective of reaching the populous Lake Victoria shore had been achieved and three new provinces were created in the area cut off from Uganda.

Part of the Old Ukambani Province was excised to form the new 'Kenia' Province embracing what were in 1961 parts of Fort Hall, Nyeri, Embu, Meru and Isiolo. Here again the subdivisions of the new province suggest the administrative convenience as the main consideration. The districts largely took their names from the most important settlements. The remainder of Ukambani included Kikuyu district (part of modern Kiambu) and most of the former Kajiado district as well as the two Kamba districts of Ulu (Machakos) and Kitui.

In the extreme west the Nyanza Province newly transferred from Uganda, roughly covered the Lake Victoria drainage area and was sub-divided into the districts of Nandi Reserve, Elgon, Kisumu, Ugaya and Lumbwa. The new province thus covered a substantial part of what is now Narok district including the settlement of Narok. Naivasha Province situated between Kenia and Nyanza

Provinces and to the south of the little known northern area was subdivided into the districts of Nandi, Baringo, Ravine, Laikipia, and Naivasha.

The evolution of administrative boundaries thus became complete first in that part of the country in which the greater portion of the country's population was concentrated. However, in considering the new administrative units it would appear that they represented areas of distinct potential. Seyidie was based in the coast rainfall region, Tanaland was clearly a riverine province and 'Kenia' covered most of the highland areas east of the Rift Valley. Ukambani was probably the poorest covering an area of low potential between the coast and the highlands.

The creation of Naivasha province brought together lands that were becoming a focus of active European settlement. It is likely for the same reason that the southern portion of Kikuyu land was included with Ulu Province in which there had been some early alienation of land. Nyanza in the extreme west was based on the potential resources of the Lake Victoria basin. To the north of the well populated part of the country lay the unstable frontier about which little was known. Before 1909 much of this area was superficially controlled from Naivasha. Marsabit, Garba Tula and Archers Post were established in 1901[12]. The new district then consisted of Marsabit, Moyale, Gurreh (Mandera), Wajir, Garba Tula, and Archers Post stations. The area became the Northern Frontier District in 1910 with headquarters at Meru following the conclusion of the Anglo-Abyssinia Border Commission. In 1911, the area between River Turkwell and the old East African Protectorate boundary had been added from Uganda.

The growing knowledge about this vast area, following a series of military expeditions, led to the transfer of headquarters from Meru to Isiolo just a little to the north of Meru. This move brings to light an important feature in the integration of the area with the more populated parts of the country. In its history, it should be noted that the administrative centre has never been located far from the main areas of settlement which constitute the wetter

[11]*Kenya: Report of the Regional Boundaries Commission* Cmnd 1899 Appendix VI Map 2 1962
[12]*Kenya: N.F.D. Miscellaneous Report* 1915–23

Figure 1.3

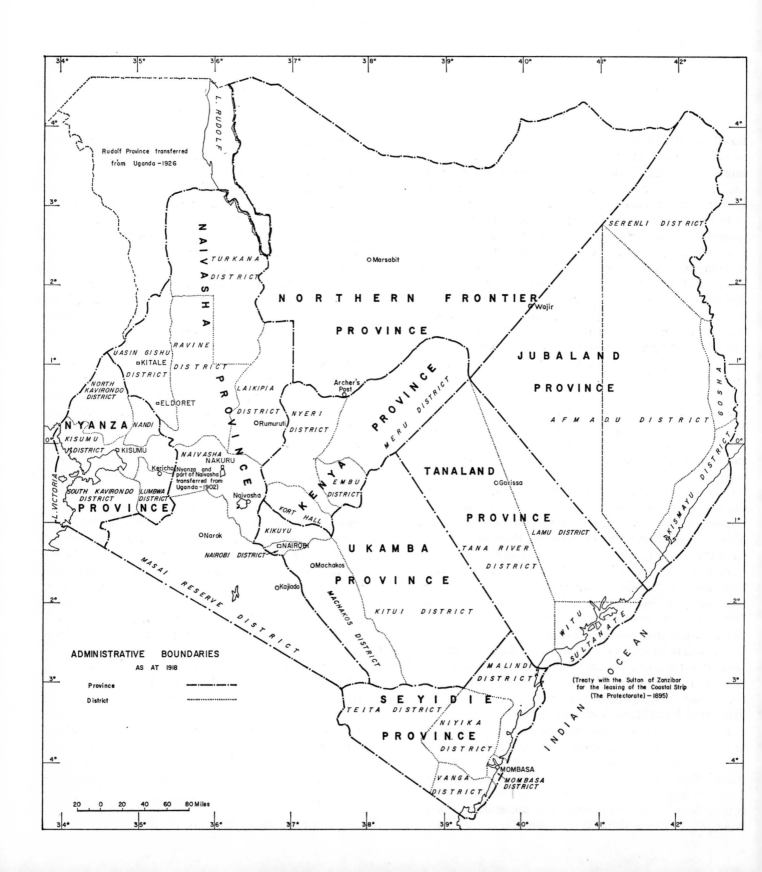

and the southern half of the country. The completion of district boundaries of the new Protectorate clearly show the dominant influence of the ethnic complexity of the areas. Quite early names such as Taita, Masailand, Kikuyu District, Laikipia, Naivasha, Baringo, Nandi, and Lumbwa appear.

The Protectorate 1918[13] (Figure 1.4)

Internal boundaries of the Protectorate at this period show important changes in the Province of Nyanza, Naivasha, and 'Kenia'. The Nyanza Province of 1909 is at this time reduced by the excision of the greater part of the old Lumbwa district. The area cut off together with the old Masailand district were combined to form the new Masai Reserve District. Further east the old Naivasha district lost the southern part of the Nandi Reserve which retained the name of Nandi district as part of a reduced Province. The remainder of the old Nandi Reserve and the old Nandi District were combined to form the Uasin Gishu District, which extended into the less known area of the north. The Naivasha Province had greatly increased in size by the addition of Masai Reserve District in the south and the addition of the Turkana District in the north. With the exception of the Rudolf Province and part of Samburu, the Naivasha Province had come close to the concept of the Rift Valley Province as we know it today.

Important changes in the area affecting the 'Kenia' Province had taken place. The addition of the new Nyeri District had greatly enlarged the Kenia Province. Internally, Fort Hall was much reduced in area by the extension of Nyeri district corridor to the boundary of Ukambani Province. The rest of what was later to evolve into the modern Central Province was divided into the new Embu and Meru Districts. In the south of 'Kenia' Province, Kikuyu District which formed part of the Ukambani appeared as a reduced unit with the creation of separate Nairobi District. Over the remainder of Ukambani Province, Ulu District had changed its name to Machakos. Jubaland Province in the extreme east had been divided into the three districts of Serenli, Afmadu, and Kismayu. In the south-west, Tanaland and Seyidie Provinces remained relatively unchanged. Summarising the changes it will be noted that the districts continued to

be organised largely on the basis of Kenya's main ethnic groups. New names such as Kavirondo, Uasin Gishu and Turkana emerged in addition to those that had appeared on the map.

The Colony and Protectorate 1924[14] (Figure 1.5)

The internal administrative organisation of the country according to proclamation No. 54 of 1924 reflects the emphasis that was now laid on the settled districts and urban areas as opposed to the predominantly African districts. In Nyanza Province, Kisumu township, the sugar area of Miwani, and the outpost of the settled area in the hills overlooking Nyando Valley up to Londiani were separated and designated Extra-Provincial District. Further east, the former Naivasha Province which had extended from the nomadic lands of Turkana to the similar pastoral Province of Masai in the south, was broken up in the formation of the new Extra-Provincial districts. Except for Turkana, the settlement districts of Trans-Nzoia, Uasin Gishu, Nakuru, Laikipia, Naivasha and Nairobi were all similarly designated and a separate administrative authority created for them. The African districts were placed under the chief Native Commissioner. This began the dual approach to development which continued to affect Kenya right up to the eve of independence period.

East of Naivasha Province North Nyeri, where settlement had developed, was separated from the predominantly African districts of Meru, Embu, Fort Hall, South Nyeri and Kiambu. Ukambani Province was for the first time enlarged to include Taita District. The Coast Province replaced Seyidie Province. However, the new province though it had lost Taita District gained in area by the inclusion of that part of Tanaland Province lying south of River Tana as well as Lamu and Witu Sultanate. Vanga District assumed the name of Digo, underlining the interest in ethnic factors. In the extreme east the reduced Jubaland Province is shown as generally lying east of the forty-first meridian.

In 1924 Proclamation of boundaries established the

[13]*Kenya: Report of the Regional Boundaries Commission* Cmnd 1899 Appendix VI Map 3 1962

[14]*Kenya: Report of the Regional Boundaries Commission* Cmnd 1899 Appendix VI Map 3 1962

Figure 1.4

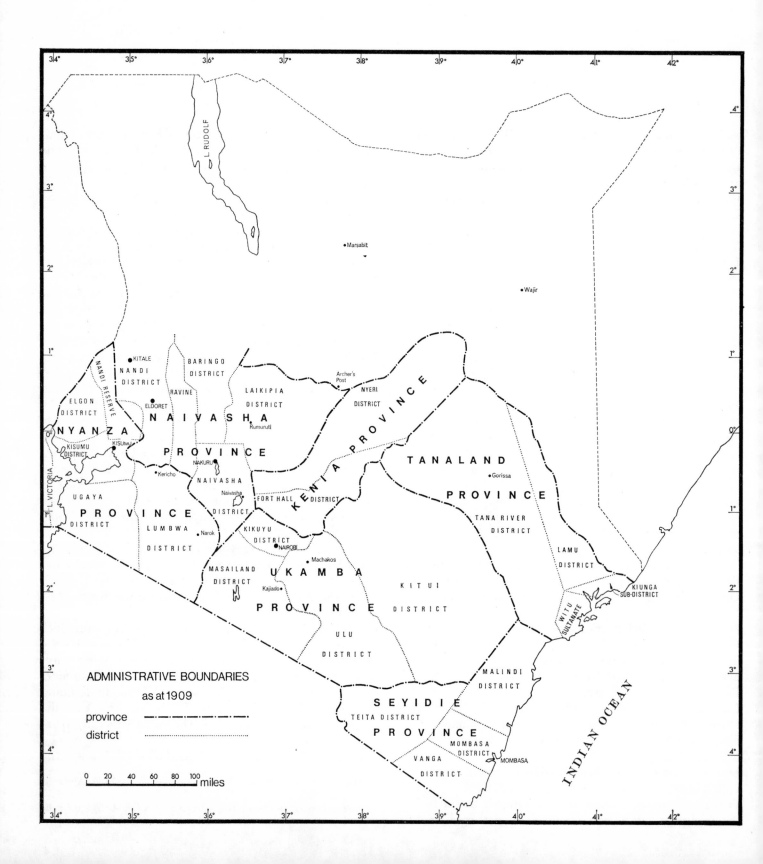

ADMINISTRATIVE BOUNDARIES

as at 1909

province ▬ · ▬ · ▬ · ▬ · ▬

district ·············

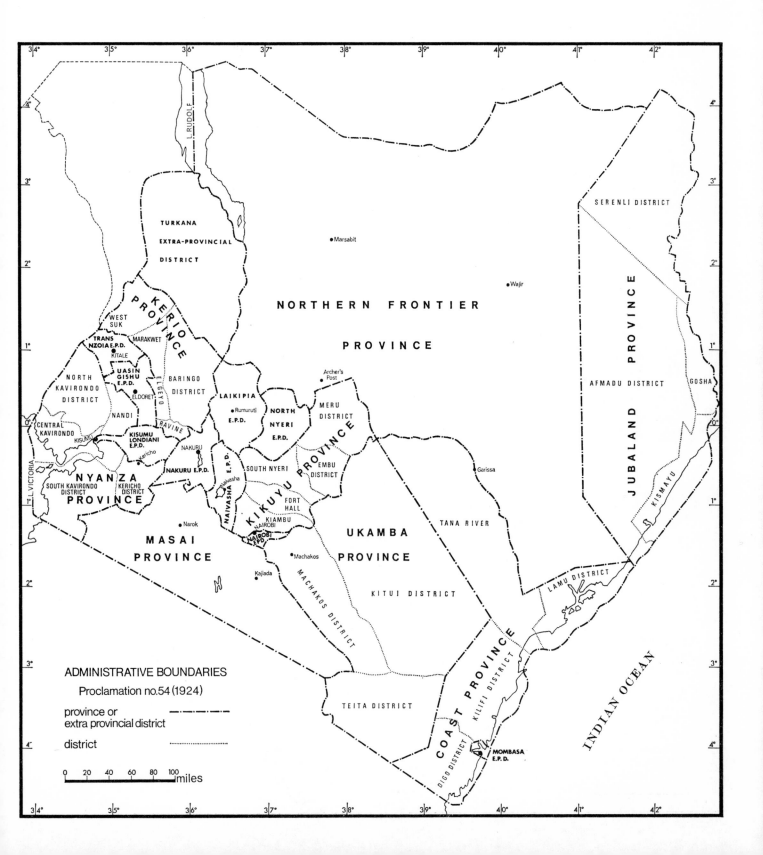

ADMINISTRATIVE BOUNDARIES

Proclamation no.54 (1924)

province or
extra provincial district

district

Figure 1.6

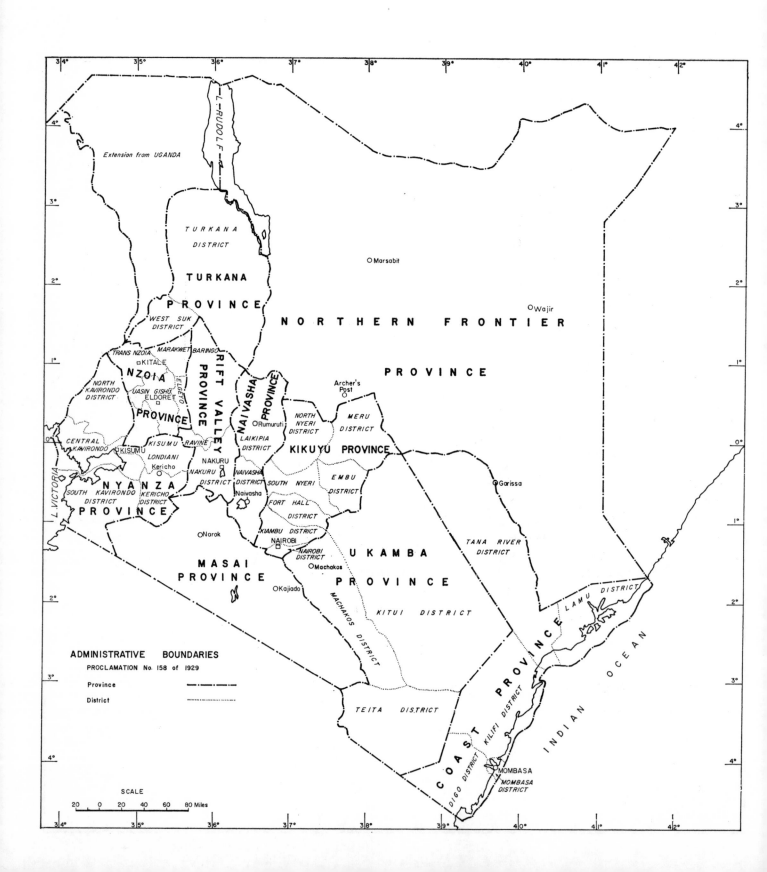

ADMINISTRATIVE   BOUNDARIES

PROCLAMATION No. 158 of 1929

Province ————————

District ························

district units which have continued to appear on the administrative maps to the present day. In summary it is necessary to stress that it aimed at normalising the difference in land policy which the rapid advance of settlement in post-war Kenya had created. Far more important the two distinct districts further represented areas in which different economic policies towards the utilization of the land were to be pursued.

The Colony and Protectorate 1929[15] *(Figure 1.6)*

For the first time the external boundaries of the Republic as we know it today appear in the Proclamation No. 158 of 1929. By these changes we see a further attempt to reorganise the administrative units of the areas between the Kikuyu and Nyanza Provinces. The Turkana Province appeared including Turkana and West Suk Districts. The old Kerio Province, which included the Extra-Provincial districts of Trans-Nzoia, Uasin Gishu and the predominantly African districts of Elgeyo-Marakwet, Maringo and Ravine, was sub-divided into an enlarged Nzoia Province including Trans-Nzoia, Marakwet, Elgeyo and Nandi and further east, the Rift Valley Province which appeared for the first time including Baringo and Ravine and Nakuru District. The Naivasha and Laikipia, Extra-Provincial districts were amalgamated to form the Naivasha Province. Further east, the settled North Nyeri district once more was added to the Kikuyu Province. In the south Ukamba Province remained unaltered with Taita District still included in the Province.

In the extreme west, Nyanza Province had been reduced by the excision of the Nandi District thus establishing a move to include the Kalenjin-speaking group together. The Coast Province remained as it was in 1924. But on the eastern border, Jubaland had been ceded to Italy. In the extreme north-west, the area of the Colony and Protectorate had been increased by addition of the area lying between Lake Rudolf, Turkana Province and the Uganda border.

Kenya Colony and Protectorate 1933[16] *(Figures 1.7)*

The evolution of modern administration and the attempt to define boundaries on an ethnically complex area naturally raised considerable boundary disputes. This had been aggravated by the progress of alienation of land and

in the west the development of mining. These two factors greatly contributed towards the boundary consciousness among the population of Kenya. The boundary outlines of 1933 as indicated by the Proclamation No. 109 of 1933 formed the background against which the Carter Land Commission worked.[17] The most important change was the amalgamation of the previous ten provinces into the four large provinces of Nyanza, Rift Valley, Central and Coast in addition to the provincial districts of Turkana and Northern Frontier.

According to this map we see that the Rift Valley had greatly increased in size but excluded the predominantly pastoral areas of Masai and Turkana in the north. For the first time the former settled districts and the African districts in the area came under a single Provincial control. Again for the first time the related Kikuyu and Kamba ethnic groups were brought together under a much enlarged Central Province which included the Nairobi District. Along the Coast, Taita District had been combined with the Coast Province, a relationship that has continued to the present. The amalgamation of provincial units into larger ones was probably largely dictated by the need for economy during a period of economic difficulties.

Kenya 1961 *(Figure 1.8)*

In 1961, the boundaries of what came to be the Republic of Kenya reflect yet a further change, this time affecting the Masai, Extra-Provincial District and the Central Province. The main changes were the inclusion of the two Kamba districts of Kitui and Machakos. On ethnic grounds it would appear that this was an attempt by the colonial government to complete the isolation of the Kikuyu areas and related Embu and Meru groups. The area of the Northern Province was enlarged by inclusion of part of the country in the Tana River bend to the south-west of Garissa in the province which reduced the area to the Coast Province.

The internal boundaries of Kenya before the 1962 boundary revision thus reflected the cumulative effect of

[15]*Kenya: Proclamation Rules and Regulations* Vol VIII Proclamation No. 158 1929, 1930
[16]*Kenya: Proclamation Rules and Regulations* Vol. XII 1933, 1934
[17]*Kenya: Kenya Land Commission Report* Government Printer, Nairobi 1933

Figure 1.7

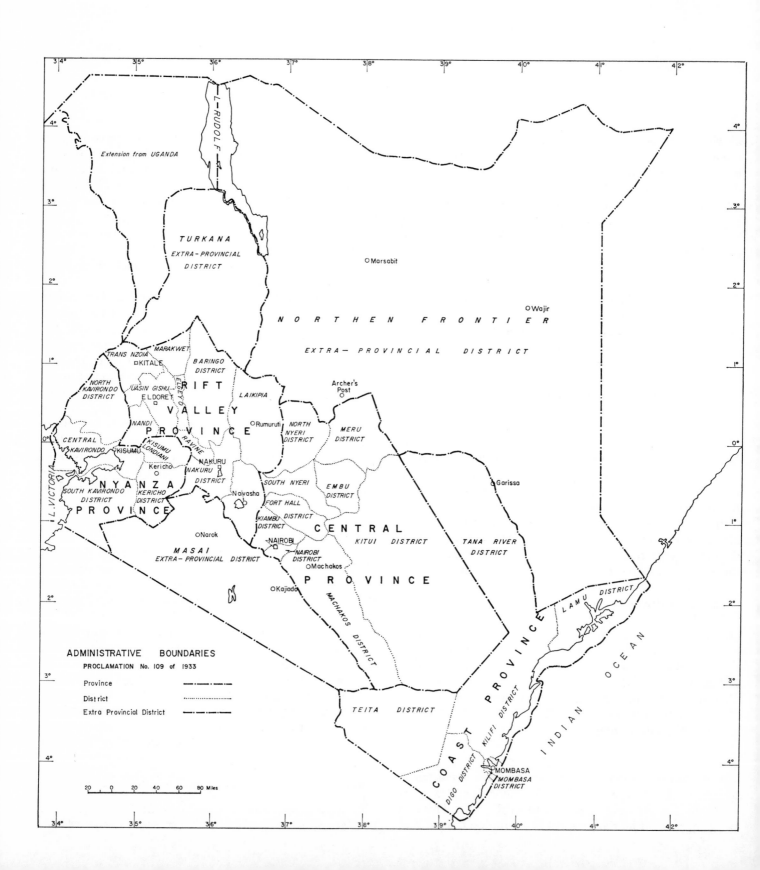

Figure 1.8

EVOLUTION OF THE BOUNDARIES OF KENYA/13

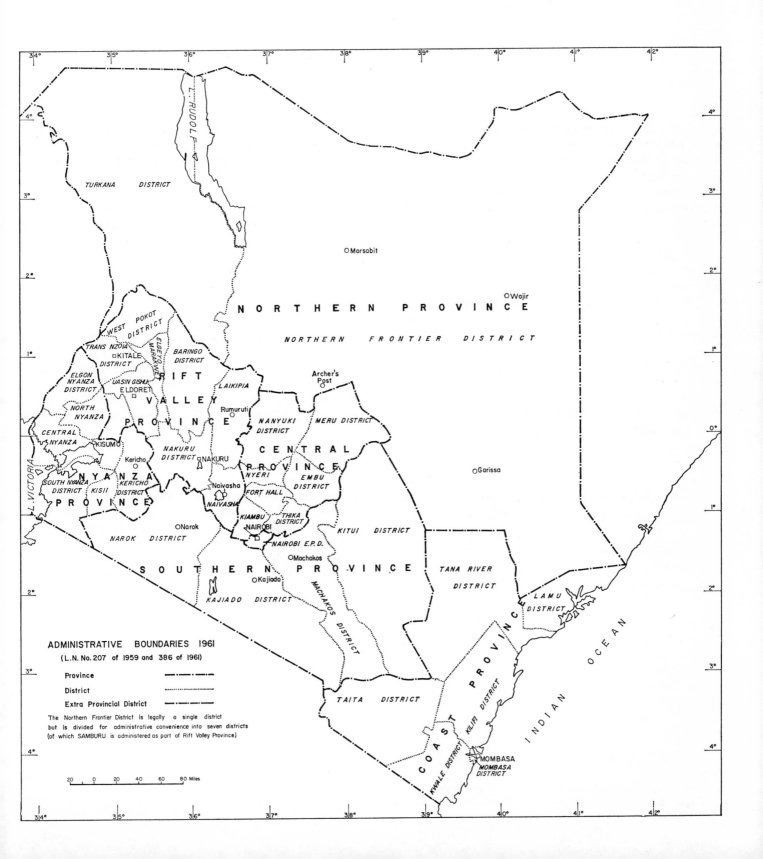

ADMINISTRATIVE BOUNDARIES 1961
(L.N. No. 207 of 1959 and 386 of 1961)

Province	
District	
Extra Provincial District	

The Northern Frontier District is legally a single district
but is divided for administrative convenience into seven districts
(of which SAMBURU is administered as part of Rift Valley Province)

20 0 20 40 60 80 Miles

the conflicting interests of the ethnic identity, the earlier land policies and political consideration. The relative stability of the Nyanza boundaries and that of the highland districts of Kikuyu to the north of Nairobi need to be stressed. The combined Southern Province was largely a reflection of the dominant attitude which followed the resistance movement of 1952–55.

The Regional Constitution Boundaries[18]
Before leaving the subject of internal boundaries it is necessary to touch on the nature of the new boundaries and the implication of the changes. The Regional Constitution which established the new boundaries was a unique step in the history of boundary evolution. The sentiments which were finally expressed in terms of actual boundaries had already been aired at the Constitutional Conference before the establishment of the Boundaries Commission. According to the agreement reached at the Constitutional Conference the Commission was set up in July 1962 with the following terms of reference.[19]

'To divide Kenya into six regions and the Nairobi area for the purposes of giving effect to the Report of the Kenya Constitutional Conference 1962 and in particular to Appendix II of that Report (Framework of the Kenya Constitution) paying particular attention to:

(*a*) The existing boundaries of the Provinces and the Nairobi Extra-Provincial District; and

(*b*) The wishes of the people in any locality to be included in any particular Region or the Nairobi area.'

For the first time in the history of the boundary changes the wishes of the people as a principle was given explicit recognition. The existing boundaries were to be examined in the light of the desire of the inhabitants. Thus the work of the Commission brought into prominence the importance of the population diversity in the demarcation of administrative boundaries. In the reduced Nyanza, the Commission set about separating the areas of claim of the

three main ethnic groups. It will be noted later that, in the West Central portion of the country, the much enlarged Rift Valley Province covered largely the north to south belt of Kalenjin-speaking group and the region that had been settled by Europeans.

In the central part of the country the Central Province had once more increased its area by addition of Nyandarua and the Kirinyaga (formerly part of Embu). The Northern Frontier Province appeared to reflect the division of opinion between the Galla-speaking group of the western half and the Somali groups in the eastern half of the Province.[20]

The western Galla-speaking groups found themselves merged with the Kamba, Embu, and Meru in the new Eastern Province which rivalled the Rift Valley in area. Further east, the Somali speaking groups were combined to form the present North-Eastern Province. In the southeast, the Coast Province once more assumed its former shape by addition of the Tana River bend area which had earlier been part of the Northern Frontier Province.

These changes in boundaries reflect a conscious attempt to organise the physical and human resources to meet specific needs. But within these boundaries of the Republic of Kenya there are distinct regions which from the earliest times of settlement have presented different problems to the utilization of resources. It is these regions and the nature of their resource bases that we need to examine as a background to development of the economy and population distributions, as well as the movements that are consequent upon the development.

[18]*Kenya: Report of the Regional Boundaries Commission* Cmnd 1899 Schedule A (ii) 1962

[19]*Kenya: Kenya Constitutional Conference 1962* Cmnd 1700, 1962

[20]*Kenya: Report of the Northern Frontier District Commission* Cmnd 1900 pp. 11–19, 1962

Part Two The Land
and Development
of the Economy

2 Major Geographical Divisions

Geographically Kenya may be conveniently divided into five broad regional divisions (Figure 2.1).

1. The Lake Victoria basin
2. The Central rift and associated highlands
3. The eastern plateau foreland
4. The Coast Region
5a/b The Semi-arid Northern, North-eastern and Southern Kenya

It will be seen that these regions do not coincide with the administrative divisions, which have changed over the years. But the nature of relationship between their resource base and the needs of the population of these areas is an important background to an appreciation of population movements.

1. THE LAKE VICTORIA BASIN

This is part of a well-watered lacustrine environment which extends into Uganda and Tanzania. On the Kenya side it embraces the plateau country sloping westwards from the highlands that border the central rift of Kenya. This plateau country is further sub-divided into two parts north and south of the gulf by the minor east-west rift of Nyanza.

Among the distinctive contrasts is a rainfall pattern varying from about 40 inches in the hotter areas around the Lake shore to well over 70 inches in the highland areas of the eastern portions. The Lake shore areas show a minimum expectation of about 20 to 35 inches in nineteen years out of twenty and present different problems of land use to people in comparison with the higher and wetter areas where the minimum expectation is 45 inches or more in nineteen years out of twenty. The potential of the land is reflected in the ecological contrast between the Lake Shore Savannah, the intermediate High Rainfall Savannah and the richer Kikuyu Star Grass areas which enjoy higher and more reliable rainfall.

It will be noted that there are important cultural differences between the populations of the lower areas generally lying between 4,500 feet and 3,700 feet above sea level and areas above 5,000 feet. A description of the early settlement which will follow shows that the lower areas generally deficient in rainfall are largely populated by the southern members of the Nilotic linguistic group whereas the higher areas seem to be more dominated by the Bantu-speaking elements in the area north and south of the gulf.

The distribution of high potential land will show that most of it is to be found in the better watered areas either underlain by soils derived from the recent volcanics or volcanics from pre-Cambrian period. Special mention should be made of the fertile highlands of Kisii, Kericho, Mount Elgon and parts of the former North Nyanza District. These areas are in marked contrast to the lower lake shore areas which though very fertile in parts suffer from flood damage during the main rainy period from March to April. During this period large rivers such as Nyando fail to contain flood waters over the flatter portion of the Kano Plains. Similar flooding characterises the lower courses of other large rivers such as Sondu-Miriu, Yala, and Nzoia.

The location of mineral resources and the distribution of tsetse fly are two environmental factors which have in varying degrees influenced population movements in the region. Unlike most parts of Kenya the Lake Victoria basin has always played an important part in the production of minerals. These minerals are found in the region of pre-Cambrian rocks which surround the lake area. The most important of these have been gold and copper. More recently other mineralised areas have been discovered in association with the denuded volcanic centres of South Nyanza. However it will be shown that the few minerals that have been discovered, though important in terms of revenue, have not had a wider regional effect on population movements.

The situation is different in the case of tsetse fly which has exercised a more widespread influence in the region. It has been shown that by 1953, approximately ten per cent of the Republic was subject to infestation with the fly.[1] But actual incidence is largely confined to the shores of Lake Victoria and the lower parts of the river basins that enter the lake. In the lake basin, the infestation has been largely of the lake side and riverside species of tsetse fly. At the turn of the century, the thicket country around the lake shore and the wooded banks of the rivers in this area became the home of several species of *Glossina*, vectors of animal and human forms of *trypanosomiasis*.

[1]*East Africa: Report of the Royal Commission* 1953–5 Cmnd 9475 p. 256 para. 12 H.M.S.O. London

Figure 2.1

MAJOR GEOGRAPHICAL DIVISIONS/17

1. Lake Victoria basin
2. The Central Rift and associated highlands
3. The eastern plateau foreland
4. The coast
5a/b The semi-arid and arid northern and southern Kenya

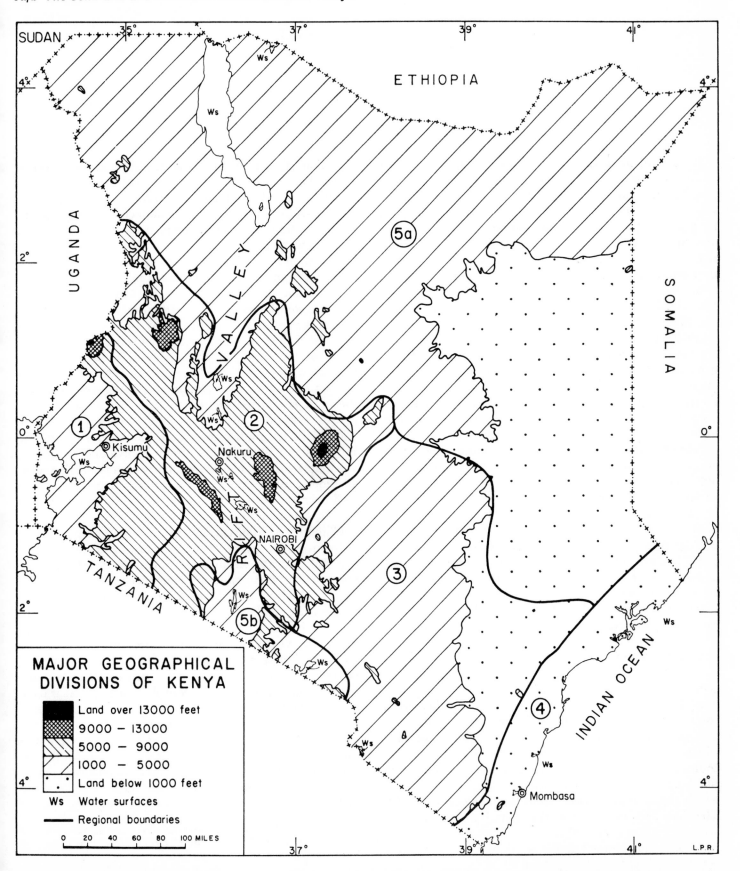

MAJOR GEOGRAPHICAL
DIVISIONS OF KENYA

Land over 13000 feet
9000 – 13000
5000 – 9000
1000 – 5000
Land below 1000 feet

Ws   Water surfaces

Regional boundaries

0   20   40   60   80   100 MILES

Records of the invasions of the fly underline the comparatively late date of encroachment of tsetse into the lake basin. Oral traditions of the lacustrine population suggest that the fly entered a well-populated area settled by a people practising fishing, agricultural and pastoral activities. Morris records three main epidemics of sleeping sickness in the area.[2] The first outbreak occurred during the period 1901–10. This was primarily an interlacustrine and island invasion from the neighbouring territory of Uganda. It led to a decimation of much of the lake shore population. Except for the island of Rusinga with its relatively high population density, the lake shore belt has not fully recovered demographically and economically from this initial invasion. Tsetse fly continues to be a major obstacle to a fuller utilisation of the land. It is therefore one of the factors which must be taken into account when considering movement of rural population from the districts that border the lake.

Administratively the greater part of the region was, according to the 1961 boundaries shown, included in the old Nyanza Province. The Province, as it was then, consisted of the rural districts of Elgon Nyanza, North Nyanza, Central Nyanza, South Nyanza, Kisii, and Kericho (Figure 1.8). On the basis of these boundaries it will be seen that the region was divided between the predominantly African rural areas and the isolated blocks of Sotik and Kericho which were settled by Europeans. In addition, the location of the narrow stretch of sugar lands covering the northern fringes of the Kano Plains and extending from Kibos to Muhoroni should be noted.

2. THE CENTRAL RIFT AND ASSOCIATED HIGHLANDS

As the name suggests, the rift subdivision of Kenya's geographical regions consists not of one homogenous unit but of a number of sub-regions linked together by a common tectonic history. Crustal deformation in this part of Kenya has given rise to important regional contrasts which make this a vital area in the economy of the country. The basic framework is of a central north-south rift flanked by imposing escarpments and plateau areas which generally slope away from the shoulder of the rift. The floor itself is highest in the central portion where it attains an altitude of well over 6,000 feet above sea level. But north and south it slopes to more arid parts at an elevation of 1,200 feet in Lake Rudolf and 2,000 feet in Lake Magadi areas. It will be seen that tectonic activities which have led to greater elevation of the floor in the Nakuru-Naivasha area have economically brought about the important regional differences associated with that area of the rift.

The pattern of elevated volcanic highlands lying east and west of the rift floor and linked in the central portion by an area similarly favoured by altitude and fertile volcanic soils forms the basic structure around which the human geography of the area may be described. In the west the diverse highland area extends from the thick lava block of the Mau-Tinderet area northwards to Kitale portion where the eroded lavas have exposed the more ancient core of the highland area. The volcanic region of the west rift highlands is matched in the east by the eastward sloping Aberdares plateau with the City of Nairobi at its south-eastern end. In the north-east, the sub-division is extended by Mount Kenya and Nyambeni volcanic region. This is a similarly diverse region with altitudes varying from about 4,000 feet above sea level to well over 12,000 feet in the case of Aberdares and 17,000 feet for Mount Kenya.

Climatic conditions in the area show important regional differences. In terms of temperature and rainfall the regional contrasts outlined above emerge clearly. For the floor yearly temperature means decrease from about 85°F in Lodwar and Magadi areas to just over 60°F. in the Nakuru-Naivasha area. The bordering plateau to the west is characterised generally by moderate temperatures, the yearly mean temperatures ranging between 56°F for Equator and 65°F for Kitale. This compares favourably with the highland areas further east where the figure ranges around 60°F. Nairobi yearly mean is 64°F and that of Thika is 68°F.

Rainfall, which is an important consideration in the agricultural activities of the highland area, shows a similar regional variation. In general, the floor of the rift valley is dry except for the Nakuru-Naivasha region which enjoys an annual mean of between 25 and 60 inches. In the highland areas of the west, the annual

[2]Morris D. R. S. 'Studies in the epidemiology of sleeping sickness in East Africa' *Transactions of the Royal Society of Tropical Medicine and Hygiene* pp. 71–86 Vol. 54 No. 1 1960

means are generally between 40 and 50 inches spread over about eight months of the year. Kericho area is the wettest part and it receives well over 70 inches of rainfall a year. East of the rift, the highland area receives annual totals ranging from 30 to 60 inches of rain except for the parts of Aberdares, Mount Kenya and Nyambeni where rainfall totals of over 60 inches are received.

However, it is more important to consider the nature of rainfall reliability in assessing the potential of the land. The 30 inches rainfall reliability map shows that the areas of reliable rainfall coincide with the highland areas where orographic effects increase the reliability of rainfall.[3] In the plateau areas west of the Rift Valley, agricultural production is dependent on the April to August rains, whereas in the area to the east the March to May rains have proved to be more important to the economy.

Among the most important resource bases of the regions are the varied soils derived from volcanic materials of different periods. These soils under varied temperatures and moisture situations are capable of a wide range of uses. In the rift floor soils derived from explosive materials are found in addition to others derived from the old river sediments and lake deposits.

But in the areas west of the rift floor materials from the volcanic explosions and other rock types dominate the nature of the soils. The Mau volcanics with their dark brown loams underlie the mountain forest community that cover the area. Further west, Kericho volcanics or phonolites underlie the dark chocolate-red soils of great depth. These soils form the basis of the successful tea farming industry and the fast changing modern agriculture of the Kipsigis. In this area it is estimated that the soil cover over the ridges may be more than 100 feet deep. Further north the Uasin Gishu plateau is characterised by red to deep or dark brown friable clays with a laterite horizon. Away from this volcanic belt the important Basement material may be seen in the increasing importance of the sandy material in the soils of parts of Nandi and part of Trans-Nzoia. However, the more fertile volcanic soils reappear in the north-west of Trans-Nzoia and Kitale.

In the highland areas to the east there is a parallel diversity in the physical conditions of the soils. Here, attention should be drawn to the deep humic brown clay, suitable for tea development in areas about 7,000 feet above sea level. At lower levels the dissected narrow ridge country on the slopes of the Aberdares with its dark-brown to yellow-red friable clays is amongst the most productive volcanic soils of Kenya. It forms a category quite different from the poorer sandy soils of the eastern fringes of this highland region.

The soils of the highland region have been described in some detail to provide the background to the important farming developments that will be considered later. But the diversity in soils types is just one aspect of the varied opportunities which the area presents to development. Differences in land potential of the highland region are also reflected in the major groupings of plant communities which characterise the area. The better watered and higher parts of the highlands are potentially areas of Highland Grassland and Highland Forests.[4] In its original form the vegetation consisted of limited stretches of forest with extensive areas of undulating open grassland. Between 6,500 feet and 9,000 feet above sea level and with a minimum rainfall of 40 inches the undulating grassland is potential area of Kikuyu grass (*Pennisetum clandestinum*). But at lower elevations and under conditions of higher temperatures the lower rainfall supports *Acacia-Themeda* grassland. The altitudinal range from 6,300 to 9,000 feet represents the most important forest zone in Kenya with considerable variations resulting from differences in aspect of slope and the varying temperature conditions. The forest belt where it has survived includes economically valuable elements such as cedar (*Juniperus procera*) and podo wood (*Podocarpus milanjianus* and *Podocarpus gracilior*.)

The Highlands Grassland and Forest region is potentially one of the most productive parts of the country. It will be seen later that in this varied environment has developed a mixed farming based on cereals, livestock and valuable plantation crops of which coffee, tea and pyrethrum are the most important. Culturally, the grassland region was the main foundation of the pastoral economy that dominated the life of much of Kenya just before the establishment of modern administration. The region has

[3]Glover J., Robinson P. & Henderson J. P. 'Provisional maps of the reliability of annual rainfall in East Africa' *Quarterly Journal of the Royal Meteorological Society* pp. 602–9 Vol. 80 No. 34 1951

[4]Edwards D. C. 'A Vegetation Map of Kenya' *Journal of Ecology* pp. 377–85 No. 128, 1940 Edwards D. C. & Bogdan A. V. *Important Grassland Plants of Kenya* Pitman, London 1951

been influenced by two different approaches to land utilization. The European settlers who were attracted by its potentials established a productive agriculture which continues to play a vital role in the economy of the Republic.

In those areas which lay outside the alienated portions it will be seen that the tendency has been for a rapid increase in population and concentrations of indigenous agricultural populations. The juxtaposition of European areas of farming and areas occupied by dense African rural communities raised problems that for long dominated the affairs of the country in the years preceding independence.

According to the 1961 boundaries the greater part of the highland region was included in the Rift Valley Province (Figure 1.8). This consisted of the African districts of West Pokot, Elgeyo-Marakwet, Nandi, Baringo, and the European settled districts of Trans-Nzoia, Uasin Gishu, Nakuru, Laikipia, and Naivasha. The remainder of the highland region was included in the Central Province which at that time consisted of the European settled districts of Nanyuki and Thika together with the African districts of Kiambu, Fort Hall, Nyeri, Embu, Meru and in Machakos District. The expanding urban area of Nairobi was a separate district.

A description of the administrative organisation of the region draws attention to the location of the former African districts of each of the two provinces in relation to the European settled districts. In the case of the Rift Valley Province, the African districts were largely peripheral to the alienated lands. But in the Central Province the African districts came to be sandwiched between the alienated lands and the associated forest areas. This locational relationship has had an important influence in the subsequent growth and movements of population.

3. THE EASTERN PLATEAU FORELAND

To the east of the rift highlands, the landscape in Kenya may be described as a vast plateau surface of ancient rocks. In places this ancient platform has resisted denudation and now stands above the general level in the form of residuals. The residuals of Machakos and Kitui in the north and Taita Hills in the extreme south have played a key role in the human geography of this vast area.

The landscape which slopes gently eastwards is in general a region of low rainfall and higher temperatures. Rainfall in most parts averages 20 to 30 inches except over the higher hills of Machakos, Kitui, and Taita. In these areas annual means in excess of 30 inches are experienced. Away from the highland fringes rainfall becomes increasingly unreliable. This intervening region between the coast and the volcanic highlands suffers periodically from intense drought conditions and has for long been regarded as one of the traditional famine regions of Kenya. It will be noted that this is a region where growing desiccation has resulted in a striking concentration of the human population in such critical areas as Taita Hills and the higher residuals of Machakos and Kitui.

Over the greater part of the region the most characteristic vegetation community is Desert Grass-Bush (dry bush with trees).[5] But in the higher parts of Machakos and Kitui, Chyulu and Taita Hills, the natural vegetation consists of Scattered Tree Grassland (*Acacia-Themeda*). The Desert Grass-Bush country is a vast area of low potential suitable only for the most extensive form of land utilization. Parts of the area are known to suffer from the tsetse fly menace. Even in the more favoured parts characterised by Scattered Tree Grassland or *Acacia-Themeda* community, more intensive forms of land utilization and in particular production of crops are seriously restricted by moisture conditions. Throughout the greater part of the region development is hampered by the extremely unreliable rainfall and poverty of grazing. This is a region where man has lived in a delicate relationship with the environment and is under constant threat of famine. It has been noted that during the brief periods of better moisture conditions, the population which has moved over to the higher residuals has tended to migrate back to the lower country only to be driven back by prolonged drought of the following years.

In conclusion it is necessary to draw attention to the results of mineral search in the region. So far despite the finds of minor mineral deposits these have not affected the population pattern of the area. There have been such discoveries as the copper deposits of the Tsavo-Galana

[5]Edwards D. C. & Bogdan A. V. *Important Grassland Plants of Kenya* Pitman, London 1951

confluence and Kanziku graphite. But these deposits are still awaiting exploitation and do not affect the attraction power of the region in terms of population. Administratively the greater part of the region is now part of the Eastern Province. However, in 1961 most of the region including the two Kamba districts of Machakos and Kitui were combined with similarly dry districts of Kajiado and Narok to form the Southern Province. (Figure 1.8).

4. THE COAST REGION

Extending along the entire length of the Kenya seaboard, the Coast Region is the third most important area of Kenya. Separated from the interior by the plateau foreland, it is one of the most clearly marked geographical sub-divisions of the Republic. But beneath this apparent simplicity the region is unique in minor varieties of potential arising from the inherent physical diversity. This complexity is directly related to the geological history of the area. The geological diversity which underlies the great variety of soil types and vegetation associations is in sharp contrast to a unity imposed by the nature of climate of the area.

The immediate coastal plain lying at an altitude of less than 100 feet above sea level is the most recent part. It is largely underlain by pleistocene deposits of corals and sands. Behind this youthful platform is a varied plateau from 200 to 450 feet above sea level largely carved out of marine shales, mudstones and limestones of Jurassic age. To the west of this the landscape rises to a line formed by the intermittent ranges of Mazeras sandstones at an altitude of about 1,200 to 1,300 feet above sea level. In the west the high edge declines to merge with the Nyika platform of Duruma sandstone.

The geological background has been outlined in detail to underline the great diversity of soil parent material. Of particular importance here is the prevalence of coral and sandstone formations which through their porosity greatly affect the fertility and moisture holding capacity of the soil. There are few areas of fertile residual soils and those derived from alluvium as in the Ramisi Valley. But for the most part, the coast soils are unsuited to intensive forms of land utilisation.

In contrast to the physical diversity outlined there is a climatic unity which is imposed by the location of the region. Most parts of the coast experience mean annual temperatures in excess of 80°F. This monotony is only relieved by the seasonal fluctuations. Rainfall distribution, however, shows the transition from the more humid south to the desert fringe near Lamu and from the humid coast plain to the arid and semi-arid plateau foreland region.

In the extreme north, Lamu enjoys a mean annual rainfall of about 35 inches a year. This rises to well over 50 inches in the area around Vanga. From the humid coast where annual means are between 30 and 50 inches, rainfall decreases westwards to about 20 inches a year. However, in an area subject to high temperatures and considerable rainfall fluctuations mean annual data are an inadequate guide to the nature of the potential of the region. A map of rainfall probability of less than 30 inches of rain a year shows that it is only a narrow band of the region south of Kilifi which has good prospects of obtaining that amount. In this restricted portion between 0–10 years in 100, rainfall is likely to be less than 30 inches. The remaining parts of the region have very poor prospects.

The vegetation of the Coast Region is basically a savannah formation with patches of residual forests in ecologically suitable areas. The distribution of these forest patches is largely governed by the complex soil differences and the history of human usage. In the hinterland, much of the country is covered by *Acacia-Euphorbia* or *Acacia-Bushland* with patches of Lowland Dry Forest. Remnants of the forest are found along the entire coast from the north to near Vanga in the south. Years of occupation in the south has virtually destroyed the forest community. The Arabuko-Sokoke Crown forest which extends over 92,000 acres is an evergreen variety of the lowland forest.

Apart from the woodland vegetation of the freely drained sands and the *Combretum* association of the coral rags, the Lowlands Rain forest is perhaps the most important member of the coastal vegetation community. This forest association is rapidly being depleted by fire, logging and extension of cultivation. Moomaw estimated that in 1960 it was less than ten per cent of its potential area.[6]

[6]Moomaw J. C. *A Study of Plant Ecology of the Coast Region of Kenya Colony, British East Africa* p. 37 Government Printer, Nairobi 1960

An assessment of the land potential in the Coast Region must include limitations of restraints to a fuller utilisation of the land. It will be noted later that despite the long occupation of parts of the area, the Coast is still largely underdeveloped agriculturally. One of the main limitations to the balanced use of the land is the prevalence of the various species of tsetse fly which affects man and livestock. The Coastal Bushland has in places been invaded by *Glossina pallidipes* and *Glossina austeni*.

Administratively, the Coast Region forms part of the Coast Province which in addition includes parts of the interior region of plateau foreland. The greater part of Tana River District and the whole of the Taita District are essentially parts of the plateau foreland region and share its physical and human problems (Figure 1.8).

5a/5b. THE SEMI-ARID NORTHERN, NORTH-EASTERN AND SOUTHERN KENYA

This is one of the most extensive geographical subdivisions of the Republic. The principal features of the sub-division include high temperatures, low and extremely erratic rainfall. Most centres in the area experience mean annual temperatures of 80°F or more except the higher spots such as Moyale and areas close to the highland fringe. In general mean annual rainfall is well under 20 inches except in parts of Masailand where 20–40 inches may be received. But there are considerable variations depending on altitude and location. Mandera has a mean figure of 9·1 inches per annum, Wajir 10·1 inches and Garrisa 11·9 inches. But Moyale and Isiolo with 27·2 inches and 25·5 inches respectively show that there are ameliorating factors to the general problem of aridity. The real problem of the region is the unreliability of rainfall. Over the greater part of the area rainfall is likely to fall below 30 inches in at least thirty out of every one hundred years.

This meagre and extremely uncertain rainfall underlies the general uniformity of the vegetation character in the area. There is in Southern Kenya, an outer core of higher rainfall which is covered by a dry bush vegetation. The Desert Grass-Bush covers approximately two-thirds of the Republic and is part of a more extensive vegetation type that extends northwards into Somalia and the Horn area. The characteristic vegetation is mostly a cover of

deciduous bushes ten to fifteen feet in height with scattered tufts of perennial grasses. In the drier core area of northern Kenya the vegetation largely consists of Desert shrub. Perennial grasses are absent in this section.

The movement of man and livestock is strictly controlled by the availability of water in the region. Generally, this is one of the most difficult environments from which to make a living. It will be seen later that in development it is also hampered by inadequate human and material resources. Intensive search for minerals is continuing in the area. But until such a diversity is achieved the region will continue to depend on the scarce resources of rainfall and minimum vegetation cover. Administratively, the southern portion in 1961 formed part of the Southern Province including Narok, Kajiado, Machakos and Kitui. Since the revision of the boundaries, this part has been added to the Rift Valley Province (Figure 1.8).

3 Transport and Resource Development

In an attempt to probe into the factors underlying the mobility of population in the Republic it is necessary now to consider first the basic network of communication and the economy that has developed with the growth of this network. The basic network may be regarded as the major arteries through which this movement takes place in response to development of the regions. But, far more important, they have created the regional differences in economic opportunities which play a crucial part in the circulation of peoples.

While considering the regional differences it is the intensity in economic development which will form the focus of interest for the student of population dynamics. Regional differences largely reflect the differing intensity in the effect of modern economy and are regarded as continuing to be the main motivating force.

I. RAIL AND ROAD COMMUNICATIONS (*Figure 3.1*)

i. *The railways*

In the study of population movements a distinction will be made between the prehistoric and historic migrations on the one hand, and on the other to the modern shifts of population which continue to take place in response to the stimulus of social and economic development. For a number of reasons a knowledge of the development of rail communication in Kenya is important for an understanding of modern population movements. In the first place whether the system developed in response to political or economic needs, it provided a new form of mobility permitting a freer and less hazardous communication between peoples. The rail pattern is a fundamental structure on which has rested the movement of manpower in the country. It is only in the period since the last war that the road communication has come into prominence as a means for long distance movement of peoples and hence as a serious factor in the direction of flow of population. But it should be noted that the evolving trunk connections by roads have been greatly influenced by the pattern which the rail communications set.

Secondly, in serving and helping in development of traffic in the productive regions of the country the linking communications may be considered as largely basic to differences in economic opportunities which underlie much of the modern movements of peoples from one part of the country to another. It has been stressed that Kenya as a unit is largely a creation of the period following the completion of railway from Mombasa to Kisumu.[1]

But thirdly, rail communication in creating traffic provides work opportunities which continue to draw manpower from the different regions of the country. The East African Railways and Harbours are one of the largest employers of labour and the trade union organisations in this area are among the most powerful of the organised bodies in the country.

Fourthly, the railway pattern is fundamental to development of urban centres and industrial opportunities. The pattern of industrial activities in the urban areas which constitute an important attraction to the working population is a subject of a later chapter. But it is necessary to stress the rail communications as an element in the geographical distribution of urban settlements and industries. The policy on location of industrial estates is indirectly a vital factor in the increase of employment opportunities. According to the 1962 Census out of a total population of 670,947 living in towns with over 2,000 inhabitants 89.9 per cent were to be found in those towns which have developed on the railways.[2]

The seven largest towns of Kenya with over 10,000 inhabitants are some of the major rail centres of the country. In these respects the pattern that has evolved provides a vital clue to the sources and destinations of the migrating population and hence the effect of economic policy on the country's human resources.

The basic pattern of rail communication which now traverses the country from the Coast to the Lake shore and across western Kenya border into Uganda are inherited from the inter-territorial system which was originally intended to link Uganda to the Coast (Figure 3.1). 'The engineers came to Mombasa in 1896 to build the "Uganda Railway" and Kenya was merely a tract of land which had to be crossed to reach the goal of Lake Victoria.'[3]

It has been stressed that the driving force in the

[1]O'Connor A. M. *Railways and Development in Uganda* East African Studies No. 18 p. 147 East African Institute of Social Research 1965

[2]Bloomberg L. N. & Abrams C. *Report of United Nations Mission to Kenya on Housing* p. 61, 1965

[3]O'Connor A. M. *op. cit.*, p. 148

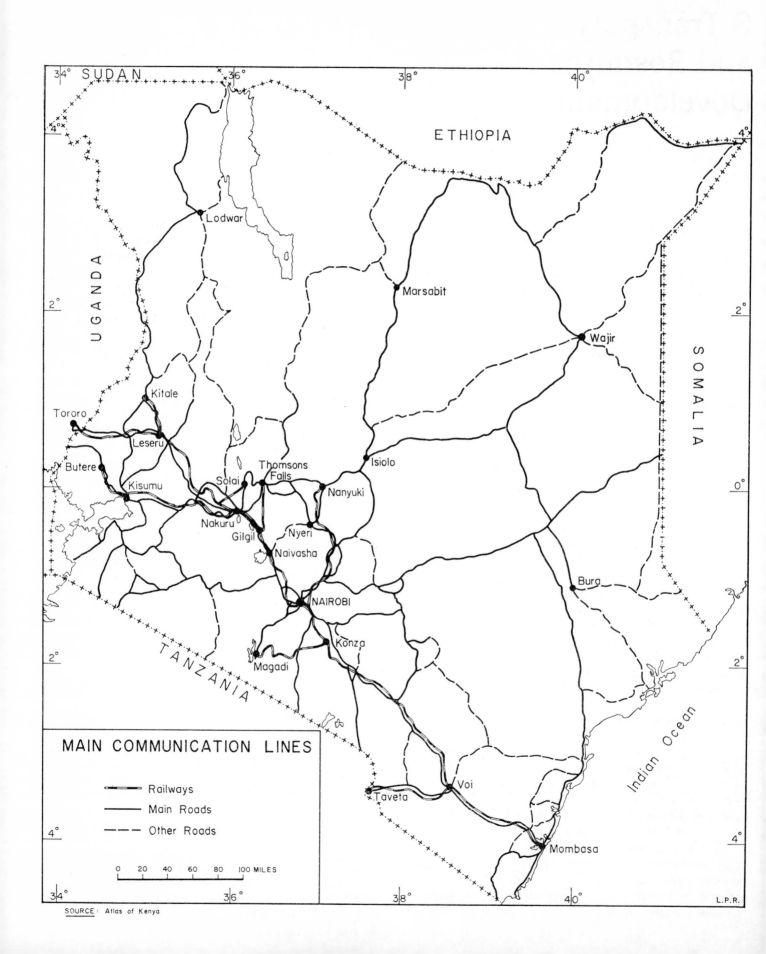

SUDAN

ETHIOPIA

UGANDA

SOMALIA

Lodwar

Marsabit

Wajir

Kitale

Tororo

Leseru

Butere

Kisumu

Solai

Thomsons Falls

Isiolo

Nanyuki

Nakuru

Gilgil

Nyeri

Naivasha

NAIROBI

Bura

Magadi

Konza

TANZANIA

Indian Ocean

Voi

Taveta

Mombasa

MAIN COMMUNICATION LINES

——— Railways

——— Main Roads

– – – Other Roads

0 20 40 60 80 100 MILES

L.P.R.

SOURCE: Atlas of Kenya

direction of the rail development was to a large extent political. The railway was thus initially not designed to develop the areas through which it subsequently passed. The main aim was to link the Kingdom of Buganda with the Coast and thus consolidate Britain's imperial ambitions in the area.[4]

Begun in 1896, the greater part of the system was complete by 1930. The 589 mile line from Mombasa reached Kisumu on the shores of Lake Victoria at the end of 1901. Kisumu thus became the focus of the traffic that was developing in the well-watered region round the Lake. The completion of the line thus laid the foundation for Kisumu to develop as one of the earliest urban centres in the country.

The Nairobi-Thika line was completed in 1913 and was finally extended to Nanyuki in 1930. Further west the Uasin Gishu plateau was crossed to the Uganda border in the 1920's and branch lines were laid to the farming centres of Kitale, Solai and Thomson's Falls by 1930. The Kisumu-Butere extension was completed in 1930. Meanwhile, the Magadi Soda line from Konza had been completed in 1914. Extensions of the branch lines to the rich farming districts represent a second stage in the motive behind the rail developments. It had become necessary to generate traffic to pay for an expensive line which had been initially built to meet political expediency. This was the rationale of the encouragement given to the settlement of Europeans in the alienated areas of Kenya. There is no doubt as to the effect of the branch extensions on the traffic increase.[5]

Meanwhile, during the First World War, the British military authorities had pushed a line from Voi across the dry plains that now form part of the Tsavo National Park to Taveta close to Tanzania border. This line was extended further west and linked up with the German line from Tanga to Moshi. This Kenya extension was retained after the war and thus continued the link with Mombasa which brought the fertile volcanic highlands of north-east Tanzania within the orbit of the port of Mombasa.[6] This is now a vital communication link for the sisal plantations of Taveta-Taita district.

ii. *Road communications*
Although the primary importance of railways in popula-

tion movement is accepted, road transport has assumed a more prominent position with the increase in vehicle numbers. Between 1954 and 1960 it is reported that the increase in vehicles averaged ten per cent and that in 1960 it was fifteen per cent.[7]

This increase can be interpreted in terms of the increase in the number of persons being moved by motor vehicles on the road. Thus while the rail pattern established the initial framework on which the interchange in manpower between the various regions of the Republic has taken place, the road systems of the country now form an essential part of the transport complex. The pattern of regional density emphasises the Nyanza, Central and the Coast Provinces. The coincidence of areas of denser road traffic network with areas of population is an important factor in the population movements. People living in such areas enjoy greater mobility and should be expected to form an important section of the migrating population.

On the contrary, the arid northern and eastern areas and the semi-arid southern portions of the country are very poorly served by roads. Extensive areas of the Republic in these parts are without road communication. Thus in considering the contribution of the regions to the moving population in Kenya, the problem of accessibility must be considered.

Apart from density patterns in Kenya, it should be noted that the trunk roads in the country generally serve the same areas as the railways. Thus from the point of view of direction of flow they underline the pattern established by the railway system of the country to which they were intended as feeders.

2. DEVELOPMENT OF THE ECONOMY
i. *Introduction*
Having considered the arteries of communication in the country we now turn to discuss the varying pace of development in different parts of the country. In this

[4]Van Dongen I. S. *The British East African Transport Complex* University of Chicago Research Papers No. 38, 1954
[5]O'Connor A. M. p. 149 *An Economic Geography of East Africa* Bell and Sons, 1966
[6]Van Dongen I. S. 'Mombasa in the Land and Sea Exchanges of East Africa' *Erdkunde* Band XVII pp. 16–37
[7]*The Economic Development of Kenya: Report of an Economic Survey Mission* p. 128 International Bank for Reconstruction and Development 1962

chapter, attention is directed to the assessment of the elements of Kenya's economy and their development which form the foundation for the study of population mobility. Analysis in this chapter is intended to establish the important distinction that still exists between the former African areas and those areas that were formerly exclusively set aside for European settlement.

Modern Kenya, unlike the more favoured states in Africa has developed largely on the basis of production of agricultural and livestock commodities from the land. In 1962, out of a total Gross Domestic Product of £103,080,000 for agriculture, livestock, forest, fishing and hunting industries, agriculture accounted for £74,890,000, livestock £21,480,000, forestry £5,710,000, fishing and hunting £1,000,000.[8] The changing role of agriculture in the total economy can be seen in Table 3.1.[9]

ii. *The Mining Industry*

Although a wide variety of metallic and non-metallic minerals have been discovered in the Republic, the range of economic minerals is limited largely to gold and related minerals, copper, trona (soda ash) and limestone.

The gold mining has been largely restricted to the pre-Cambrian rocks in the Nyanza and Western Provinces. The discovery of gold was made during the world trade depression in the 1930's and led to a rapid but short lived influx of miners into the areas concerned.

The value of gold produced rose steadily until the early years of the World War. But the production returns for the period after 1939 show a sharp decline. Over the twenty years from 1940 to 1960 gold production declined from over £500,000 to about £100,000. In 1940 the value of refined gold amounted to £648,783.[10] But in 1961 this had decreased to £154,000.[11] During that period the largest gold mine had closed down. Table 3.2 gives a picture of relative importance of various minerals between 1956 and 1963.

The rapid decline of the gold mining activity in the Nyanza and the Western Provinces has been as striking as was its swift expansion. Rosterman Mines, the largest in the area north of the gulf was abandoned later in 1952. Ngiga Mines Company went into liquidation early in 1953 and Sakwa Mines ceased operation in 1955.

Large scale mining of gold has ceased north of the gulf,

Table 3.1 GROSS DOMESTIC PRODUCT BY INDUSTRIAL ORIGIN

	1954 %	1960 %
Outside Recorded Monetary Economy		
Agriculture	21·2	15·6
Livestock Products	6·4	4·9
Forestry	1·1	1·3
Fishing and Hunting	0·2	0·1
Total	28·9	21·9
Recorded Monetary Economy		
Agriculture	12·5	13·1
Livestock	4·0	4·2
Forestry	0·3	0·4
Fishing and Hunting	1·0	0·2
Total	17·8	17·9
Mining and Quarrying	0·6	0·5
Manufacturing	8·9	9·6
Construction	4·0	3·5
Electricity and Water	0·8	1·2
Transport and Communication	7·5	9·0
Wholesale and Retail Trade	13·7	12·9
Banking, Insurance and Real Estate	0·9	1·6
Rents (including ownership)	3·0	3·9
General Government	8·8	10·3
Services	5·0	7·0
Government Officers Salaries Revision	—	0·8
Total	53·2	60·3
Grand Total	100·0	100·0

SOURCE: *The Economic Development of Kenya: Report of An Economic Survey Mission* p. 243. International Bank for Reconstruction and Development 1962

[8] *Economic Survey 1965* p. 2 Table 1 Statistics Division, Ministry of Economic Planning and Development, Kenya 1965

[9] International Bank for Reconstruction and Development Report p. 243

[10] Pulfrey W. 'The Geology and Mineral Resources of Kenya' p. 288 *Bulletin of the Imperial Institute* pp. 277–99 Vol. XLV No. 3 1947

[11] *Kenya Census of Industrial Production* 1963, p. 16, 1965

[12] International Bank for Reconstruction and Development Report p. 103

[13] Kenya 1962. *Kenya African Agricultural Sample Census* 1960/61 p. 1 Part I, Economics and Statistics Division, Kenya 1962

Table 3.2 THE MINING INDUSTRY IN KENYA

Principal Minerals	Unit	1956 Production	1956 Value (£ 000)	1963 Production	1963 Value (£ 000)
Soda ash and Soda	Long tons	146,326	1,590·9	104,175	1,283·6
Copper	Long tons	859	189·0	2,212	504·7
Salt	Long tons	21,885	186·2	32,683	140·1
Gold	Fine oz troy	13,842	172·5	10,193	128·9
Lime and Limestone	Long tons	13,281	81·5	16,188	97·4
Diatomite	Long tons	4,837	95·7	3,283	71·0
Carbon Dioxide	Long tons	677	49·2	509	54·2
Silver	Fine oz troy	54,689	16·5	52,422	25·2

SOURCE: *Statistical Abstract* p. 64. Economics and Statistics Division, Ministry of Finance and Economic Planning, Kenya 1964

but some gold is still produced in association with copper at Macalder Nyanza mine in South Nyanza. The output of the mining industry is still dominated by the Macalder Nyanza mine. The ores consists of auriferous mixed sulphides of which the most important constituent is copper. But in addition, it produces silver and gold. However, the copper industry which became important in 1951 with the first production from Macalder Nyanza mine is expected to decline in importance as the more productive ores are exhausted.[12]

Apart from the gold and copper some mining of diatomite and soda ash continues in the Rift Valley and occupies a limited number of workers. The Magadi Soda Works recently suffered a setback with the elimination of the established markets in the Republic of South Africa. Apart from these two minerals the remainder of the mining manpower is concerned with the production of Portland Cement.

Between 1957 and 1961 cement production increased by about 14 per cent by value. In terms of quantity the increase was 60 per cent and gave an equivalent growth rate of 12·5 per cent per annum. Kenya became self-sufficient in cement production in 1957 and by 1961 the productive capacity had exceeded 500,000 tons. The two factories have been sited close to the limestone sources of the coast and the Athi Plains near Nairobi. Efforts continue towards a fuller mapping and assessment of mineralised areas in the Republic. But so far the mining activity does not contribute significantly to population movements on a national scale.

iii. *The pattern of land classification*

The present movement of population is primarily the outcome of the policy of land usage which became established with the modern administration in Kenya. By 1961 the land in Kenya was divided into four broad divisions.[13] In the first category was the predominantly leasehold land and occasionally freehold land held by Europeans and Asians and from 1961 by Africans. These holdings totalled some 7·7 million acres. Up to 1961 this area was specifically alienated for non-African farming. It is this acreage of land in Kenya and its utilisation that underlies the pattern of population movement that is dealt with at length in this book. About one-half of the acreage of this category of land is suitable for arable farming and the other half is largely pastoral land. This first division of land prior to opening it up for African farming was referred to as the 'Scheduled Areas'. The Coast alienated land was also included in this category. The evolution of agriculture in the former scheduled area will be treated separately. But it is important to note that up to the Second World War most attention was directed to this category of land which provided the bulk of Kenya's revenue. Even up to the present, its contribution is still a vital factor in the revenue earning capacity of Kenya's agricultural land.

The vast majority of Kenya's African rural population in 1961 were to be found occupying approximately one million peasant holdings covering some 18 million acres. This large acreage was for the most part worked by traditional techniques. It will be seen that in some areas population pressure had reached a serious level. Up to the Second World War, the production of this category of land was largely directed to meet subsistence needs. But in a few areas it will be noted that some attempt had been made to establish a limited range of cash crops.

This category of land has in a few areas witnessed important changes in methods of tenure and in the output of land. Consolidation of land has appeared in much of the Kalenjin landscape and during the Emergency the greater part of Kikuyu landscape was enclosed. These were the non-scheduled areas prior to the opening of the scheduled areas for African farming. It will be noted that the momentum of economic development established in these areas and the consequent gap in economic opportunities between these and the former African lands have provided the basis for the movement of population.

Reflection on the regional background to movements of population brings to light yet a third category of land which includes those areas into which no significant movements have taken place. In 1961 these comprised some 110 million acres or some 173,000 square miles which were outside the former scheduled areas. These areas were in effect the semi-arid and arid areas of extremely low rainfall inhabited largely by the nomadic pastoral peoples in the north-east and southern Kenya. Little change has taken place in these areas, and they still constitute the principal famine regions of the Republic.

Table 3.4 LAND USE CATEGORIES IN NON-SCHEDULED AREAS BY PROVINCE

	Ai	Aii	Aiii	Aiv	Total A	Bi	Bii	Biii	Total B	SQUARE MILES C	D	TOTAL
Central	1,784	—	234	104	2,122	1,058	156	194	1,408	2,782	—	6,312
Nyanza	4,192	—	399	1,297	5,888	809	755	636	2,200	—	—	8,088
Southern (excluding Masai Districts)	435	—	—	—	435	1,108	1,177	1,190	3,475	4,179	3,861	11,950
Masai (Kajiado, Narok)	1,535	1,023	485	987	4,030	520	—	—	520	3,618	6,548	14,716
Rift	1,277	345	291	224	2,137	1,343	455	1,195	2,993	1,491	754	7,375
Coast	445	—	474	643	1,562	425	601	679	1,705	2,640	14,995	20,902
Northern	—	—	—	—	—	15	—	—	15	130	121,727	121,872
Total	9,668	1,368	1,883	3,255	16,174	5,272	3,144	3,894	12,316	14,840	147,884	191,214

SOURCE: *Kenya African Agricultural Sample Census* 1960/61 p. 2

The fourth category of land use included the Forest areas where a substantial number of labourers have moved in to work on the re-afforestation schemes or for the saw-millers permitted to tap these forest resources.

Summarising the state of land classification, by 1961, some 15,621 square miles of the country consisted of water and parks. This area was considered unavailable for agriculture or grazing. The Forest areas covered some 5,952 square miles, the former scheduled areas 12,173 square miles and the former non-scheduled areas 191,214 square miles.[14]

iv. *Land use in the former non-scheduled areas*
Before the constitutional changes which opened the scheduled highland region to African farming the African area constituted 85 per cent of the total area of the Republic. For agricultural purposes this land could be sub-divided into four broad categories on the basis of rainfall.[15]

A. High potential land with adequate rainfall (35 inches or more).

B. Medium potential land with 25 to 35 inches a year.

C. Low potential land receiving between 20 and 25 inches and suited mainly to ranching except for irrigation.

D. Nomadic pastoral land, with less than 20 inches of rainfall. This type of land is considered mainly suitable for wild life and the poorest type of ranching.

Table 3.5 summarises in percentage form the land use categories by provinces at the time of the 1960–1 African Agricultural Sample Census.

[14]*Kenya African Agricultural Sample Census* 1960/61 Part 1, p. 2
[15]*Kenya African Agricultural Sample Census* 1960/61

Table 3.5 LAND USE SUMMARY BY PROVINCES

Former Non-Scheduled Areas

LAND CATEGORIES

Area	A %	B %	C %	D %
Central Province	33·6	22·3	44·1	—
Nyanza Province	72·8	27·2	—	—
Southern Province:				
(i) excluding Kajiado and Narok	3·6	29·1	35·0	32·3
(ii) Kajiado/Narok	27·4	3·5	24·6	44·5
Rift Valley Province	29·0	40·5	20·2	10·1
Coast Province	7·4	8·1	12·6	71·7
Northern Province	—	—	0·1	99·9
Percentage of Total Area	8·4	6·4	7·8	77·3

SOURCE: *Kenya African Agricultural Sample Census* 1960–61

Table 3.6 LAND USE SUMMARY BY PROVINCES[1]

Former Non-Scheduled Areas

LAND CATEGORIES (SHARE OF NATIONAL TOTAL)

Area	A	B	C	D
	Percentages of National total			
Central Province	13·1	11·4	18·7	—
Nyanza Province	36·4	17·9	—	—
Southern Province:				
(i) excluding Kajiado and Narok Districts	2·7	28·2	28·2	2·6
(ii) Kajiado and Narok Districts	24·9	4·2	24·3	4·4
Rift Valley Province	13·2	24·3	10·0	0·5
Coast Province	9·7	13·8	17·8	10·1
Northern Province	—	0·1	0·9	82·3
National Total	100·0	100·0	100·0	100·0

SOURCES: *Kenya African Agricultural Sample Census* 1960–61 p. 2

According to the above classification, 77·3 per cent of the total area of the former non-scheduled lands consisted of the nomadic pastoral land with less than 20 inches of rainfall (Table 3.5). About 99·8 per cent of the area of the Northern Province consisted of this category of land. But of the total area under this category of land 82·3 per cent was in Northern Province, 10·1 per cent in the Coast Province, 4·4 per cent in the two Masai districts of Narok and Kajiado and 2·6 per cent in the Kamba districts of Machakos and Kitui (Table 3.6). The land potential thus revealed the vast extent of African land unit that was of little value except for the most extensive pastoral form of land use.

Approximately 8 per cent of the former non-scheduled land was of low potential. It has been noted that this land received a total of 20 to 25 inches of rainfall and could, except under irrigation, support only poor quality ranching or wild life. The bulk of the Republic's African population depended largely on just under 15 per cent of the total land area made up of 6·4 per cent of Medium Potential Land and 8·4 per cent of High Potential Land.

The distribution of Medium Potential Land showed that 28·2 per cent was in the Kamba Districts of Kitui and Machakos, 24·3 per cent in the Rift Valley, 17·9 per cent in Nyanza, 13·8 per cent in the Coast Province, 11·4 per cent in the Central and less than 1 per cent in the Northern Province.

The High Potential Land with adequate rainfall comprised 8·4 per cent of the total land area. But of this, Nyanza Province had the highest percentage with 36·4 per cent followed by Kajiado and Narok Districts with 24·9 per cent. The Rift Valley Province had 13·2 per cent, Central Province 13·1 per cent, Coast 9·7 per cent and Kamba districts of Kitui and Machakos 2·7 per cent.

3. DEVELOPMENT OF THE RURAL ECONOMY

i. *Nyanza Province* (*non-scheduled*)

In considering the nature of population mobility, reference will be made to pre-colonial movements which formed part of the continent wide adjustments to environmental conditions. This section is concerned with the modifications of the traditional economy as a result of a new concept of land utilisation. It includes two main stages.

The first stage concerns the establishment of the basic exchange crops in the ecological and traditional setting and the second stage, a move towards a fuller utilisation of the crop and livestock potential of the area.

The first stage which coincides with the spread of rail and road communications in the area is described by Hugh Fearn.[16] It forms part of the early chapter on economic differentiation of the country. The second stage belongs to the post-war period when the stimulus of a growing population and political pressure against the established interest of European settlers made the need for a change in the economic policy necessary. In this survey a provincial approach is adopted as a basis for a later summary on the economic and social causes of migration. These administrative units formed important areas of application of official policies. But before examining the implications of the changes it is necessary to attempt a brief reconstruction of the economy of rural Nyanza at the turn of the century.

The economy of Nyanza has evolved against the background of two broad ecological regions; *Acacia-Combretum zone* and the higher areas of Kikuyu/Star Grass zone. A further subdivision will be made in the *Acacia Combretum zone* to distinguish the lower areas near the Lake shore from the intermediate zone (High Rainfall Savannah) which lies between the wetter Kikuyu/Star Grass areas and the Lake shore Savannah ecological zone.

According to a 1953 estimate which preceded the 1960/61 Sample Census it was reckoned that of the utilisable land available the *Acacia-Combretum* zone had 2,510 square miles of which 550 square miles were in North Nyanza, 1,000 square miles in Central Nyanza, 840 square miles in South Nyanza and 120 square miles in Kericho District. There were a total of 2,548 square miles of utilisable Star Grass area of which 1,250 square miles was located in North Nyanza, 226 square miles in Central Nyanza, 912 square miles in South Nyanza and 160 square miles in Kericho District.

The more limited area of the Kikuyu Grass ecological zone covered 1,200 square miles. Of these, 100 square miles were in North Nyanza, 600 square miles in South Nyanza and 500 square miles in Kericho District. At a much higher altitude the High Cold Mountain zone

[16] Fearn H. *An African Economy* pp. 63–90

Table 3.7

i. CENTRAL NYANZA

Ginnery	1950/51	1955/56
Samia	5,510,196	1,732,674
Ndere	1,360,955	1,427,413
Kibos	394,218	1,845,687

ii. SOUTH NYANZA

Homa Bay (including Kendu Bay)	1,989,553	2,888,397

SOURCE: District Agricultural Offices

covered some 60 square miles of North Nyanza District.[17]

When the modern era of administration began in Nyanza about the turn of the century, the subsistence economy of the area was dependent mainly on agriculture in the higher and wetter areas and the keeping of livestock which was more important in the more open areas of the Lake shore, the intervening plateau and the plateau grasslands of the area.

The predominantly agricultural groups had concentrated mainly on what has been defined as Kikuyu/Star Grass areas. Traditional interest in livestock in these areas north and south of the gulf were confined to social functions. But over the plateau areas between the Kikuyu/Star Grass and the lake shore regions and around the lake shore itself, pastoralism played a more important role, the significance depending on the cultural inclination of the group. Pastoralism was thus less influenced by the ecological zonation which has been noted in the area. The fertile highlands of Kericho had become the base of a distinctly pastoral group for which cultivation was of a very minor importance. This was the case with the Nandi plateau which bordered the Lake basin further to the north of Kericho.

But the plateau area between Mount Elgon and the high rainfall core of Kakamega district also supported a number of important ethnic elements for whom pastoral occupation was just as important as cultivation. In the areas further west towards the lake shore, pastoralism formed part of a dual economy which in the immediate vicinity of the lake was further complicated by the influence of fishing.

(a) *The Lake Shore Savannah areas.* The first attempt to diversify the economy outlined began with the establishment of the peasant-grown cotton in this region and within the framework of existing systems of land tenure. For much of the period from 1903 up to 1922 the development of cotton was a virtual failure and it was only after 1931 that the cotton could be regarded as having been well established.[18]

The cotton experiment was begun in the lake shore savannah areas and chiefly in the heavy black cotton soils of the rift floor and the fringing lake lowlands. The areas chosen for this were the flat plains of the east of Kisumu and the lower areas towards the Uganda border.

The cotton belt of the eastern sector of the lake basin now falls into two contrasting zones. The lower areas surrounding the gulf below 4,000 feet above sea level forms part of the lake shore savannah ecological zone. But the production of this peasant-grown crop has subsequently spread to the lower portion of the intervening plateau areas lying below 4,500 feet above sea level. This section forms part of the high rainfall savannah ecological zone.

In South Nyanza the main cotton zone forms a narrow belt from Miriu-Sondu delta to Homa Bay and embraces the location of Karachuonyo, North Nyokal, Kanyada and parts of Lambwe Valley. Cotton planting in this southern area began about 1925, that is later than in the areas north of the gulf. Renewed interest in the crop resulted in further plantings about 1930 and the first ginnery was erected at Kendu Bay about 1932. During the peak cotton boom of 1938–9 a second ginnery was built at Homa Bay. But with the post-war decline in the cotton output the first ginnery has since been closed. Cotton ginning in the area now takes place at Homa Bay. From this southern portion, the cotton belt continues into the lake shore areas of Tanzania.

In Central Nyanza the main cotton areas include the greater part of Bondo Division (Sakwa, Asembo, Yimbo, Uyoma), West Alego and the present Bunyala and Busonga locations. This was the original area for cotton. But the main producing areas of cotton at present lie some 40 to 50 miles west of Kisumu town. A yield of about 100 lb. of seed cotton per acre has been noted on the plains, but the estimated yield of peasant-grown cotton is about 100 to 150 lb. of seed cotton per acre.

The output of cotton from different parts of the cotton region can be gauged from the ginnery returns of seed cotton purchases in Table 3.7. Although there is considerable overlap in the ginnery tributary areas, it will be seen that the Samia area accounted for about 60 per cent, Ndere area 26 per cent and the Kibos area 7 per cent of the Central Nyanza output in 1950–1 season.

The climatic limitation to crop production and land

[17]Swynnerton R. J. M., Booth J. E. P. & Moon J. T. *Agricultural Problems and Potential of the African Lands of Kenya* p. 25 Technical Memorandum February 1953 Department of Agriculture (unpublished)
[18]Fearn H.

tenure have restricted the range of crops which could be used for a further diversification of the economy in the area. Attempts to experiment with low altitude *Excelsa* coffee has been abandoned due to world market conditions for the coffee crop. These plots were located in the lake shore areas where cotton has been established as the major crop. Some parts of the region, notably Uyoma in Central Nyanza and Karachuonyo in South Nyanza have developed groundnuts as an important export crop. But the future of the region does seem to lie in a fuller utilisation of the excess flood water for irrigation purposes.

Although parts of the flat plains of the lake shore region are well suited to irrigation, it is surprising that little progress has been made by peasant effort around the lake shore. Interest in irrigation has been confined to patches of swamp fringes in the plains east of Kisumu where rice has been the focus of attention. The recent Kenya Nile Water Resources Survey (1956)[19] examined the irrigation potential of the swamps in aggraded river valleys and flood plains where the plateau rivers enter the plains. These are areas where the tremendous volume of water from the surrounding highland areas causes widespread flooding annually.

The largest of these potential areas is the Kano Plains east of Kisumu where a massive irrigation project is proposed. The crop pattern envisaged include paddy rice and sugar cane. But the institution of these schemes requires a revolutionary change of outlook on the system of land holding and settlement pattern. The development of the Kano Plains will involve the utilisation of 30,000 acres. A second area of interest is in the lower Yala Swamp and includes an area of about 20,000 acres of swampland.[20] However, apart from this development in cotton by African peasants, for diversification of the economy we must turn to non-African initiative during this early period.

Experiments were made by European firms to introduce the growing of rubber and sisal in the Kisumu neighbourhood. The rubber experiments failed. Sisal experiment was located at Maseno at an altitude of about 5,000 feet above sea level on a 982 acre estate belonging to the East African Industries Limited.[21] The experiment, which began in the first decade of the present century, was eventually abandoned. Sisal is well suited to the hot lake shore savannah areas of Nyanza. A small output comes from the hedge cuttings in scattered parts of the area. But in general it has never developed as an important crop among the peasants of the low lying areas.

One of the most important developments in the lake shore savannah areas of Nyanza has been the establishment of plantation sugar in the Kibos-Miwani and Muhoroni areas. But this development will be more conveniently treated under the 'Former Scheduled Areas'.

Among the activities affecting the economy of the area is the fishing industry. This activity is one of the main pillars of the subsistence economy, but it is also an important part of the modern exchange economy which affects the economic opportunity in the area around the lake.

Although the traditional fishing economy depends on a wide range of species, commercial fishing is largely concentrated on the two well known species of *Tilapia esculenta* and *T. variabilis*. Both are phytoplankton feeders and are often found in the same areas but *T. esculenta* is the predominant species in the shallow gulfs and bays whereas *T. variabilis* tends to be common off the more exposed shores.

T. esculenta which has for long dominated the commercial fish trade is more readily available during the months of April to May when large catches are normally made. But *T. variabilis* is caught in highest numbers just about June, July and August. This is the period when the catches of *T. esculenta* are at their lowest.

Due to the individual and scattered nature of traditional fishing, figures are lacking for the total number of persons supported by this industry and the actual output. The scope of generalisations regarding the place of the industry in the total economy is therefore limited.

Commercial fishing which occupies a number of persons has depended largely on the use of introduced devices and crafts. Two types of nets have been used in the trade. Early in the 1950's the legal method of catching tilapia

[19]Gibb, Sir A. & Partners *Kenya Nile Water Resources Survey* 1956

[20]Kenya: Development Plan 1964–1970 pp. 60–1

[21]Fearn H. p. 96

[22]Lowe (McConnell), Rosemary H. *Observations on the Biology of Tilapia (Pisces-Cichlidae) in Lake Victoria, East Africa* Supplementary Publication No. 1 Uganda Argus, Kampala 1956

was by use of 5 inch gill nets, the indigenous traps already described, and for some time seine nets (1–3 inch mesh).

The 5 inch gill net was introduced into the area during the second decade of the present century. Trade in the net reached a boom in 1925 and in 1930. It was used to supply fish to the developing trade focused on the railhead at Kisumu. The use of the net resulted in a rapid rise in total catches. By 1954–5 some 250 miles of gill nets were being set nightly in the gulf area. During that same period, it was estimated that about 4,000 fishermen were earning the greater part of their living from the activities in the 250 square miles of the gulf waters.[23]

Before 1954 some 30 seine nets were allowed to operate in the gulf area. Reports were made that immature fish were being taken out by the seines. With the rapidly declining catches of tilapia it was decided to close the gulf for seine net fishing after 1 April 1954. This restriction was subsequently lifted because of the difficulty of enforcing the restriction when Uganda and Tanganyika continued to permit the use of seines. It had proved impossible to patrol the 500 mile coastline of the Kenya waters with the available personnel.

Although fishing has continued as an important aspect of the economy of the lower parts of Nyanza and Western Provinces, the industry appears to be in a depressed state and has not recovered from the heavy fishing associated with the high rural population densities for the areas nearby. It is sometimes stressed that the seasonal rhythm of fishing interferes with the agricultural activities and proper care of the land. However, despite these disadvantages, regional planning of the lake shore areas must take into account the continued importance of this natural resource of the Republic.

(b) *The High Rainfall Savannah Zone* (*Acacia-Combretum Zone*). In between the lake shore savannah areas and the richer Kikuyu Grass and Star Grass zones of the Nyanza and Western regions is a zone that has experienced even less development. This is the High Rainfall Savannah region. Agricultural activity of this intervening region is based largely on production of the staple food crops of sorghum, maize and finger millet, varying in importance according to the altitude and rainfall pattern.

In addition to the above staple cereals, cassava has recently increased in importance as a famine relief in response to agricultural policy. It now plays a more important role in the cropland acreage of the area. Banana is a favourite on the wetter fringes but generally conditions become more unsuitable and precarious for the crop towards the margins of the lake shore savannah. South of the gulf, maize, sorghum, beans, potatoes and cassava are the dominant crops in the higher parts below Kisii Highlands. Over the lower parts, severity of the dry season and the general poverty of the soils are reflected in the importance attached to sorghum. Increasing unreliability of rainfall, and poor lateritic soils are among the limiting factors.

Broadly a similar range of crops exist in the area north of the gulf. But the rise of maize to a position of importance from the 1930's has no parallel in the more isolated southern area. This period coincided with the introduction and popularisation of the plough, of the white maize variety and of a major cotton planting drive. The introduction of the plough enlarged the scope of the peasant cultivators and enabled maize to rise to the position of an important cash crop. Thus maize in the higher areas and cotton in the lower parts became the principal cash crops of this ecological zone. The success story of the maize in the northern areas of the present Kakamega and Bungoma Districts was in part a story of transport improvements. It was the extension of the railway from the coast across the area into Uganda in the early decades of the present century which set the pace for important development in peasant-grown maize. During this period the recorded increase of maize production for sale was 2,800 per cent between 1931 and 1936 in the present Bukusu location as compared to 21 per cent for the whole of the former North Nyanza.[24]

Apart from the importance of maize in the region as a whole, cotton continues to be the most successful cash crop. To the north of the gulf the cotton producing areas include the hotter and lower locations of Malakisi, Itesio, Buhayo, Marach, Buholo, North and South Ugenya.

[23]*Lake Victoria Fisheries Service: Annual Report* 1954/55 East African High Commission
[24]Wagner G. *The Bantu of North Kavirondo* Vol II pp. 19–60 Oxford University Press, London 1956

Wagner (1956) recorded an increase of 600 per cent between 1931 and 1937 for the four locations (Marama, Marach, Buhayo and Malakisi). In the area south of the gulf, parts of South Nyanza have been found suitable for sugar. There are plans to develop 80,000 acres of potential sugar lands in East Konyango area of South Nyanza.

In conclusion, it should be noted that, unlike the lake shore savannah areas, the cash crop development has been wholly a peasant activity. The region has not experienced large scale development of agriculture comparable to the lake shore sugar industry. Further, it should be added that in common with the lake shore areas agricultural activities have for long suffered from the restrictive effects of the traditional land tenure in the area. There have been developments of consolidation throughout the area, but most of the land is still held under traditional tenure.

(c) *Kikuyu and Star Grass Zones*. These areas are of special importance because they are part of the limited lands of high potential on which the agricultural economy of the country is based.[25] In addition it will be noted in the chapter on population that the population of the country has tended to concentrate in these areas. However, despite the potential of the land and the availability of manpower, with the exception of Kericho area now included in the Rift Valley Province, the regions have lagged behind in economic development. This slow rate of economic development has been due to a number of factors. In the first instance, the economic policy of the colonial government was more concerned with the development of the European agriculture in the former 'Scheduled Areas'. Secondly, the regions by virtue of their concentration of manpower were used mainly as sources of labour supply for the rapidly developing economy of the highlands. Finally the traditional systems of tenure which had developed in these areas militated against the adoption of more scientific forms of land utilisation. The increasing emphasis which is now placed on the development of these regions indicate a new orientation in economic policy but also an increasing awareness of the importance of a more scientific use of the land in these areas.

At a time when cotton and sugar were being established in the lower areas of Nyanza, these regions remained under the traditional subsistence economy. The striking changes which have taken place in the land utilisation and which will in the future have an important bearing on population mobility are the outcome of developments in these regions mainly since the Second World War. The changes have involved a modification in the crop range of the traditional subsistence economy which prevailed during the earlier years. New cash crops have been introduced which were formerly restricted to European farming areas.

Perhaps more important for the future, the efforts to match these changes with those in the traditional forms of land tenure have begun to take effect. Although the regions are capable of supporting a wide range of crops, the traditional economy placed emphasis on the basic subsistence crops.

In Kisii Highlands, the rural economy was characterised by emphasis on maize, finger millet and sorghum with additions of beans, sweet potatoes and bananas. The increasing importance of bananas in the area is regarded as a relatively recent development coming mainly from the areas further north of the gulf.

To the north of Kisii Highlands, the small patch of high potential land in Nyabondo plateau area supported broadly similar subsistence crops. Here maize, finger millet, beans and sweet potatoes were the main crops. Maize was particularly favoured by the deep loam soils which developed over the weathered lava flows. In common with Kisii Highlands, bananas are now a well established part of the crop complex.

The rapid spread of bananas in this region and elsewhere in recent years has been largely due to their importance as an alternative source of starch in the area of rapidly growing population. In this respect it has assumed the important role of a major cash crop and is now a common feature of homesteads in the area.

The food crops of the similar parts to the north of the gulf include finger millet, sorghum, sweet potatoes, bananas and sesame. Maize has become the most important cereal though formerly finger millet and sorghum were the leading cereals.

[25]*Kenya: Development Plan* 1964–1970 p. 45 para 3 Government Printer, Nairobi 1964

Table 3.8

Crop	Percentage of total weight
Maize	35
Sorghum	13
Finger Millet	5
Beans, peas	18
Sweet Potatoes, Cassava	14
Bananas	15
Total	100

Table 3.9

District	Coffee	Pyrethrum ACRES	Tea
North Nyanza	8,000	—	10,000
South Nyanza	15,000	15,000	8,000
Kericho	—	—	16,000

In the Maragoli area, Wagner (1956) recorded the crop ratios in Table 3.8.[26]

Except for the pioneer fringe around Mount Elgon, the Kikuyu Grass and Star Grass regions have experienced pressure on available land resources because of the increasing population. In Kisii, parts of Central Nyanza and North Nyanza the pressure on land resources is reflected in the cropping practice. For many years, the subsistence farmers in these areas have been faced with the problems of diminishing space and falling yields of the basic cereal crops. It is against this background that the growing popularity of bananas may be viewed. Further the problems partly explain the common practice of interplanting of crops which is more elaborate here than in the areas of lesser potential. The basic pattern involves a mixture of a staple cereal and one of the many pulses grown in the region. But in certain areas it is common to find more than two cereals in one field. With the introduction of bananas and cassava these have been added to the crop complex. This practice of mixed cropping renders the estimates of crop acreages unreliable. In general the cereal maize tends to be more dominant over the deeper loam soils.

Particular mention must be made of the development of maize which has made rapid strides in the High Rainfall Savannah Zone. Whereas maize has dwindled as an export commodity in other areas, the foothill locations of Mount Elgon are leading surplus areas today. It is the emphasis of maize and other cash crops that accounts for the recent rapid increase in land devoted to crops.

But the growing contribution of the Kikuyu/Star Grass Zones of the former Nyanza to the economy of the Republic is a reflection of the relatively late introduction of the four basic cash crops of coffee, pyrethrum, tea and wattle. These crops were established earlier in the other parts of Kenya where European farming had developed to a high degree of efficiency.

Tables 3.8 and 3.9 indicate the targets set for the former non-scheduled areas of Nyanza by the Swynnerton Plan.[27]

Coffee. Although parts of the lower plateau areas of Nyanza with high rainfall are suitable for the Robusta type of coffee, Arabica is the principal species to have been developed in these areas of Nyanza. It will be noted that the Swynnerton Plan envisaged an eventual coffee acreage of 8,000 for the growing areas of North Nyanza and 15,000 acres for South Nyanza. The bulk of the South Nyanza acreage was planned for Kisii Highlands where a combination of climate and soil provided ideal conditions.

In the South Nyanza area, the story of coffee began with a small acreage of the half-Kents variety and half-French Mission type in the first District Council Nursery in 1933. This had an uncertain start with coffee suffering a major set-back with the outbreak of the 1939–45 war. The present producing acreage is wholly the outcome of post-war changes in policy which permitted cautious development of coffee farming in the non-scheduled areas. Before this it had been argued that an expansion of coffee growing by Africans would result in a rapid spread of coffee diseases and hence endanger the plantation-grown coffee on which the economy of the country depended.

In Kisii Highlands the main development has been a replacement of the earlier Kents variety with Blue Mountain type which is more tolerant of high altitude conditions. Table 3.10 shows the trend of coffee production in South Nyanza between 1951 and 1955.

Between 1955 and 1957 South Nyanza production from Kisii Highlands placed the District third among the African growing areas of Kenya.[28] The official policy is to confine the production of Arabica to a zone ranging from 4,800 feet to 6,400 feet above sea level. The coffee harvest here is fitted into the seasonal rhythm with a light harvest from late April to May and a heavy harvest from September to November. Arabica yield is estimated at 8 hundred-weight per acre and marketing is on a co-operative basis. It was forecast that the export of coffee from the area by 1965 would reach 2,715 tons.[29]

Developments in the former North Nyanza Districts

[26] Wagner G. Vol. II p. 20

[27] Swynnerton R. J. M. A Plan to Intensify Development of African Agriculture in Kenya p. 18 Government Printer, Nairobi 1954

[28] International Bank for Reconstruction and Development Report 1962 p. 82

[29] Kenya: Report of the Committee to Carry out an Economic Survey of South Nyanza and Kericho District p. 36, 1957

Table 3.10

	1951	1952	1953	1954	1955
Number of growers	1,470	1,746	2,923	3,425	4,584
Acres planted	370	472	756	1,136	1,707
Acres in bearing	182	205	281	360	471
Parchment Coffee (marketed in tons)	26·51	41·1	46·4	90·0	—
Buni Coffee (marketed in tons)	—	26·2	54·8	117·0	—

SOURCE: *South Nyanza District Agricultural Gazetteer*

have been equally recent. The first commercial plantings took place here in 1955 and the total area planted increased from 76 acres at the end of the year to 121 acres at the end of 1956. A phased development has been followed beginning with the fertile southern locations of Bunyore, Maragoli, Nyangori and Teriki. Under strict supervision plantings have since been extended to the remaining Star Grass Zone. By 1963, there were two coffee pulping stations in Maragoli location, one in Bunyore and one in Nyangori location.

Unlike the areas already described, the expansion of coffee in the foothill parts of the former Elgon Nyanza District has taken place in an area with more land. Returns from the coffee Board of Kenya showed that production of coffee by 1955–6 had placed the Elgon Nyanza District fifth among the African coffee producers in Kenya. The area is now one of the important Arabica coffee regions of Kenya. It includes the greater part of the 8,000 acres which were set by the Swynnerton Plan for the District.

Pyrethrum. The pyrethrum plant was first introduced into Kenya before World War II and rapidly became one of the most important export crops. Its importance in the economy of Kenya is due to the use of the flower as a natural insecticide. Kenya is now the most important producer of this natural insecticide in the world.

Developments in Nyanza Province have been confined to Kisii Highlands where climatic conditions and soils are particularly suitable. The Swynnerton Plan envisaged an ultimate target of 15,000 acres of pyrethrum for the old South Nyanza production area. Thus when the target is reached, South Nyanza including Kisii will be the largest producer among the former non-scheduled areas of Kenya. This activity will be wholly concentrated in the present Kisii district. Pyrethrum production in Nyanza is a peasant activity carried on a co-operative basis. In 1963, there were twenty-four pyrethrum societies alone in the Kisii District and they sold a crop worth about £100,000.[30] It has become one of the most valuable crops in the diversification of the rural economy of Kisii Highlands and the neighbouring parts of Kericho District. The area available is limited by restriction of the altitudinal range to between 6,400 to 7,000 feet above sea level.

Tea. This is the third important crop in a drive for a fuller utilisation of the higher ecological zones of the former Nyanza. Tea is primarily a plantation crop. Its history and significance to population mobility will be discussed in the section on Kericho production area. It was introduced into Kenya in the 1920's and the total acreage in the whole country was 51,000 acres in 1962. In that year this acreage produced 36·2 million pounds of tea worth £6·7 million.[31] For nearly thirty years development of tea was restricted to former scheduled areas where it was planted on large commercial estates. Since that time development of peasant-grown tea has been limited by the location of the capital equipment needed for processing the crop. Before 1960 there were only 1,572 acres of tea on small holdings. The Swynnerton Plan which opened the way to development of the crop in former African areas set a target of 10,000 acres for North Nyanza (including the Elgon Foothills), 8,000 acres for South Nyanza and 16,000 acres for the African areas of Kericho District. Although less important than coffee, it is one of the important cash crops which has been established in the Kisii Highland area. Experiments are continuing with the establishment of tea in the restricted areas of the Kakamega district. Here Kaimosi area has forged ahead of the remainder of the ecologically suitable parts of the district.

Wattle. Development of the wattle bark industry in the Nyanza area is recent. For many years the main interest in the former non-scheduled area was limited to Central Province which in 1950 provided two-fifths of all dried wattle bark. The main districts in the old Nyanza with possibilities are Kericho and Kisii. A target of 30,000 acres was set for the Kipsigis and Kisii non-scheduled area. Kisii area should by 1965 have had 17,000 acres of wattle. There is however, less interest in the crop at the moment as farmers turn to tea.

Situated in the south-eastern corner of the former Nyanza province is Kericho District which is one of the most important and developing farming areas of Kenya. The greater part of the district falls within the Kikuyu/Star Grass Zone and the whole area is now included in

[30]*Industry in East Africa* 1964–5 p. 71
[31]*Industry in Kenya* 1964–65 p. 69

the Rift Valley Province as a result of the 1962 boundary revision. As part of former Nyanza Province this is one of the two areas which has been intensively affected by non-African agricultural activity. The land was formerly divided into eight subdivisions including the predominantly African areas of Sotik, Buret and Belgut, the European settled parts of Sotik and Kericho, the former Kericho European area located north of the railway line as well as the forest reserve in the extreme east of the district.

In terms of ecology, the Buret Division is similar to Kisii Highland and is suitable for the same range of crops. This area contains some of the best tea growing lands in Kenya. The northern half of the former African areas of Sotik also share similar characteristics. But the southern half is less rich though some useful cash crops are also possible. The Belgut section consists of two dissimilar parts. To the east and bordering the Kikuyu/Star Grass and similar parts of Kericho settled areas is an extremely fertile country. But further west, the land changes to a savannah country with inferior soils, low rainfall and higher temperatures.

The former settled area of Sotik though less rich is nevertheless a high potential land area suited to a wide range of agricultural products, north Sotik is specially well suited to tea, coffee and wattle production. But the central and western portion of this area has developed into an important breeding centre for livestock. A portion of the former Kericho European area lying south of the railway line is devoted principally to tea growing. But the rest of the land is also well suited to balanced farming.

The northern half of the former Kericho European area includes the foothills of Tinderet which are well suited to coffee farming. But administratively it also includes the low country of Muhoroni-Chemelil and Songhor which now form part of the new Central Nyanza District. These flattish areas have been included in a description of the sugar farming.

In the exteme east of the district is the Crown Forest Reserve covering the upper slopes of the Mau. This is a vital water catchment area lying above the productive tea lands and other agricultural areas of Kericho. Experiments have been conducted to ascertain the possible effects of expansion of tea cultivation in the area.

In this experimental programme the 1,700 acre Sambret Valley excised from the Forest Reserve was leased for full development to the Brooke Bond (East Africa) Company.[32] Before the European settlement in the area the occupied parts supported the predominantly pastoral Kipsigis and land was held in common. Individual rights to land were confined to the period of cultivation.

The Kipsigis originally depended on finger millet as the main cereal. But with the introduction of maize in the area in the second decade of the present century by European farmers and the popularisation of the steel plough, the rural economy underwent a revolution which has changed the entire landscape of the Kipsigis country. With the use of the plough, cultivation, formerly undertaken by women, became more and more a male occupation. Between 1930 and 1940 the area made great strides in land consolidation.

Summary. In summarising the Nyanza economy as a background to migration, the impact is striking of the introduction of new crops and types of farming by non-Africans. Later this becomes the official policy of administration as a means of improving the rural areas in which the majority of the Africans live. But against this development there is the general stagnation of the greater part of the economy in which utilisation of the land is directed largely to production of subsistence crops. The importance of the subsistence economy in Nyanza emerges clearly in the following figures (Table 3.11 to 3.13).

The dominance of subsistence crops such as finger millet, maize, sorghum, pulses, cassava and traditional livestock is a reflection of a different approach to resource development. The chief cash earners which underlie the wealth of the principal areas of modern farming are noted for their small acreages. Considered against this background, the islands of large scale farming in the province assume an added importance in the migration of labour force.

ii. *The Rift Valley Province (non-scheduled)*
Extending across the rift and its associated highlands the old Rift Valley Province occupies a strategic location in the farming lands of Kenya. Although in the north and

[32]Pereira H. C. 'The Development of Tea Estates in Tall Rain Forest' *East African Agricultural and Forestry Journal* pp. 16–21 Vol. 27 Special Issue, March 1962

Table 3.11 NYANZA PROVINCE

Acreage of Temporary Crops by Districts (Total of both Crop Cycles)

CROP	Elgon Nyanza	North Nyanza	Central Nyanza	South Nyanza	Kericho	Nyanza Province
			'000 ACRES			
Wheat	—	—	—	—	—	—
Rice	4·4	—	1·8	—	—	6·2
Millet	1·5	—	0·9	29·8	—	32·2
Wimbi	52·1	40·2	87·4	77·8	24·8	282·2
Sorghum	59·0	96·8	160·5	28·2	0·2	344·9
Maize	133·6	290·5	216·8	176·1	91·4	908·4
Pulses	12·9	141·5	65·3	42·5	0·7	263·0
Potatoes	1·3	1·1	0·6	0·7	0·2	3·9
Sweet Potatoes	5·4	4·0	2·0	8·2	0·3	19·9
Cassava	50·3	31·6	43·4	31·1	—	156·4
Sugar Cane	3·8	3·8	—	1·5	0·2	9·3
Cotton	27·3	—	6·2	4·1	—	37·5
Ground Nuts	2·2	1·7	6·2	10·3	—	20·2
Sesame	2·7	—	—	5·1	—	7·8
Pyrethrum	—	—	—	4·2	—	4·2
Vegetables	—	—	—	0·3	—	0·3
Others	—	1·3	0·6	0·1	0·3	2·3
Aggregate Acreage of Crops	356·5	612·5	591·7	420·0	118·1	2,098·7
Acreage under Temporary Crops	246·9	377·5	348·9	311·7	103·7	1,388·6

SOURCE: *Kenya African Agricultural Sample Census* 1960/61 Part II p. 55 Appendix Table 96

Table 3.12 ACREAGE OF PERMANENT CROPS

CROP	South Nyanza	Central Nyanza	North Nyanza	Elgon Nyanza	Kericho	TOTAL
			'000 ACRES			
Bananas alone	2·4	2·3	18·7	8·4	0·2	32·0
Bananas associated	2·9	1·5	5·3	4·8	0·7	15·3
Pineapples	—	—	—	—	—	—
Other Fruit	0·6	—	—	0·2	0·8	1·6
Total Fruit	5·9	3·8	24·0	13·4	1·7	48·9
Coffee	5·6	0·1	0·7	2·6	0·1	9·1
Tea	—	—	—	—	0·2	0·2
Sisal	—	—	—	—	—	—
Wattle	1·5	—	—	—	2·6	4·1
Total Industrial Crops	7·1	0·1	0·7	2·6	2·9	13·4
Total Permanent Crops	13·0	3·9	24·8	16·0	4·6	62·3

SOURCE: *Kenya African Agricultural Sample Census* 1960/61 p. 59

Table 3.13 NYANZA PROVINCE

Numbers of Livestock by Districts

LIVESTOCK	Elgon Nyanza	North Nyanza	Central Nyanza	South Nyanza	Kericho	Nyanza Province
Cattle	260·4	111·0	No census	311·5	303·9	986·9
Sheep	31·4	73·2	279·4	136·9	367·8	888·7
Goats	54·9	54·0	269·2	156·2	225·3	759·6
Pigs	0·5	—	—	5·1	—	5·6
Poultry	359·2	643·7	1,058·8	529·3	202·7	2,793·2

SOURCE: *Kenya African Agricultural Sample Census* 1960/61 p. 59

south the Province is characterised by lands of low potential, the well-watered highland areas and the more elevated portion of the rift floor are amongst the best farming lands in the Republic.

At the turn of the century this portion of Kenya was predominantly a pastoral world with cattle as the mainstay of the nomadic groups which roamed over the area. Its importance as a goal for the shifting population is largely due to the inclusion of the bulk of the former scheduled lands in the area. Prior to the opening up of the former scheduled areas for settlement by non-Europeans, the Rift Valley could be defined largely as alienated land with the peripheral African districts of Nandi in the extreme western margin and the Baringo, Elgeyo-Marakwet and West Suk in the extreme north. In these two land units, different approaches to land utilisation have led to wide differences in economic opportunities.

Development of the rural economy of the former non-scheduled areas of the province has been influenced by the nature of the five main ecological zones of the area (Table 3.14). These are:

(a) The High Cold Mountain Zone.
(b) Kikuyu/Star Grass Zone.
(c) Perennial ranching lands at 4,500 feet to 6,500 feet above sea level.
(d) *Acacia-Commiphora*/*Commiphora Sansevieria* Bush.
(e) Steep to precipitous escarpment land mainly given over to shifting ledge cultivation, at an altitude of 3,500 feet to 8,000 feet above sea level.

(a) *High Cold Mountain Zone.* A summary division of the former African areas by ecological zones showed that allowing for 5 per cent waste land, these areas had 855 square miles of utilisable land in the High Cold Mountain Zone at an altitude of 8,000 to 10,000 feet above sea level. The land enjoys a rainfall of over 40 inches, well distributed over 7 to 8 months. Most of it was in Elgeyo and West Suk districts. Growth rate is poor because of cold conditions and thin soil. The zone has been used mainly for cattle and sheep ranching. Some rotational grazing schemes have been introduced in the area. In some parts attempts have been made by the inhabitants of the area

to grow maize. But due to high altitude and cold conditions, maize takes about nine to ten months to mature. The resulting crop is generally poor and subject to frost.

(b) *Kikuyu Grass/Star Grass Zone.* This is the most productive zone in the area. It comprises a total of 860 square miles, the bulk of this utilisable land was in the Nandi and Baringo districts. The region falls into the two subdivisions of the Kikuyu Grass Zone and the Star Grass Zone. Within the Rift Valley the altitude ranges from 6,000 to 7,500 feet above sea level. Rainfall varying from 25 to 40 inches is reliable and is well distributed over six to seven months. Conditions in this zone are highly favourable to arable farming but at higher levels plant growth rate is slow due to low temperatures. The best areas are found in the Nandi, Baringo, Elgeyo and West Suk. It is reckoned that about three-fifths of the Nandi District consists of land within this category.

The majority of Africans in this zone are pastoral but, in recent years, there has been expansion of maize monoculture particularly in Nandi. In Elgeyo especially along the Uasin Gishu border, wheat is grown for sale.

(c) *Perennial ranching area.* The second most extensive ecological zone in the Rift Valley lies at an altitude of 4,500 to 6,000 feet above sea level. Rainfall ranges from 20 to 30 inches spreading over five to seven months. Typical of this type of land are the better grazing lands of Samburu and Baringo. It is a marginal area for crop production but is more suited to beef ranching in large rotational grazing blocks. The area has tended to suffer from overstocking and uncontrolled grazing. It will be necessary to improve water supplies in order to raise the productivity.

(d) *Acacia-Commiphora and Commiphora-Sansevieria Bush.* Situated largely on the semi-desert fringe it is natural that this should form the most extensive ecological zone. The zone is characterised by a low and unreliable rainfall generally less than 25 inches a year. The high temperatures and high rate of evaporation place severe strain on plants in the area. Agriculture is hardly possible. The bulk of this type of land is to be found in Samburu,

Table 3.14 AREA OF UTILISABLE LAND AVAILABLE (SQUARE MILES)

Ecological Zones

DISTRICT	(a) (Less 5 per cent for waste)	(b) (Less 10 per cent for waste)	(c) (No deduction)	(d) (Less 10 per cent for waste)	(e) (Less 10 per cent for waste)	TOTAL
Nandi	—	500	—	—	16	516
West Suk	380	90	130	585	120	1,305
Elgeyo	380	90	100	270	60	900
Baringo	—	180	375	2,520	80	3,155
Samburu	95	—	670	5,751	—	6,516
Total	855	860	1,275	9,126	276	12,392

SOURCE: Swynnerton R. J. M. Booth J. E. P. & Moon J. F. *Agricultural Problems and Potential of the African Lands of Kenya* p. 25 Technical Memorandum 23 February 1953 Department of Agriculture

Table 3.15 ACREAGE OF TEMPORARY CROPS BY TYPE

CROP	Total Crop Acreage '000 ACRES
Wimbi	0·5
Maize	39·3
Pulses	0·5
Potatoes	0·1
Sugar Cane	0·1
Vegetables	0·1
Others	0·2
Aggregate Acreage of Crops	40·8
Acreage under Temporary Crops	40·7

SOURCE: *Kenya African Agriculture Sample Census 1960/61* p. 116

Table 3.17 NUMBERS OF LIVESTOCK

LIVESTOCK	Nandi District THOUSANDS
Improved exotic cattle	1·9
Improved native cattle	1·0
Unimproved local cattle	257·3
Total Cattle	260·3
Sheep	94·8
Goats	46·1
Pigs	—
Poultry	80·5

Table 3.16 ACREAGE OF PERMANENT CROPS

CROP	Eastern Division	Southern Division	Northern Division '000 ACRES	Central Division	Nandi District
Bananas alone	—	—	—	—	—
Bananas associated	—	—	—	0·1	0·1
Pineapples	—	—	—	—	—
Other Fruit	—	—	—	—	—
Total Fruit	—	—	—	0·1	0·1
Coffee	—	—	0·1	—	0·1
Tea	—	—	—	—	—
Sisal	—	—	—	—	—
Wattle	0·9	0·3	0·9	0·1	2·2
Total Industrial Plants	0·9	0·3	1·0	0·2	2·4
Total Permanent Crop	0·9	0·3	1·0	0·2	2·4

SOURCE: *Kenya African Agricultural Sample Census 1960/61* p. 122

Baringo and extends into neighbouring districts. Here the dominant form of land use is very similar to zone (*c*). The proposed grazing blocks would require longer periods of resting. Soil erosion is a far more serious problem. The greater part of the districts covered are unsuited to agriculture.

(*e*) *Steep to precipitous escarpments.* Due to tectonic influences on topography, a considerable proportion of land in the Rift Valley Province consists of steep to precipitous escarpments ranging from 3,500 to 8,000 feet in altitude. The lands experience a wide range of conditions and are unsuited to balanced farming or pastoral occupations because of the excessively steep slopes.

In various parts of the Province, this type of land is used for temporary patch cultivation and fallow. Under traditional practice the fertility of the land was protected by the system of shifting cultivation which allows for restoration over a period varying from three to fifteen years. Table 3.14 shows that this type of land was to be found in the Nandi, West Suk, Elgeyo and Baringo districts.

Summary. Development in the Nandi district, the best endowed of the former African districts in the Rift Valley, reflects the same slow change we have noted in the other predominantly African Districts. The acreage from the African Agricultural Sample Census for Nandi gives an indication of the economy of the area (Tables 3.15–3.17). We may conclude that the economy of the Nandi District in respect of the potential cash earners is undeveloped. There was in 1960–1 a marked dependence on unimproved livestock and the newly introduced maize as a cash crop. It is unlikely that such an economy would attract a large labour supply. Similarly the economy in the pastoral areas described could be regarded as basically subsistence in orientation. The underdeveloped nature of the economy of these areas will be seen as presenting a marked contrast with the adjacent activity in the former scheduled areas.

iii. *The Central Province (non-scheduled)*
Situated in the heart of the country, and almost coinciding with the core of high rainfall centred on the Aberdares and Mount Kenya-Nyambeni region, the Central Province in 1961 included the two scheduled districts of Nanyuki, Thika and the five African Districts of Kiambu, Fort Hall, Nyeri, Embu and Meru. The situation in Kiambu was affected by the presence of considerable areas of alienated land and plantation farming.

The former scheduled districts will be considered together with the rest of the former alienated lands. But it is necessary to note the peripheral distribution of the former scheduled areas in the exteme north and southern fringes of the districts. In the south-west this important region merges into the rapidly growing urban region of Nairobi.

The history of land use in the region has shared in the problems of the other former African districts in the Republic. However, with its population problem, and situated centrally to the areas of vastly different economic development, its economy has received a more powerful impact and the motivation for change. The population features of the region will be treated at a later stage. But it is necessary to describe the main aspects of the economy as it has developed.

The contrast between the tilted plateau of the Aberdares, Mount Kenya and the Nyambeni mass with the lower and drier country to the east has already been mentioned and the effect of altitudinal differences on the ecology of the Aberdares, Mount Kenya, Nyambeni areas have also been considered. However, it should be noted that the rural economy which supports the dense population concentration of the Central Province is based on the varied potential of the following six main ecological zones into which the former non-scheduled lands can be subdivided:

(*a*) The High Bracken zone.
(*b*) Kikuyu Grass zone.
(*c*) Star Grass zone.
(*d*) The Grass Plains Savannah or Grass Woodlands.
(*e*) *Acacia-Combretum* zone.
(*f*) *Acacia-Commiphora* and *Commiphora Sansevieria* Bush.

This traditional economy had begun to differentiate itself into two forms in the initial period of settlement of the area. The vast majority of the people who now form part of the Central Province were essentially cultivators practicing some hunting. But livestock was subsidiary except in the lower country where prior to the spread of

Table 3.18		Table 3.19	
District	Area (SQUARE MILES LESS 10 PER CENT)	District	Area (SQUARE MILES LESS 10 PER CENT)
Kiambu	129	Kiambu	149
Fort Hall	99	Fort Hall	216
Nyeri	132	Nyeri	112
Embu	108	Embu	124
Meru	112	Meru	432

SOURCE: Swynnerton R. J. M., Booth J. E. P. & Moon J.T. *Agricultural Problems and Potential of the African Lands of Kenya* p. 10

tsetse, conditions were more particularly suitable for cattle. With more settled conditions and under the influence of economic and land policy of the colonial administration the following patterns have emerged within the six ecological zones.

(a) *High Bracken Zone.* The zone lying at an altitude of 6,500 to 7,500 feet above sea level includes the lands below the forest edge on the Aberdares and Mount Kenya. The rainfall is 60 to 80 inches and is well distributed for agricultural purposes. But cold conditions inhibit plant growth and hence agricultural activities. The soils are poor, light and powdery. Agricultural activities in Kikuyuland included shifting cultivation of maize with sweet potatoes, English potatoes and some bananas. On the slopes of Mount Kenya, in Embu and Meru, foxtail and bulrush millets are important.

Because of infertility of the soil it has only been possible to raise one or two crops before bush fallow. Such a system could only support a low population density. Because of this it tended to be less fragmented than the other area. If Kikuyu grass and exotic leys can be established dairying with limited areas of potatoes, tea and pyrethrum and wattle could be more successful. The bulk of this land is in Fort Hall.

(b) *Kikuyu Grass Zone.* The second ecological zone in the Central Province is a subdivision of the balanced mixed farming area. In the Central Province it lies at an altitude of 5,500 to 6,500 feet above sea level. Rainfall ranges from 30 to 50 inches and is distributed between two planting seasons. This is one of the most important ecological zones in the Central Province and is heavily populated. The figures in Table 3.18, excluding land unsuited to agriculture, show a relatively even distribution between the districts of Kiambu, Nyeri, Embu and Meru.

The traditional practice in this area before enclosure was shifting cultivation, with maize and beans as the main crops. Some potatoes and sweet potatoes are grown as well. With the concentration of population, there has been a tendency for the fallow period to be very short. It is a zone which before enclosure move was severely fragmented. The present cash crop policy in the region is to develop tea in the upper part of the ecological zone and Arabica coffee at lower levels. The farming system envisaged for the zone may thus be defined as an intensive balanced system including an arable ley rotation, permanent pasture, wattle and cash crops. The zone is also well suited for dairying. Among the cash crops, tea and pyrethrum are particularly suitable for most parts of the Kikuyu districts and for the whole of the region covered in Embu and Meru. Pineapple growing is well established in the Kiambu District and Fort Hall. In addition, there is a large production of flowers, vegetables, charcoal and firewood in Kiambu and Fort Hall for the Nairobi market.

(c) *Star Grass Zone.* The altitude of this ecological zone ranges from just about 5,000 to 5,500 feet above sea level. By 1953 the distribution of utilisable land available was as in Table 3.19.

Rainfall in this region varies from 25 to 40 inches and is distributed between two planting seasons. Temperatures are higher and more favourable to plant growth. Together with the Kikuyu Grass Zone, this is the most heavily populated and productive part of the Central Province. Until quite recently the region was primarily a shifting cultivation zone with maize as the main cereal. In addition, legumes are also grown either interplanted or in pure stand. In Meru and Embu section, millet is far more important both in the short and during the long rains. The climate of the zone permits, in addition, subsistence crops such as sorghum, bulrush millet, finger millet, wheat, beans, cowpeas and pigeon peas. Quite common are potatoes and sweet potatoes, cassava and colocasia, bananas and sugar cane, in swamps.

(d) *Grass Woodland Zone.* In the Central Province, this region includes land generally between 4,000 and 5,000 feet above sea level. Rainfall varies from 25 to 35 inches a year and in common with higher areas it has two planting seasons. The zone is important because it includes areas with the greatest potential for irrigation. The figures in Table 3.20 indicate the distribution of utilisable area of this type of land in the five districts of the former Central Province.

In common with other ecological zones where traditional agricultural practices have been dominant, this has

Table 3.20

DISTRICT	Area (square miles less 10 per cent)	DISTRICT	Area (square miles less 10 per cent)
Kiambu	9	Embu	263
Fort Hall	54	Meru	414
Nyeri	16		

SOURCE: Swynnerton, Booth, and Moon

Table 3.21 ACREAGE OF TEMPORARY CROPS BY DISTRICTS

'000 ACRES

CROP	Kiambu	Nyeri	Fort Hall	Embu	Meru	Central Province
Wheat	—	1·3	—	1·5	—	2·7
Rice	—	—	—	—	—	—
Millet and Wimbi	—	0·9	2·3	44·4	73·8	121·4
Sorghum	—	0·1	0·2	0·8	2·1	3·2
Maize	115·2	96·1	176·8	122·1	212·0	722·1
Pulses	92·7	99·5	121·7	120·4	149·5	583·7
Potatoes	49·5	27·5	2·8	3·7	19·7	103·1
Sweet Potatoes	32·4	18·0	20·5	1·9	5·2	78·1
Arrow root	5·0	2·7	5·6	0·6	1·3	15·1
Yams	10·5	3·1	3·5	4·3	55·6	77·0
Cassava	8·2	0·6	2·8	0·7	5·5	17·8
Sugar Cane	7·3	3·2	4·6	4·8	23·1	43·1
Cotton	—	—	—	—	—	—
Tobacco	—	0·1	—	0·4	—	0·5
Pyrethrum	4·8	1·6	—	—	—	6·5
Vegetables	8·2	1·4	0·3	0·9	—	10·8
Others	0·3		0·6	0·2	4·0	5·0
Aggregate Acreage of Crops	334·1	256·1	341·7	306·7	551·8	1,790·1
Acreage under Temporary Crops	144·0	137·9	200·0	141·0	385·7	1,008·8

SOURCE: *Kenya African Agricultural Sample Census 1960/61 p. 6*

Table 3.22 ACREAGE OF PERMANENT CROPS BY DISTRICTS

'000 ACRES

CROP	Kiambu	Nyeri	Fort Hall	Embu	Meru	TOTAL
Bananas alone	2·8	1·8	4·4	2·1	12·7	23·8
Bananas associated	28·6	3·2	16·9	12·2	27·8	88·7
Pineapples	5·8	0·1	0·2	—	—	6·0
Other Fruit	—	0·1	—	—	—	0·1
Total Fruit	37·2	5·1	21·5	14·3	40·5	118·6
Coffee	3·4	3·1	5·2	3·7	16·3	31·7
Tea	0·5	1·4	0·3	0·3	—	2·5
Sisal	0·1	—	—	—	—	0·1
Wattle	64·4	7·2	8·5	2·5	1·7	84·3
Total Industrial Plants	68·4	11·7	14·0	6·5	18·0	118·6
Total Permanent Crops	105·6	16·8	35·5	20·8	58·5	237·2

SOURCE: *Kenya African Agricultural Sample Census 1960/61 p. 10*

Table 3.23 NUMBERS OF LIVESTOCK BY DISTRICT (EXCLUDING MERU)

'000

LIVESTOCK	Kiambu	Nyeri	Fort Hall	Embu	Central
Improved exotic cattle	1·3	2·0	—	0·8	4·1
Improved native cattle	5·5	12·7	0·5	3·6	22·3
Unimproved local cattle	60·7	68·6	125·5	69·0	323·8
Total cattle	67·5	83·3	126·0	73·4	350·2
Sheep	48·1	56·7	60·1	30·7	195·6
Goats	25·0	18·7	57·4	16·7	117·7
Pigs	1·6	1·4	3·3	4·6	10·9
Poultry	117·0	44·1	136·3	83·2	380·6

SOURCE: *Kenya African Agricultural Sample Census 1960/61 p. 10*

in the past been a zone largely devoted to shifting cultivation to meet subsistence needs. In the Kikuyu districts the maize-legume mixture was common. But in Embu and Meru, millets and legumes have been the most important combination. Fragmentation, in the whole of this area except Kiambu, was less severe in the early 1950's. The zone is capable of supporting a balanced agricultural system especially in the upper part. This higher area is suitable for arable grass leys with fodder for dry season feeding. Drought resistant grains and root crops are a necessity. Part of the Mwea-Tebere Grassland with scattered trees which occurs within the woodland zone now supports a thriving agriculture based on irrigation.

(e) Acacia-Combretum Zone. Away from the volcanic landscape the lower areas of the former Central Province lying on metamorphic rocks receive about 25 to 35 inches a year. These areas are confined to parts of Embu and Meru which extend far eastwards over the crystalline platform and lie beyond the volcanic slopes of Mount Kenya and Nyambene. The traditional agriculture is based largely on sorghum and millets with some legumes. Some cassava and sweet potatoes have been encouraged as famine relief crops. The soils are easily eroded. A rather precarious balanced system of farming may be possible with a heavy dependence on fodder or silage in the dry season. Drought resistant crops are vital. Sorghum, bulrush millet, cassava for food, pigeon peas and grams are advisable for cash crops. In this part, sisal could do well as one of the cash crops. The zone may be regarded as suitable for a semi-intensive form of agriculture. This type of land includes 159 square miles in Embu and 315 square miles in Meru.

(f) Acacia-Commiphora and Commiphora-Sansevieria Bush. The districts of Embu and Meru extend over a semi-arid landscape with a mean annual rainfall of less than 25 inches a year. It has already been noted that even this amount is highly unreliable, spasmodic and of short duration. The high temperatures characteristic of the region and the high evaporation that results provide serious obstacles to agriculture without the aid of irrigation. It is naturally most important in Meru district which extends eastwards and north-eastwards into the

Table 3.24 AREA UNDER PERMANENT CROPS BY DISTRICT

District	Province	'000 Acres	Per cent of total
Kiambu		105·6	32·3
Nyeri		16·8	5·1
Fort Hall		35·5	10·9
Embu		20·8	6·4
Meru		58·5	17·9
	Central Province	237·2	72·6
South Nyanza		13·0	4·0
Central Nyanza		3·9	1·2
North Nyanza		24·8	7·6
Elgon Nyanza		16·0	4·9
Kericho		4·6	1·4
	Nyanza	62·3	19·1
Machakos		22·5	6·9
Kitui		2·5	0·7
	Southern Province	25·0	7·6
Nandi		2·4	9·7
	SURVEY TOTAL	326·9	100·0

SOURCE: *Kenya African Agricultural Sample Census 1960/61 Vol. I p. 44*

Table 3.25 AREA OF UTILISABLE LAND

Square miles (less 10 per cent for wasteland)

	Machakos	*Kitui*
Star Grass	130	—
Grass Plains—Savannah or Grass Woodland	306	36
Acacia Combretum	948	1,089
Acacia Commiphora *Thorn Commiphora* and *Sansevieria* Bush	2,357	7,425

SOURCE: Swynnerton, Booth & Moon p. 25

semi-desert landscape of the present North-Eastern Province. The meagre population of the area practice some form of shifting cultivation coping with the uncertain rainfall with legumes and drought resistant crops. In this area, it is necessary for a family to cultivate a much larger acreage to make up for the uncertainty of the harvest. Cultivation depends on adequate bush and grass for a good burn. In Embu and Meru it has been common to cut the bush and leave it to grow for a year before burning.

Because of thin population, fragmentation is not a danger in the area. But close to water overstocking is general. In the land use preferred for the region, cultivation should be reduced to the minimum. The best crops are bulrush millet and cassava. Sisal may be possible in more favourable areas. The main factors affecting the distribution of population and livestock are the lack of water supplies in many areas and the danger of tsetse fly in the lower bush country. It is these factors that increase the cost of putting the land to productive use. A survey of utilisable land available showed that in 1953 Meru had 1,214 square miles and Embu 687 square miles.

We may summarise the African areas of the old Central Province as lands of varied potential but where modern farming had not developed. The Sample Census of the African areas in 1960–1 indicated continued dependence on subsistence crops and on unimproved livestock (Tables 3.21–3.24).

Unlike the predominantly pastoral districts of the Rift Valley, a summary of the total acreage of temporary crops in the Central Province shows a much higher acreage devoted to these crops. The emphasis is here on the subsistence food crops such as maize, pulses, millet, wimbi (finger millet) and potatoes. The millets are far more important in the north-eastern districts of Embu and Meru. However, the importance of the Central Province in the development of cash crops is reflected in the following acreages. Out of an estimated acreage of 326,900 for the areas surveyed, some 237,200 acres or 73 per cent was contained by Central Province (Table 3.24).[33]

The figures in Table 3.24 show the distribution by district and provinces in the area covered. Out of a total acreage of 237,200 for the Central Province, bananas and other fruits accounted for 118,600 acres. Much of this was to be found in Kiambu, Fort Hall and Meru Districts. The acreage of industrial plants was much higher than the other districts. The surveys showed that some 118,600 acres were for the four industrial crops including coffee, tea, sisal and wattle. Of the four, wattle was the most important, having been grown in the districts of Kiambu and Fort Hall for many years. Kiambu district had the largest acreage (68,400 acres) out of a total of 84,300 for the whole of Central Province.

iv. *The Southern Province*
The Southern Province, as it was in 1961 and just before the 1962 Census, included the two Masai districts of Narok and Kajiado as well as the two Kamba districts of Machakos and Kitui. The former stretched across the southern section of the Kenya rift and over the bordering plateau and the latter covered part of the eastward sloping plateau foreland. Although the area covered by these districts shared the problem of unreliable rainfall, the two Masai districts with their cultural distinctiveness presented a subdivision which needs to be noted. They differ from the Kamba districts which embrace within their borders residual uplands of higher potential and which have from the early years of settlement formed an important focus of human activity. The economy of the two areas will therefore be treated as two distinct subdivisions. This important difference is illustrated in the location of the parts of the Machakos district which became alienated and therefore formed part of the scheduled lands of Kenya. The economy of the former Southern Province may best be understood against the background of the following four main ecological zones of the area:

(a) The Star Grass Zone
(b) The Grass Woodland Zone
(c) *Acacia-Combretum Zone*
(d) *Acacia-Commiphora* and *Commiphora-Sansevieria* Bush

The estimates in Table 3.25 give some idea of the distribution of utilisable land by ecological zones in the early 1950's.

[33]*Kenya African Agricultural Sample Census* 1960/61 Part I p. 44

Table 3.26 AREAS COVERED BY 1960/61 SAMPLE CENSUS OF AGRICULTURE

District	Agricultural Division	Area in '000 Acres
Machakos	Yatta	272·0
	Central	178·0
	Southern	353·8
	Western	204·5
	Eastern	265·6
	Northern	149·9
	TOTAL	1,423·8
Kitui	Central (including *Acacia* Ecological zone)	588·8
	Migwani (including *Acacia* Ecological zone)	486·4
	TOTAL	1,075·2

SOURCE: *Kenya African Agricultural Sample Census 1960/61* Vol I p. 5

(a) The Star Grass Zone. Traditionally the Star Grass zone confined to the higher parts of Machakos District formerly supported shifting cultivation based almost exclusively on maize and some legume, inter-planted or grown pure. Because of the pressure for such lands of high potential, the fallow period has been considerably shortened as in the Kikuyu areas. In Machakos, this has been a problem area with land heavily fragmented and poorly used. It will be noted later that this is one of the main sources of migratory population. Under suitable management it has been noted that the region could support a balanced mixed farming. An intensive grass ley economy with a high priced cash crop is possible. The Swynnerton Plan set a development target of 2,500 acres of coffee for the region.

(b) The Grass Woodland Zone. This is the third most extensive ecological zone with the greater portion lying in the Machakos district. It includes the areas of the district between 4,000 and 4,500 feet above sea level and is largely developed on ancient crystalline rocks. The traditional land practices have been based on shifting cultivation with considerably adverse effects to the land. Maize and legume combination has been the dominant feature of subsistence farming in the area. Deterioration of the land has been accelerated by the clearance of vegetation through human and livestock agency. Although fragmentation is less severe within this ecological zone in the Kikuyu districts considered earlier those parts of Machakos which come under this zone have shown signs of heavy fragmentation.

(c) Acacia-Combretum Zone. With the greater portion of the Kamba districts lying under 4,500 feet above sea level the second most important ecological zone is the *Acacia-Combretum* zone with a rainfall range of 25 to 35 inches a year. The zone is underlain by soils developed from Pre-Cambrian metamorphic rocks in Machakos and Kitui districts. Because of the uncertainty of rainfall, the zone can only support a precarious balanced system of farming with heavy dependence on fodder or silage during the dry season. Drought resistant crops are essential and sisal has bright prospects. It is regarded as a zone suitable for semi-intensive agriculture.

The traditional economy has taken the form of shifting cultivation with maize and legume as well as some sorghum and bulrush millet. In Ukambani this zone has greatly deteriorated due to shortening of fallow and communal overgrazing particularly near the watering spots. Fragmentation has affected only limited parts of the zone.

(d) Acacia-Commiphora and Commiphora Sansevieria Bush. This is the most extensive ecological and the most typical of the Kamba districts of Machakos and Kitui. It is much more characteristic of the Kitui district which embraces large areas of arid and semi-arid lands bordering on the desert country of north-eastern Kenya. Some 2,357 square miles in Machakos and 7,425 in Kitui were regarded as utilisable land.[34] Rainfall is generally below 25 inches and is notoriously unreliable. The high temperatures and consequent high evaporation rates militate against a stable agriculture. There is the problem of food shortage and grazing difficulties arising from the prolonged periods of drought in the region. The presence of tsetse fly in some parts add to the difficulties of livestock and population distribution in the area.

The traditional economy is largely shifting cultivation with millets and drought resistant legumes in Kitui and maize in parts of Machakos. The torrential nature of spasmodic rainfall together with the destructive methods of land use have been the major problems of the area. In common with the previous ecological zone, there has been a tendency to overstocking with serious effect to the land particularly close to sources of water supply. Recommended form of land use envisages reduction of cultivated land to a minimum.

With adequate control of densities this could be primarily a stock country specialising in goats which can utilise the wide range of vegetation in the zone. But even where such control is possible it could not carry high densities of human and livestock population. The pattern of agriculture recorded in the African Sample Census of 1960–1 covered the acreages in Table 3.26.

In summarising the districts of Machakos and Kitui, they have emerged as areas largely marginal to agriculture except in the better watered areas which are limited in extent (Tables 3.26–3.28). The two districts being

[34]Swynnerton, Booth & Moon p. 25

situated on the drier fringe of Kenya's agricultural land have presented a considerable problem to administration in terms of progressive land usage.

By 1946, the Akamba land unit in Machakos was largely regarded as derelict. The countryside was in many areas marked by 'bare red patches, draining into ever-deepening gullies and ending in ever-widening sand rivers'.[35] At that time it was estimated that a population of well over a quarter of a million were occupying some 1,700 square miles at a density of about 200 to the square mile. Large parts of the same district at a slightly lower altitude than the more populated parts were unoccupied because of tsetse fly or lack of water.

The attack on deteriorating landscape of Machakos district during the post war period represented a major resource investment. The total Aldev expenditure up to June 1955 amounted to £333,458. Most of this went to development of water supplies, resettlement, and conservation of land. One of the most important projects was the Yatta Farrow construction to facilitate the irrigation of the thirsty Yatta plateau.

Schemes for conservation of the soil have extended to the Kitui section of Akamba land unit. Kitui is essentially a pastoral district. Conditions here have been less serious than in the denuded landscape of Machakos. Methods used have included contour ditches, grass planting and enclosure. In a number of cases the search for water has been disappointing. Wells in the area tend to dry up in bad years. Between 1945 and 1956, a total of £63,312 was spent in the district on betterment schemes. These schemes have been aimed largely at ameliorating the adverse physical conditions and at conservation of the land. However, they have not resulted in any large influx of people into the district.

The western portion of the former Southern Province is Masailand which extends over approximately 15,000 square miles in the southern part of the Republic. It is bordered in the east by the Chyulu Hills and the Kenya-Uganda railways which separate it from the Akamba country. In the west it is bordered by the Mau Escarpment, the Kipsigis, Kisii and Kuria lands and by the 250 mile length of the Kenya-Tanzania border. In the extreme south-east it is bordered by the western limits of the Tsavo National Park. The Rift Valley divides it into two dissimilar sections. The western section is more varied and includes some well watered country suitable for intensive forms of agriculture. In the east the landscape is chiefly plains broken by hill remnants. Ecologically the area covers a wide variety of habitats varying from limited areas of dense highland forest to bush, open grassland and hot, low-lying, semi-desert areas.

Although there are limited and better watered areas of high potential, the greater part of Masailand is *Acacia-Commiphora* landscape. This is low potential land where physical difficulties and pastoral traditions of the occupants can only support a sparse population. Agriculture has been adopted in only a few ecologically suitable areas and herding remains the dominant economic activity. Recently there has been deterioration in the quality of the land due to restriction of movement and overstocking in some areas. It is possible that with future change of emphasis to agriculture in ecologically suitable areas the carrying capacity of land may be increased.

Masailand is vital to the economy of the country because of its wild animals and importance to tourism. However, large areas are classified as land of low carrying capacity where man is constantly at war with elements of weather. In addition to the physical disabilities over most parts, isolation is extreme in all except the areas around Narok and Kajiado. It is this isolation which has been partly responsible for economic retardation of the Masai districts of the former Southern Province. Livestock continue to suffer from fluctuations of climate and availability of grazing over most parts of the two districts. In some of the lower areas, prevalence of tsetse fly has added to the difficulties.

v. *The Northern Province*

Forming more than 50 per cent of the total land areas of the Republic, arid and semi-arid northern Kenya is one of the most distinctive features in the human geography of the country. It has already been noted that rainfall is far below the minimum required for agriculture and indeed large areas receive amounts well below 10 inches

[35] *African Land Development in Kenya* 1946–55 p. 13

Table 3.27 ACREAGE OF TEMPORARY CROPS

CROP	Machakos	Kitui	Southern Province
Wheat	—	—	—
Rice	—	—	—
Millet	70·5	81·3	151·8
Wimbi	—	—	—
Sorghum	35·0	70·9	105·8
Maize	469·6	274·3	743·9
Pulses	400·1	279·3	679·5
Potatoes	0·9	—	0·9
Sweet Potatoes	30·4	6·7	37·1
Cassava	24·5	19·5	44·0
Castor	—	69·1	69·1
Sugar Cane	5·6	1·9	7·4
Vegetables	1·4	—	1·4
Others	3·1	3·6	6·7
AGGREGATE ACREAGE OF CROPS	1,041·1	806·6	1,847·6
ACREAGE UNDER TEMPORARY CROPS	554·6	411·5	966·1

SOURCE: *Kenya African Agricultural Sample Census* 1960–61 Part II p. 105

Table 3.28 ACREAGE OF PERMANENT CROPS

	'000 ACRES		
CROP	Machakos	Kitui	Southern Province
Bananas alone	1·7	0·1	1·8
Bananas associated	6·7	—	6·7
Other Fruit	1·0	—	1·0
Total Fruit	9·4	0·1	9·5
Coffee	1·3	—	1·3
Sisal	8·1	2·4	10·5
Wattle	3·7	—	3·7
Total Industrial Plants	13·1	2·4	15·5
Total Permanent Crops	22·5	2·5	25·0

SOURCE: *Kenya African Agricultural Sample Census* 1960–61

a year except over the higher mountains and the uplands in the area.

According to the African Agricultural Sample Census of 1960–61 the Northern Province consisted of 121,872 square miles. Out of this 121,727 were classified as nomadic pastoral land suited only to very poor type of ranching or wild life exploitation. The utilisation of this vast tract of country and hence its capacity to sustain population is strictly governed by availability of water for livestock and crops and the general paucity of other resources. Further, the depressions bordering the main rivers into the area have proved suitable habitats for tsetse fly which restricts the area available to livestock. Parts of the Turkwell and Kerio basins in the north-west, the Ewaso Nyiro and Tana River in the east have reported the presence of various species which restrict the movement of cattle.

The main sources of water supply in the area are River Turkwell and Kerio in the north-west, Lake Rudolf, the Uaso Nyiro which disappears in the Lorian Swamp, the Danu River from Abyssinia and the Tana River in the south-east. Apart from these the water needs of the area are provided by a number of important wells. The most important of these are found in Marsabit area, El Wak (Wells of God), Wajir and Garba Tula. These are wells located in the limestone areas and the water from them is hard and variable in quality.

Agriculture, the least important form of land use is severely restricted by the erratic nature and meagre rainfall. The crops cultivated in the more favourable areas include millet, sorghum and green gram. In Isiolo area, sorghum, maize, pigeon peas and annual pulses are grown. In the better watered slopes of Marsabit, teff is the most important crop, but in addition to teff, wheat, barley, maize, beans, potatoes, sweet potatoes and cassava are produced.

In Moyale district during the April rains maize, barley, wheat, sorghum, beans, pigeon peas, finger millet and pulses are grown. During the October rains there is a tendency to concentration on teff, finger millet, beans, cowpeas, and green gram. In Mandera District crop cultivation is a serious gamble. Sorghum is the only important crop. In the hot and low areas of El Wak, Wajir, Habaswein and Muddo-Gashi, crop growing is extremely risky and there is a tendency for concentration on camels and small stock.

The extreme north-west covering Turkana produce subsistence millet as the main crop. It is generally produced in small plots cultivated by the women. Further south, the Hill Suk cultivate millets, maize and more recently tobacco.

In summarising agricultural activity in the area, it should be noted that the pattern is that of restricted agricultural islands surrounded by vast areas where no cultivation is possible. With the severe limitation on agriculture the northern part of Kenya is thus deprived of one of the essential conditions for a higher population capacity.

The mainstay of the scattered population of the region is nomadic pastoralism. It is this form of land use which reflects an adaptation to the climatic conditions that has had the effect of presenting a high degree of cultural uniformity throughout the area. In the survey of the vegetation pattern we have noted the dominance of two main types, the Bushland Thicket and Scrub and the semi-desert vegetation. The Bushland Thicket and Scrub consists of open dry bush formation with sparse desert grass and is the most important vegetation type. It extends from the north-west to the north-east, where it is slightly modified by the sea. Here the higher humidity has resulted in denser bush formation mainly of *Commiphora* and *Acacia* spp. The semi-desert vegetation is chiefly represented by Desert Scrub formation of dwarf trees and bushes. It is generally characterised by a sparse undergrowth and annual grasses. A virtual absence of permanent grass is a distinctive characteristic of the vegetation community. To the south-east of Lake Rudolf it expands to include the arid desert country.

Of the two main categories of vegetation, the Desert Grass Bush is the most productive. It is on this that the cattle section of the livestock depends and must continue to depend. The Desert Scrub Vegetation provides mere temporary pasturage and browse for cattle. This form of usage is only possible for brief periods of the year. But this scrub vegetation is the chief camel and goat pasturage. Open Desert Grassland has considerable potential but much of it cannot be used because of lack of water. The herbage is highly nutritive but it is necessary to provide adequate water points to make it productive.

In the evolution of land use the distribution of watering sources has had an important effect. It has been noticed that degeneration of pasture in the area is localised in areas near permanent water, particularly in the Desert Grass Bush country. This deterioration has been primarily due to the inadequate distribution of livestock. Shortage of water has led to concentration in a few points. The areas affected tend to be within twenty to thirty miles of all permanent water points.

It is not merely the economy restricted to nomadic pastoralism that creates conditions unfavourable to an inflow of population. Economically, the area has lagged behind the more favoured agricultural parts of Kenya. Communication is most difficult partly because of terrain but more so because there has been little stimulus, apart from military needs, to expand roads in the area. Mobility is thus severely restricted to the slow pace of pastoral occupation. At present the most practical method of moving about the area is by air.

vi. *The Coast Province*

Isolated from the more developed up country provinces, the Coast Province is an important area of population movements. The economy of the area is based on three main ecological regions of unequal extent:

(a) Kikuyu Grass-Star Grass Zone
(b) *Acacia Commiphora* and *Commiphora Sansevieria* Bush
(c) The Coastal Belt (including the Tana River Delta)

A summary of the utilisable land available in 1953 indicated that in Taita district, some 265 square miles was under Kikuyu Grass and Star Grass. The remainder of the utilisable land covered 14,235 square miles of *Acacia-Commiphora* and *Commiphora Sanseveria* Bush.

Of the above total Lamu had 1,500 square miles, Tana River 1,000 square miles, Kilifi 4,100 square miles, Kwale 1,900 square miles and lower Taita 5,735 square miles. Lamu had an additional 400 square miles of utilisable land in the Coastal Belt, Kilifi and Kwale each had 650 square miles.[36] We may now consider the main ecological zones outlined in greater detail.

[36]Swynnerton, Booth & Moon p. 25

(*a*) *Taita Hills* (*Kikuyu Grass-Star Grass*). Taita Hills including the outlying residuals of Kasigau and Sagalla rise from a low-lying bush covered platform to a height of 7,000 feet above sea level. From about 5,000 feet above sea level, the land comes within the Kikuyu Grass-Star Grass ecological zone and it is this that gives character to the population distribution and land use in the area. The hills are surrounded by a deeply eroded country in places filled by detritus deposited by the swift streams from the upland area. The area of the hills is about 340 square miles. But the high rainfall of 40 to over 50 inches is confined to some 48 square miles. The part of the hills receiving 20 to 40 inches covers 212 square miles.

Within this region population growth has created one of the most congested parts of Kenya. By the 1950's pressure of population on cultivable land had reached critical proportions and considerable areas of steep hillside were being cleared for cultivation with disastrous results. Fragmentation has been one of the major problems of land use in the area.

Between 1948 and 1955 the Taita Betterment Scheme spent £23,168 in an effort to relieve population pressure and save the land from complete destruction. Part of this scheme involved the encouragement to plant cash crops. Crops now grown in this region include coffee, vegetables, black wattle, maize, beans, sugar cane and a variety of fruits. In addition to plans for the Hills, Taita families have been assisted to settle in parts of the Coast Province to relieve the pressure on the limited Kikuyu Grass-Star Grass region. The Swynnerton Plan envisaged a target of 1,000 acres of coffee for the region. Apart from these developments, the Taita-Taveta District is an important sisal plantation area. It will be seen that these play an important role in the movement of up-country and coast population into the area.

(*b*) *The Tana River Delta and Flood Plains.* The Tana River was among the first areas of Kenya to attract attention as a possible irrigation site. The importance of the river is enhanced by its location in a region which suffers from serious moisture shortage. For purposes of considering the land potential, the river may be conveniently subdivided into three sections. The upper section extends upstream above Bura and the middle section continues from Bura to Garsen. The delta section lies between Garsen and the Indian Ocean. It is the middle and lower section, roughly from just below Bura to the Indian Ocean which concerns the Coast Province. In 1953 the African Land Utilization and Development Board estimated a total of 200,000 acres in the lower and middle reaches as potential irrigation areas by use of gravity and pump schemes.[37]

In the lower section, the river flows in a raised bed which lies above the general level of the surrounding flood plain. The cost of protective works in this section has been mentioned as one of the problems of developing the area.

In the region of Galole, it is estimated that some 300,000 acres of suitable and commandable soils could be irrigated and that at least some 75,000 acres could be irrigated without storage. A pre-investment survey costing about £250,000 is in progress.[38] These riverine lands are the home of the Pokomo who have developed considerable skill in cultivation of irrigated rice. Their output of rice has tended to fluctuate widely with the variability of Tana floods. Here also the riverine community which entirely depends on the flood water for sustenance follows the receding flood on the plains by planting with maize, green gram and to a limited extent, cotton. Rice is planted in depressions and old river arms after the water level has fallen to less than a foot. The amount of land available for this migratory type of agriculture depends on the extent of flooding. Other crops produced from the area, include coconuts, green gram and bananas, along the river bank.

(*c*) *The Acacia-Commiphora and Commiphora Sansevieria Bush region.* It has been noted that this type of vegetation zone receives less than 25 inches a year and that rainfall is spasmodic, unreliable and of short duration. This hinterland vegetation is useful primarily for grazing and for wild life purposes. It is considered mainly as a cattle country with cultivators attempting to eke out a precarious subsistence from the soil. Shifting cultivation is widely practised. In the Coast intermediate zone, under sound management the stock carrying capacity is rather

[37] *East African Royal Commission Report* 1953–1955 Cmnd 9475 p. 271 H.M.S.O. London

[38] International Bank for Reconstruction and Development Report p. 56

better and pockets of land suitable for cultivation are available. It is on this type of land that the Mariakani Milk Scheme has been based.[39]

In general water is the main limiting factor in this section of the Coast. Tsetse infestation is low to moderate and can be controlled by use of drugs or vegetation clearance. The carrying capacity for cattle is reckoned at 30 to 50 acres per head where the bush is under control and about 100 acres in areas of dense bush.[40] Cultivation should be reduced to a minimum with bulrush millet, and cassava as the most suitable crops. Sisal is a possible cash crop. This type of country is typical of the coast hinterland environment. It is suitable largely for the extensive pastoral form of land use. The region includes approximately over 70 per cent of the former African areas of the Coast Province.

In the Taita-Taveta District, it forms the southern half of the Tsavo National Park and controlled hunting areas. The Tsavo National Park is one of the few great elephant areas of the world. Together with ecologically similar parts of south-east Machakos and Kitui area this is one of the largest game parks of the world. Although much of the park formerly consisted of low dense bush with scattered large trees much of the woody vegetation has been destroyed by overcrowding of elephants and fires started by honey hunters. The park is a problem area in animal-plant-climate relationship and the need for much research in wild land management is already well recognised.

(d) *The Coastal Belt (former non-scheduled areas)*. This ecological zone in the Coast Province falls into two sub-divisions. In the first place, there is the belt of country lying inland between the tsetse infested coastal belt proper and the semi-arid hinterland stock country. It is a sub-division capable of supporting a moderate stock density provided the human population is sufficiently dense to keep down the tsetse menace. Typical areas included in this zone are the Shimba Hills and the parkland areas to the east and south of Ndavaya in Kwale, and the area to the west of Kaloleni. The altitude in Kilifi and Kwale hinterland ranges from 500 to 800 feet above sea level and rainfall varies from 35 to 50 inches a year.

The second sub-division includes the Coastal Belt proper. It covers a belt stretching over the whole length of the Kenya Coast and is about 10 miles wide. The rainfall decreases from about 55 inches in the south to 35 inches in the north. The soils are light sandy to sandy loam. It is agriculturally the most productive part of the Coast Province.

Because of the heavy infestation of tsetse fly parts of the Coastal Belt are unsuitable for cattle rearing. Agriculture is the mainstay of the population of this sub-division of the Province. The traditional agricultural practice consisted of shifting agriculture with three years of crop and a bush fallow of nine to twelve years. To cultivate the land the bush is cleared by burning and the seeds are often planted without prior cultivation.

Subsistence agriculture is based on a range of cereals, root crops and pulses. But there are in addition to these important fruit and tree crops whose produce are used to meet subsistence needs and for cash.

Maize, which is among the important cereals, is found most adapted to areas where annual rainfall exceeds 30 inches. The ideal cereal crop for most parts of the Coastal Region is sorghum. The crop does particularly well over the coastal sands. It is better suited to these areas because it can withstand the effects of high temperatures and drought better than maize.

Rice cultivation is a further activity that adds to the subsistence needs of the region. It is particularly important in Vanga area and in the other swampy parts of the coastal belt. Apart from maize, sorghum and rice, cassava and sweet potatoes play an important part in the rural agricultural activities. A wide variety of pulses add to the crop complex. Among the most important pulses grown are green gram and pigeon peas. Pigeon peas are particularly important for resting the land after a period of arable use.

The culture fruit and tree crops is one of the distinctive features of coast agriculture. Among the common fruit and tree crops are bananas, coconuts, cashew nuts, mangoes and pawpaws. Bananas are widely grown, and eaten, along the coast especially in areas of heavy rainfall.

[39]Swynnerton R. J. M. *A Plan to Intensify the Development of African Agriculture in Kenya* Government Printer, Nairobi 1954 p. 48

[40]Moomaw J. C. *A Study of Plant Ecology of the Coast Region of Kenya Colony, British East Africa* p. 2, 1960

They have the disadvantage of being easily damaged by wind. The mango fruit is another characteristic crop of the Coast and it is found growing generally within the 35 inches rainfall zone.

Coconut palm has for a long time been an important element in the Coast farming. Like cashew nuts it is produced from small farms in African areas as well as from some large plantations in the former alienated parts of the Coast. Although once the most widely grown crop, coconut farming is now in a depressed state. The decline in the cultivation has been attributed to inadequate rainfall and poor yield. It still remains an important crop to the local people who use its fruit and leaves for a variety of purposes. Among its most valuable products is copra from which a cooking oil is extracted. In 1960 a total revenue of £289,000 accrued to producers from small farms and £120,000 to large farms. In 1961 the figures were £286,000 for small farms and £120,000 for large farms.[41] Between 1956 and 1959 the number of coconuts produced from African areas increased from 4 million to just over 18½ million fruits. But 1959/60 production from these areas fell to just over 2 million.[42]

Cashew nuts, which are an important cash crop at the Coast, have the advantage of withstanding poor soils and limited rainfall. They are ideally suited to the environmental conditions of the coast region. The bulk of the export crop has in the past been taken by India. Interest in the crop has suffered due to the declining consumption by the Indian market. Between 1960 and 1962, the export revenue declined from £323,000 to £92,000.[43]

The cotton crop is one of the main sources of cash in the region. The crop is more important in the drier northern half of the coast particularly in Malindi area. Cotton is less suited to wetter conditions of the southern half of the coast and cultivation is therefore concentrated in the area north of Mombasa. It prefers an annual rainfall of at least 30 inches. The most critical months are July and August when adequate rainfall for the swelling of the bolls is important.

Among the problems in the area is the tendency for the farmers to interplant cotton with maize. There is scope for considerable increase in the cotton acreage where this practice can be abandoned. The crop is liable to pests such as leaf sucking aphides and other insects. Picking starts in September and may continue for two months.

(e) *The Coastal Belt (former alienated areas)*. The coastal belt includes large areas of land which had been alienated and were formerly included in agricultural censuses with the 'scheduled' areas or the 'White Highlands'. According to 1962 Census these areas along the coastal strip had 39 holdings with a total land area of 123,000 acres.[44] Agriculture in these areas has for many years been based on a limited range of crops. In terms of employment and population movements, sugar and sisal have been the most important.

The coast is the second sugar growing region of Kenya. Analysis of crop concentration of temporary industrial crops in the scheduled areas and the Coastal Strip showed that in 1958 the coast accounted for 24·1 per cent of the sugar acreage. In 1962 it accounted for 31·0 per cent of the total.[45]

Plantation production of sugar in this region is concentrated in the Ramisi area where there is one of the oldest sugar mills, established in the early decades of the present century.

The plantation now covers an area of 42,000 acres (gross). Of this total, 8,000 acres had been planted with sugar. Production has ranged around 600 tons a day and the target is to rise up to 1,000 tons a day. Originally the estate included the Gazi sisal block. In 1966, the estate employed 2,000 workers including 600 regulars and 400 seasonal workers. About 25 per cent of the workers on the estate were from Nyanza. Most of the workers are now from the coast, but in addition there are a number of Kamba Taita and settled Makonde workers. Formerly the agents used to run a recruitment drive in Nyanza. Direct recruitment has now stopped but a number of Nyanza elements are still coming, following earlier

[41] *Kenya: Statistical Abstract* 1963 p. 52 Table 82

[42]Brown, L. H. *A National Cash Crop Policy for Kenya* Parts I & II p. 101 Government Printer, Nairobi 1963

[43]*Kenya: Statistical Abstract* 1963 p. 23 Table 37

[44]*Kenya Agricultural Census* 1962 'Scheduled Areas and the Coastal Strip' p. 4, 1963

[45]*Kenya Agricultural Census*, 1962 'Scheduled Areas and the Coastal Strip' p. 20 Table 23, 1963

arrivals. The importance of the Nyanza element will be noted in population movements into Kwale District.

Sisal is an important plantation crop mainly in the area north of Mombasa. The large plantations of Vipingo and Kilifi have been important destinations for up-country as well as the coast local workers. Vipingo Estate began with a modest 1,000 acres in 1934. By 1966 the Estate had grown to 24,000 acres mainly through purchase from local Arab and Indian landowners. About 1,000 acres has been given to Government for resettlement purposes. This is one of the estates which suffers from the squatter problem.

The labour force in 1966 consisted of about 1,200 regulars and about 600 contract workers who are mostly local. Originally acute shortage of labourers led to recruitment from Tanga area in Tanzania and from up-country. The Luo form a large proportion of the up-country workers. A mid-1964 count showed that the labour force consisted of 65·3 per cent Mijikenda, 14·4 per cent Luo, 10·0 per cent Makonde, 4·9 per cent Kamba, 0·8 per cent Kikuyu and 1·0 per cent others.

vii. *The Former Scheduled Areas* (*Figures 3.2 and 3.3*)
(*a*) *Background.* Movement of population in the Republic of Kenya is an aspect of the modern exchange economy. Chronologically it synchronises with the beginnings of the non-African activities in the building of the modern rail communications and subsequent resource development that has followed. In no other field has this effect been more fundamental than in the organisation of agriculture in the former 'White Highlands' of Kenya. The statistical sources on which a detailed analysis of the economy of the former 'Scheduled Areas' is based includes lands of similar status at the coast. The nature of agricultural activities in the former alienated areas of the coast and their impact have been considered in the section on the Coastal Belt.

This is not the appropriate section for a detailed study of the circumstances that led to the creation of the land unit which subsequent boundary changes have divided between at least five Provinces excluding the Coast. The close association of the early evolution of the boundaries of the highlands in relation to the railways is an important

feature. But the final shape that it took must be regarded as belonging also to a later chapter in the evolution of the transport pattern in Kenya.

Before 1901 little alienation of land had taken place. It was the completion of the rail link with the lakes and the desire to generate revenue that stimulated the move to press forward with the offer of land to potential European and South African settlers.

The first Land Regulation of East African Protectorate which had been published in 1897 and on which the limited alienation of land had taken place were replaced by the Crown Lands Ordinance of 1902.[46]

The intending settlers were encouraged by granting of freeholds or ninety-nine year leases, and some of these were later converted to 999 year leases. At an early stage it was decided that the highland area between Kiu and Fort Ternan should be exclusively reserved for Europeans. The move to exclude all others but Europeans from acquiring land in the area was further written into the Crown Land Ordinance 1915 which replaced the 1902 Ordinance. In this ordinance, a covenant was inserted which explicitly excluded non-Europeans from acquiring land, or from managing any of the leased land in the area. A distinction was made between the 'White Highlands' and the areas already settled by Africans and from which land grants and leases were excluded. But this did not prevent the acquisition of land by Europeans in areas that were considered African.

Whereas the first land ordinance allowed settlement along the railway, with the extension of settlement after the 1914–18 War, the ex-soldier Settlement Scheme and the Crown Land Ordnance of 1921 had the effect of extending settlement well away from the railway line. Between 1902 and 1922 rapid alienation had taken place extending the areas affected by European settlement well beyond the limits of Kiu and Fort Ternan. It is during this period that settlement reached Uasin Gishu and Trans-Nzoia. By 1926 the alienation of land was virtually complete in what later came to be designated, the 'White Highlands'.

The evolution of the boundary of this land unit which began at the turn of the century was given public

[46]Morgan W. T. W. 'The "White Highlands of Kenya"' *Geographical Journal* pp. 140–55 Vol. 129 Part 2 1963

Figure 3.2

TRANSPORT AND RESOURCE DEVELOPMENT/53

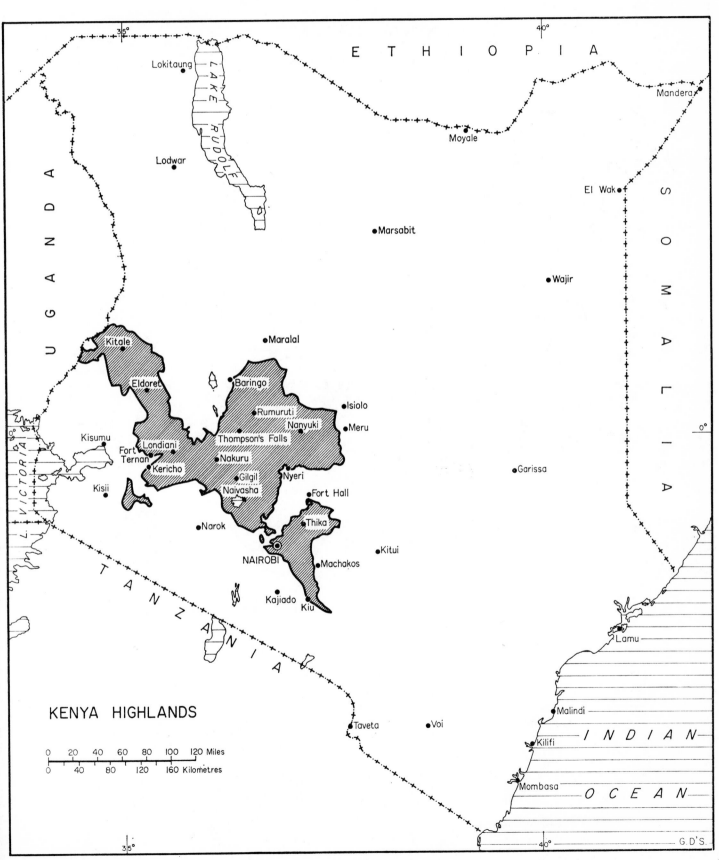

KENYA HIGHLANDS

KENYA HIGHLANDS
FARMING TYPES AND ZONES

Mixed Maize.

Mixed Wheat.

Cattle Beef or Dairy.

Plantation Crops.

Forest Areas.

Boundary of Sub Committee Production Areas.

0 10 20 30 40 50
MILES

Source : Troup Commission's Report.

recognition by the Wyn Harris Commission in 1939. After this Commission the boundaries of Highlands demarcating an area for persons of European origin was given legal effect by the Seventh Schedule of the Crown Lands Ordinance under authority of the Kenya (Highlands) Order in Council 1939.[47]

Whereas the above developments could be seen as a move to separate areas of European farming from the rest of African land units, subsequent administrative evolution had the effect of fragmenting this area between the Nyanza, Rift Valley, Central and Southern Provinces. The bulk of the scheduled areas so defined came within the boundary of the Rift Valley and Central Province. Nyanza Province and the Southern Province had a rather limited share. Within this boundary, there has been unity of approach to land tenure but varied agriculture and pastoral activities in response to the ecology of the land.

(b) *Ecology of the area.* The former scheduled lands form four unequal blocks of country including the isolated Sotik area in the extreme south-west and the Thika-Nairobi and Athi-Plains section in the south-east. The main blocks extends over the diverse rift and associated highlands.

To the west of the rift is the Trans-Nzoia, Uasin-Gishu, Londiani and Molo-Kericho farming area. This is one of the richest farming areas of the Republic and is linked to the Laikipia, Nanyuki, Kinangop farming areas to the east of the rift by a broad corridor of land which covers the floor of the rift in the Nakuru, Naivasha section. This main farming area is broken by blocks of Forest reserves of which the main ones are Mount Kenya, Aberdares, West Mau, Tinderet, Nandi and Elgon.

The Elgon slopes are forested but from the edge of the forest, much of the north-western section forms part of the Scattered Tree Grassland (Low Trees, High Grass) country. A similar vegetation complex occurs over the northern portion of the Thika-Athi Plains section. The greater portion of the area including the highland shoulder on either side and the elevated portion to the north of Lake Nakuru forms part of the Highland Grassland and Highland Forest country.

To the north-east of the Highland Grassland and High-land Forest country is a similar ecological zone covering the slopes of Mount Kenya and separated from the main blocks by a southern extension of Laikipia portion of the Scattered Tree (*Acacia-Themeda*) Grassland which extends north-west from the foothills of Mount Kenya. Scattered Tree (*Acacia-Themeda*) Grassland is also characteristic of the floor of the rift from Nakuru southwards. This is the same type of vegetation which covers the plains extending from Nairobi south-eastwards. From the foregoing, brief description of the ecological background it will be noted that the former scheduled areas form diverse environments offering scope for a wide range of farming activities. A brief description of these activities will now be made.

(c) *The farming regions of the west rift highlands.* This extensive and diverse plateau region bordering on the rift in the west includes the Trans-Nzoia-Kitale producing area in the extreme north, the Uasin-Gishu plateau in the central portion and in the south Songhor-Nandi Hills, the Molo-Kericho and Sotik areas.[48] This region thus includes that former portion of Nyanza Province which has played a vital role in the internal migrations in that Province and in the exchange of population with the other Provinces.

Trans-Nzoia Kitale area. In the extreme north the Trans-Nzoia-Kitale forms a rich farming country with a mean annual rainfall of 40 to 50 inches and with good prospects of receiving 30 inches more. This sub-division is the leading producer of maize. Some pedigree cattle are kept and on the slopes of Mount Elgon coffee is produced.

The importance of the farming sub-region emerges clearly in the statistics in Table 3.29. According to these figures, Trans-Nzoia production area accounted for a mere 4·1 per cent of the total wheat acreage for the whole former scheduled lands including the Coast, 2·3 per cent of barley and 2·1 per cent of oats. But it produced the bulk of the country's maize accounting for 41·6 per cent of the total acreage of the former scheduled areas.[49] Of the temporary industrial crops, Trans-Nzoia production area accounted for 1·9 per cent of pyrethrum acreage

[47]Morgan, W. T. W. p. 142
[48]*Kenya Agricultural Census* 1962 p. 20
[49]*Kenya Agricultural Census* 1962 p. 20

Table 3.29 DISTRIBUTION OF CEREALS BY DISTRICTS 1962

	Wheat %	Maize %	Barley %	Oats %
Laikipia	6·0	5·1	9·7	10·5
Naivasha	21·3	1·7	37·0	23·6
Nakuru	19·5	22·3	37·0	37·7
Trans-Nzoia	4·1	41·6	2·3	2·1
Uasin Gishu	41·5	24·8	7·5	19·9
Lumbwa/Songhor	0·1	1·2	0·3	0·5
Kibos/Chemelil	—	—	—	—
Kericho/Nandi	—	0·1	—	—
Sotik	0·1	1·0	—	—
Nairobi	—	0·2	0·3	0·5
Mount Kenya	7·4	0·9	6·2	5·8
Thika	—	0·3	—	—
Machakos	—	0·3	—	—
Voi	—	0·4	—	—

SOURCE: *Kenya Agricultural Census* 1962 p. 20

Table 3.30 DISTRIBUTION OF TEMPORARY INDUSTRIAL CROPS BY DISTRICT 1962

	Pyrethrum %	Sugar %
Laikipia	13·1	—
Naivasha	28·7	—
Nakuru	37·9	—
Trans-Nzoia	1·9	0·2
Uasin Gishu	11·4	0·2
Lumbwa/Songhor	0·9	9·6
Kibos/Chemelil	—	58·7
Kericho/Nandi	0·2	—
Sotik	—	—
Nairobi	0·9	—
Mount Kenya	4·7	0·2
Thika	—	—
Machakos	—	—
Voi	—	—

SOURCE: *Kenya Agricultural Census* 1962 p. 20

Table 3.31 DISTRIBUTION OF PERMANENT INDUSTRIAL CROPS BY DISTRICT 1962

	Coffee %	Tea %	Sisal %	Wattle %
Laikipia	0·1	—	—	0·3
Naivasha	—	—	—	1·2
Nakuru	8·4	—	15·0	0·8
Trans-Nzoia	9·9	0·7	1·0	3·0
Uasin Gishu	1·9	3·5	4·0	85·0
Lumbwa/Songhor	5·4	1·6	3·9	—
Kibos/Chemelil	—	—	—	—
Kericho/Nandi	0·8	76·6	—	0·4
Sotik	1·2	7·5	—	5·0
Nairobi	25·5	9·1	1·2	4·0
Mount Kenya	3·8	—	0·2	0·1
Thika	42·0	—	31·7	0·3
Machakos	0·9	—	14·1	—
Voi	—	—	20·0	—

SOURCE: *Kenya Agricultural Census* 1962 p. 21

Table 3.32 DISTRIBUTION OF DAIRY AND BEEF HERDS 1962

	Dairy %	Beef %
Laikipia	5·6	16·8
Naivasha	10·3	9·4
Nakuru	21·7	15·3
Trans-Nzoia	19·4	13·3
Uasin Gishu	17·1	13·3
Lumbwa/Songhor	4·9	3·5
Kibos/Chemelil	0·1	—
Kericho/Nandi	0·3	0·1
Sotik	3·7	3·5
Nairobi	3·1	0·3
Mount Kenya	8·5	15·0
Thika	1·6	4·9
Machakos	3·5	4·6
Voi	—	—

SOURCE: *Kenya Agricultural Census* 1962 p. 39

Table 3.33 MILK UTILIZATION BY DISTRICT 1961/62

	Sold as whole milk %	Converted %
Laikipia	8·2	79·4
Naivasha	40·4	49·7
Nakuru	28·4	60·6
Trans-Nzoia	15·1	77·5
Uasin Gishu	33·9	55·3
Lumbwa/Songhor	21·8	66·8
Kibos/Chemelil	35·9	6·1
Kericho/Nandi	17·3	54·3
Sotik	59·2	33·0
Nairobi	77·8	8·0
Mount Kenya	14·3	72·0
Thika	69·3	10·6
Machakos	88·7	4·5
Voi	6·5	

SOURCE: *Kenya Agricultural Census* 1962 p. 43

Table 3.34 ANALYSIS OF SHEEP POPULATION BY DISTRICTS 1962

	%
Laikipia	12·7
Naivasha	20·7
Nakuru	34·3
Trans-Nzoia	3·1
Uasin Gishu	6·9
Lumbwa/Songhor	0·2
Kibos/Chemelil	—
Kericho/Nandi	0·1
Sotik	0·6
Nairobi	0·2
Mount Kenya	19·5
Thika	0·5
Machakos	1·0
Voi	—

SOURCE: *Kenya Agricultural Census* 1962 p. 52

Table 3.35 AFRICAN EMPLOYEES BY DISTRICT 1958–62

	'000	
	1958	*1962*
Laikipia	7·9	10·3
Naivasha	14·7	20·1
Nakuru	36·6	40·7
Trans-Nzoia	20·3	23·9
Uasin Gishu	20·6	24·0
Lumbwa/Songhor	8·3	8·1
Kibos/Chemelil	5·1	6·1
Kericho/Nandi	33·2	28·7
Sotik	6·7	7·0
Nairobi	23·3	24·3
Mount Kenya	10·1	9·0
Thika	42·5	33·6
Machakos	5·7	5·3
Voi	3·9	4·5

SOURCE: *Kenya Agricultural Census* 1962 p. 121

and 0·2 per cent of the sugar acreage. The picture was brighter for the permanent industrial crops. The district accounted for 9·9 per cent of coffee acreage, 0·7 per cent of tea, 1·0 per cent of sisal and 3·0 per cent of wattle in 1962 (Table 3.31).

About 60 per cent of the total land was classified as meadows and pasture, a factor underlying the importance of the dairy industry in the area (Table 3.32). The district accounted for 19·4 per cent of the total population of dairy cattle placing it second among the producing areas. Much of the milk is converted to cream. In 1962 77·5 per cent of the milk produced was used for this purpose (Table 3.32). In addition the area included 13·3 per cent of the beef cattle, taking a third place in the list of major producers. The sheep population of the district accounted for a mere 3·1 per cent of the overall scheduled area total (Table 3.34). Analysis of Gross Farm Revenue for the district showed an increase from £2,689,000 in 1958 to £3,141,000 in 1962. The number of African employees rose from 20,300 to 23,900 including children (Table 3.35).

Uasin Gishu area. Situated in the Central portion of the West Highland farming region the Uasin Gishu plateau is clearly one of the richest farming districts of the Republic. Mean annual rainfall varies from 40 to 50 inches. Uasin Gishu is primarily a mixed wheat farming area, but it also accounts for a large proportion of the maize acreage.

In 1962 the District accounted for 41·5 per cent of the wheat acreage, 24·8 per cent of barley and 19·5 per cent of oats in the scheduled areas including the Coast. In contrast to Trans-Nzoia the farming pattern is more diverse and the volcanic soils richer. Of the temporary industrial crops, the district had 11·4 per cent of pyrethrum acreage and 0·2 per cent of sugar acreage. In addition the farming activity included 1·9 per cent of coffee acreage, 3·5 per cent of tea, 4·0 per cent of sisal and

85·5 per cent of wattle acreage. This then has been the principal wattle growing district among the former 'Scheduled Areas'. About 60 per cent of the total land in 1962 was uncultivated pasture.

The Uasin Gishu district is the third most important dairying and beef cattle area in the Republic. In 1962 the district accounted for 17·1 per cent of the dairy cattle and 13·3 per cent of the beef cattle (Table 3.32). But little of the milk was sold as whole milk. In 1962, 33·9 per cent of the milk of the district was sold as whole milk and 55·3 per cent converted to cream. It shared the same characteristic with Trans-Nzoia in having a low percentage of sheep population (6·9 per cent, Table 3.34). The district is clearly one of the major employment areas. The number of African employees increased from 20,600 in 1958 to 24,000 in 1962 (Table 3.35).

The Molo-Kericho-Nandi area. The southern farming region of the West Highlands of Kenya consisted of blocks of land including the Molo-Kericho areas, the Songhor-Nandi Hills areas and the isolated Sotik area. In addition the sugar lands lying to the south of Nyando escarpment in the Kibos-Chemelil areas have been included for convenience. The last area is ecologically a part of the Lake Shore savannah region but, for statistical and land tenure purposes, has been included with the former Scheduled Areas.

The Molo-Kericho area receives much higher rainfall. Kericho on the edge of Mau Forest experiences amounts well over 70 inches a year. The greater portion of this is included in the Nakuru District figures of crop acreages. It is a well established farming area specialising in the high altitude crops such as pyrethrum, wheat, barley and oats. It is this area that accounts for the rather high percentages of wheat, barley, oats and pyrethrum acreages of the Nakuru district (Tables 3.31). On the livestock side it includes a large portion of the dairy and beef cattle and sheep of Nakuru District. Molo is a famous sheep country.

The economy of the African areas of Kericho District has already been discussed in the section on Nyanza Province. But there remains the tea lands which constitute the south-western extension of the former scheduled areas of the Republic. The area included the bulk of the 41,800 acres of developed tea lands of Kenya by the end of 1962. In that year, the Kericho/Nandi production area accounted for 76·6 per cent of the total tea acreage in the former scheduled areas as against 83·3 per cent in 1958. The greater part of the acreage was to be found in the area south and north of the Molo-Kericho highway and in the smaller tea growing area of Nandi on the flanks of Tinderet mountain. The tea area of Kericho-Nandi considered above is part of a larger tea region which extends to the former African areas of the rest of Kericho District, Nandi, North Nyanza and Kisii districts. It is reckoned that a further 10,000 to 12,000 acres of tea could be developed in these areas outside the former scheduled lands.[50] Between 1958 and 1962 acreage of tea in the Kericho-Nandi area increased from 27,400 to 33,200. In 1962 Kericho District alone had 24,100 acres and Nandi 9,100 acres. The growing importance of Kericho-Nandi area in terms of employment may be seen in the changing magnitude of employment. According to 1962 Census it had 28,000 African employees. This figure was in fact lower than earlier years. A total of 34,000 African employees were recorded in 1961 and 33,200 in 1958.[51] In 1958 and 1962 it occupied the third place in the total employment of Africans, but in 1961 it came second after Nakuru District.

In the former Nyanza scheduled areas, employment avenues have been considerably augmented by the development of non-African sugar farming activities in the Songhor, Chemelil, Miwani and Kibos areas. Before 1930 a number of Asian families had been settled on the gently sloping plains below the Nyando escarpment and to the north of the Miwani-Kibos section of the railway line. During that year, 56 Asian families in the area were occupying some 15,000 acres of land of which 9,120 acres were under sugar. In addition, two further sugar plantations, one of Victoria Nyanza Sugar Company and the other of Muhoroni Sugar Company had been established at Miwani and Muhoroni respectively. By 1955 some 18,400 acres of sugar were being grown in the Kibos-Muhoroni area and 100 acres in the Lumbwa/Songhor area. In 1962 some 4,400 acres of sugar was reported in the Lumbwa/Songhor area. The acreages of the Kibos/Chemelil section were:[52]

	Acreage
Kibigori/Chemelil	9,800
Miwani	9,600
Kibos	6,800

The Kibos/Chemelil area accounted for 58·7 per cent of the sugar acreage for the whole of the former scheduled areas. But in addition by 1962 the Lumbwa/Songhor area had 5·4 per cent of the coffee, 1·6 per cent of tea and 3·9 per cent of sisal. Part of the Lumbwa/Songhor area is now included in the Nyanza resettlement scheme.

The employment of Africans in these two areas had also shown change. Between 1958 and 1962 the Lumbwa/Songhor figures showed a decrease from 8,300 to 8,100 adults and children and the Kibos/Chemelil area an increase of from 5,100 to 6,100 adults and children. The special importance attached to the sugar industry in the area is to be seen in plans for opening up two further factories in the area with a total capacity of 90,000 tons of sugar.[53]

To the south-east of Kericho farming area is the isolated Sotik farming block. The settlement was established in the first decade of the present century as a buffer area between the Nilo-Hamitic Kipsigis from the Mau slopes and the Kisii from the highland area to the west. The emphasis of farming in this area is on pastoral potentialities. But some areas also produce tea. In 1962 this farming area accounted for 0·1 per cent of wheat acreage, 1·0 per cent of maize (Table 3.29) of the permanent industrial crops (Table 3.31). Sotik area accounted for 1·2 per cent of coffee acreage, 7·5 per cent of tea and 5·0 per cent of wattle in the former scheduled areas.

On the livestock side, Sotik had 3·7 per cent of the dairy and 3·5 per cent of beef livestock population (Table 3.32). Analysis of milk utilisation showed that the emphasis of farming is on the selling of whole milk (Table 3.33). About 60 per cent of the milk produced was sold as whole milk and only 33·0 per cent was used for conversion to cream. The nearby Kericho township and tea areas form a convenient market for the whole milk of the

[50]Brown L. H. *A National Cash Crop Policy for Kenya* Parts I & II p. 18 Government Printer, Nairobi

[51]*Kenya Agricultural Census* 1962 p. 121

[52]*Kenya Agricultural Census* 1962 p. 94

[53]*Industry in Kenya* 1964–65 p. 71

area. Between 1958 and 1962 the number of African employees in Sotik rose from 6,700 to 7,000.

(d) *The central rift farming region.* The existence of a productive farming area in the central portion of the Kenya section of the Gregory Rift is largely due to the topographical features of the floor. It has been noted that the floor of the rift rises from the Magadi area in the south and from the Lake Rudolf area in the north reaching a peak in the Naivasha area.

Traversed from south to north by the railways it has thus developed into a farming area of great importance to the economy of Kenya. It plays a major part in the movement of population into the Rift Valley Province. The ecological contrasts in the area give rise to three distinct farming sections, a northern section with rainfall totals between 30 and 50 inches and a southern section with amounts less than 30 inches and the Kinangop plateau.[54] The southern section is a predominantly ranching country with emphasis on beef cattle or sheep in higher parts. This is in contrast to the northern half which is more of a mixed farming area with crops such as maize, wheat, barley, oats, pyrethrum and some sisal. This northern section especially the Subukia area is well known for its pedigree herds.

Overlooking the rift valley floor but at a slightly higher level is the downfaulted plateau of Kinangop lying at an altitude of some 7,000 to 8,000 feet above sea level. The Kinangop plateau now forms an important farming region with such crops as wheat, barley, oats and pyrethrum. In addition to these it is an important dairy, sheep and pig area.

A summary of the distribution of cereal acreages by percentages indicated that in 1962 Nakuru district had 19·5 per cent of wheat, 22·3 per cent of maize, 37·0 per cent of barley and 37·7 per cent of oats (Table 3.29). It had 37·9 per cent of pyrethrum and was thus the leading producer of this crop in that year (Table 3.30). Of the permanent industrial crops Nakuru district accounted for 8·4 per cent of coffee, 15 per cent of sisal and 0·8 per cent of wattle out of the total for the former scheduled areas (Table 3.31).

It was clearly the most important dairying region in Kenya with 21·7 per cent of the dairy cattle. On beef cattle, Nakuru district came second with 15·3 per cent of the total beef herds (Table 3.32). The emphasis in the dairy industry is on production of cream which used 60·6 per cent of the milk in 1961/62 leaving 28·4 per cent to be sold as whole milk. About 34 per cent of the sheep population in the former scheduled area was concentrated in the district (Table 3.33 and 3.34). Nakuru district with its diverse agriculture naturally has a high demand for labour. Between 1958 and 1962 the number of African employees rose from 36,600 adults and children to 40,700 (Table 3.35).

The Naivasha area which extends east to include Kinangop Plateau had 21·3 per cent of the wheat acreage in 1962, 1·7 per cent of maize, 37·0 per cent of barley, 23·6 per cent of oats and 28·7 per cent of pyrethrum (Table 3.29). In terms of livestock Naivasha had 10·3 per cent of the dairy herds and 9·4 per cent of the beef herds. About 40 per cent of the milk was sold as whole milk and 50 per cent converted to cream (Table 3.33). Naivasha was the second most important sheep area. In 1962, it had 20·9 per cent of the total sheep population of the former scheduled areas (Table 3.32).

Its importance as an employment area is indicated in the increase of African employees from 14,000 in 1958 to 24,100 in 1962 (Table 3.35). The two districts and the farming areas of the west rift highlands account for the importance of the Rift Valley Province as an area of economic opportunity for the African workers.

(e) *The Laikipia Plateau and the former Scheduled areas of the old Central and Southern Provinces.* An important farming region of the Republic extends from the plains of Laikipia in the north to the residual hills of Machakos. The region falls into three distinct sub-divisions. In the extreme north are the plains of Laikipia which continue to embrace much of the district of Nanyuki. In the central portion are two blocks of forest lands covering the slopes of Mount Kenya and the higher parts of Aberdares. Much of this central portion is included in the forest reserve. But in its southern tip is an important plantation farming area of Nyeri and Kiambu districts. It will be seen from the map of the farming types and zones that much of the lower portion of this forested belt has been cleared for settle-

[54]Morgan W. T. W. p. 150

ment. This appears as the blank area which severs the outlying block of former scheduled area from the main part to the north of Nairobi. To the south-east of Nairobi-Thika line, the remainder of the scheduled lands form an isolated but homogenous block extending to the hills of Machakos. Laikipia production area is the most northerly portion to the east of the Rift Valley. It is a peneplain largely of basement complex rocks which merge west and east into the younger lavas of the tertiary period. The general altitude of the plains varies from about 6,000 to about 7,000 feet above sea sevel. About the turn of the century, they were part of the Masai grazing area and were evacuated as a result of a treaty to unite the two Masai reserves.

Situated on the drier fringe of Kenya's farming land the region experiences a rainfall varying from 15 inches to about 30 inches. For most of the area, the rainfall is likely to be below 30 inches for at least 6 years in 20 years. Practically the entire area is Scattered Tree and Open Grassland (*Acacia-Themeda* grassland). Conditions in this farming region are ideal for ranching. Extensive ranches have replaced the former nomadic pastoral occupation of the Masai. In 1962 there were 7 out of a total of 13 estates of over 50,000 acres. Out of a total of 119 holdings of between 10,000 and 49,999 acres twenty were in Laikipia.[55]

Although the region specialises in beef cattle with some dairy, a considerable acreage is devoted to cereals. In 1962 the region accounted for 6·0 per cent of wheat acreage, 5·1 per cent of maize, 9·7 per cent of barley and 10·5 per cent of oats. Some 13·1 per cent of the pyrethrum in the former scheduled areas was in Laikipia district. But being rather dry it is not an important producer of crops which require low temperature and high rainfall. In 1962, Laikipia had 5·6 per cent of the dairy herds and 16·8 per cent of the beef herds (Table 3.32). It was therefore the chief area of concentration of beef cattle followed by the nearby Mount Kenya. It merges south-east into the dairy and maize country of Mount Kenya slopes.

The lands rising from the plains of Laikipia to the slopes of Mount Kenya are among the most important livestock areas of the country. In 1960 Mount Kenya region showed that 89·2 per cent of the total land area was uncultivated pasture. In 1962 the uncultivated

pasture constituted 84·9 per cent of the total land surface. For the same years the region accounted for 8·5 per cent of the number of dairy cattle in the whole country. Mount Kenya is primarily a beef producing area. In 1958 it had 14 per cent of the beef cattle and in 1962 it held the third place with 15·0 per cent of the total beef cattle. Between 1958 and 1962 the region declined from second place to third place in the total number of sheep. The actual proportions were 22·5 per cent of total for 1958 and 19·5 per cent for 1962.[56] In addition to livestock population, Mount Kenya Region was specially noted for its contribution to the cereal production. According to 1962 Census, the region accounted for 7·4 per cent of wheat, 0·9 per cent of maize, 6·2 per cent barley and 5·8 per cent of oats from the former scheduled areas. In the same year it accounted for 3·8 per cent of coffee acreage.

The Central portion of the former scheduled lands, which were originally forested, now forms the basis of a thriving plantation agriculture. This activity is found in two widely separated blocks. In the extreme north-east is Nyeri area and in the south are the important plantations of the Nairobi area and its vicinity. Majority of the plantations are to be found in a line lying north-west of Nairobi-Thika axis. In the better watered areas these are mainly coffee plantations. But in the cooler parts such as Limuru, tea plantations are important. Apart from the coffee and tea plantations this is a mixed farming area, with livestock forming an important element in the landscape. In the area between Nairobi and Thika sisal plantation is an important element in the utilisation of the land. The remainder of the area south of the Nairobi-Thika axis is an important cattle farming area with emphasis on beef production and dairy in the area close to Nairobi. In 1962 Nairobi area had 3·1 per cent of the dairy cattle, and 0·3 per cent of the beef cattle. A total of 46·2 per cent of the land was uncultivated pasture.

At the same time, Nairobi area accounted for 25·5 per cent of coffee, 9·1 per cent of tea, 1·2 per cent sisal and 4·0 per cent wattle in the former scheduled areas. Thika production area accounted for 42·0 per cent of coffee, 37·7 per cent sisal and 0·3 per cent sisal. Over one-half

[55]*Kenya Agricultural Census* 1962 p. 77
[56]*Kenya Agricultural Census* 1962 'Scheduled Areas and the coastal strip' pp. 34, 39 & 52

of the land (58·1 per cent) was classified as uncultivated pasture. The Nairobi and Thika areas are therefore among the most productive areas of Kenya.

It has been noted that in the extreme south-eastern portion the former 'White Highlands' extended to parts of Machakos District. This portion of the former Scheduled Area covered the north-western and northern section of the district. It will be noted that area included the wetter and higher residuals more favoured by rainfall as well as the drier Athi-Kapiti plains.

The higher parts of the district are suitable for such plantation crops as coffee and wattle. In 1962, Machakos District accounted for 0·9 per cent of the total coffee acreage of the former Scheduled Areas. However, its principal contribution to the economy of the 'Highlands' was in sisal. In 1962 it accounted for 14·1 per cent of the sisal acreage.

The ecology of the area favours pastoral activities. In 1962, the proportion of land under uncultivated pasture was 88·8 per cent. In that same year it had 3·5 per cent of the dairy and 4·6 per cent of the beef cattle. The district specialised in production of whole milk. During the 1961/62 season, 88·7 per cent of its milk produced was sold as whole milk. Between 1958 and 1962 the number of African employees decreased from 5,700 to 5,300.

Since its formation, the 'White Highlands' has made great strides in the establishment of modern farming in the heart of rural Kenya. The economy that has developed rapidly in the former scheduled lands is the basic factor which underlies the economic opportunities for the labour force of the country. We may now take up the story of urban developments and industrial growth which have added to the strength of areas of non-African investment.

4 Urbanisation

The geographical pattern and intensity of population movements do not merely reflect the underlying importance of the resources of the country. The process of urbanisation and the location of the urban centres in Kenya are important elements in the mobility of population. The cumulative influence of the growth of urban centres and the diverse functions which support their population form part of the disequilibrium distinguishing those parts of the country supplying or receiving migrating population.

But the importance of the urban centres goes beyond the sphere of internal migrations which is the subject of this book. Urban centres have become important planning targets. The solution to economic and social problems of the country require a careful consideration of problems that have emerged with the rapid growth of the urban centres.

1. THE URBAN TRADITION IN KENYA

Although we are primarily concerned with the more recent history of the urban centres and their relationship to population movements, along the coast of Kenya the urban tradition is of considerable antiquity. Commenting on the origins of towns in East Africa, the Royal Commission stated that: 'Except on the coast there were few towns in East Africa prior to the establishment of European administration. Many of the coastal ports have a long history and were described as important centres of population by such early travellers as Ibn Batuta, and Vasco da Gama.'[1]

These ancient small trading centres have added to their original nucleus, modern sectors of the European planning period. Others such as Gedi suffered eclipse and finally declined. Apart from these ancient coastal settlements, the remaining urban centres are a European creation and form a part of the evolution of modern administration in Kenya. These centres grew along routes established into the interior, in particular the railway routes and the roads that penetrated different parts of the country. Transport developments, which included the use of Lake Victoria as a waterway, led to the establishment of Kisumu on the Lake shore.

In considering the impact of urbanisation in Kenya, it is important to note the effect of restrictive policies which not only curbed the growth of non-African activities but also effectively restricted the attraction of the rural population. For many years the towns were regarded rather as bases for administrative and commercial activities than as centres for permanent African settlement and participation. The central portions of the towns developed as areas where the non-African could live in healthy surroundings.

Settlements began either as trading posts or administrative centres and were later declared townships and trading centres. Most of the existing townships were gazetted during the first quarter of the present century as the modern administration began to take shape. In Kenya one-third of the total number of townships listed in 1948 had been declared by 1914.[2]

2. DEFINITION OF URBAN CENTRES

One of the main problems in a comparative study of urbanisation is the nature of the criteria used. Petersen[3] has suggested economic, political and demographic considerations as the three kinds of index used in varying combinations to measure urbanisation.

The economic index relies on the proportion of non-agricultural employment. He mentions that a nation may be considered urban if less than half of the occupied males are engaged in agriculture. On this basis Kenya is overwhelmingly rural in character. Table 4.1 shows the proportion of rural and urban population in Kenya.[4] It is also common to include within the terms urban those settlements which are politically or administratively recognised as such. A large number of such settlement are to be found in Kenya where because of the history of administration the centres have been long recognised as urban in status. There are a large number of settlements with less than 2,000 persons which have served as administrative centres.

Perhaps the most favoured criterion for distinguishing the urban from non-urban centres is the demographic factor. Here the number of persons living in the settlement or in a conglomeration is the measure. It is the varied use of these criteria that creates difficulties in regional studies of urbanisation and related problems.

[1]*East Africa Royal Commission Report* 1953–1955 Cmnd 9475 pp. 200–3 H.M.S.O. London 1955

In the Nigerian Census 1931, the distinction between the rural and urban settlements was made on the basis of a total population of 2,000 persons or more. According to the 1952/3 Nigerian Census, urban centres were referred to as places with a total population of 5,000 or more. A similar tendency to change in the index used has been noted in other countries. The Ghana Population Census of 1960 defined as urban area localities with a population of 5,000 or over. On the basis of this index there were only seven settlements which ranked as urban in Kenya in 1948 and eighteen in 1962 (Table 4.2).

The normal criteria used in studies of urbanisation is a population of 20,000[5] or more inhabitants. If this is applied to the 1962 Census there were only four urban centres in this category.

During the Kenya Population Census 1962 a four-fold classification of urban settlements (Municipalities, Grade 'A' Townships, Grade 'B' Townships and Trading Centres) was used and found unsatisfactory for Census purposes. Blacker considered as urban areas in Kenya towns with a total population of 2,000 or more inhabitants.[6] On the basis of Blacker's definition there were thirty-four towns with a total population of over 2,000 persons. Blacker (1965) has shown that the aggregate population of these towns came to 670,945 or 7.8 per cent of the total population of Kenya.

3. DISTRIBUTION AND RATE OF GROWTH OF THE URBAN POPULATION

Geographically it will be found that apart from the coastal belt, the majority of these urban centres are concentrated in an hour-glass shaped region with a north-west to south-east axis and distinctively broader at both extremities.

In the north-west, the region is broadest where the highlands which rim the Lake Basin merge into the West Rift Highlands of Kenya. At the opposite end it is broadest along the Nairobi-Isiolo axis. The narrower point is in the region of Gigil and Thomson's Falls.

A careful examination of the potential of this region shows that majority of the towns fall within the region enjoying good to fair prospect of obtaining 20 inches of rainfall.

This is the economic heartland of Kenya whose im-

portance in the economy of the country has already been mentioned. Further the most important of these towns are located in that part of the country which administratively formed the former 'White Highlands'. Its resource base and transport advantages have already been mentioned.

According to the 1962 Census the pattern of distribution of urban centres with a population of above 2,000 persons showed wide regional contrasts. The pattern revealed a clear dominance of the highland region in the heart of Kenya.

Within these broad divisions population was markedly concentrated in a few urban centres. In the Lake Victoria basin, Kisumu township had 73.5 per cent of the total urban population for the whole region. The Rift and Highland region in the centre showed the overwhelming importance of Nairobi. The city of Nairobi accounted for about 63 per cent of the total population for the highland region whereas Nakuru accounted for 9.0 per cent, Eldoret 4.6 per cent and Thika 3.2 per cent. In the same year Nanyuki's population was about 2 per cent of the total population of the region. Of the urban population of the coast 92.9 per cent was concentrated in the Mombasa Municipality in 1962.

The limited urbanisation suggested by the figures in the Lake basin, the plateau foreland and the drylands of Kenya reflect the importance of the non-African activities in the origins of these centres and the significance of the economic development in the highlands in the last sixty years of the present century. It is this together with extra-territorial demands of the hinterland that are reflected in the growing importance of Mombasa which dominates the population picture along the coast.

The overwhelming importance of the City of Nairobi in the Highlands and similarly situated towns on the one hand and the dominance of Mombasa at the Coast are vital factors in the intensity of population movements in Kenya.

[2]*East African Royal Commission Report* 1953–1955

[3]Petersen W. *Population* pp. 183–9 Macmillan Co., New York 1961

[4]Blacker J. G. *Population Growth and Urbanisation in Kenya* pp. 59–63 United Nations Mission to Kenya on Housing Appendix A 1965

[5]Barbour K. M. Prothero R. M. &c *Essays on African Population* p. 252 Routledge and Kegan Paul, London 1901

[6]Blacker J. G. C. 1965

Despite the restrictive policies of the initial phase, urban centres in Kenya have shown a marked increase in population. A comparison of the 1948 picture and that of 1962 show the nature of this change.

At the time of the 1948 Census, there were seventeen towns in the regions mentioned with a population of 2,000 or more each. These accounted for a total of 285,445. By 1962 towns of this size had increased to thirty-four and the total population involved had risen to 670,945 in a country with an overall total of 8,636,263 persons. About two-thirds of the urban population at the time of the Census was accounted for by the City of Nairobi and Mombasa. In 1948 these two giants accounted for (203,722) 71·36 per cent of the total population in the country. There is therefore evidence of growth of urban population in the other parts of the country.

By comparing the total urban population at the Censuses of 1948 and 1964 Blacker showed a rise of 135 per cent or an average rate of 6·3 per cent per annum over the fourteen year period. Within this period it is reported that the number of urban Africans increased by 174 per cent as against 85 per cent for the non-Africans.[7] Out of total urban population of 670,945, about 90 per cent are served by rail centres and only 10 per cent are in non-rail centres.

4. URBAN CENTRES OF THE LAKE VICTORIA BASIN

Apart from the small administrative towns of Kisii, Kakamega and Kericho, urbanisation in the Lake Basin is dominated by Kisumu, the former administrative and commercial centre of the old Nyanza Province. (*Figure 4.1*)

Kisumu is the largest of the urban centres in the region and it stands on a downfaulted lava ridge in the floor of the Nyanza Rift. The town is situated at a focal point of the transportation round the eastern end of the Lake shore and from the Coast and the Highlands to the east. Originating as a railhead and a minor administrative centre it has grown considerably with the addition of distributive and collecting functions for the greater part of Western Kenya.

Its pattern of land use shows a core of built up area surrounded by developing but as yet relatively empty

[7]Blacker J. G. C.

land. For many years Kisumu accommodated the Provincial headquarters of the old Nyanza Province.

Kisumu is the major port of Lake Victoria and accommodates the headquarters of Marine Services of the Lake. The survival of the town has depended largely on the regular employment offered by the Marine Workshop and on the associated maintenance and engineering services. Although it functions primarily as a major distributive and collecting centre in the Lake Basin, its administrative function is a further important element in its employment opportunities.

It has the advantage of rail-served industrial estate situated about a mile from the town centre on the north side of the lava ridge on which the town is sited. About a quarter of this estate has already been allocated. Apart from the oil storage installations close to the shore, light industries have developed parallel to the railway and on both sides of the Kisumu-Mumias road.

The town is linked to the other ports by a regular steamer service. Permanent surfaced road communication now links the town with the most populous parts of the Kakamega district and with Nairobi. Beyond Kakamega and towards the Uganda border, it is hoped to continue the all weather surface to link the main trunk routes of Kenya with those of Uganda to the West.

Kisumu is strategically situated in the middle of a productive land extending from the foothills of Mount Elgon to the Tanzanian border. Within this area products from the agricultural activities north, south and southeast of the gulf and the modest contribution of the surviving mining industry of the area south of the gulf pass through Kisumu as the main gateway.

Copper and livestock products from South Nyanza District, maize from Kisii and North Nyanza, and cattle from Kericho District are among the most important products that have been used the port and its facilities. Its pre-eminence as an urban centre has been in part due to its nodal position and even more to its role as the main rail centre for the whole of the former Nyanza Province.

While it would be misleading to infer exceptionally rapid growth from a crude comparison of the intercensal differences in the size of the total population, it is worth noting that between 1948 and 1962 the average rate of

Table 4.1 URBAN AND DISTRICT POPULATION BY RACE 1962 CENSUS

	Urban		Rural	
	NUMBER	%	NUMBER	%
African/Somali	441,739	5·3	7,924,203	94·7
Asian	164,992	93·4	11,621	6·6
European	34,865	62·5	20,894	37·5
Arabs	26,030	76·5	8,018	23·5
Others	3,319	85·1	582	14·9

Table 4.3 DISTRIBUTION OF URBAN POPULATION BY REGION: 1962 CENSUS

REGION	Population Total	% of National Total
Lake Victoria Basin	32,007	4·77
Rift and Associated Highlands	423,560	63·13
Plateau Foreland	9,332	1·39
The Coast	193,302	28·81
Semi-arid northern and Southern Kenya	12,744	1·90
TOTAL	670,945	100·00

Table 4.4

Kisumu Township	Africans	Non-Africans	Total
1948	5,336	5,563	10,899
1962	14,119	9,407	23,526

Table 4.2 TOWNS WITH 5,000 OR MORE: 1948 AND 1962

1948

Nairobi	118,976
Mombasa	84,746
Nakuru	17,625
Kisumu	10,899
Eldoret	8,193
Kitale	6,338
Lamu	5,868

SOURCE: *Statistical Abstract* 1963 p. 13

1962

Nairobi	266,794
Mombasa	179,575
Nakuru	38,181
Kisumu	23,526
Eldoret	19,605
Thika	13,952
Nanyuki	10,448
Kitale	9,342
Nyeri	7,857
Kericho	7,692
Gilgil	6,452
Lamu	5,828
Malindi	5,818
Athi River	5,510
Isiolo	5,445
Fort Hall	5,389
Thomson's Falls	5,316
Embu	5,213

SOURCE: *Statistical Abstract* 1963 p. 9

Figure 4.1

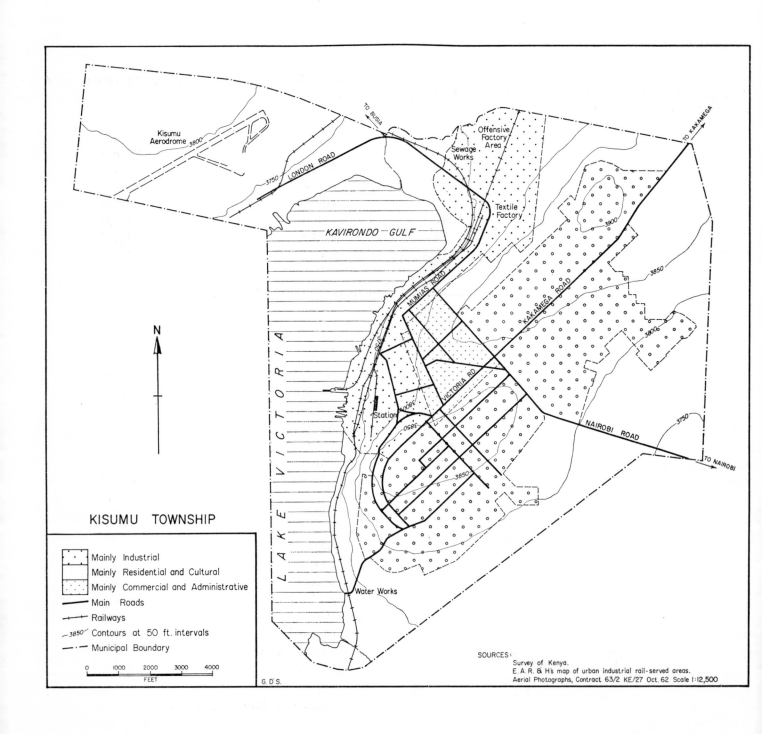

KISUMU TOWNSHIP

	Mainly Industrial
	Mainly Residential and Cultural
	Mainly Commercial and Administrative
	Main Roads
	Railways
3850	Contours at 50 ft. intervals
	Municipal Boundary

0 1000 2000 3000 4000
FEET

G. D'S.

SOURCES:
Survey of Kenya.
E. A. R. & H's map of urban industrial rail-served areas.
Aerial Photographs, Contract 63/2 KE/27 Oct. 62 Scale 1:12,500

growth has been 5·6 per cent per annum. The highest increase has been among the indigenous African population. The non-African population has not increased much since the last Census was taken. Unlike Kisumu urban developments have been restricted to such administrative centres as Kakamega and Kisii. Kakamega, the main administrative centre of the former North Nyanza has shown marked stagnation in the years following the Second World War. It has suffered from its location between the two main arteries of traffic through Eldoret and through Kisumu.

Kakamega was chosen as the headquarters of the North Nyanza district in place of the older established caravan route centre of Mumias further west. As a distributive centre it is in competition with both Kisumu and Eldoret. The built-up area has continued to occupy a relatively small portion of the total township land.

With the closure of the transient mining activity, the town lost an important economic stimulus. The recent choice of the alignment of Mau-Summit Tororo road to Uganda was a further setback to the development of the township. However, the existing permanent road surface from Kisumu will undoubtedly give a further stimulus to the development of the township.

The 1962 Census revealed that Kakamega had a total population of 3,939, which consisted of 3,155 Africans and Somali, 601 Asians, 84 Europeans, 91 Arabs and 8 others. In 1948 the total population of the township was 4,978, made up of 56 Europeans, 563 Indo-Pakistans 41 Goans, 24 Arabs and 2 others. The decline in the total population between 1948 and 1962 is indicative of the economic stagnation of the area which has affected the development of the township.

To the south-east of Kisumu, Kericho township is an important district headquarters. It is also the centre of the thriving plantation and peasant-grown tea of the Kipsigis country. Apart from the tea factories scattered in the estates, the built-up area consists mainly of administrative and shopping facilities.

In 1948 the total population of Kericho township was 3,218. This figure included 211 Europeans, 709 Indo-Pakistani, 49 Goans, 5 Arabs and 1 other. By 1962 Kericho's population had increased to 7,692, made up of 5,950 Africans and Somali, 1,462 Asians, 231 Europeans,

25 Arabs and 24 others. The average growth rate per annum for Kericho of 6·4 per cent between the censuses is one of the highest in Kenya. To the south-west at the head of Riana Valley is Kisii Township, the old administrative headquarters of the former South Nyanza District and now the headquarters of Kisii District.

Unlike Kericho, Kisii has remained largely an administrative centre. Despite its location in a highly productive area, there has been no marked expansion of its built-up area in terms of transport. In 1948, the town had a total population of 2,436 made up of 56 Europeans, 332 Indo-Pakistani, 16 Goans, 10 Arabs and 6 others.

5. URBAN CENTRES OF THE RIFT AND ASSOCIATED HIGHLANDS

Towns of the highland region, which accounted for just about two-thirds of the urban population in Kenya in 1962, range widely in size. At one end of the scale is Eldama Ravine which had a population of 2,315 and at the very other end are the City of Nairobi and Nakuru Township with 266,796 and 38,181 respectively.

The close association of the major towns with non-African economic activity may be clearly seen in the distribution of the townships and their size. The majority of the townships are to be found in that portion of the highland region which formerly constituted a part of the 'White Highland' of Kenya. None of the towns situated in the former African land units in the highland area had reached the 10,000 mark at the time of the 1962 Census.

The majority of the highland towns were small settlements of mostly between 2,000 and 10,000 persons. Because the greater part of these are rail centres they have exercised an important influence on employment. A combination of factors internal and external to the economy of Kenya has resulted in a faster growth of a few of these centres.

Nairobi has developed from a small railway station at the beginning of a major change of gradient to one of the largest cities in Eastern Africa. Close by are the industrial towns of Thika and Athi River. In the heart of the Rift Valley, Nakuru has developed rapidly to become the leading town of the Rift Valley. In the Highlands, west of the Rift Valley, Eldoret and Kitale are the most important settlements.

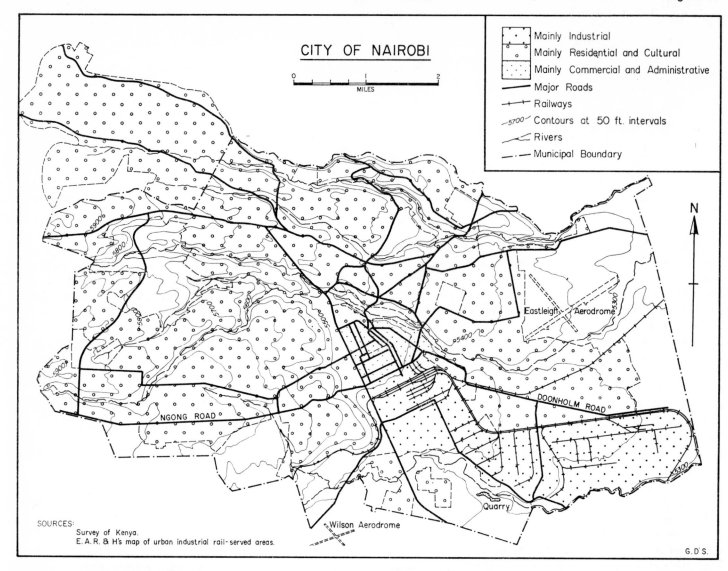

CITY OF NAIROBI

0   1   2
MILES

Legend:
- Mainly Industrial
- Mainly Residential and Cultural
- Mainly Commercial and Administrative
- Major Roads
- Railways
- 5700 Contours at 50 ft. intervals
- Rivers
- Municipal Boundary

SOURCES:
Survey of Kenya.
E.A.R. & H's map of urban industrial rail-served areas.

G.D.S.

i. *The City of Nairobi* (Figure 4.2)

A closer examination of the location of the City shows that it is situated at the south-eastern end of the agricultural heartland of East Africa. This strategic position has been enhanced by transport planning which began at the Coast towards the end of the last century.

The City heart is located where the spurs of the tilted plateau to the west merge into the flat plains to the east. The change of gradient is marked by a distinctive bluff at an altitude of about 5,500 feet above sea level.

The eastern half of the City extending from the City centre towards Embakasi Airport is a flattish landscape lying generally between 5,000 and 5,400 feet above sea level. In the west the streams merging from the highlands have cut quite deep valleys. Eastwards these open out to accommodate the sluggish streams.

The immediate environment consists of the productive highland area extending northwards and westwards to embrace the rich farming lands of the Rift Valley and the Lake Victoria Basin in Western Kenya.

In its present position, the City enjoys the advantages of four major land routes from the Coast, the Rift Highlands of Western Kenya, the Mount Kenya-Nairobi

axis and, towards the south, the route to Arusha and Moshi. It is also the commercial and air communication centre for the whole of East Africa. Nairobi's developing facilities for air communication now ranks it as one of the leading international airports in eastern Africa.

By comparison with the Coastal centres, Nairobi is a youthful settlement. From its beginnings towards the end of the last century its development in the initial period reflected the early uncertainties that characterised the farming developments in the highlands of Kenya.

Its development was most rapid after World War II. Judged by the rate of increase of privately owned buildings, activities in Nairobi rose rapidly between 1945 and 1952. But evidence of the rapid expansion of Nairobi activities is not confined to the decade following the end of the Second World War. Nairobi's growth has been part of the general economic growth not only of Kenya but of East Africa as a whole and in particular Uganda.

Between 1920 and 1945 the value of cotton goods imports for Kenya and Uganda increased from just under £912,000 to £2,677,000. This represented an increase of 293 per cent.[8] Indices of the economic progress

[8]White L. W. T. &c *Nairobi Master Plan* p. 79 H.M.S.O. London 1948

Table 4.5 URBAN POPULATION 1962

Towns of 2,000 or more persons

	Total Population by racial groups	Nairobi's share	Percentage of total
Africans/Somali	441,739	156,246	35·37
Asians	164,992	86,453	52·39
Europeans	34,865	21,477	61·60
Arabs	26,030	982	3·77

of the Nairobi area show a steep rise from about 1920 to the end of the war. During the period 1906 to 1944 available estimates indicated that the population of Nairobi had grown from about 10,000 to well over 100,000.[9]

During the period 1952–3 the rate of growth of Nairobi was much faster than that of Dar-es-Salaam and Kampala. The onset of the Emergency in 1952 and the associated uncertainties was reflected in a slower rate of growth in 1953 and 1954.[10]

Nairobi includes among its important activities the role of the capital City of Kenya. Its function until recently as the headquarters of the East African Common Services Organisation has been a vital element in its employment situation although future developments may alter this role. However, in addition to these important administrative functions, Nairobi has developed healthy commercial and industrial functions.

The thriving industrial activity which has developed in the City has been encouraged by the setting aside of about 700 acres of rail-served industrial land. In the Old Station Warehouse areas some twelve acres of industrial land close to the City heart have all been allocated. The commercial street about two miles from the City centre is now mostly taken up and some sites are due for redevelopment. Following the rapid development of the post-war period the New Industrial Area from London Road eastwards was opened. This rail-served industrial area covers 648 acres and lies about four miles from the City centre.

Functional differentiation of the City has already produced three main distinct parts. In the centre of the City is the Commercial centre and parks. The developments in the industrial estates have already been mentioned.

Perhaps one of the most important functional differentiations is the varied character of the City residential area. Nairobi was originally strictly planned on racial lines with the European residential areas limited to the western, north-western and northern parts of the City. The Asian residential area extended from Eastleigh and parts of Westlands to include portions of the City close to the shopping centre. Another Asian residential area was to be found in the southern part of the City. The African residential units have sprawled eastwards from the railway residential property close to the centre of the City. These

rigid boundaries are breaking down though Eastlands is still predominantly African.

Until quite recently the City's expansion has largely been determined by its location in the former scheduled area. The direction of expansion has been more towards the east and within the boundaries of the outlier of former scheduled land which borders Machakos District to the west and north-west.

The most recent boundary changes extended the new limits of the Nairobi Area to include the neighbourhoods in the eastern, southern and western sectors of the City. With this expansion Nairobi boundaries now extend east to include Embakasi Airport and in the north the former Kahawa military base, Kamiti Prison and the peri-urban area. In the west, parts of the former Kiambu district have now been included.[11]

An impression of the growth of Nairobi before the first national census may be obtained from estimates and partial records.[12] The first national Census in 1948 gave a total population of 118,976 for the City of Nairobi. Of this total 64,397 were Africans and 53,579 non-Africans. The figure for non-Africans included 10,830 Europeans, 37,935 Indo-Pakistani, 3,875 Goans, 626 Arabs and 1,313 others. By 1962, the total population of the City had risen to 266,794. This figure excluded a total Peri-Urban population of 47,966 which together gave Nairobi (Extra-Provincial District) a figure of 314,760 persons.

If the boundary adjustment of the 1962 is taken into account the 1963 limits of Nairobi would have given a total population of 344,000. On the 1962 old boundaries the annual rate of increase in population has been given as 5·9 per cent.[13]

Although the City is one of the most important attractions to the African population, in 1962 it had only 156,246 Africans and Somali out of the national total of 441,739 in towns with over 2,000 persons. The proportion of the Africans in the capital was 35·37 per cent of the above national total.

[9]White L. W. T. &c pp. 82–4
[10]Walmsley R. W. *Nairobi: The Geography of a New City* p. 10 East African Literature Bureau 1957
[11]*Report of the Regional Boundaries Commission* Cmnd 1899 H.M.S.O. London 1962
[12]White L. W. T.
[13]Blacker J. G. p. 62

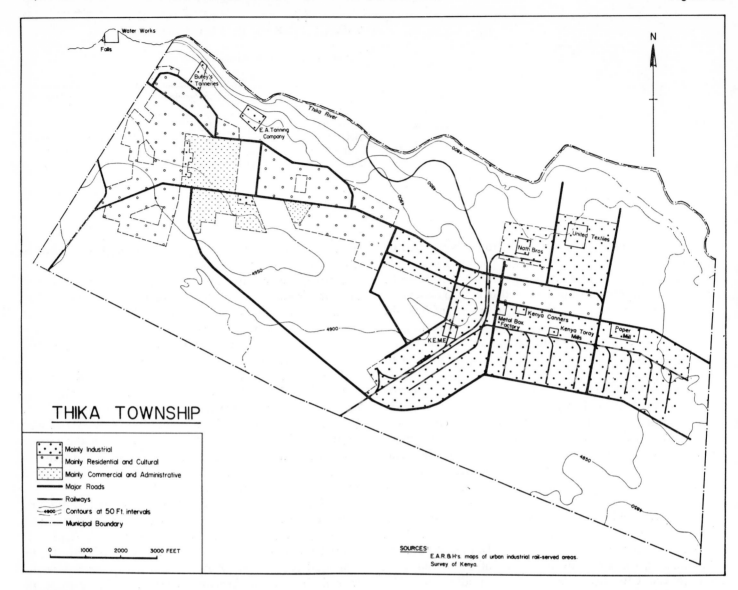

THIKA TOWNSHIP

Mainly Industrial
Mainly Residential and Cultural
Mainly Commercial and Administrative
Major Roads
Railways
Contours at 50 Ft. intervals
Municipal Boundary

0   1000   2000   3000 FEET

SOURCES:
E.A.R.&H's. maps of urban industrial rail-served areas.
Survey of Kenya.

In the same year Nairobi had 52·39 per cent of the Asian population and 61·60 per cent of the European population living in urban centres with 2,000 or more persons. The proportion of the Arab population in these towns accounted for by Nairobi was 3·77 per cent of the total. The concentration of the European and the Asian population is a reflection of the commercial, industrial and administrative importance of the centre in the Kenya and East African setting.

The productive resources of the Nairobi area and the proximity of the services offered by the City have stimulated development of industrial activities and development of the towns of Thika (Figure 4.3) and Athi River. These two smaller towns are important elements in the attraction of the labour to the peri-urban areas of Nairobi.

Thika township is a medium sized highland settlement located at an altitude of 4,897 feet above sea level and about twenty-six miles from Nairobi. The town is sited at the lower end of the north-west to south-east ridge lying between the Chania one of the main tributaries of the Tana River and Ndarugu, a tributary of the Athi River. The immediate environment of the settlement is a

productive farming country specialising in plantation crops, beef cattle or dairy. Among its advantages that have attracted industry are abundant labour supply, power and water facilities.

Thika's industrial area is located about two miles from the centre of the town and has provided an ideal opportunity for industries that require cheap land and plenty of ground for expansion. The town has shared in the growing prosperity associated with the investment in the modern farming of the surrounding lands.

In 1948, Thika had a total population of 4,435 including 2,806 Africans, 1,353 Indo-Pakistani, 163 Europeans, 30 Goans, 65 Arabs and 18 others. In 1962, the total population had increased to 13,952, made up of 11,352 Africans and Somali, 2,336 Asians, 179 Europeans, 41 Arabs and 44 others. Blacker (1964) computed an average growth rate of 8·5 per cent giving the town a lead over all the main towns including Nairobi. This increase among the Asians has not been as high as that of the Africans.

In the south-east, is the satellite town of Athi River. This area now provides accommodation for one of the

Figure 4.4

URBANISATION/71

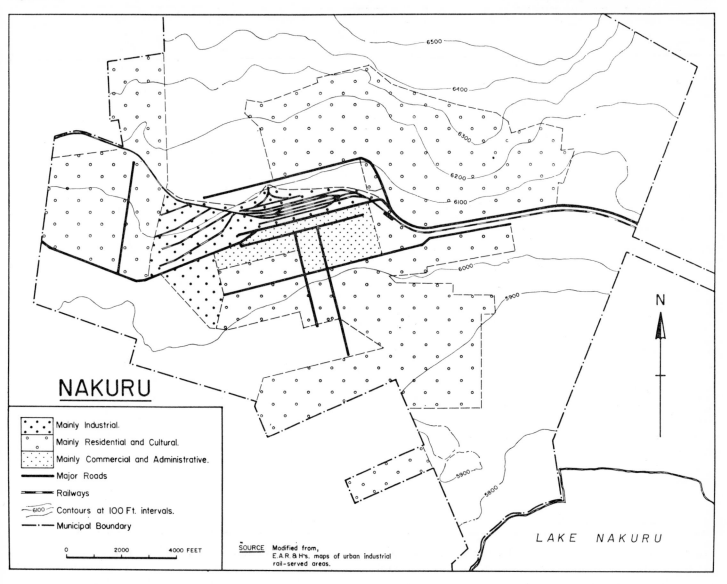

NAKURU

Legend:
- Mainly Industrial.
- Mainly Residential and Cultural.
- Mainly Commercial and Administrative.
- Major Roads
- Railways
- 6100 Contours at 100 Ft. intervals.
- Municipal Boundary

0   2000   4000 FEET

SOURCE Modified from,
E.A.R. & H's. maps of urban industrial
rail-served areas.

LAKE NAKURU

two cement factories in Kenya and the most important meat cannery in the country. In 1962 Athi River had a total population of 5,510 including 5,216 Africans and Somali, 118 Asians, 88 Europeans and 87 others.

ii. *Nakuru Township* (*Figure 4.4*)

Nakuru, the chief town of the Rift Valley and the provincial headquarters is an important rail junction in the heart of the richest farming province in Kenya. It is situated in a narrow gap between the lower slopes of Menengai Crater in the north and Lake Nakuru in the south. Because of this limited site the town has expanded literally, especially on the southern side of the railway. The better residential areas are situated on the slopes of Menengai to the north of the railway line.

The selection of the site of the town as a major rail junction is part of the long history of the economics of rail construction. Having carried the rail construction meridionally to the latitude of Nakuru, the next problem was to negotiate the steep escarpment that borders the rift to the west.

The main task of the builders of the railways was to design a cheap railway line along the easiest route from the Coast to the shores of Lake Victoria. Two alternative routes were considered, the one over the Mau Escarpment via Nyando Valley to the Lake shore and a more northerly route to River Nzoia and eventually to the Lake. Since the shortest convenient route to the Lake was an important factor the Nyando Valley route had an advantage over the Nzoia route.

When the need to extend the railway line to Uasin Gishu plateau was realized, Nakuru's choice was well established. The Uganda branch crosses the Mau just south of Eldama Ravine from where the escarpment branches into two arms to form the Kamasia Hills and the Elgeyo escarpment. Nakuru was the centre from where trains negotiating the western wall along the two routes could be serviced. But Nakuru's growth is only in part due to its strategic location in relation to the rail transportation to West Kenya and Uganda. It is the natural centre of a rich farming Province producing wheat, maize, beef, dairy products and pyrethrum.

Situated at an altitude of 6,071 feet above sea level it is easily the largest highland town after Nairobi. Its

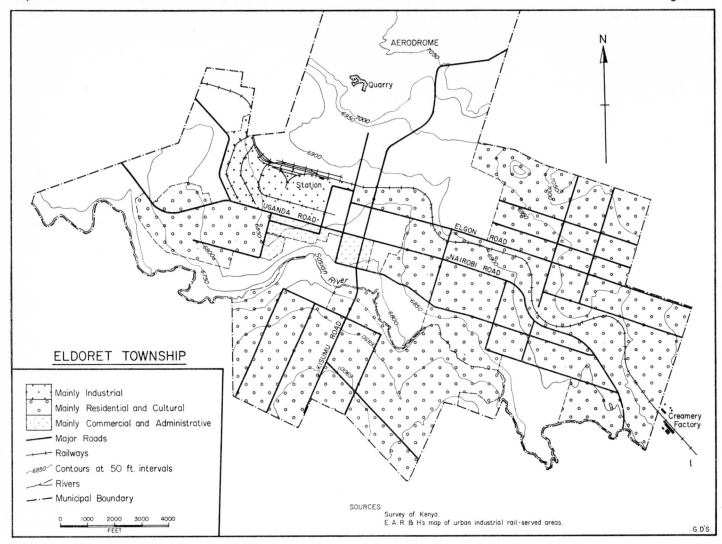

ELDORET TOWNSHIP

Mainly Industrial
Mainly Residential and Cultural
Mainly Commercial and Administrative
Major Roads
Railways
6850 Contours at 50 ft. intervals
Rivers
Municipal Boundary

0   1000   2000   3000   4000
FEET

SOURCES:
Survey of Kenya.
E. A. R. & H's map of urban industrial rail-served areas.

G. D'S.

growth has reflected the needs of the farming community for processing the products of the farming industry and purchasing the goods needed by the farmers. Of its rail served industrial estate of about eighty-six acres, over half has been allocated.

In 1948 Nakuru had a total population of 17,625 including 12,845 Africans, 2,912 Indo-Pakistani, 1,159 Europeans, 335 Goans, 173 Arabs and 201 others. At the time of the 1962 Census, Nakuru Municipality maintained its place as the third largest town in Kenya with a total population of 38,181 including 30,189 Africans and Somali, 6,203 Asians, 1,414 Europeans, 181 Arabs and 194 others.

Blacker (1964) worked out an average growth rate of 5·7 per cent per annum in the period between the 1948 and 1962 Censuses. In common with the remaining highland towns Nakuru does not show any special concentration of the non-African population. It has thus been essentially a centre of the farming community. At the time of the Census, it had only 4 per cent of the total European population in towns of 2,000 persons or more and 3·76 per cent of the Asian population.

iii. *Eldoret and Kitale*
To the west of the Rift Valley development of farming and transport facilities has stimulated the growth of the

towns of Eldoret and Kitale. Eldoret is the administrative headquarters, as well as being an agricultural and industrial centre, for the Uasin Gishu Plateau. Lying at an altitude of 6,875 feet above the sea level it has rail served industrial land of about twelve acres (Figure 4.5).

In 1948 Eldoret was the fifth largest town in Kenya with a total population of 8,193. This consisted of 5,408 Africans, 888 Europeans, 1,761 Indo-Pakistani, 84 Goans, 31 Arabs and 21 others. At the time of the 1962 Census, the total population of Eldoret had increased to 19,605. It thus retained its fifth position. This total was made up of 15,059 Africans and Somali, 3,758 Asians, 664 Europeans, 38 Arabs and 86 others. Eldoret was until recently the main centre of the Boer farming community in Kenya. Following on independence the European population has been further reduced by the outflow of farmers. Blacker (1964) reckoned a growth rate per annum for Eldoret of 6·4 per cent between the 1948 and 1962 Censuses. This gave the township one of the highest growth rates in the country. It was higher than Nairobi, Mombasa, Nakuru, Kisumu and a number of other Kenya towns. The growth of the town has been closely linked up with the prosperity of the farming industry of the area in which it is situated.

Kitale further to the north-west is a small town located

Figure 4.6   URBANISATION/73

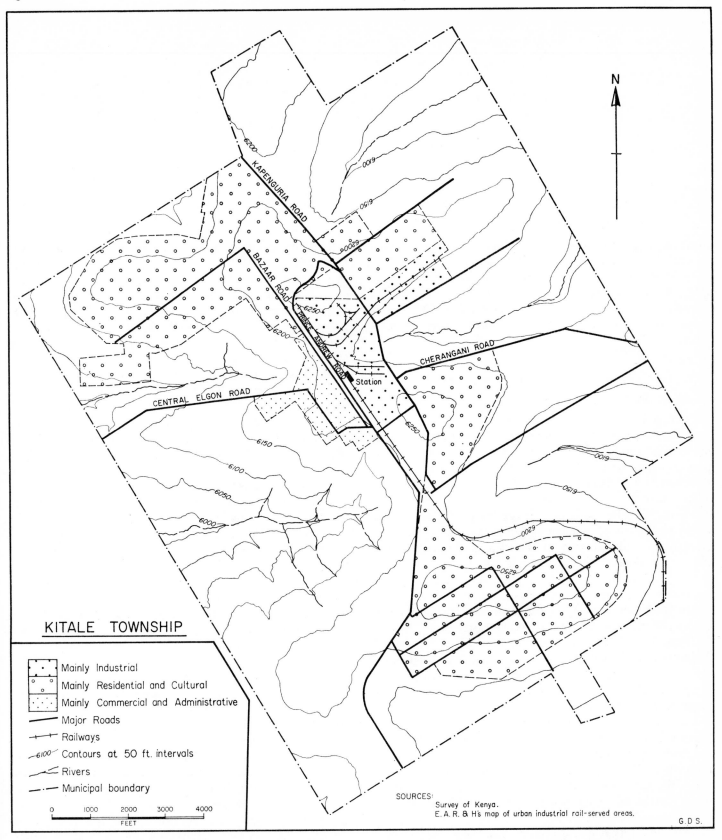

KITALE TOWNSHIP

	Mainly Industrial
	Mainly Residential and Cultural
	Mainly Commercial and Administrative
	Major Roads
	Railways
	Contours at 50 ft. intervals
	Rivers
	Municipal boundary

0   1000   2000   3000   4000
FEET

SOURCES:
Survey of Kenya.
E. A. R. & H's map of urban industrial rail-served areas.

G.D S.

on the edge of the productive island of west central Kenya (Figure 4.6). The town is the chief centre of the Trans-Nzoia District, as well as the collecting and distributive centre of one of the most important maize growing areas. The land around has important pastoral potential. Situated at an altitude of 6,220 feet above sea level it has remained a small town serving this thriving agricultural area. Industrial activities have been encouraged by the allocation of some sixty-nine acres of rail-served estate close to the centre of the town.

At the time of the 1948 Census, Kitale was the sixth urban centre in Kenya in terms of size. In 1962 although

Table 4.6 **A.** MOMBASA PORT TRAFFIC

YEAR	No. of steamships	Total net tonnage	Total cargo tonnage	Gross Earnings (£)
1948	806	2,433,099	2,344,066	1,341,023
1952	917	3,037,239	2,910,435	2,045,673
1956	1,233	3,839,606	3,175,102	2,968,000
1960	1,330	4,469,754	2,651,383	3,542,000
1962	1,422	4,610,787	2,873,227	3,796,000

B.

IMPORTS	Bulk oil	Bulk coal	EXPORTS	Bunker coal	Bunker oil and Bunker coal
1940	210,666	117,547	1940	11,938	53,047
1950	589,598	37,280	1950	20,781	157,496
1960	1,023,586	42,671	1960	—	129,396

the total population was higher it had lost the sixth place to Thika township.

In between the two Censuses, Kitale has grown much more slowly than the main urban centres which have already been described. Blacker (1965) worked out a growth rate of 2·8 per cent per annum between the two Censuses.

6. URBANISATION IN THE COAST REGION

Mombasa (Figure 4.7)

Mombasa attracts attention because of its ancient history and participation in the commerce of the Indian Ocean basin. The modern phase of the town is preceded by a period of activity following the establishment of the settlement by a group of exiled Shirazi princes.[14]

Its expansion is to a greater extent the history of the economic development of a large part of East Africa embracing parts of Tanzania, Kenya and Uganda. This is a phase which began in the closing decades of the nineteenth century. Mombasa has become the principal port of Kenya, Uganda part of the Congo and northern Tanzania. The quotation below vividly captures the vision of Mombasa at the zenith of its early prosperity and before the European phase of its development. 'There is an island hard by the mainland, on which is a town called Mombasa. It is a very fair place with lofty stone and mortar houses, well aligned in streets. . . . This is a place of great traffic, and has a good harbour, in which are always moored crafts of many kinds and also great ships. . . .'[15]

But that urban centre differs vastly from the modern port and the activities which have developed in the area following the penetration of the railway to the productive hinterland. Developments by 1926 had made it vital to begin the first phase of the construction of modern deep water berths on which the prosperity of Mombasa to a great extent depends.

From this initial phase pressure resulting from a more rational use of the land resources of the hinterland had led to reciprocal expansion of harbour facilities on the north-west of the island and west mainland. These modern expansions of the first half of the twentieth century mingle in the eastern sector of the island with what remains of ancient Mombasa around Fort Jesus.

The emergence of a modern port on what is generally a coral bound coast is due to the natural advantages of the site with which Mombasa surpasses the other ancient coastal settlements. The port occupies a portion of the submerged seaboard and a natural defensive site. At this point on the African coast is the Island of Mombasa three miles long by two and a half miles wide with access through a one and one-fifth mile opening in the coral shelf. Most of the island consists of coral, but lagoonal sands cover the north-west tip of the parts of mainland. Shales and Magarini sands underlie Changamwe and areas north-east of Port Tudor and south-west of Port Reitz. On this foundation had developed the town of Mombasa which lies mostly between the 50 and 100 foot contour. Only parts of Changamwe rise up to about 250 feet above sea level.

The area of the municipality is now about 100 square miles of which some 20 per cent is covered by water. The little used old Mombasa Harbour lies in the east of the island. Sailing craft found this eastern harbour was safer to navigate in comparison with the more difficult entrance to Kilindini Harbour. The old harbour is still used for sail or motorised craft belonging to Greeks, Indians and Africans on trade along the coast and between south-west Asia, India and the East Africa. It has no rail connection and cargo is handled manually.

ii. *Development of the modern port of Kilindini*

The development of Mombasa deep water harbour and related growth of the commerce and industry of the town are vital factors in the movement of population in the coast region and Kenya as a whole.

The story began with the construction of the first jetty on the southern side of Ras Kilindini in 1896; this was followed by the construction of deep water berths in 1926. By 1931, five berths and an oil jetty had been completed at Shimanzi and at the close of the Second World War seven berths had been completed. By 1955, the harbour works on Mombasa Island were completed. Two years later, the Kipevu causeway opened a new phase for development of Changamwe.

[14]Van Dongen I. S. *Mombasa in the Land and Sea Exchanges of East Africa Erdkunde* Band XVII, 1961 pp. 16–361
[15]*Mombasa Master Plan* 1962 p. 3 Mombasa Municipal Council 1963

Figure 4.7 **URBANISATION/75**

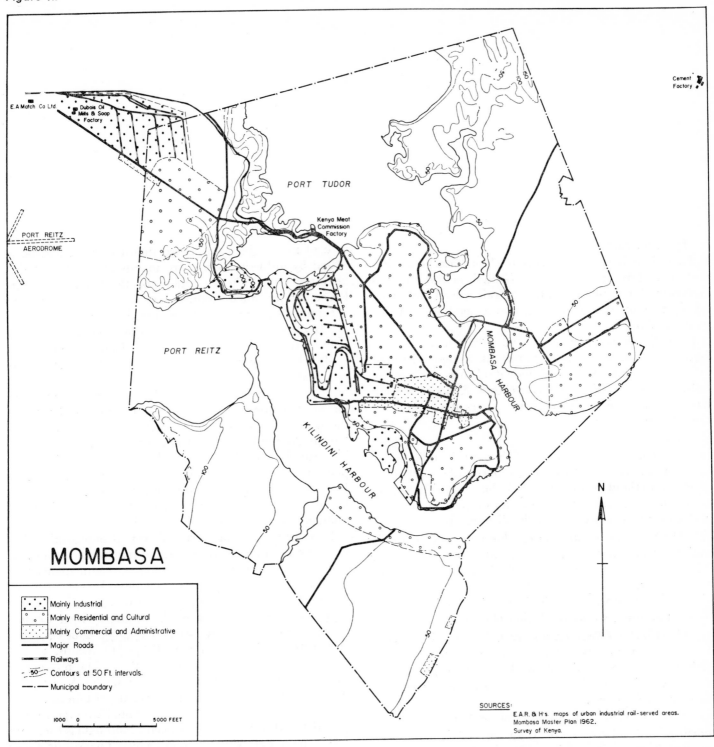

MOMBASA

Legend:
- Mainly Industrial
- Mainly Residential and Cultural
- Mainly Commercial and Administrative
- Major Roads
- Railways
- 50 Contours at 50 Ft. intervals.
- Municipal boundary

1000   0   5000 FEET

SOURCES: E.A.R. & H's. maps of urban industrial rail-served areas.
Mombasa Master Plan 1962.
Survey of Kenya.

iii. *Growth of traffic* (Table 4.6)

The need for heavy investment in the port facilities of Mombasa to serve the demands of its hinterland may be seen from the fact that the number of steamships calling increased from 255 in 1908 to 1,330 in 1960 and the aggregate tonnage involved rose from 738 to 4,469,000 in between the two periods.[16] Most of this rapid expansion happened after the Second World War.[17]

The port of Mombasa derives its traffic largely from the cotton and coffee produce of Uganda and from the plantation crops of Kenya such as coffee, sisal, tea and pyrethrum. It is only to a limited extent that its increasing volume of trade has been drawn from the northern highlands of Tanzania. It controls almost all the entire coffee trade of East Africa. Petroleum products form about one-third of the port traffic and about half of all imports. The port is linked with the hinterland north by a road through the Nyali pontoon bridge and south by the Likoni ferry. Through these come the products of sisal, coconut and sugar estates as well as the products of the African rural farmers.

[16]*Mombasa Master Plan* 1962

[17]Othieno-Ochieng N. A. *The Port of Mombasa: A Summary Review of Port Facilities* Table I–III (unpublished report)

iv. *Industrial estates*

Industrial activity of the Port of Mombasa is an important feature of its economy. Growth of industry has been stimulated by reservation of rail served industrial estates first on the island and now extending over the west mainland.

In 1926, about 950 acres of land were reserved on the Island for industrial development associated with the activities of the Port. Two additional schemes south of the railway station and in the Whitehouse Road area were later added. The main industrial estates now consist of the following units:

The island of Mombasa

(a) *Kilindini high level godown.* This area is mainly for warehousing associated with the import and export trade of the hinterland of the port. It is here that the export trade in coffee and associated factories are concentrated and land in the area is virtually all used up.

(b) *The Shimanzi industrial area.* This industrial sector is mainly for light industry and refrigerator storage facilities. This area is again fully developed. To the north-west of the sector and opposite the tanker berths, are situated the oil companies' storage installations. In this same area are found the allied works producing chemicals.

(c) *The Whitehouse Road industrial area.* This unit is adjacent to the railway marshalling yards and accommodates such industries as the aluminium works, concrete prefabrication, the maize and rice mills. There is no more space for further development.

(d) *North and South of the Railway Station.* Extending to the north of the railway station is an area of light industry around Nizarali Street. The area south of the railway station is largely devoted to motor vehicle repair, vehicle assembly and ancillary trades.

(e) *Around Mbaraki Creek.* This area south of the island mainly accommodates shipyards, marine and general engineering. Land is extremely limited in this sector by the coral cliff. There is no further room for expansion of industry in this section of the island.

The New Industrial Area of the West Mainland

(a) *Changamwe Area.* This extension now covers an area of about 550 acres. The area is linked by road and rail to the main docks and harbour area. By 1962 some 20 per cent of the originally proposed industrial area had been leased by individual concerns, mainly oil companies and ancillary users. The remainder of the area has been leased by the Shell Company of East Africa and now accommodates the newly constructed oil refinery.

(b) *Makupa Causeway.* This small industrial estate is served only by road. Here the Kenya Meat Commission factory deals with some 7,500 head of cattle, sheep and goats every month.

(c) *North and South Mainland.* Provision has been made for industrial development in the area north and south of the Island. So far the cement factory in the north mainland is the most important development. The expansion here suffers from lack of a rail connection. A bulk silo plant for bulk loading of cement has been erected at English Point opposite the old harbour. The south mainland has remained undeveloped except for the coral quarrying and local service industries.

Mombasa's thriving port and related industrial activities have been matched by a rapid rise in population. At the time of the 1948 Census, Mombasa Municipality had a total population of 84,746 including 42,853 Africans, 23,847 Indo-Pakistani, 13,485 Arabs, 2,027 Europeans, 1,733 Goans and 801 others. According to 1962 Census, the total population had reached 179,575. This consisted of 111,847 Africans and Somali, 43,713 Asians, 17,740 Arabs, 5,305 Europeans and 970 others. The number of Europeans is likely to fall further but the Arabs have shown a rate of increase of 25 per cent per annum.

Blacker (1965) worked out an annual average rate of growth for Mombasa of 5·5 per cent. Mombasa is therefore one of the fast growing towns in Kenya. The Municipality is planning for a total population of 250,000 by 1980. Of this total 112,000 is planned for on the island and about 140,000 will be accommodated on the adjacent mainland.

In 1962 Mombasa had only 25·31 per cent of the total African and Somali population in towns with more than 2,000 persons. But at the same time, the Municipality had 68·15 per cent of the total Arab population in these towns. The Asians recorded in Mombasa accounted for 26·49 per cent of the total population resident in towns of over 2,000 persons. The proportion of Europeans was 15·21 per cent of the total.[18]

[18] *Mombasa Master Plan* 1962

5 Distribution and Types of Manufacturing Industries

I. DISTRIBUTION OF MANUFACTURING INDUSTRIES

The development of resources of Kenya and the growing diversity of the needs of her population have stimulated a modest but significant manufacturing industry. The pattern of this industry is influenced by the degree of urbanisation and by the economic factors which govern the location of these industries.

As a general rule, it has been noted that there is a distinct tendency for the concentration of industries in the vicinity of Nairobi. Such industries as are located elsewhere are those that must be close to their raw material source or which provide small-scale consumer goods to meet the needs of local population. Processing of agricultural, forest or mineral products generally takes place near the sources of raw materials; this is particularly true of the processing of dairy products, sugar and sodium carbonate at Magadi.

i. The Nairobi Extra-Provincial District

The pattern of distribution of industrial establishment brings out the overwhelming importance of the Nairobi Extra-Provincial District. In 1957 the area accounted for 41 per cent of the total industrial establishments in the country. In 1961 Nairobi Extra-Provincial District had maintained its lead with 43·27 per cent of the total industrial establishments (Table 5·1).

The Census of manufacturing industry in 1957 revealed that there were 17,689 persons employed in the Extra-Provincial manufacturing area. This figure accounted for 36·71 per cent of the total number of employees engaged in industry. In 1961 the area still held the lead in employing 41·43 per cent of the industrial employees (Table 5.2). It should be noted that this overwhelming lead is due largely to the influence of the City of Nairobi, which is most important for the metals and association industries and least in textiles, leather and clothing.

ii. The Coast Province

The Coast has continued to hold the second most important place in the development of manufacturing activities. But the importance of the province is here clearly inflated by the contribution of the municipality of Mombasa. By 1961 the presence of Mombasa in the Coast Province had led to the value added by manufacture being

Table 5.1 PROVINCIAL DISTRIBUTION (1957 & 1961)

Number of Industrial Establishments by Province

	1957	%	1961	%
Nairobi EPD	344	41·00	344	43·27
Coast	157	18·71	146	18·36
Rift Valley	152	18·11	140	17·61
Central	83	9·89	69	8·68
Nyanza	83	9·89	82	10·31
Southern	20	2·38	14	1·76
Total	839	99·98	795	99·99

SOURCE: *Kenya Census of Manufacturing 1961 pp. 78–9*

Table 5.2 NUMBERS ENGAGED

	1957	%	1961	%
Nairobi EPD	17,689	36·71	20,593	41·43
Coast	8,495	17·63	8,045	16·19
Rift Valley	8,686	18·03	7,605	15·30
Central	6,712	13·93	6,760	13·60
Nyanza	3,706	7·69	3,698	7·43
Southern	2,769	5·74	2,874	5·78
Northern	127	0·26	130	0·26
Total	48,184	99·99	47,705	99·99

SOURCE: *Kenya Census of Manufacturing 1961*

Table 5.3 NUMBER OF ESTABLISHMENTS

TOWNS	1957	% of Total	1961	% of Total
Nairobi City	330	53·83	335	54·30
Mombasa Town	137	22·35	136	22·04
Nakuru	40	6·53	37	6·00
Eldoret	20	3·26	26	4·21
Kitale	17	2·77	14	2·27
Thika	21	3·43	20	3·24
Kisumu	48	7·83	49	9·94
TOTAL	613	100·00	617	100·00
NATIONAL TOTAL	839		795	

Main towns as a percentage of National Total	73·06	77·61
Nairobi as a percentage of National Total	39·33	42·14
Mombasa as percentage of National Total	16·32	17·10

about 50 per cent above that of either the Rift Valley, the Central or Southern Province.[1]

The type of industry which has developed in the area also differs considerably from those of other Provinces. The Coast Province has little of the food and beverage industry but is rather more important in the sphere of the metal industry.

In 1961, 32 per cent of the metal and associated industries was assigned to the Province. It is important to note that the metal products and ship repairing industries which are in themselves large industries are based at Mombasa. Away from Mombasa Island, the cement industry already mentioned and one of the oldest sugar factories form part of the industrial pattern that enhances the importance of the Coast Province as an employment area. The completion of the British Standard Portland Cement factory at Bamburi has now made Kenya self-sufficient in this commodity. The factory is based on the extensive coral and shale raw materials of the area. Capacity of the two cement factories in Kenya now exceeds 500,000 tons.

It has already been noted that rural Coast Province is noted for its important plantations of which Vipingo Estate Limited is the largest north of Mombasa. The sisal factory in 1965 produced about 4,000 tons of fibre and the target is to raise the figure to about 5,000 tons. In the section of the Coast south of Mombasa, Jafferali Coconut Estate and Madhvani Estate Limited are the most important establishments processing products of the area. The Madhvani Sugar Estate already mentioned in Ramisi area was formerly the Kenya Sugar Limited. In recent years production has been generally below 3,000 tons a year. In 1957, the combined output of the Coast and Nyanza sugar factories was 20,000 tons. By 1961 this figure had gone to 32,600 tons. The value-added total rose from £918,000 in 1957 to £1,562,000 in 1961.

In 1957 the Coast Province was the second most important manufacturing area with 18·71 per cent of the total establishments and 17·63 per cent of the labour engaged in manufacturing activity in the whole of Kenya. During this year, it had slightly fewer people employed than the Rift Valley Province. In 1961, the Province had 18·36 per cent of the total number of establishments and 16·19 per cent of the labour employed. This gave the

Province a lead both in the concentration of the percentage of establishments and in the number of people employed over the Rift Valley.

iii. *The Rift Valley*

Containing the bulk of the former Scheduled lands, it has been noted that the Rift Valley is one of the most important farming areas of Kenya. It produces much of the agricultural export of the country and has as well a high demand for consumer goods. Its importance in manufacturing is due to the presence of a variety of establishments processing dairy products, grains and raw materials, including pyrethrum for insecticides.

The Rift Valley is the most important Province in the timber industry. In 1961 nearly 3,700 persons were engaged in the industry in the Province. This represented about two-thirds (64 per cent) of the total engaged in the timber industry in the whole country.

Although the town of Nakuru plays a similar role to that of Nairobi and Mombasa in their respective areas, the town does not hold the same dominant role in the distribution of manufacturing activities, for they are more diffused.

It will be noted that in 1957 the Province accounted for 18·11 per cent of the total number of manufacturing establishments and in 1961 it had 17·61 per cent. The total contribution of the Province, to the employment of people in manufacturing was 18·03 per cent in 1957 and 15·30 in 1961.

iv. *The Central Province*

This area is clearly less important in manufacturing activity than the Nairobi, Coast and Rift Valley areas. It is the fourth most important manufacturing area for a variety of reasons.

Proximity of Nairobi and advantages of services offered has attracted a number of plants to the Province. But the most important contribution is from the small industrial complex at Thika about thirty miles from Nairobi. Close to Nairobi are two large breweries. The large factory making sisal products such as mats, sacks and twine at Kalimoni, east of Ruiru contributes to the lead of the

[1]*Kenya Census of Manufacturing 1961*, Nairobi, 1963

Table 5.4 NUMBERS OF PERSONS ENGAGED

TOWNS	1957	% of Total	1961	% of Total			
Nairobi City	15,915	57·67	19,236	57·62	Main towns as a percentage of National Total	58·03	67·16
Mombasa Town	6,242	22·62	6,711	20·10			
Nakuru	1,284	4·65	1,958	5·87	Nairobi as a percentage of National Total	33·03	38·70
Eldoret	867	3·14	1,302	3·90			
Kitale	363	1·32	310	0·93	Mombasa as a percentage of National Total	12·95	13·50
Thika	1,485	5·38	2,395	7·17			
Kisumu	1,441	5·22	1,472	4·41			
TOTAL	27,579	100·00	33,384	100·00			
NATIONAL TOTAL	48,148		49,705				

Province over the remaining industrial area. Most of the important Central Province industries are within thirty miles of the City of Nairobi.

By 1957, the Central Province accounted for 9·89 per cent of the total establishments and in 1961 it had 8·68 per cent of the total number of establishments. In terms of the number of persons engaged, the Province was more prominent. Its industrial establishment in 1957 employed 13·93 per cent of the total in employees in manufacturing industry for the whole of Kenya. In 1961 it accounted for 13·60 per cent of the total number of persons engaged in manufacturing.

v. *Nyanza Province*

The pattern of distribution of industrial establishments and employment showed Nyanza to be relatively undeveloped. In 1957 the Province accounted for 9·89 per cent of the establishments which employed some 7·69 per cent of the total labour force involved. In 1961, it had higher proportion of the establishments (10·31 per cent) due to changes in other Provinces. But the total number of persons engaged had fallen slightly to 7·43 per cent of the total number engaged in manufacturing industry. The bulk of this industrial activity was largely concentrated in Kisumu, Miwani and Kericho areas.

vi. *The Southern Province*

Poor in resources and with an undeveloped economy the Province lags behind the areas already considered. Most of the industrial activity in the area is dominated by the contribution of the Cement Factory and the Kenya Meat Commission canning factory at Athi River some twenty miles from Nairobi. The only remaining important industry in the province is the sodium carbonate industry of Lake Magadi located on its raw material source.

According to 1957 Industrial Census, the Southern Province accounted for 2·38 per cent of the total number of industrial establishment in the country and in 1961, 1·76 per cent. The number of persons engaged remained at just under 6 per cent of the total for the whole country, including a small contribution of the Northern Province in the Meat industry.

2. MANUFACTURING INDUSTRIES IN THE MAIN TOWNS AND THEIR IMMEDIATE SURROUNDINGS

The concentration of industries in the few urban centres and national importance of the individual towns and their location in providing employment opportunities is clearly reflected in the figures for the seven main towns of Kenya.[2] (Tables 5·3–5·4).

3. TYPES OF MANUFACTURING INDUSTRIES IN THE MAIN TOWNS

The manufacturing industry in Kenya is primarily an urban activity and is highly concentrated in the seven main towns listed above. Analysis of the 1957 Census of manufacturing industries showed that these main towns between them accounted for 73·06 per cent of the industrial establishments. In 1961 the concentration had intensified. During this census year approximately 78 per cent of the total number of establishments were found in the seven rail-served urban areas. Nairobi City accounted for 39·33 per cent of the total national establishments and Mombasa 16·32 per cent in 1957. By 1961 Nairobi had increased its share to 42·14 per cent of the National Total and Mombasa 17·10 per cent.

In the total number of persons engaged, the concentration in these areas, though still evident, was not so marked as in the number of establishments. In 1957, the seven main urban centres accounted for 53·03 per cent of the total persons engaged in the manufacturing industries and in 1961 this figure had increased to 67·16 per cent, thus reflecting the same trend as in the number of industrial establishments.

Out of the national total in 1957, Nairobi contributed 33·03 per cent of industrial employees. In 1961, the area had increased its share to 38·70 per cent. Mombasa which in 1957 contributed to the employment of nearly 13 per cent of the persons engaged in manufacturing industry, increased its share rather slowly to about 14 per cent of the national total in 1961. Nakuru's figures increased from 2·66 per cent to 3·94 per cent and Thika 3·08 per cent to 4·82 per cent. There was actually a decrease in industrial employees at Kisumu from 2·99 per cent of the national total in 1957 to 2·96 per cent in 1961.

[2] *Kenya Census of Manufacturing* pp. 79–85

i. *Nairobi City*

The dominance of the City of Nairobi in manufacturing industry can be seen in its share among the seven main urban centres of Kenya. In 1957, it had 53·83 per cent of the total number of establishments. By 1961 Nairobi had raised its share to 54·30 per cent of the establishments in the seven main urban centres of the country. Its share of the number of persons engaged was even greater during the two Census years. In 1957 it accounted for 57·67 per cent of the number of persons engaged in manufacturing industries of the above urban centres and in 1961 it had maintained the lead with 57·63 per cent of the total.

The importance to employment position of the role of Nairobi as the headquarters of the East African Transport and communication institutions should be noted.[3] These institutions which include the railways, post and telecommunications and airways are part of the public services which account for a large number of employees. The function of Nairobi as the capital of Kenya provides a wide range of employment possibilities. The City Council is also one of the biggest employers.

The main establishments of Nairobi include grain milling, beer and malt, sawn timber, metal products, furniture and fixtures, printing and publishing, clothing, tobacco, soft drinks, bakery products and soap. In addition to these, electricity and building construction employ a large number of persons.

In 1961 industrial establishments in Nairobi were responsible for a total sale of goods worth £25,213,000. The rate of establishment of new factories in and around the City has been accelerated since the introduction of the six year Development Plan in Kenya's economic planning.

Nairobi now accommodates the only two tobacco manufacturing plants in Kenya following the closure of the Nakuru plant in 1962. In 1961, 68 per cent of those engaged in the manufacture of soft drinks were to be found in Nairobi as against 60 per cent in 1957. Over 50 per cent of the paper and paper products establishments were located in Nairobi in 1961 and the same proportion of the printing and publishing establishments were also to be found in the area.

[3]Walmsley R. W. pp. 39–44

ii. *Mombasa District*

In 1957, Mombasa had 22·35 per cent of the total number of manufacturing establishments and 22·04 per cent in the seven major towns of Kenya in 1961. It had about the same share of the total number of persons engaged in the manufacturing industry in the seven main towns.

Mombasa accommodates some of Kenya's largest industries such as the establishments of the Kenya Aluminium Works Limited, Sheet Manufacturers Limited, the recently established Kenya Rayon Mills, African Cotton Industries Limited, the Kenya Casements Limited, Mombasa Match Factory, Kenya Glass Works and the British Portland Cement Factory already mentioned.

In addition to the above industrial establishments, it has establishments processing meat and dairy products, grain mills, factories producing beer and mineral waters, clothing and sawn timber. It has important furniture, printing and publishing and soap, metal and paperboard products, and it processes the basic industrial chemical, clay and concrete products.

But Mombasa's importance as an employment area is largely due to the Port and associated institutions. Since the late 1950's the port labour force has been about 6,000 men employed permanently and semi-permanently in operations normally handled on a two shift basis. More recently the oil refinery has added to the industrial complex.

Industrial development in Mombasa is geared primarily to the export and import trades on which its prosperity and growth has depended. The industrial bias is not on manufacture but on facilities for storage, assembly, packing, sorting, grading and distribution. Despite its excellent port facilities, there are virtually no heavy industries.

iii. *Nakuru*

In terms of number of establishments, Nakuru ranked fourth among the major towns of Kenya in 1957 and in 1961. In 1957 it had 6·453 per cent of the total number of establishments and in 1961 6·00 per cent. But in the total number of persons engaged the town rose from fifth place with 4·65 per cent of the total numbers engaged, to fourth place in 1961 when it had 5·87 per cent of the total number of persons engaged.

The pattern of industries reflect the role of the town as the focus of the farming activities of the Central portion of the Rift Valley Province. In 1961 it included among its important industries, miscellaneous chemical industries and an important textile establishment. The importance of grain milling and sawn timber reflect two of the most vital sources of the wealth of the Province. In addition to the above industries, Nakuru is a major centre for processing of dairy products. It is an important centre of printing and publishing.

iv. *Kisumu*
According to industrial Census of 1957, Kisumu had 7·83 per cent of the total establishments in the seven main towns of Kenya. By 1961 the town had increased its share to 7·04 per cent of the total. In number of establishments it thus held the third place after Nairobi and Mombasa.

Most of these establishments employ very few people. A Census of the number of persons engaged showed that in 1957 it had 1,441 employed in manufacturing industry nearly the same number as the smaller town of Thika. Kisumu's share at that time was 5·22 per cent of the total number of persons engaged. By 1961 the share of Kisumu had fallen to 4·41 per cent of the total number of persons, placing it fifth after Nairobi, Mombasa, Thika and Nakuru.

The most important industry in the town is steamer and boat building and repair at the Marine Engineering workshop. It is also an important centre for the production of sawn timber, soap and grain milling. Kisumu is a centre of printing and publishing and has in addition establishments producing non-electrical machinery.

A number of important industrial establishments are now scheduled for completion to add to the limited list of industries described. The Kisumu Cotton Mills financed by the Khatan Group of Bombay has already been established in the town. The factory has a target employment of 2,500 workers by 1968 and annual production of 20 million yards of cloth. Direct employment is planned for about 2,600 with an additional 2,000 to 3,000 to be absorbed in indirect employment. The industry is located in the centre of one of East Africa's major cotton producing regions. It is the second of the three cotton mills round Lake Victoria which will provide a market for part of the cotton crop in the region.

v. *Thika*
The growth of the economy of the town has been stimulated by a prosperous agricultural environment and the attractions of the site for industrial developments. In this respect, Thika is in a far happier position than many Kenya towns. It has attracted some important industrial establishments.

The Kenya Canners Limited was one of the original industries to be drawn to the site. By 1965 the establishment was employing just under 500 permanent members of staff and is the largest fruit and vegetable cannery in East Africa. By 1965 annual handling capacity rose to 20,000 tons of pineapples and some 2,000 tons of vegetables. Thika has the advantage of being located in the heart of Kenya's pineapple growing country. Some 16 million cans are packed a year from the factory. This is a factory with an annual output of £1 million which, under normal conditions, exports some ninety per cent of its products. Recent changes in the East African Common Market arrangements have caused a set-back to the prospects of the industry. To this important establishment we must add the rice, milk and sugar confectionery.

Close by, is the Metal Box Company of East Africa which in 1965 employed about 500 people. In 1961 the establishment had about 450 persons employed at the site. The original factory building was opened in 1949 and has since been expanded by the addition of 50,000 square feet of factory space. Production is now restricted to open top cans intended for perishable products.

In 1950 the Nath Brothers established a Rayon Cloth Factory based upon imported raw materials at Ruaraka. However, in 1960 the factory was transferred to Thika to manufacture sports shirts and underwear. In 1963 another company, United Textiles (Kenya) Limited also established a £1 million factory in Thika. The most recent arrival is the Toray Mills Limited established by the Japanese. In addition to these establishments Thika has the important Kenya Paper Mill which fulfills a variety of the needs of the country. Mention must also be made of Bulleys Tanneries, Kenya Wattle Extract Factory and Thika Tiles. These are just some of the important establishments which make up the sizeable manufacturing complex of the township area.

Thika's future as an industrial town is bright. In 1957, it accounted for 3·43 per cent of the total number of establishments among the seven main towns of Kenya and in 1961 it had 3·24 per cent of the total. During the same period, Thika's share of the total number of persons engaged increased from 5·38 per cent to 7·17 per cent of the total. It thus maintained its third place in 1961 in terms of the total number of employees.

vi. *Kitale and Eldoret*
The two remaining major towns compare unfavourably with the above centres. The highland town of Eldoret is primarily a collecting and distributive centre. Among its important industries are sawn timber, grain milling and dairy products. Kitale shows an even smaller range of industries largely associated with the products of the farming activities of the area around.

In 1957, Eldoret had 3·26 per cent of the total number of establishments. By 1961 it had increased its share to 4·21 per cent of the total. Kitale's share of the establishments declined between 1957 and 1961 from 2·77 per cent to 2·27 per cent.

Of the two towns, Eldoret is far more important. In 1957 it accounted for 3·14 per cent of the total number of persons engaged and in 1961, 3·90 per cent. Kitale's small share fell from 1·32 per cent in 1962 to 0·93 per cent in 1961.

Part Three Population and Migrations

6 The population of Kenya

I. TOWARDS A SCIENTIFIC STUDY OF POPULATION

Interest among developing countries in a scientific study of population resources is gathering momentum. This mounting interest is largely because of the realisation that possession of accurate and up-to-date information on the composition and patterns of changes of population is crucial to intelligent decision-making in any modern state. In poor countries faced with shortage of resources for development it is even more vital to know the population size, rate of growth and factors underlying the growth of population.

But the history of interest in population problems in Kenya shows a slow start and a period of stagnation. A survey of the literature on population indicates a remarkable lack of interest in an accurate survey of resources of population almost up to the end of the last World War. It is possible to argue that this period of complacency about an inadequate knowledge of population probably reflected limitation of facilities for a more scientific analysis of our human resources. However, alternatively the slow development in this field could be taken as indicating a lack of awareness of the need for accurate information and a thorough analysis of our population characteristics.

Until quite recently the administration appeared to have been content with the most crude methods of Kenya's population estimates. Interest in a fuller analysis was confined to non-Africans for whom the compulsory recording of vital statistics had become an early part of administrative policy.

Even today the study of population as a necessary instrument of policy must still be regarded as a novel idea. In a number of important sectors of the activities of our government, policy makers have yet to be won over to the importance of framing policies in the light of the realities of our population resources. Further, it is still necessary for students of population in Kenya to be vigilant in ensuring that resources are made available for this vital aspect of our periodic national inventory.

It could be concluded that the slow germination of interest in the colonial period and the period following independence is indicative of the prevailing ideas on the utilization of resources. During much of the colonial period the African population was primarily regarded as a labour reservoir for islands of non-African economic activities. The governments of the day were noted for the meagreness of the social and economic programmes which affect the masses of the population of the country.[1]

However, recent developments indicate that we are entering a new phase. The background to this change now sweeping through other developing countries is summarised by Dudley and Nortman: 'In developing countries the rising rates of population have led to fears that these will out distance economic growth. There is concern that economic progress will be dissipated in supporting more people with little or no improvement in individual well-being. All too often this is the reality in the developing countries today.'[2]

Two related developments have helped to focus attention towards the economic implications of population size and its growth. Among the African population there has been political pressure during the colonial period for more land to be made available to relieve congestion in certain areas. The land issue is one of the oldest administrative and political problem in Kenya.

The increasing refinement of the African approach to the land as a means of solving the population problem has had the effect of stimulating colonial administration to respond more carefully to the problem of population pressure on land resources. In its early interest on the practical problems of population, the administration tended to be preoccupied largely with the relationship between the total numbers, rates of increase and land available for absorbing the increases.

In the introductory chapter to one of the despatches on the subject, the position in East Africa is set out as follows.

i. The population of East Africa is increasing steadily, and in certain districts where the increase is most rapid, there is already serious congestion on the land. At the same time large parts of East Africa produce nothing of value and support only a very thin population.

ii. A solution for the problems of congestion commonly suggested in Kenya is that more land should be added to

[1]Harlow V., Chilver E. M. & Smith A. *History of East Africa* Vol II pp. 209–64 Clarendon Press, Oxford 1965
[2]Dudley K. & Nortman D. *Population Policies: The World Scene* First African Population Conference, Ibadan 1966

the areas affected for occupation and cultivation by Africans on traditional tenures and by traditional means. This suggestion is examined and rejected for reasons to be stated. The importance is stressed of the need to make it clear to those who suggest this solution that the addition of more land with no change in methods of farming is in fact no solution at all.

The position in the problem areas of Kenya is further summarised in the following paragraph from the Governor's despatch.[3]

It is perhaps unnecessary here to do more than to repeat the general conclusion of all these documents which is that in certain districts, notably the Kikuyu and Machakos Districts of the Central Province, the Maragoli-Bunyore-Kakamega area of North Nyanza, the Taita Hills and the Kisii Highlands, the pressure of people on the land is more than it can properly bear even if the standard of farming were to be greatly improved.

While these problems have continued to engage the attention of the administrators and legislators, important developments have taken place since the last World War in providing the initial statistical information for a more accurate assessment of the population situation. The first major step was the successful completion of the first national census for Kenya in 1948 which formed part of the general census of East African countries. This was followed by a second census in 1962 for Kenya. An account of these two censuses and their significance is discussed in a special paper by Lury.[4]

The invitation of a Population Mission by Kenya Government in 1964 to advise on the population question marks yet another landmark in the official interest on the population issue. Thus facts about our population and policies on population may now be regarded as an important field of study that requires the attention of all the relevant disciplines.

2. GEOGRAPHICAL INTEREST IN THE STUDY OF KENYA'S POPULATION

The geographical discipline is among a number of disciplines which find in the population study a fruitful field of research. In its concern with the content of space and relations of reality in space lies its contribution to our knowledge of the nature of our population resource. The geographer's view of the intellectual significance of the study of population is underlined thus by Trewartha: 'Population is the point of reference from which all the other elements are observed and from which they all, singly and collectively derive significance and meaning. It is population which furnishes the focus.'[5]

However, within this fertile area of research, the application of geographical methodology is directed to specific areas of interest. Geographers have for long been closely interested in the design and collection of population data. In a scientific analysis of information on population, students of geography may be interested in the historic past of the population, its early settlement and how our knowledge about it has changed over the years.

But a major field of activity lies in the detailed consideration of population numbers and the patterns presented by the distribution of numbers. However, while our main interest appears to have been largely confined to treatment of numbers, the qualities of population and their regional patterns provide a rewarding field for geographical research.

Limitation of data forces our attention in this volume to be focused on the less well investigated aspect of population mobility and its implications to social and economic development. Such a study requires a careful analysis of the total population and in particular those aspects which help towards identifying the movements and its selective impact on our varied population.

3. GROWTH OF THE TOTAL POPULATION

The first national Census in Kenya taken in 1948 gave a total population of 5,405,966 made up of 5,251,120 Africans and 154,846 non-Africans. Warning of a possible error of five per cent has been made for this Census[6].

By 1962 the total population of the country had increased to 8,636,263 Africans and non-Africans. The Africans comprised 96·9 per cent of the total population

[3]*Land and Population in East Africa* Colonial Office No. 290 1952
[4]Lury D. A. *Population Data in East Africa* Discussion Paper No. 18 Institute for Development Studies, University College, Nairobi 1966
[5]Trewartha, Glenn T. 'A Case for Population Geography' *Annals of the Association of American Geographers* pp. 71–97 Vol. XLIII No. 2 June 1953
[6]*East African Royal Commission* 1953–1955 Cmnd 9475 p. 463 H.M.S.O., London 1955

Table 6.1 URBAN AND RURAL POPULATION BY RACE: 1962 CENSUS

RACE	Urban NUMBER	%	Rural NUMBER	%
Africans/Somali	491,739	5·3	7,924,203	94·7
Asians	164,992	93·4	11,621	6·6
Europeans	34,865	62·5	20,894	37·5
Arabs	26,030	76·5	8,018	23·5
Others	3,319	85·1	582	14·9
Total	670,945	7·8	7,965,318	92·2

SOURCE: Blacker J. G. C. 1965 p. 62

and the non-Africans 3·1 per cent. The Asians who formed the largest section of the non-African population comprised 2·1 per cent of the total population.[7]

On the basis of these two Censuses a mean growth rate in the intercensal period of 3·3 per cent is suggested. This growth rate has been questioned. It has further been suggested that the median rate which was 2·94 per cent and the modal rate of 2·64 per cent per annum might be a more appropriate measure.[8]

In 1946 and with unreliable information the Government Development Committee assumed a rate of increase of 2·5 per cent per annum. Earlier evidence before the Carter Commission (1933) assumed a rate of about 1·5 per cent per annum.

The suggestion of a rising rate of population increase lends strong support to the need for a population policy if programmes of social and economic development are not to be undermined.

Taking the old provincial boundaries before the revision by the Regional Boundaries Commission the share of the 1962 population showed wide differences. Some 34·88 per cent of the total population was within the old Nyanza boundary, 29·29 per cent in Central, 12·14 per cent in the Rift Valley, 11·74 per cent in the Southern, 8·42 per cent in the Coast, 6·38 per cent in the Northern Province and 3·64 per cent in the Nairobi Extra-Provincial District.

Adjustment of Provincial shares of population on the basis of the new boundaries gave the Coast 8·58 per cent, North Eastern 3·11 per cent, Eastern 18·04 per cent, Central 15·33 per cent, Nairobi 3·98 per cent, Rift Valley 20·28 per cent, Nyanza 18·93 per cent and the Western Region 11·75 per cent.

The rural-Urban share of the total population is shown in Table 6.1.[9]

Since this study is primarily concerned with the African population, it is largely an examination of the impact of development on rural population.

4. THE MAJOR ETHNIC GROUPS OF THE AFRICAN POPULATION[10] (*Figure 6.1*)

Ethnic identity is important Census information in Kenya. For a predominantly rural population such as Kenya, this provides a valuable source of information for analysing mobility of population and the selective impact on the various sections of the rural population. But the ethnic pattern also provides an insight into the modifications of the population distribution by economic development. A brief analysis of the major ethnic divisions of the African population may now be made.

The African population of Kenya derives from four main ethnic sources, Bantu, Nilotic, Nilo-Hamitic and Hamitic. These are linguistic classifications and are already questioned. They must only be regarded as giving the most general groupings of a population with a very complex linguistic, social and political past.

The broad distribution of the four ethnic elements is partly a reflection of the location of Kenya in one of the major culture contact areas of Africa. For ethnic purposes Kenya's administrative unit is imposed. The regional distribution within the country gives a general idea of the nature and direction of the early movements that brought the groups to the confines of the present-day Kenya. But the pattern is further an indication of the extent to which economic development of the country has stimulated movement away from the main population source areas. The mingling of the peoples of Kenya in areas of economic growth has taken place largely in the southern half of the country.

Geographically the population has shown greater mixing in that part of the country favoured by reliable rainfall. This includes the Lake Victoria Basin, the Highlands and the Coast Region.[11] This latter movement is likely to intensify and it is the main object of this study. It is essentially a drift from the rural to urban areas of the country and from the less developed parts of the land to the developing sectors of what Fair (1963) has described as Kenya's 'chief economic island'.[12] The economic island

[7]Etherington D. M. 'Projected Changes in Urban and Rural Population in Kenya and the implications for Development Policy' *East African Economic Review* New Series Vol. I No. 2 pp. 1–19

[8]Etherington D. M. p. 2

[9]Blacker J. G. C. *Population Growth and Urbanisation in Kenya* United Nations Mission to Kenya on Housing Appendix A p. 62 1965

[10]Ominde S. H. *The Ethnic Map of the Republic of Kenya* Occasional Memoir No. 1 Department of Geography, University College, Nairobi 1963

[11]Glover J. &c 'Provisional maps of the reliability of annual rainfall in East Africa' *Quarterly Journal of the Royal Meteorological Society* Vol. 80 pp. 602–9 1954

[12]Fair F. J. D. 'A Regional Approach to the Economic Development of Kenya' *South African Geographical Journal* Vol. 45 pp. 55–77 1963

Figure 6.1

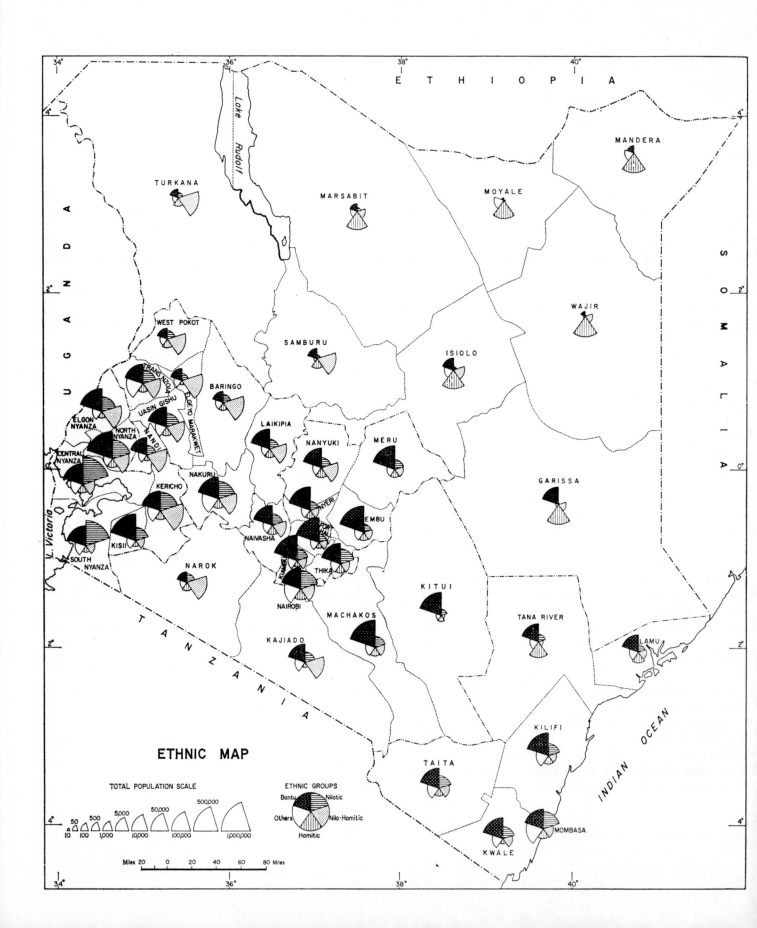

ETHNIC MAP

had been brought to reality by an inflow of capital in the development of former scheduled areas of Kenya. Changes in the pattern of employment in this area are certain to have a profound effect on the intensity and direction of population movements.

i. *The Bantu-speaking peoples*

The Bantu-speaking peoples of Kenya fall into three main geographical divisions—the lacustrine, central and coastal. These broad geographical groupings are necessary for an understanding of different influences which have affected this group.

According to the 1962 Census, the Bantu population of Kenya numbered 5,412,574 or 64·69 per cent of the total population of the country. The Bantu distribution show that they are mainly concentrated in the southern half of Kenya. In this portion they are found in varying concentrations which reflect the complex influences of early migrations, the resource base of the country and subsequent land policy of the colonial government.

The lacustrine group in the west include the Abaluhya of the Western Province, the Gusii and Kuria in the South Nyanza district. It will be seen that these groups are now generally found either spread over the plateau area to the east of Lake Victoria and in the case of the Gusii almost coinciding with the boundary of the highlands unit which stands as a residual above the westward sloping plateau surface. In this varied environment the Bantu have been influenced by the subsequent spread of the Nilotic and the Nilo-Hamitic peoples.

The Bantu-speaking people of the lacustrine region are separated from the Central group which include the Agikuyu (Kikuyu), Embu, Meru, Tharaka and the Akamba by a broad band of country extending from the region of Lake Rudolf in the north of Kenya, southwards into the arid steppes of northern Tanzania. In this intervening region the Nilo-Hamitic element is more prominent except for the Nakuru and Naivasha districts into which a large flow of central highland Bantu and the lacustrine group have moved in search of employment and more recently land.

The majority of the central group of Bantu are based on the fertile highlands to the east of the Kenya section of the East African Rift Valley. From this base they have spread into the farming districts of the Rift Valley Province and to a lesser extent, other parts of Kenya. The remainder of the group are to be found in the dry plateau foreland situated to the east and south of Rift Highlands. In this region of unreliable rainfall the main concentrations of the Bantu are to be found in such residual uplands as the hills of Machakos and north Kitui and the Taita-Taveta area of the Coast Province. The hills of Machakos and Kitui form the home base of the Akamba tribe. Most of the Taita people are to be found in the hilly country which, until the recent road improvement, only had difficult access routes.

The central Bantu are a part of a much larger group referred to as the 'Eastern Bantu' in ethnographical writings on Africa.[13] In this group are included the Chagga, Pare and the rest of Taveta groups in Tanzania. In Kenya's Coast Province, important sections of this group of Bantu include the Pokomo of the Tana river and related tribes, the Mijikenda and the Taita. The last groups have been described under the title 'The Coastal Tribes of the North-Eastern Bantu'.[14]

The coastal Bantu differ from the central and the lacustrine groups in the intensity of external influences which they have experienced over the millenia of their settlement in the Coastal region. Thousands of years of contact with the maritime communities of south-west Asia and the more recent waves of Hamitic penetrations, especially in the northern half of the Coast, have brought about an important degree of mingling of people and cultural diffusion. It is in this respect that the coastal Bantu differ markedly from the interior communities.

The pattern of distribution of the Bantu-speaking peoples outlined above is part of a major series of movements of a semi-continental nature. The Kenya Bantu are part of these great waves of movements which are believed to have led members of the 'Niger Congo linguistic family' from a dispersal centre somewhere in the Nile-Congo watershed into the Congo basin, Southern Africa and parts of Eastern Africa.[15]

[13]Seligman C. G. *Races of Africa* 3rd Edition Oxford University Press, London 1957

[14]Prins A. H. J. 'The Coastal Tribes of the North-Eastern Bantu' *Ethnographic Survey of Africa* Part II, London 1952

[15]Greenberg J. H. *Studies in African Linguistic Classification* Compass Publishing Co. New Haven 1955

The dating of the first dispersal movement of the Bantu is uncertain. However, it has been suggested that by about the fifteenth century the greater portion of East Africa appears to have been covered by members of the group.[16] The actual direction of movements seems to have been greatly influenced by the major land features such as swamps and Lake Victoria. Further the movements have been complicated by the human environment and in particular the later migrations.

The present concentration of the Bantu element of the population roughly south of a line from the north of Mount Elgon, south-east to just about north of Lamu at the Coast is a result of adjustment to the more recent migrations of the Nilo-Hamitic and the Hamitic peoples who have spread into Kenya and added to its ethnic diversity.

Lewis, in 1960, stated that before the southerly migrations of the Hamitic Galla and Somali elements, the Bantu populations were living to the east of the present Kenya-Somali border. Elements of this early Bantu population, described by Prins in 1952 as 'stragglers who lost contact with the main body of Shungwaya migrations . . . .', are still to be found in parts of southern Somali.[17]

The legendary dispersal centre of 'Shungwaya' somewhere between the banks of lower Juba river and Patta island appears in the traditions of most member tribes belonging to the North-Eastern Bantu. However, less clear is the geographical origin of the Central Bantu, who are now mainly settled on the fertile highlands to the east of the Kenya rift. It is possible that they also originated from the Shungwaya source at the time of the southerly migration of the Hamitic Galla and Somali peoples.

Commenting on the settlement of the highlands east of the rift Lambert (1949) considered the Mbere, Embu, Gichugu, Ndia and the Agikuyu as part of a general wave of migration from the east. The movement of the Agikuyu is described by Lambert as coming from the east and southern end of Mount Kenya to what is now the southern part of Nyeri and northern Muranga districts.[18]

In the chronology of this movement which eventually brought the groups to the east of the rift, it is generally acknowledged that in the initial stages of settlement of the northern area, hunting was far more prominent. But that by the time Kiambu and Southern Muranga were settled, cultivation had become more important.[19]

Examination of the pattern of distribution in the western districts of Kenya stress the complexity of the region now inhabited by the lacustrine Bantu. All the districts show substantial numbers of Nilotic and Nilo-Hamitic groups. The degree of intermixture with the other ethnic groups in the area appears to be much greater in this part of the country. The lacustrine Bantu of Kenya occupy part of a region that has been described as a 'Linguistic, cultural and racial "shatter-belt" '. The complex ethnic pattern here is the result of a series of migrations which confirm the area as one of the most ancient corridors of movements in East Africa. It was still an unstable area at the time of the establishment of the British Administration in East Africa.

Oral traditions of most of the Bantu-speaking elements who now live in the Lake basin of Kenya trace their migrations from the Uganda side of the border, indicating their connection with the lacustrine Bantu communities of that country. The majority suggest a route through the narrow corridor of low country between Mount Elgon and the shores of Lake Victoria. But the island on the northern side of the Lake certainly assisted in the short distance movements. The islands on the western shores of South Nyanza have elements which trace their movements from what is now southern Buganda and Busoga.

But other traditions also suggest the land area on the western side of Lake Victoria as an important route of migration into Tanzania. Some of the Bantu groups in South Nyanza may have settled in the area from this end. However, the large group of Bantu now based in Gusii Highlands certainly entered the present territory from the north with the majority of the lacustrine Bantu of the present Western Province. This is confirmed in Gusii tradition which mentions the Kano Plains to the east of Kisumu as one of the places where they paused for some time.

The presence of members of the different elements of

[16]Ogot B. A. 'Movements of Peoples in East Africa' *East Africa* pp. 36–48 *Editions Presence Africaine* Paris 1964

[17]Lewis I. M. 'Somali Conquest of the Horn of Africa' *Journal of African History* Vol. I No. 2 pp. 215–30

[18]Lambert H. *The Systems of Land Tenure in the Kikuyu Land Unit* Part I. Communications from the School of African Studies, New Series No. 22, University of Cape Town 1949

[19]*Report of the Native Land Tenure in Kikuyu Province* p. 16, Kenya 1929

the Bantu group away from their original area of settlement is an important indication of the nature of population movement in Kenya.

ii. The Nilotic peoples

The peoples of Nilotic origin constitute one of Kenya's major ethnic groups. Their distribution throughout the country and in other developing areas of East Africa provide a striking evidence of the force or pull of economic development on the rural population. At the time of the 1962 Census, there were 1,148,335 Nilotic people in Kenya, some 13·7 per cent of the total African population of the Republic. Greenberg (1955) grouped them together with the Nilo-Hamitic peoples, as members of the Eastern Sudanic subgroups of African languages. He distinguished the Nilo-Hamitic language as having had superficial word borrowing from the Hamito-Semitic or what he termed 'Afro-Asiatic' languages of North-Eastern Africa.[20]

The distribution map of the ethnic groups shows the Nilotic element as dominant in the former districts of Central Nyanza and the present South Nyanza District. The presence of substantial numbers of the Nilotic elements in the Bantu areas towards the Uganda border has already been mentioned as reflecting the trend of early historic migrations.

Away from the lacustrine districts in which the Nilotics are concentrated it will be shown that there are three other areas where the ethnic group appear in numbers. Firstly, there are the districts of the Rift Valley Province including Trans-Nzoia, Uasin Gishu, Kericho, Nakuru and the former Naivasha District. Secondly, Nairobi-Extra-Provincial district and the neighbouring areas which formerly constituted parts of the Thika District. Finally, there are large numbers of Nilotics in certain parts of the Coast such as Taita, Kwale, Mombasa and Kilifi-Malindi.

Migrations of the Nilotics from their base districts adjacent to Lake Victoria is again a result of recent economic development of Kenya and urbanisation following this change. The arid north-eastern half of Kenya and the districts of Narok, Kajiado, Machakos, Kitui, Tana River and Lamu have up to now not attracted this ethnic group. These are the districts which have not experienced important agrarian and economic revolution.

Although no agreed date has been put forward for the arrival of the Nilotics in the various parts of East Africa, beginning of the fourteenth century has been suggested as a probable date of entry into the area now occupied by the lacustrine kingdoms of Uganda.[21]

It would appear that the early waves of Nilotic invaders probably entered what is now the Western Province of Kenya somewhere about the seventeenth century and that by the eighteenth century they had began to spill into what was formerly the Western parts of Central Nyanza District. By the end of the nineteenth century the advance guard of the settlement wave was well established in what is now the South Nyanza District. The movement from Central Nyanza to South Nyanza into Musoma and north Mara areas of Tanzania continued well into the twentieth century.

The present pattern of Nilotic distribution which extends into Uganda and Tanzania is the result of a complex series of migrations and of the processes of assimilation which accompanied these movements. The migrations are part of the movements on a semi-continental scale which affected Eastern Africa. In historical perspective they are closely related to Hamitic migrations into north-eastern Kenya and to similar movements which brought the Eastern Sudanic linguistic groups, including the Masai, Nandi and others, into the rift region of Kenya and its bordering highlands.

Movements of the Nilotics from their source region in the Sudan and through Uganda and their results have been described in three memoirs (1950, 1951 and 1954) by J. P. Crazzolara.[22] Researches into these movements provide an important framework for the investigation of the important history of settlement of the greater part of Southern Sudan, Uganda and Western Kenya. But interest in this particular series of movements is not only confined to the complexity which it has introduced into the Lake Victoria basin. The movements are an important element in an understanding of evolution of the population regions of Western Kenya.

[20]Greenberg, J. H.

[21]Ogot B. A. pp. 36–48

[22]Crazzolara J. P. *Lwoo Migrations* Vol. I Instituto Missioni Africani Verona 1950; *The Lwoo* Vol. II *Traditions* Editrice Nigrizia, Verona 1951; *The Lwoo* Vol. III *Clans* Editrice Nigrizia, Verona 1954

iii. *The Nilo-Hamitic peoples*

The Nilo-Hamitic group of peoples form one of the most distinct cultural units in Kenya. The 1962 Census showed that there were 1,373,876 Nilo-Hamitic peoples in the whole of Kenya. The group thus comprised 16·42 per cent of the total African population of the country. They occupy a belt of country stretching from the north-west Kenya and Lake Rudolf area southwards into Central Tanzania. In the Kenya section they formerly spread over much of the highland country in west-central Kenya including the Rift Valley.[23][24][25]

It will be noted that in Kenya, the Nilo-Hamitic group impinges on the lacustrine Bantu and Nilotic elements in the west and on the central and Coastal sub-divisions of Bantu group in the east. Within the Nilo-Hamitic group are included such elements as the Turkana, Suk, Iteso, Nandi, Kipsigis, Elgeyo and Marakwet, Sabaot of the Elgon slopes and surrounding plateau, the Masai, Samburu, Tugen, Nderobo and the Njemps.

There has been considerable discussion about the origin of this ethnic group. Huntingford (1963) suggests a common geographical dispersal centre in the Nile Valley. He mentions that the Nilotics were probably in the Western part of the area south-east of Bahrel Ghazal region and the Nilo-Hamitics somewhere in the north or north-east of Lake Rudolf.[26]

About the time the Nilotic waves of migrations were penetrating northern and western Uganda, it appears that the northern areas of Kenya began to receive advance waves of Nilo-Hamitic peoples which included the Masai and related groups. The Masai are now largely found in the southern portion of the Nilo-Hamitic band of territory which extends into the northern part of Central Tanzania. Although they have been primarily pastoral, there has been among them a growing interest in cultivation. The present pattern of Masai distribution is the outcome of internal conflicts of the nineteenth century and the land settlement policy of the colonial government which followed in the early part of the twentieth century.

The Suk, Turkana and the Samburu who occupy the more arid stretches in the northern section of the Nilo-Hamitic area are still predominantly pastoral. But there are pockets of higher rainfall where small groups such as the hill Suk practise some form of cultivation. Further

changes are to be expected in the economic organisation of this group as a result of the government policy of resettlement and concentration on development of the resources of the areas they occupy.

Perhaps the economically most important of the group are the Nandi and the Kipsigis who occupy the extreme western section of the Nilo-Hamitic country, for they are now among the most progressive farmers in modern Kenya. In common with the other Nilo-Hamitic elements the Nandi and the Kipsigis were distinguished by a strong cattle complex. In the early days of settlement of Kenya Highlands they depended more on cattle. It is possible that a series of disasters may have forced a new emphasis following the loss of the cattle base of the economy.

One of the most striking changes in this West-Central area has been the rapid post-war development of land consolidation. As a result of this development alongside the thriving plantation farming based on tea, Kericho District is now one of the major area of attraction to farm labour from the more populated parts of the Nyanza and the Western Provinces.

Some comment must be made on the geographical distribution of the Nilo-Hamitic peoples and in particular their relationship with the Hamitic peoples to the north-east. In general their distribution suggests a predominantly north to south migration, which became possible as a result of pressure from the north, north-east and east. It is possible to see this pressure in terms of the spread of the Hamitic peoples. However, the effect of climatic changes on a predominantly pastoral people might have had as significant an effect as the human invasions.

The Nilo-Hamitics form an important proportion of the urban population chiefly in those urban areas located in or close to their main zone. In Nairobi and Mombasa

[23]Huntingford G. W. B. 'The Northern Nilo-Hamites' *Ethnographic Survey of Africa* Part IV London 1953

[24]Huntingford G. W. B. 'The Southern Nilo-Hamites' *Ethnographic Survey of Africa* Part VIII London 1953

[25]Gulliver & Gulliver 'The Central Nilo-Hamites' *Ethnographic Survey of Africa* Part VII London 1953

[26]Oliver R. & Matthew G. (ed.) *History of East Africa* Vol. I pp. 58–93 Clarendon Press, Oxford 1963

THE POPULATION OF KENYA/91

districts, they form only a small part of the urban African population.

iv. *The Hamitic peoples*

The fourth important ethnic constituent of Kenya's population is the Hamitic element. The distribution of the Hamitic element in the country underlines the position of the Republic at cross roads of major semi-continental migrations. Although this element of the population of the country is found in small numbers in most parts of Kenya's towns and small urban type settlements, it is in the north-eastern sector of the country where they form a majority of the population.

Geographically it will be seen that the bulk of the Hamitic peoples is found chiefly in that portion of Kenya regarded as arid or semi-desert. This, as has been noted, is a region which suffers from serious moisture deficit and its conditions are unsuitable for agricultural activities. Over the greater part of the region the annual rainfall in a five year period is likely to fall below 10 inches.

At the time of the 1962 Census, there were 372,116 Hamitic peoples in Kenya representing 4·44 per cent of the total African population of the Republic. The ethnic group consists of two main sub-divisions and a collection of minor groups. The detailed distribution of the various elements of this population is again the outcome of different streams of migration and internal adjustments.

The two main groups represented in Kenya are, firstly, the Rendille-Galla group and, secondly, the Somali-speaking group. In the first group, the Boran element is the most numerous. The Boran in Kenya cover an extensive and sparsely populated territory stretching from the southern border of Ethiopia to Tana River in the south and represent one of the earliest waves of migration whose influence extends into neighbouring Ethiopia. The Rendille whose origin is uncertain have settled in a large portion of the Marsabit District. Together with the Galla-speaking Borans they form the main part of the pre-Islamic wave of migration. Other Galla-speaking elements in the area include the Gabbra of Marsabit District, the Orma of Tana River and the Sakuye of Moyale District.[27]

The Somali element form the largest single group of the Hamitic peoples in Kenya. They are predominant over that part of the country extending from the north of Lamu District to Ethiopian border. They are therefore situated to the east of the Rendille-Galla group and are thus the most easterly and also the most recent of the Hamitic peoples in the area.

The Somali group includes the Darod element mainly located in the southern half of the present Somali belt and the Hawiye branch which is in the main located in the districts lying to the north of Wajir. Since they are the most numerous in the area they dominate the relationship between the State of Somalia and her neighbours.

The territorial distribution of the various elements of the Hamitic population in Kenya reflects the end stages of a series of movements which began in the Horn of Africa about the tenth or the eleventh century. The movement probably began under the stimulus of changing climatic conditions or an increase of population in an environment of limited agricultural and pastoral potential.

The situation about the nineteenth century suggests that the present area in Kenya occupied by the Somali and related Hamitic groups was still under a 'pre-Hamitic Zengi' population.[28] This was a mixed-Negroid or Bantu population which was probably related to the remaining continental spread of the group in the eastern part of Africa.

In these series of movements which gathered momentum during the following centuries, the Somali succeeded in pushing the Galla population from the main part of the Horn of Africa westwards into Ethiopia and to the south. In some places the original Galla population was by-passed and remained as pockets within the later movement. But as the Galla population withdrew, the negroid predecessors were pushed further into Kenya.

Frequent clashes over grazing ground, which became inevitable with such migrations, were a constant source of anxiety in the early stages of the establishment of the administration. It is these clashes between the earlier and later Hamitic waves of migration that led to the establishment of the Somali-Galla line by the British Administration under 'the Special Districts (Administration)

[27]*Kenya: Report of the Northern Frontier District Commission* Cmd 1900 H.M.S.O. 1902
[28]Lewis I. M. pp. 213-29

Figure 6.2

1. *The Lake Victoria Basin*
2. *The Rift and Associated Highlands*
3. *The Eastern Plateau Foreland*
4. *The Coastal Region*
5. *The Southern and Northern Drylands of Kenya*

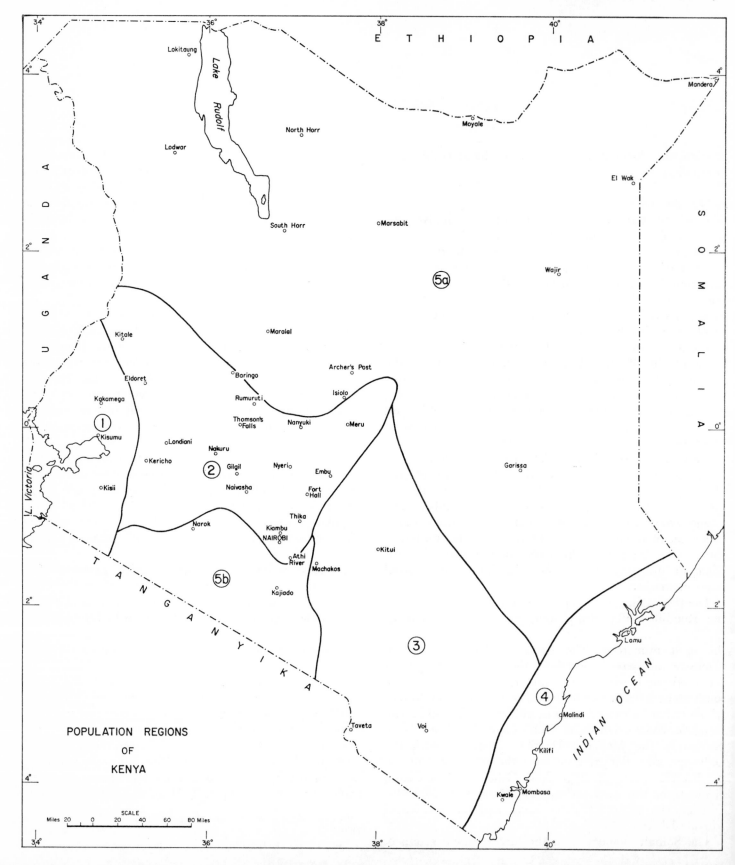

POPULATION REGIONS
OF
KENYA

SCALE

Miles 20   0   20   40   60   80 Miles

Ordinance of 1934.'[29] The line ran roughly from the Tana River bend just east of the Meru district boundary northwards to Ethiopian border west of Mandera settlement.

The large scale movement of the Somali into the eastern parts of the present-day Kenya coincided roughly with the establishment of the British Administration in the area. Since that time a small number of Somali and other Hamitic elements have moved into various urban settlements and trading centres in most parts of Kenya mainly in response to the livestock trade. Some of the Hamitic elements represented on the ethnic map are recent immigrants from Somalia. As the Hamitic population moved southwards, they came into contact with an environment more favourable to cultivation. Some of the groups have adopted methods of cultivation from the Bantu population with whom they came into contact.

It has been noted that the area occupied by the group is hostile to cultivation. There has not been any significant movement into the area from other parts of the country. In this sense the area differs from the main productive areas of Kenya which have become scenes of increasing mixing of the various ethnic elements.

Further, because of difficulties of communications even the movement out of the area is extremely restricted. Increased productivity from the area will depend on the solution to the problems of water or communications or the discovery of important mineral resources.

5. THE GEOGRAPHICAL DISTRIBUTION OF POPULATION (*Figure 6.2*)

The concern of geographers with mapping the pattern of distribution of total population and the nature of areal concentrations has been one of the most fruitful fields of geographical research. Donald J. Bogue (1959) has defined the field of study of population distribution as: 'the study of a nation's or a community's population in terms of areal subdivisions such as regions, state, socio-economic areas, urban, rural residence, and census tracts.'[30]

In this study the concern is with the rural to urban mobility and rural urban flow of population. Analysis of the regional pattern of distribution and in particular the

problems of the major population regions is thus essential.

From a consideration of the history of population research in Kenya, there have been attempts from the early part of the present century to present a pattern of population distribution. Such analysis to be meaningful requires well-defined units, base maps and reliable census material.

The progress in collecting reliable data has been considered in an earlier chapter. A second major difficulty has continued to limit a fuller or a dynamic analysis of population distribution. This is the problem of the boundary changes, which was treated in the first chapter of this volume.

We may conclude that for the purposes of a comparative study of the present position of population distribution and the early part of the present century we have a hiatus which cannot be bridged directly. There is a further danger that continuing boundary changes could for many years hamper valuable research which is needed for urgent social and economic planning.

In the period between the two national Censuses, there have been important boundary changes at the Provincial district and location or ward level. Thus except in limited parts of the country a comparative study of trends in the distribution of population between 1948 and 1962 is virtually impossible without a laborious adjustment of the 1962 census results. Progress in provision of a reliable base map is still hampered by lack of agreement over the boundaries of enumeration units in certain parts of the country. But allowing for these limitations the analysis of population pattern in Kenya on the basis of 1962 figures provides a landmark in the study of areal distribution.[31, 32]

The sharp physical contrast which is a pattern of Kenya's geography is closely reflected in the geographical distribution of its population. The regional background thus provides the most fruitful approach to analysis of the areal pattern of total population.

[29]*Kenya: Report of the Northern Frontier District Commission* 1962 Map II

[30]Bogue D. J. *Population Distribution. The Study of Population* (see Hauser and Duncan pp. 383–99) 1959

[31]Morgan W. T. W. *Kenya 1: 1M. Population Distribution Map* 1962 Department of Geography, University College, Nairobi 1963

[32]*Kenya 1: 1M. Density of Population Map* 1962 Department of Geography, University College, Nairobi 1964

i. *The Lake Victoria population region*

The ethnic survey has already shown that the region is dominated by members of two major African linguistic families, the lacustrine Bantu of the Niger-Congo linguistic family and the Nilotic Luo of the Southern section of the Eastern Sudanic linguistic group. It has already been noted that the more diverse Bantu group consists of Baluhya, the Gusii and Kuria. At the time of the 1962 Census there were 1,086,409 Baluhya, of which 925,370 were recorded in the Lake Basin. Out of the 538,343 Gusii in Kenya 530,728 were in Nyanza Province. The Kuria group which numbered 41,885 in the whole of Kenya had 40,481 living within their base in Nyanza Province. The bulk of the Kuria group live in Tanzania just across the international boundary. During 1948 and 1957 censuses, Tanzania recorded 67,908 and 85,090 Kuria living in the country. Out of the total Kenya Nilotic population of 1,148,335 some 1,061,621 were at the time of the 1962 Census in the old Nyanza Province.

Lake Victoria region is part of a well defined zone that includes the lacustrine regions or parts of Tanzania and Uganda. With relatively minor breaks it is one of the distinctive features of the East African and the African population scene. Knowledge of the Lake Basin as a population region of importance in East Africa emerges at a comparatively late period in the history of the political evolution of the area. Joseph Thompson's[33] impression of a dense settlement of villages and his surprise at the contrast with the areas that lay across his route underline the fact that the explorer had entered one of the main population concentrations in East Africa.

Commenting on the impressions of the early travellers at the turn of the century, Wrigley (1965) says: 'In the Central Rift Valley there were only a few groups of Masai herdsmen, loosely occupying a vast area with their wandering flocks and herds. The whole of the western section of the highlands was very lightly peopled and parts of it, notably the Uasin Gishu plateau north of the railway line were practically uninhabited. Only two areas were at all densely occupied. There were the numerous Kavirondo tribes of the Lake Basin, and there were the Kikuyu and allied peoples of the eastern highlands whose settlements reached northwards from Nairobi to the slopes of Mount Kenya.'[34]

The Lake Basin concentration is therefore one of the oldest features of the human geography of the area. Through its continuation into Uganda it played a major part in the direction of the early railway plans. As a major population region in Kenya its role in the economic development of Kenya has been grossly underrated.

The distribution map of rural population in this region shows two well defined cores located north and south of the Nyanza rift valley. In the north of the gulf, the core region extends from the higher parts of the Kakamega district in the east across the southern part of the northern plateau to Uganda-Kenya border.[35]

From this east-west core population becomes less concentrated northwards towards the foothills of Mount Elgon and south towards the gulf. The Nyanza rift zone including the Kano Plains and the lacustrine fringes are generally lightly populated. Further, there is a marked sparsity of population towards the Uganda border. In the area south of the gulf the main population belt extends from the highlands of the south-east including Kisii and Kericho northwestwards to the Lake shore locations of Kanyada, and Karachuonyo.

In 1948 the core locations to the north of the gulf varied in density from about 300 persons per square mile to just about 900 persons per square mile. Maragoli (23 a. and b.) the most heavily populated location had a density of 938 persons per square mile. South Ugenya and Buholo (14, 15) in the extreme west had 380 and 307 persons per square mile each. On the northern fringes Marama had 334 persons per square mile and Isukha (11) south of Kakamega forests 357 persons per square mile. In the south Kisumu location (28) had 420 persons per square mile. There were in this core region (Figure 6.3) locations with densities above 400 persons per square mile.

Analysis of land use figures for the area in 1948 gave the overall densities per square mile of cropland varying from 621 for Idakho location (24) to 1,187 for Maragoli. Cropland densities for Kajulu (27) and Kisumu were 966

[33]Thompson J. *Through Masailand* Law, London 1884

[34]Harlow V., Chilver E. M. & Smith A. (Editors) *History of East Africa* Vol. II p. 212 Clarendon Press, Oxford 1965

[35]Ominde S. H. *Land and Population in the Western Districts of Nyanza Province, Kenya* (Ph.D. Thesis, University of London, Unpublished)

Figure 6.3

The Western Districts of Nyanza Province

Population Density 1948 Census
(excluding Reserved Forests)

N.B. For location index see appendix

Figure 6.4

The Western Districts of Nyanza Province

Population Density 1962 Census
 (excluding Reserved Forests)

N.B. For location index see appendix

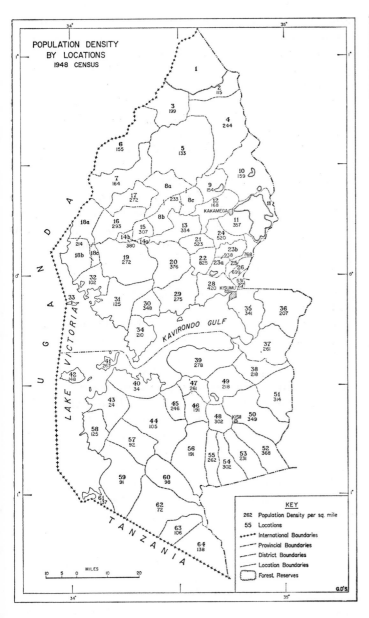

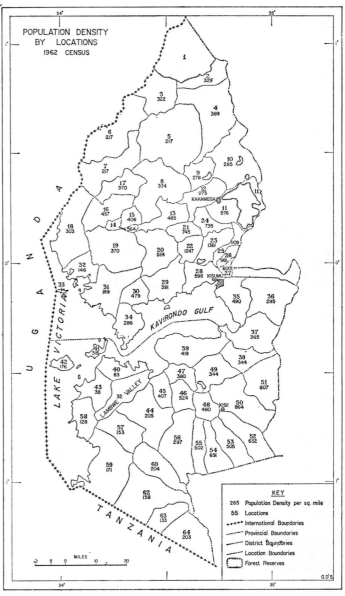

Table 6.2 NORTH AND CENTRAL NYANZA: 1962 CENSUS

LOCATIONS	Density per square mile	LOCATIONS	Density per square mile
North Nyanza		*Central Nyanza*	
Maragoli	1,361	Kajulu	600
Bunyore	1,247	Kisumu	598
Tiriki	1,109	South Ugenya	564
Nyangori	981	Gem	524
Kisa	745	West Kano	490
Idakho	735	Asembo	479
Isukha	576	North Ugenya	457
Marama	485		
Buholo	406		

Table 6.4 1962 CENSUS

LOCATION	Density per square mile	LOCATION	Density per square mile
North Nyanza		Alego	370
Wanga	334	Nyakach	365
Kabras	285	Samia	303
Bunyala	278	East Kano	295
Butsotso	273	Uyoma	286
Elgon Nyanza		*South Nyanza*	
Kimilili	389	North Nyokal	380
Marach	370	Kasipul-	
Elgon	329	Kabondo	344
Malakisi	322	Rusinga	318
		East Nyokal	297
Central Nyanza		Gem	282
Seme	391		

Table 6.5 1962 CENSUS

LOCATION	Density per square mile	LOCATION	Density per square mile
Elgon Nyanza		*South Nyanza*	
Bukusu	218	Mfangano	176
Itesio	217	West Konyango-	
Bukhayo	217	Mohuru	171
		Suna	158
South Nyanza		West Nyokal	153
East Konyanyo	205	Butende	133
Kanyamkago	204	Gwassi	128
Bukuria	203	Kasigunga	83
		Kaksingiri	38
Under 200 persons per square mile:		Lambwe Valley	32
Central Nyanza			
Sakwa	169		
Yimbo	146		

Table 6.3 SOUTH NYANZA AND KISII DISTRICTS: 1962 CENSUS

LOCATION	Density per square mile	LOCATION	Density per square mile
Kitutu	864	South	
North		Mugirango	502
Mugirango	808	Wanjare	480
Majoge	651	Karachuonyo	419
Nyaribari	632	Kanyada	407
Bassi	505		

and 711 respectively. The ratio of cropland to total area for the same period ranged from 60 per cent to well over 80 per cent. The number of acres of cropland per head of population varied from 0·5 for Maragoli to 1·0 for Kisa (21) and Idakho.

In 1962 the number of locations with over 400 persons per square mile had increased (Figure 6.5 and Table 6.2). In the area south of the Gulf, the 1948 Census showed much lower density figures for the core areas. The 1948 density map shows that none of the Kisii Highland locations had reached the 400 persons mark. Majority of these locations had densities between 300 and 400 persons per square mile. It will be seen later that this area was probably under-enumerated. The 1962 figures revealed increases which could not be attributed to the natural intercensal growth of population.

In 1962 the density pattern for the locations extending from the Lake shore to the highlands in the south were as in Table 6.3.

In the extreme east most of the Kericho locations had slightly lower densities. These were generally between 250 and 500 persons per square mile.

The majority of people in the Lake districts of Western Kenya lived over a varied region with densities between 200 and 400 persons per square mile. In the north of the gulf this area surrounding the core touches the Uganda border in the region of Samia location. The locations in this Western fringe area includes Samia (18), Marach (17), Wanga (8), and Alego (19) locations.

In 1948 most of these locations had densities of between 200 and 300 persons per square mile of cropland. The acreage of cropland per head of population was between 1·0 and 3 acres. The land use survey of the area showed that the proportion of cropland to total area ranged from 50 per cent to about 80 per cent. By 1962 densities for the locations were generally much higher (Table 6.4).

The third and most distinctive population region in the Lake Basin include those areas which had densities of less than 200 persons per square mile. From the regional point of view, these are to be found in three main areas. In the area north of the gulf it covers that part of the plateau stretching from the foothills of Mount Elgon to the more populous locations that surround the high density belt.

Nearer the Lake shore the sparsely populated parts include the Central Nyanza locations of Yimbo (32) and Sakwa (31). But in the area south of the gulf, the lightly populated region lies to the west of a line drawn from Homa Bay south-east to the Masai border with South Nyanza.

In 1948, this region showed densities well below 200 persons per square mile. Yimbo and Sakwa both had less than 50 persons per square mile and in the South Nyanza District a large tract of country had less than 100 persons per square mile.

At the time of the 1962 Census, the density figures had become much higher and most locations showed a range between 200 and 299 persons per square mile (Table 6.5).

Figures for cropland density in 1948 showed that the locations here had a range of 200 to 500 persons per square mile of cropland. But the majority had a range of 200 to 300 persons per square mile of cropland.

Factors underlying the distribution of population. The distribution of rural population of the Lake Victoria basin is closely related to the physical conditions of the area. Such is the adjustment of the rural population to the land resources that the core areas of population closely coincide with areas of high and reliable rainfall.

The main population cores in the area are situated where the mean annual rainfall is 45 inches or more and a minimum expectation is 35 inches or more in 19 years out of 20. The most densely peopled areas north and south of the gulf experience a minimum expectation of 55 inches or more in 19 out of 20 years.

Although rainfall is the most important single factor, it is not to be inferred that this is the sole explanation of the concentration of population. The soils are fertile but this is not universally the case. They vary from the limited areas of acidic and heavily leached soils of the granite belt north of the gulf to the highly fertile loam soils developed from the pre-Cambrian sediments and lavas as well as the Tertiary volcanic material.

In these heavily populated regions a double harvest is assured by the highly reliable rainfall and over most areas bananas and maize are an important element of diet. These regions are lands of high potential and their population densities may be taken as indicative of the carrying capacity of the land. However, although the physical and economic conditions have no doubt favoured such concentrations of population, the exceptionally high densities cannot be entirely explained by these two factors.

The tribal movements outlined earlier suggest the importance of the historical situation which might partly explain these concentrations. The population cores which have emerged may be regarded as partly a result of adjustment to historic movements which have reduced the land available to certain groups. Oral traditions of the ethnic groups in the area show shortage of land as a major factor in the inter-tribal clashes.

However, a description of the population pattern in the Lake Victoria basin is incomplete without reference to the role of the spread of the tsetse fly. The significance of the tsetse fly to population distribution and land use lies in the comparatively late date of entry of the fly into the area.

Morris (1960) outlined three main epidemics in the area. The first outbreak in the area was from 1901 to 1910 and was part of an inter-lacustrine and island invasion from the neighbouring territory of Uganda. Violent outbreaks of sleeping sickness on the mainland and a virtual decimation of the lake shore population is mentioned. Reference has already been made to the fact that except for the island of Rusinga, the Lake shore belt has not recovered demographically from this initial invasion.[36] It is during this period that the fly gained a foothold in the Kuja-Migori system. In these areas, despite active measures of fly eradication, the problem remains an important factor in the intensity of population concentration round the Lake shore.

Intercensal population increases. Etherington (1965) has drawn attention to the unsatisfactory nature of considering population growth on crude comparison of the 1948 and the 1962 Censuses. The figures given in Table 6.6

[36]Morris D. R. S. 'Studies on the epidemiology of sleeping sickness in East Africa' *Transactions of the Royal Society of Tropical Medicine and Hygiene* pp. 71–80 Vol. 54 No. 1 1960

Table 6.6 INTER-CENSAL POPULATION IN-CREASES IN THE WESTERN DISTRICTS OF NYANZA

LOCATION	% increases	LOCATION	% increases
Elgon Nyanza		Kisumu	42
Kimilili	59	West Kano	44
Elgon	184	Kajulu	13
Malakisi	62	Kisumu Town	113
Bukusu	64		
Iteso	40	*South Nyanza* (New District)	
Bukhayo	32	East Nyokal	55
Marach	36	Kanyada	65
		Gem	47
North Nyanza		Karachuonyo	51
Bunyore	51	North Nyokal	45
Maragoli	39	Kasipul-Kabondo	57
Tiriki	45	East Konyango	47
Nyangori	40	West Nyokal	46
Isukha	61	Gwasi	2
Idakho	42	Mfang'ano	19
Kisa	42	Rusinga	19
Marama	45	Kasigunga	53
Buholo	32	Kaksingiri	30
Wanga	43		
Kabras	80	*South Nyanza*	
Bunyala	80	West Konyango-	
Butsotso	62	Mohuru	74
Kakamega Town	0·19 (—)	Kanyamkago	85
		Bukuria	46
Central Nyanza		Butende	25
Alego	36	Suna	119
Samia	42		
North Ugenya	56	*Kisii*	
South Ugenya	48	Kitutu	148
Seme	42	North Mugirango	157
Gem	39	Wanjare	59
Nyakach	40	Nyaribari	72
East Kano	43	Majoge	115
Uyoma	37	Bassi	118
Asembo	38	South Mugirango	92
Sakwa	35		
Yimbo	43		

have been adjusted to take account of the minor boundary changes in the old Nyanza Province.

It is not possible to make comparisons of this nature throughout the country. But these figures for the Western Districts of the old Nyanza Province raise certain problems.

In the first place they range from 2 per cent to 148 per cent. Such increases cannot be considered normal. Analysis of the increases suggest that they are partly associated with locations which were in 1948 lightly populated such as Elgon, Bunyala and Kabras in the north, and Suna and Kanyamkago in the area south of the gulf. It is probable that more research might show that these high increases were a result of immigration or movement from adjacent locations.

But such a movement cannot explain the increases in Kisii Highland locations. It is likely that there may have been errors arising from under-enumeration in Kisii area at the time of the 1948 Census.

The distribution of the increases show that the main population core of the area north of the gulf, the lower and drier Lake shore areas of the western Districts showed generally low figures.

ii. *The population regions of the Rift Valley and associated highlands*

The rift population region though diverse is one of the most important regions in Kenya. At the time of the 1962 census, it had the vast majority of the 1,373,876 Nilo-Hamitic peoples in Kenya. Further, in the highlands that lie to the east of the rift proper the region accounted for the majority of the Central group of Bantu already mentioned. Out of the 2,215,805 Kikuyu-Embu and Meru peoples in Kenya 1,802,981 were to be found in the Central Province. However, the nature of the regional concentration of population may best be understood by subdividing the region into the three distinct parts. These are the rift highlands of the east, the floor area including the Nakuru-Naivasha area and finally the west rift highlands.

The east rift highlands (Figure 6.5). The east rift highlands extend from the plains of Laikipia and Nanyuki in the

Figure 6.5

Location Population Density of the Kikuyu, Embu and Meru Districts of Central Province: 1962 Census (excluding Reserved Forests)

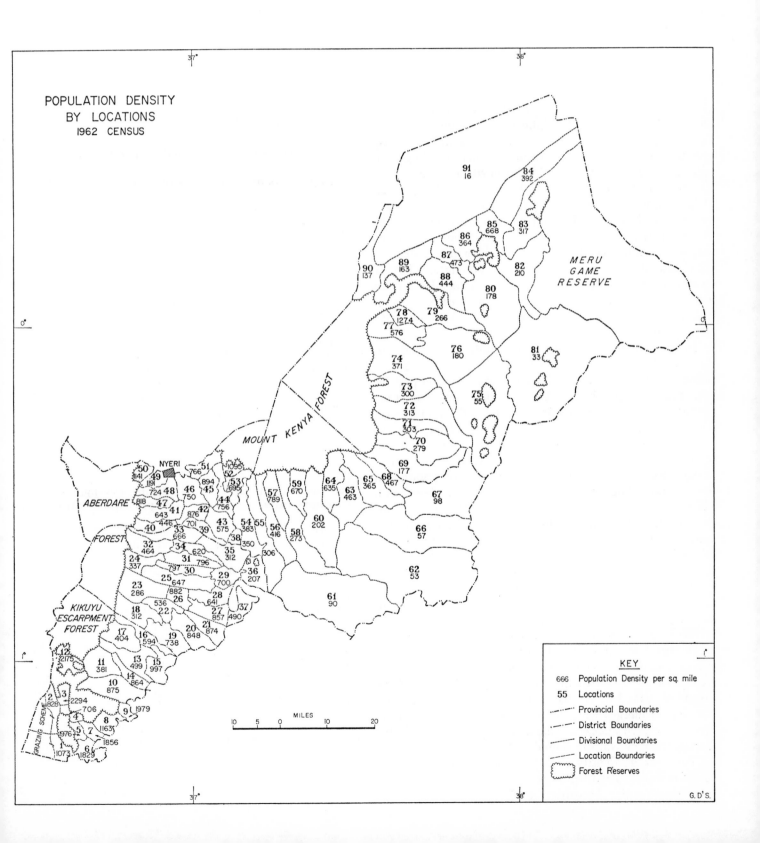

POPULATION DENSITY
BY LOCATIONS
1962 CENSUS

MERU GAME RESERVE

MOUNT KENYA FOREST

NYERI

ABERDARE

FOREST

KIKUYU
ESCARPMENT
FOREST

GRAZING SCHEME

MILES

KEY	
666	Population Density per sq. mile
55	Locations
·-··-··-	Provincial Boundaries
·-·-·-	District Boundaries
-------	Divisional Boundaries
------	Location Boundaries
⌇⌇⌇	Forest Reserves

G. D'S.

north to include the Nyambeni Hills, Mount Kenya and the Aberdares plateau. The influence of this diverse region on the population pattern is further complicated by the history of the land settlement which involved the setting aside of large areas in the north and the Thika District in the south-east for European settlement. In these former settled areas particularly in the north, population is sparse. The 1962 census revealed that in many parts population density was less than 25 persons per square mile. In the forested slopes of the Aberdares and Mount Kenya the density of population hardly exceeded 10 persons per square mile. Thika District in the south-east had much higher densities with many of the wards having an average density of about 100 persons per square mile.

In the remaining former African districts of Kiambu, Fort Hall, Nyeri, Embu and Meru the mean district densities varied from just about 100 to about 600 persons per square mile (Figure 6.5). Meru had an average density of 125 persons per square mile and Kiambu with the highest mean density had an average of 557 persons per square mile. However, the above mean district densities and the presence of game reserves and forest areas give a false picture of the nature of population distribution. The population regions fall into three main subdivisions: The Aberdares slopes, Mount Kenya-Nyambeni region and the low platform which lies to the east and south-east of the Aberdares and Mount Kenya-Nyambeni region. In both the Aberdares and the Mount Kenya regions, population concentration become less intense near the forest zone. This feature is most marked in the upper reaches of northern Kiambu locations and the western fringes of Fort Hall. Within these broad subdivisions there are further differences.

In the Aberdares, the distinct population sub-region which had developed extends from the foothills of Mount Kenya in Nyeri District in a southerly direction to extreme south of Kiambu. At its southern end the population sub-region merges with the urban settlement of Nairobi. Parts of it have since the boundary revision been included within the new Nairobi boundary.

The average density of population allowing for forest areas in 1962 varied from 500 to well over 2,000 persons per square mile. Towards the forest limit the average

Table 6.7 DENSITY RANGE (1962 CENSUS)

1,000 persons or more per square mile

LOCATION	Density per square mile	LOCATION	Density per square mile
Kiambu		3	536
Lari	2,175	4	848
Limuru	2,294	5	874
Kabete	1,856	6	857
Muguga	1,976		
Dagoretti	1,829	*Nyeri*	
Karai	1,073	Aguthi	750
Kiambaa	1,163	Tuegenge	724
Ndumberi	1,979	Muhitu	876
		Gikondi	701
Nyeri		Gethi	575
Tetu	1,191	Othaya	643
Muhoya	1,141	Mahiga	818

500–999 persons per square mile:		**From 200–499 persons per square mile:**	
Kiambu		*Kiambu*	
Ndeiya	829	Gatamaiyu	381
Githunguri	875	Ndarugu	404
Komothai	864	Kiganjo	499
Ngenda	997		
Chania	594	*Fort Hall*	
Ngecha	706	(Muranga)	
		15	312
Fort Hall		20	207
8	647	2	286
10	797	17	490
11	700	9	337
12	796	19	464
13	620	16	312
14	666		
7	641	*Nyeri*	
18	882	Lower Muhito	350
1	738	Chinga	446

Table 6.8 DENSITY RANGE (1962 CENSUS)

1,000 and more persons per square mile

LOCATION	Density per square mile	LOCATION	Density per square mile
Nyeri (East) Magutu	1,095	Ruguru Iriani	766 695
Meru Ntima	1,274	*Embu* Inoi Baragwe Ngandori	790 670 635

500–999 persons per square mile:

Nyeri		*Meru*	
Kirimukuyu	894	Upper Abothuguthi	576
Konyu	756	Nija	668

200–499 persons per square mile

Embu			Muthambe	303
Kiine	383		Karingari	279
Mwerua	306		Nkuene	371
Mutira	416		Igoje	300
Kabare	273		Nyaki	266
Ngariama	202		Akachiu	210
Kyeni	467		Maua	317
Gaturi	463		Ithima	392
Kagaari	365		Mathura	364
			Kianjai	444
Meru			Akithii	473
Mwimbe	313			

Table 6.9

Under 200 persons per square mile

LOCATION	Density per square mile	LOCATION	Density per square mile
Embu		Tharaka North	33
Thiba-Mwea	90	Kiirua	163
Evurore	98	Kibirichia	137
Nthawa	57	Mikinduri	178
Mavuria	53	Lower Abothuguchi	180
		Game Park	0·57
Meru		Northern Grazing	
Magumoni	177	Area	16
Tharaka South	85		

densities for locations decreased to between 200 and 499 per square mile.

A marked feature of the detailed pattern of population concentration is a sharp rise in densities in the southern portion of the Kiambu District and to a lesser extent in the vicinity of Nyeri township. In 1962 the average rural density for Kiambu allowing for forest areas was 925 persons per square mile.

But eight out of the seventeen locations in Kiambu had densities of over 1,000 persons per square mile. In Nyeri two locations in the Aberdares region had densities of over 1,000 persons per square mile. Table 6.7 shows the kind of rural densities which characterised this region at the time of the 1962 Census.

Rural densities that appear in this region are not a common feature of the African rural population patterns except in limited areas such as the Nile Delta. The pressure on land resources and consequent development of a landless class are to be expected as a result of such concentrations.

Mount Kenya-Nyambeni Region. The locations (Table 6.8) show the pattern of distribution in the region that covers the populated slopes of Mount Kenya which lies to the north-east of the Aberdares. The Mount Kenya-Nyambeni region located to the north-east of the Aberdares population region in general shows slightly lower densities than those that occur in Kiambu, parts of Fort Hall and Nyeri section of the Aberdares. The populated region is situated mainly between 4,500 feet and 7,000 feet above sea level. A favourable rainfall and fertile soils of the mountain slopes supports densities ranging from 200 to well over 1,000 persons per square mile. It appears as a virtual island of dense population surrounded by low and dry country which is very sparsely peopled. Kiine (54), Mwerua (55), and Mutira in Embu all had less than 500 persons per square mile.

In the Nyeri location of Magutu (52), the density of population was well over 1,000 persons per square mile. A similar concentration was a feature of Ntima location in Meru (78). Over the slopes of Mount Kenya, densities of more than 500 persons per square mile appeared mainly in those parts which were formerly forested. In Embu, locations such as Baragwe (59) and Ngandori (64) had

8

81-159007

more than 600 persons per square mile. Inoi (57) recorded over 700 persons per square mile. However, those locations which straddle the forest belt and the drier country to the south and east generally had lower densities.

The sparsely populated areas of Embu and Meru (Table 6.9). Embu and Meru Districts form a sharp contrast to the closely settled districts on the slopes of the Aberdares. This is because considerable parts of the two former districts extend to include large areas of the drier country to the east. The Mwea-Mbere and Tharaka landscape generally lies below 4,000 feet above sea level. The country is generally hot and suffers from low and unreliable rainfall. It extends north-east to include much of the country below the Nyambeni slopes. Typical of such densities are the locations such as Tharaka North (81) and Mavuria (62). The lowest densities were to be found in the drier country of Embu and in particular Meru where the Northern grazing area (91) had 16 persons per square mile in an area of 640 square miles. Meru Game Park had less than 1 person per square mile.

While the density pattern is important in examining the causes of mobility of population, the inadequacy of mean densities must be stressed. The 1962 Census figures for the districts showed that approximately 15 per cent of the total population of the five African districts in the area was concentrated in twelve locations with more than 1,000 persons per square mile. These locations accounted for no more than 168 square miles of the country or approximately 3 per cent of the total surface area of the locations excluding forest reserves.

However, the majority of the people were found to be living in locations with densities ranging from 500 to 999 persons per square mile. These locations formed about 15 per cent of the land surface, excluding forests, but accounted for just over 40 per cent of the total population of the area. About 34 per cent of the total population was spread over thirty-two locations with average densities between 200 and 499 persons per square mile. But these locations covered some 28 per cent of the total surface area of the land. The remaining 10 per cent of the population was thinly spread over 53 per cent of the total surface area of thirteen locations mainly in Embu and Meru.

But having examined the pattern of rural population, the factors underlying the varying concentrations may now be considered. In the first place there is an obvious correlation of the main areas of population concentrations and the major geographical subdivisions. The physical environment and its carrying capacity is thus an important factor in the concentrations defined. We have already noted that the concentrations on the slopes of Nyambeni, Mount Kenya and the Aberdares are located in areas receiving ample and reliable rainfall and characterised by fertile volcanic soils. These areas have a superior resource base which set them apart from the basement complex country to the east with its infertile soils, low and unreliable rainfall. The concentrations would appear to reflect a close adjustment to the agricultural opportunities of the area.

However, such an interpretation is clearly an oversimplification of the complex history of this population region. It is necessary to set the pattern against the background of the ethnic movements already noted as well as against the more recent policy of land settlement and subsequent economic development of the area.

The population geography of the area east of the rift has also been deeply affected by the creation of European settlement and the disposition of the former 'Schedule Areas'. The European settlement crossed the line of the south-westerly advance of the Agikuyu group and followed the zone then sparsely occupied by the pastoral communities of the Masai and related ethnic groups. The rapid progress of land alienation across the line of Agikuyu advance which followed in the wake of the rail construction introduced a barrier to the expansive movements which had begun in the northern reaches of Kikuyuland. We may conclude that what had begun as a response to environmental factors and probably as a repercussion to other migrations became confined by rigid boundaries. It is within this boundary that population has increased under the stimulus of other social factors. Densities in southern Kiambu are clearly among the highest rural densities in the world. The influence of the developing urban centre of Nairobi in these high densities should also be noted.

The social and economic problems which have emerged as a result of the growing pressure on available land resources are extremely relevant factors in the explanation of migratory movements of population in the area.

The central rift population region. The central rift population region is important as a bridge between the population region of the east rift highlands and those of western Kenya. It is part of an hour glass shaped region with a base in the west. Eastwards the main populated part of Kenya broadens to include the Kikuyu-Embu and Meru axis already described.

Thus the central rift is not merely a physical but is also a distinctive human sub-region in marked contrast to the heavy population concentration at either end. North and south, this narrow waist of population belt is bordered by virtually empty or sparsely populated parts of Baringo and Narok districts. The mean densities of the districts that lie partly in the rift floor showed the mentioned decrease north and south of the central portion. In 1962, Baringo district in the north had an average population density of 32 persons per square mile and Narok district in the south had an average density of 15 persons per square mile. In the central portion the more populated Nakuru District had 97 persons per square mile and Naivasha district 52 persons per square mile.[37]

But a closer examination of ward densities showed considerable diversity. In the extreme north, vast areas of Baringo district had densities of less than 25 persons. This district may be described as an area of sparse population with pockets of higher densities in the south-west and west. The extremely low density marked the transition from the highland proper to the semi-arid and desert conditions further north and north-east. In the extreme south, extensive areas of Narok district similarly had densities of less than 25 persons per square mile. But most parts of the district actually had densities of 2 to 10 persons per square mile.

The remainder of the rift region stretching from Longonot and Naivasha neighbourhood northwards to Nakuru formed a complex patchwork of densities ranging from 25 to 50 persons per square mile to between a 100 to 250 persons per square mile. This belt of populated country follows the productive farming area that lies just below the Bahati escarpment and continues across the floor of the rift westwards beyond Nakuru township to link up with Njoro Ward.

In attempting to explain the pattern of rural density of the rift floor, it is important to stress the effect of the history of settlement dating back to pre-European times. The varied ethnic groups which have come to occupy the rift have left a distinctive mark in its pattern of population distribution. In the early stages of the land occupance, we have noted that the rift had come to be dominated primarily by pastoral communities where the Nilo-Hamitic peoples practised an extensive form of land utilisation. This form of occupance could not support a high concentration of rural population.

The European settlers who displaced the Nilo-Hamitic pastoralists from much of the rift floor and surrounding plateau practised a mixed economy which came to depend more and more on livestock and cereal cultivation. This was later strengthened by introduction of new plantation crops. The type of economy followed by the new settlers brought about influences that have continued to dominate population pattern of the region up to the present.

Describing the form of economy that the early farmers chose in the area Wrigley (1965) says: 'But for the most part the gentlemen settlers preferred the types of agriculture to which they were accustomed—the breeding of sheep and cattle and the growing of wheat.'[38]

These very settlers needed labour that could not be adequately met from the nearby resources. Thus in one sense, the settlers have contributed to continued sparsity of population. However, by attracting labour from outside they set in motion a movement which still continues as a part of the economic and social system of Kenya. On the whole, the nature of densities of this middle section of our populated zone is clearly a reflection of the importance of the physical conditions, primarily rainfall and soils. This is the section of the rift that enjoys a high and reliable rainfall and is a close correlation between the rainfall map and the distribution of population.

It will be noted that mean district densities in the area

[37]*Statistical Abstract* p. 8. Economics and Statistics Division, Ministry of Finance and Economic Planning, Kenya 1963

[38]Wrigley C. C. 'Kenya: The Pattern of Economic Life 1902–1945' *History of East Africa* Vol. II p. 217 Oxford 1965

Table 6.10 THE WEST RIFT HIGHLANDS (1962 CENSUS)

DISTRICTS	Density per square mile (1962 Census)	DISTRICTS	Density per square mile (1962 Census)
Elgeyo-Marakwet	160	Uasin-Gishu	61
Nandi	167	West Pokot	30
Trans-Nzoia	81		

west of the rift tend to be higher particularly in the former African districts (Table 6.10). But because of inclusion of certain forest areas and lands unfit for human occupation these average densities are not of much value. They merely point to considerable diversity that exists particularly between the former settled areas and the African districts.

Rainfall and temperature which are serious limitations in the central rift are here far more favourable to agricultural activities. The west rift highlands thus differ from the central portion in some very important respects. The highlands are generally wetter and the favourable rainfall covers an extensive area. Because of the high potential of the land considerable parts are capable of sustaining higher densities.

The pattern of rural densities is influenced in the main by the history of settlement. In common with most parts of the west-central Kenya, this was pastoral domain just before the settlement activities which introduced large scale European farming into the area. In the course of the settlement by Europeans, the earlier Nilo-Hamitic pastoralists were restricted to certain well-defined reserves. These reserves such as Elgeyo-Marakwet and Nandi unlike Baringo, West Pokot and Narok are located in some of the most productive lands in Kenya. With population increase within these limits they now appear as islands or ribbons of high density areas in an environment which is generally lightly populated.

By comparison, population density of the wards and locations of the west rift highlands were higher in 1962 than those of the rift floor. The higher parts of Elgeyo-Marakwet above the escarpment formed a well populated tract with densities of 100 to 700 persons per square mile. The northern portion and the southern location in 1962 had densities of 500 to 700 persons per square mile. These areas were among the most crowded portions of the west rift highlands. There were limited areas with densities of well over 700 persons per square mile. In the extreme west of the highlands the eastern part of Nandi district had densities of well over 500 persons per square mile. Most parts of Nandi district however had densities ranging from 100 to 250 persons per square mile. The least populated areas were the former 'scheduled lands' and the drier parts of West Pokot with an average of 25 to 50

persons per square mile. It is in the south of Uasin Gishu, and the Trans-Nzoia districts where densities of over 50 persons per square mile could be found. But even when all factors have been considered, the basic feature which emerges is of the central rift and the highland to the west as an area of low population density set between two heavy concentrations of population at either extreme.

iii. *The population region of the eastern plateau foreland*

A vast region extends from the lower reaches of the eastern rift highlands and from the Tana River to the Coast region in which the population distribution assumes a distinctive pattern. Generally this region may be described as a vast expanse of very sparsely populated country with islands of denser concentrations. It is only in the extreme north-west where it borders the eastern rift highlands that higher densities of population are encountered. In the extreme north-west are the Kitui and Machakos Hills which are in themselves areas of important population concentrations. These two areas form the home base of the Akamba population.

Machakos is by far the most closely settled area. The almost bare hills form a marked contrast with the parched ground in the rest of the district; they are reminiscent of the physical difficulties that face man in his attempt to wrest a living from the soil in this area. The north-western half of the district contains the vast majority of the population of Machakos.

In this north-western half location densities range from 500 to 750 in the hills to the north of Machakos township. Most parts of the district immediately south-east of Machakos showed location densities ranging from 250 to 500 persons per square mile. This north-western part of the district ranks as one of the major population problem areas and it will be seen later that this is one of the major sources of working population in Kenya.

In the southern half of the Machakos district there is a rapid decrease in density of population over the low platform. In this area there were parts of the country with less than 2 persons per square mile.

East of Machakos district, Kitui Hills though less densely populated formed a sharp contrast to the rest of the sparsely populated area. Much of Kitui had less than 100 but over 50 persons per square mile. The central hills

THE POPULATION OF KENYA/105

of Kitui carried a higher density generally between 100 to 250 persons per square mile.

There was a distinct fall in density of population towards the Tana River flood plain. In this eastern portion density of population showed a decrease from between 10 and 50 persons per square mile to well under 2 persons per square mile. Except for the areas bordering the Tana River in the east, much of Kitui may be regarded as a continuation of the population characteristic of the extreme eastern portion of the eastern rift highlands.

Lying between the coast and the Machakos-Kitui population concentrations are the population islands of Taita and Taveta. The Taveta sub-division is in effect a continuation of the population region which skirts Kilimanjaro foothills. Here location densities in 1962 were between 50 to 100 persons per square mile.

The population island of Taita is one of the unique features of the eastern plateau foreland. Densities in the lower parts of the district between Masa and Bura range between 50 to 100 persons per square mile. In the area south of Voi similar densities were encountered. These are the lower portions of the district which share in the problems of the dry plains around.

But in the hilly parts of the district densities of well over 100 persons per square mile were common. The steep slopes have been cleared of vegetation to provide sustenance for the increasing population of the area. Areas around Wundanyi had densities of well over 250 persons per square mile. In the extreme north-east the Tana river flood plain formed an oasis of higher population density generally less than 25 persons per square mile.

The remainder of the dry parts of the plateau foreland were virtually empty. Most parts showed densities of less than 2 persons per square mile. This is the dry scrub country that forms the hinterland of the coast region and the home of a variety of wild life including such big game as the elephant. Tsavo, the largest National Park of Kenya is located in this region and represents the typical appearance of much of the uninhabited parts of the plateau foreland.

The pattern of population described shows the plateau foreland as deficient in human population. Over its extensive grasslands have roamed the ethnic groups that are now found sheltering in the more favourable hills

with better agricultural prospects. Water is still the major limitation. But the soils of the area are also poor.

The population problem in this region is twofold. There is the acute shortage of land for man and stock in the residuals which have become crowded with population from the surrounding plains over the years. In the rest of the country the sparsity of population makes improvements in means of communications extremely expensive. Isolation is one of the major drawbacks of this region. It is likely to remain a sparsely-populated land of little value for agricultural purposes until the problem of the water shortage is solved.

iv. *The coast population region*
The coast region is perhaps the most clearly defined of Kenya's three major population regions. It lies approximately 200 miles from the nearest large concentration of population in the interior. The only intervening island of population in between is the Taita Hills region which lies some thirty miles from the coast population belt and has already been considered.

The coast population region extends from Lamu in the north-east and continues south-westwards across the international boundary into Tanzania. It falls into two distinct sub-divisions on either side of Tana River mouth.

The least populated section of this region extends north-eastwards from Formosa Bay to include the Tana River delta and Lamu District. This northern sub-division is the most sparsely peopled section of the whole coast region. Over the greater part of the sub-division average densities are below 10 persons per square mile.

The island of Lamu had in 1962 an average density of 20 to 50 persons per square mile and was thus the most populous part of the sub-division. Away from Lamu Island, Tana River floodplain, Patta Island and the surrounding areas had low densities ranging from 10 to 25 persons per square mile. This section is in actual fact an extension of the population region of the semi-arid and arid parts of north-eastern Kenya. With the decline of the ancient centres of trade and commerce the area has fallen behind the southern half of the coast. The mean district density for Lamu in 1962 was 8 persons per square mile.

The southern half of the coast population belt extends

southwards from the latitude of Ras Ngomeni. In the northern section it stretches inland to about twenty-five miles. Further south and north-west of Mombasa the population region deepens inland to about fifty miles from the coast. But in the extreme south it narrows again to about thirty miles from the coast. In the area south of Mombasa, the presence of the Shimba Hills has reduced the average density in some parts to less than 2 persons per square mile. Geographically the most important feature is the decreasing density of population from the humid coast to the drier interior. But there is also a general increase in population concentration from the north and from the south towards Mombasa and its surroundings.

Most of the coast population is to be found in the lagoonal sands and pockets of fertile soils along the coast plain. In general average density of population for the coastal plain is well over 100 persons per square mile. But within this average density there are pockets of much higher densities of which Mombasa, the mainland north and west of Mombasa had in 1962 a density of 1,000 to 1,500 persons per square mile whereas the south mainland had an average of 500 to 750 persons per square mile. The land of high density extends inland along the main route out of Mombasa. Mombasa's density is influenced by its urban role and attraction and must therefore be considered apart from the rural densities of the rest of the region.

Away from the Mombasa cluster, the most important concentrations are to be found in and around Malindi and in Kilifi as well as its immediate neighbourhood. There are patches of concentrations such as in Takaungu and Vipingoni. Most of the immediate hinterland of Malindi, Kilifi, Gazi and Shimoni had an average density of 100 to 250 persons per square mile.

From the higher densities of the coastal plain there is a distinctive fall in density to the hilly country that lies west of the coast plain. The coast hills are more prominent in the area south-west of Mombasa. Here they are represented by the deeply eroded Shimba Hills. Although the average density of population in Shimba Hills forest areas is well below 2 persons, where the hills have been reduced considerably the average density lies between 50 and 100 persons per square mile. Further west there is a rapid decrease in population density to well below 50 persons per square mile. The broad belt of Nyika country that lies in the extreme west of the coast plain had an average density of between 25 to 50 persons per square mile.

As a population region the coast compared unfavourably with the major population concentrations of the interior. We have noted that the vast majority of the coast people live in the southern half of the region. This pattern of distribution is a direct result of the operation of environmental factors.

In general, the coast population region roughly coincides with that part of the coast where in 10 to 20 years out of 100 the rainfall is likely to be less than 20 inches. But the main concentration is actually located in that section of the coast where in 10 to 20 years the rainfall is likely to be less than 30 inches. The major concentration of the coast population thus appears to be directly related to prospects of good rainfall.

But within this broad distribution the sharp changes in the character of soil and underground water conditions which is a common feature of the coast also play a vital part in the distribution of population. The immediate coastal fringe with its coral rags either exposed or covered by a thin veneer of sandy material, is generally sparsely populated. In the interior the heavy soils which have developed over the Jurassic shales also tend to be avoided in preference for the more freely drained sites. Hilly remnants of the interior sandstone formation also have a negative effect on population concentration. The prevalence of sandy material in most parts of the coast lowers the carrying capacity of the land.

Analysis of the factors underlying the distribution of population along the coast would be incomplete without reference to the economic activities associated with Mombasa and smaller centres along the coast. The activities of the port of Mombasa now dominates the entire region and accounts for the increasing concentration of population in the areas around. This development is likely to intensify as the port expands its activities further.

v. *The population pattern of the southern and northern drylands of Kenya*

Lying to the south and to the north of the main populated

portion of Kenya are two diverse regions which share the common characteristic of aridity. The southern region has a higher rainfall in general and contrasts with the northern region in which conditions deteriorate and give way to a desert environment extending from Lake Rudolf south-east to Tana River Valley.

In the southern section mean annual rainfall varies between 10 and 20 inches. But in the extreme north it is only the highland fringe and the area towards Somali border which receives this amount. Over much of the Northern Province mean annual rainfall is less than 10 inches.

Rainfall probability shows that throughout the area in 30 out of 100 years the rainfall is likely to be less than 30 inches. Average density is meaningless in a region which is everywhere sparsely populated. It will be seen that its contribution to Kenya's population mobility is modest.

The southern sub-region is thinly covered by pastoral Masai. There is still migration from place to place in search of pasture. In the extreme south this migration cuts across the international boundary which separates Kenya from Tanzania. According to 1962 Census most parts of the southern dryland had an average density of about 2 to 10 persons per square mile. Higher densities were only encountered in areas which border the main population regions.

In the extreme northern section although the average density was around 2 to 10 persons per square mile, there were large tracts of country with densities of less than 2 persons per square mile.

7 Migratory Movements of Population

1. GENERAL CONSIDERATIONS

In the earlier chapters an attempt was made to study in some detail the factors which have a likely bearing on the problem of mobility of population. It has been implicit in these early chapters that mobility might be stimulated by favourable or adverse conditions. But in these studies the ground has also been laid for the study of those areas where the nature of population movement and their effects can be most usefully studied. One of the main difficulties of studying mobility of population in developing countries is the absence of the necessary data. In Kenya, this limitation is both a question of quality and also of time. The material used here in analysing mobility are birth place statistics supplemented by sample data on age and sex-structure of the population obtained from the 1962 Census.[1]

The study considers the dynamic aspects of our population. But the main objective is to examine in detail the selective impact of population movement on the various sections of the African population. The study is therefore focused on the rural and urban areas, the two poles of African population movements.

Geographically, these areas have growing problems arising from migratory movements which closely concern the government of the country. However, the study of migrations is a field of interest to a number of disciplines. In this study the emphasis is on the geographically significant aspect of population mobility. Thus if some of the demographically important problems are not treated in depth it is in order to concentrate on spatial aspects and on the factors underlying such areal differences in our human resources.

Demographers and geographers are vitally interested in the study of migration because it is one of the major determinants of the number and distribution of population. But the study of migration has far deeper social and economic implications. In Kenya we are slowly becoming aware of the implications of the exodus of a large number of people from one part of the country to another or from our homeland to neighbouring countries. These problems are not new. During the colonial period the effects of a large influx of people into the expanding urban areas stimulated a series of restrictive legislation.

Soon after independence in Uganda and Tanzania, the concern of these governments with the presence of large numbers of Kenyans in their countries and the implications of their competitive position in the labour market became a policy question attracting considerable public attention.

In post-independence Kenya, we have already become involved in urging our people to remain on and develop the land in a desperate bid to solve the mounting problem of unemployment in our extensive rural and more limited urban areas. Our preliminary study of the main population regions of Kenya brought to light the unusual concentrations of population in the Lake Victoria basin and in the area east of the rift valley. The problem of land and the need for redistribution of population have always been important areas of dispute in Kenya. Even today resettlement of population is a vital area of activity of the Kenya government. We are therefore inevitably drawn to take the study of population mobility as matter basic to the consideration of serious policy issues.

2. CLASSIFICATION OF MIGRATIONS

In this study the terms migration and mobility of population are used interchangeably. To students of population the term migration is used to cover all movements in physical space. The spatial aspect of this movement and the underlying factors are of special interest to geographers.

We have already covered the early pre-colonial movements that resulted in the physical occupation of the present-day Kenya. Migration of population is a continuing feature of human resource dynamics. In population studies the movements are commonly reduced to two main classes.

There is, first, the international movement on which a number of standard works have been written in other parts of the world. In a sense Kenya is also affected by international migration involving neighbouring countries. There are the periodic movements of pastoral population including the Galla and Somali, and the Masai of Kenya in search of pasture across international boundaries. The relationship between the ethnic patterns of Kenya and

[1]'Birth Place. Analysis by Tribe, Sex and Five Year Age Groups (African)' 1962 Census Ministry of Economic Planning and Development, Kenya

Table 7.1 IMMIGRANT TRIBES IN TANZANIA

	1948	1957
Taita	8,658	3,395
Kamba	2,348	10,865
Baluhya	2,611	1,634
Kikuyu	3,918	856
Sabaot	621	—

Table 7.2 SEX RATIO BY PROVINCE 1962

PROVINCE	Sex Ratio	PROVINCE	Sex Ratio
Nairobi (E.P.D.)	154	Rift Valley	105
Central	94	Southern	91
Coast	101	Northern	110
Nyanza	93		

Table 7.3 NAIROBI EXTRA-PROVINCIAL DISTRICT 1962

	Sex Ratio		Sex Ratio
Nairobi City	149	Nairobi (E.P.D.)	154
Nairobi Peri-Urban	181		

those of the surrounding countries are such that there are considerable movements across the national boundaries.

There is evidence that Kenya is affected by a flow of people from within her borders to the neighbouring countries in search of employment or better economic opportunities. According to the 1959 Uganda Census there were 37,648 Luo and 43,255 other Kenya tribes in Uganda.[2] The Tanganyika Census of 1957 listed the following comparative figures of immigrant tribes in the country from Kenya[3] (Table 7.1).

Southall (1961)[4] has described these as post-colonial movements resulting from trade along the routes from the coast to the interior and also based on the interior network of communication which had developed. He suggested broad distinctions which could be made in areas of East Africa on the basis of such movements. These little studied international movements, though of great significance within the East African setting, are not the main objective of this book. We are concerned here with the internal component of similar movements which lead to absence in some areas of an important section of the population or to inter-provincial shift of population.

There is little doubt about the social and economic importance of the internal movements of population in many African countries in the form of large shifts in population from the rural to urban or from less prosperous rural to richer rural areas. But with the present limited refinement of census material it is possible to measure this movement only in the most general form. It is in filling this gap, that the birthplace statistics of the 1962 Census of Kenya are important in a study of population movements in the country.

However, it is not possible from such general information to obtain a full picture of the migration streams and causes of these migrations. The information from birth-place statistics must therefore be supplemented by other data to obtain a more complete view of the dynamic aspect of our population. There is a further difficulty arising from boundary changes which have been numerous. The student of population mobility is therefore working with areal variables which tend to restrict the comparability of data.

3. THE SIGNIFICANT DEMOGRAPHIC CHARACTERISTICS IN THE STUDY OF MIGRATIONS

For analysis of the nature of population mobility certain characteristics of its composition are most important. We have already considered the ethnic composition of the African population of Kenya. The demographic and other effects of the early migratory movements are now a matter of the past history of the population.

In the following study we will now concentrate on analysis of the age-sex distribution as a vital factor in the understanding of the regional dynamics of our population. Here the two most important characteristics are the age-sex ratio and the age-sex pyramids which are analysed for the total population and for the different ethnic groups and sub-groups.

i. The sex ratio

As one of the most important indices of population change, the sex ratio is conventionally expressed as a percentage of males to 100 females. The value of such data is affected by the degree of accuracy in the statement of ages. When the ratio is over 100, then the males are in excess and when less, then the females predominate.

Just as it varies with regions at any one time, so does it change with the differences in the socio-economic character of the population. The ratio also varies with the time and is thus a valuable index of the trend of population. It is one of the most important clues to the effects of population movements. The nature of the burden of dependents on the adult section of the population can be easily examined from the pattern of the sex ratio. The sex ratios shown below vary from province to province

[2]Uganda Population Census 1959 p. 18 Government Printer, Kampala 1961
[3]African Census Report 1957 pp. 41–4 Government Printer, Dar-es-Salaam 1963
[4]Barbour & Prothero (Editors) pp. 157–92 Essays on African Population Routledge and Kegan Paul, London 1961

Table 7.4 CENTRAL PROVINCE 1962

	Sex Ratio		Sex Ratio
Embu	91	Nanyuki	125
Fort Hall (Muranga)	89	Nyeri	89
Kiambu	95	Thika	127
Meru	94		

Table 7.5 COAST PROVINCE 1962

	Sex Ratio		Sex Ratio
Kilifi-Malindi	90	Mombasa	134
Kwale	94	Taita	97
Lamu	97	Tana River	98

Table 7.6 NYANZA PROVINCE 1962

	Sex Ratio		Sex Ratio
Central Nyanza	89	Kisii	96
Elgon Nyanza	91	North Nyanza	88
Kericho	109	South Nyanza	93

Table 7.7 RIFT VALLEY PROVINCE 1962

	Sex Ratio		Sex Ratio
Baringo	99	Nandi	98
Elgeyo-Marakwet	103	Trans-Nzoia	110
Laikipia	101	Uasin Gishu	108
Naivasha	108	West Pokot	94
Nakuru	113		

and from district to district, and suggest a number of important consequences[5] (Table 7.2).

The figures show the significant differences between Nairobi Extra Provincial district, the Coast, Rift Valley, the Northern and the three provinces of Central, Nyanza and Southern. There is an obvious excess of males over females in the Nairobi area which suggests a strong influence of migrations in the sex ratio. The low figures for males in the other three main districts of population concentration may at this stage suggest the influence of migration out of these areas.

But the high figures of males for the Northern Province is more difficult to explain. It may be due to errors in recording the numbers of children; or, on the other hand, the disparity may be due to under-enumerations of females. More information is needed. A closer examination of the district pattern provides a useful indication as to the population characteristics of the various parts of the country (Table 7.3).

For Nairobi a conclusion may be reached that the high proportion of men over women is due to the combined effect of the City and to a lesser extent that of the Peri-Urban area. In the Central Province, there is a striking difference between the former African districts of Kikuyu, Embu and Meru areas and those districts that were formerly included in the 'White Highlands' such as Nanyuki and Thika. This contrast is similarly clear in the age-sex pyramids of the district (Table 7.4).

The proportion of males is clearly low for the Central Province districts of Embu, Fort Hall (Muranga), Meru and Nyeri. Fort Hall and Nyeri are particularly low and it will be noted later that these are the districts which contribute a large proportion of migrating population (Table 7.4).

In the Coast Province, Mombasa District stands apart from the rest of the districts. Here it will be noted that this particular district shows a high proportion of males in the population. The districts immediately north and south of Mombasa in 1962 showed a slight deficiency of males (Table 7.5). A similar deficiency was noted for the districts of Embu, Fort Hall, Meru, Kiambu and Nyeri. These deficiencies are a result of migration and will be explained in more detail in the text.

Nyanza is predominantly a rural province. But even in this area there are significant differences between Kericho and the remaining districts (Table 7.6). Kericho shows a slight surplus of males over females. But the districts of Central Nyanza and North Nyanza both indicate deficiency in male population. South Nyanza, Kisii and Elgon Nyanza are about normal although they also show slight male deficiency. On the whole Nyanza as a province is a male deficient area. This feature will be more fully explained in the treatment of migrations which follows.

A survey of the pattern of sex ratio in the Rift Valley districts on the whole tends to show a surplus of males. On the basis of such information, it is possible to divide the districts into two categories. There are the former African districts of Baringo, Nandi and West Pokot which all show a slight deficiency in the male population. These districts differ from those which formerly constituted a part of the 'White Highlands' of Kenya. In districts such as Trans-Nzoia, Uasin Gishu, Laikipia, Nakuru and Naivasha, there are indications of predominance of males. The sex ratio in all these is above 100 (Table 7.7). The high male figures for the Elgeyo-Marakwet is not easy to explain and needs more investigation.

The Southern Province has more in common with the male deficient districts of the Central and Nyanza Provinces. Only Kajiado district shows a slight male dominance over females. But Kitui, Machakos and Narok districts all show low male figures (Tables 7.8).

Except for Turkana, and Samburu, all the districts in the Northern Province had surplus of males. Garissa, Isiolo, Mandera, Marsabit, Moyale and Wajir all had a ratio of over 100. Such a high ratio cannot simply be explained in terms of migrations and could be due to errors of enumeration (Table 7.9).

District sex ratios in Kenya have revealed a distinction between those parts of the country which clearly show either deficiency in male population or a surplus. In each of these categories are both rural and urban areas, but the figures for Nairobi and Mombasa do not alone establish the overwhelmingly masculine character which is a feature of Kenya's towns.

[5]The figures are derived from: *Kenya Population Census* 1962 Tables, Advance Report of Vols. I & II, Vol. 2 (Ministry of Economic Planning and Development, Nairobi), Ministry of Finance & Economic Planning, Nairobi 1964 and 1965

Table 7.8 SOUTHERN PROVINCE 1962

	Sex Ratio		Sex Ratio
Kajiado	102	Machakos	90
Kitui	89	Narok	93

Table 7.9 NORTHERN PROVINCE

	Sex Ratio		Sex Ratio
Garissa	127	Samburu	100
Isiolo	115	Turkana	97
Mandera	117	Wajir	117
Marsabit	105	Province	110
Moyale	109		

Table 7.10 URBAN SEX RATIO (AFRICAN) 1962

	Sex Ratio		Sex Ratio
Nairobi	187	Kitale	133
Mombasa Municipality	151	Nyeri	162
Nakuru Municipality	150	Gilgil	158
Kisumu	158	Lamu	125
Eldoret	145	Malindi	186
Thika	151	Athi River	213
Nanyuki	152	Isiolo	128

The following data show more clearly the masculinity of the urban centres of this part of tropical Africa. This feature is of great importance in revealing the presence of migration (Table 7.10).

The contrast between the urban centres and the rest of the rural areas and also that between the former African rural districts and the 'scheduled' areas may be expressed in terms of the percentage of children in the total population.

Analysis of the results of the 10 per cent Sample Census of African in Kenya in 1962 reveals that children below the ages of 15 formed about 30 per cent of the total population. Some 29·55 per cent of the total population of Nairobi in 1962 were children below the age of 15. In the Peri-Urban area the figure was even 24·12 per cent. In Mombasa the proportion of children in the African Somali section of the population was 32·6 per cent. These figures were much lower than those of the rural districts.

The Nyanza rural districts had percentages ranging from about 45 to 50. Kisii had the highest percentage with 50·16 per cent of the population falling below 15 years of age. In the Central Province, Kiambu, Fort Hall, Nyeri and Meru each had a population of which over 50 per cent were children. But in the settled districts of Thika (41·03) and Nanyuki (39·50) the proportion of the child population though relatively low suggested that different influences were affecting the structure of the population. For most of the African districts of the Rift Valley, the proportion of child population varied between 45 and 50 per cent.

We can therefore say that there is a basic contrast in the character between our urban and rural population and that even among our rural population there are important differences between certain districts and the others. Most striking is the extremely youthful character of the African population, particularly in the main population source areas of the Lake Basin, the Central Province and the Coast.

ii. *The age-sex pyramid*

Perhaps one of the most vital pieces of information on population characteristics is the age-sex distribution which is commonly represented by the age-sex pyramid. It constitutes one of the most sensitive characteristics or peculiarities of population in any area and is therefore a most useful tool for a geographical analysis of the regional character of population. We have already noted the importance of the sex ratio in describing the imbalance or balance of the characteristics of sex distribution in any population. The age-sex pyramid provides a striking visual perspective of the impact of various factors on the population as a whole over several generations. However, although it is relatively simple to construct, it is important to bear in mind the complex story that it represents. 'The age-sex distribution of a given population is a record of nearly a century of societal experience. Just as the geologist may read much of the earth's history by examining the exposed strata near its surface, one familiar with the subject may see reflected in the profile of a given society's age-sex distribution many important events which have occurred over the century prior to the census involved.'[6]

However, important though the age-sex pyramid is in the study of the history of a population it is subject to certain errors for which allowance must be made. The reliability of the age data partly depends on the level of literacy. There is also the tendency to prefer certain numbers. In certain cases, many persons tend to report their ages and ending in zero. The younger members of the family may be omitted. But the commonest errors are understatement of age and numbers of population. The diagrams prepared for the various population samples to be considered are therefore liable to these errors. These are but a few of the problems facing students of population geography in a country such as Kenya. Further in the nationwide survey of the age-sex pyramids, a number were rejected by the author for the smallness of samples. The distortions to which these diagrams are subject may therefore be a result of the nature of the sample taken. But when these have been allowed for, the age-sex pyramids of these African population samples are clearly significant in the detailed analysis of migratory movements of population and their impact. (See note on derivation of percentages. Percentages are based on the total numbers for each sex sample.)

The age-sex pyramids for total population in the five

[6]Smith Lynn T. *Fundamentals of Population Study* p. 155, Lippincot, New York 1960

Figure 7.1

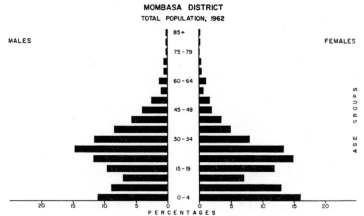

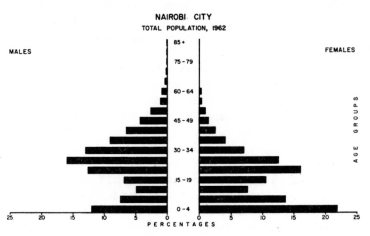

provinces included two broad categories. In the first category are the urban sample pyramids represented here by Nairobi City, Nairobi Peri-Urban and Mombasa District (Figure 7.1). In the second category are the rural district pyramids (Figure 7.2–7.11). These rural pyramids show distortions which are significant geographically in a national study of population movements.

The urban age-sex pyramids all show the standard distortion between the ages of 15 and 54. There is a bulge reflected in the pattern for both sexes. The distortion is due to the presence of a large number of persons of working age. This kind of distortion will be a valuable index in a general survey of migrations and especially in the analysis of inter-district population movements.

Throughout rural Kenya, the majority of the age-sex pyramids shows that the population is overburdened by a broad base of dependants including children below the age of 15 years. To this must be added the female adult population left behind by selective migration which will be examined later (Figures 7.2–7.11).

However, for a more detailed picture of the imbalance of numbers, we need to go back to the age-sex ratio. The analysis in Table 7.11 of the African age-sex ratio for the City of Nairobi and Mombasa District are derived from the 10 per cent sample Census of 1962 and are a valuable indication of the regional and selective impact of migration.

Nairobi City and Mombasa may be taken as representative samples of urban settlements which have continued to draw rural population consisting largely of males. A comparison of the 1962 and the 1948 position has shown however that the masculine character of the African urban population is on the decrease largely due to an increased inflow of females particularly dependants (Blacker 1965).[7] Among the urban areas the difference between Nairobi and Mombasa calls for comment. Nairobi appears more masculine than Mombasa, above 24 years. Mombasa is a much older settlement though still dominated by inward migration.

But leaving aside the striking features of the major urban centres the regional differences in the effect of migrations are also indicated by the age-sex ratios of the various rural districts. The first obvious distortion is

[7]Blacker J. G. C. p. 60

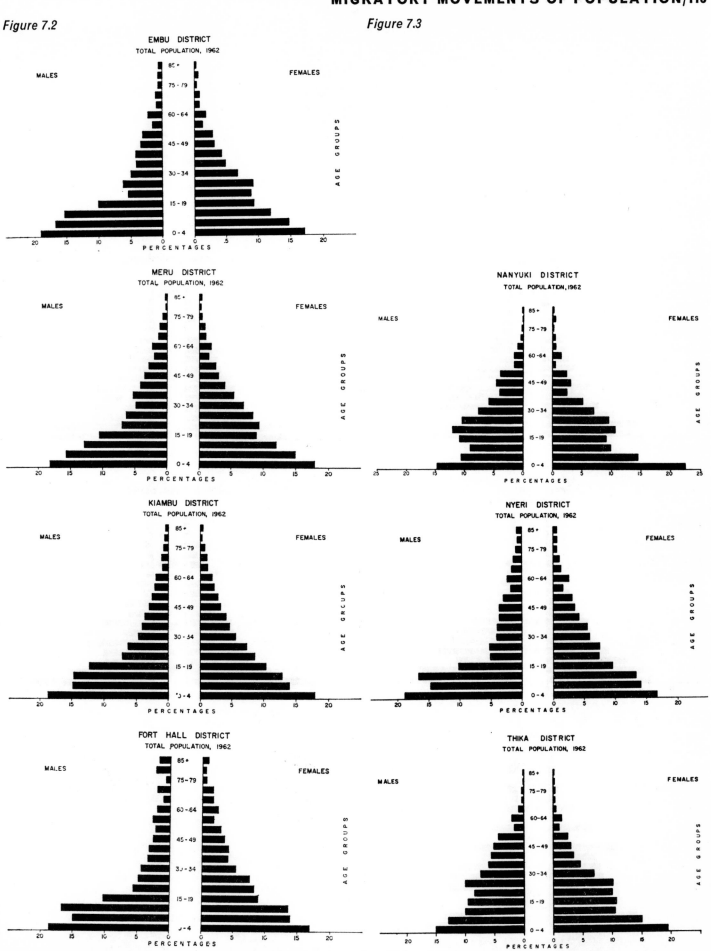

Figure 7.2

Figure 7.3

Figure 7.4

Figure 7.5

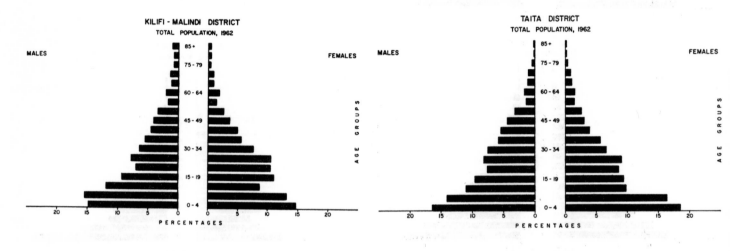

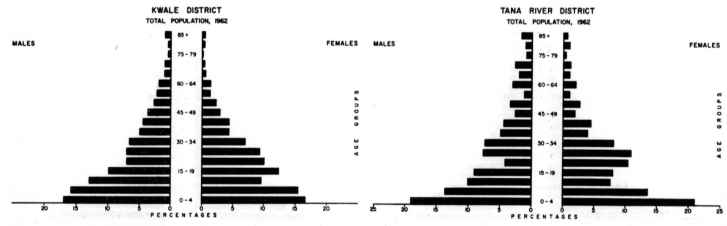

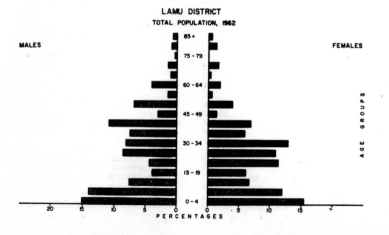

Figure 7.6   Figure 7.7

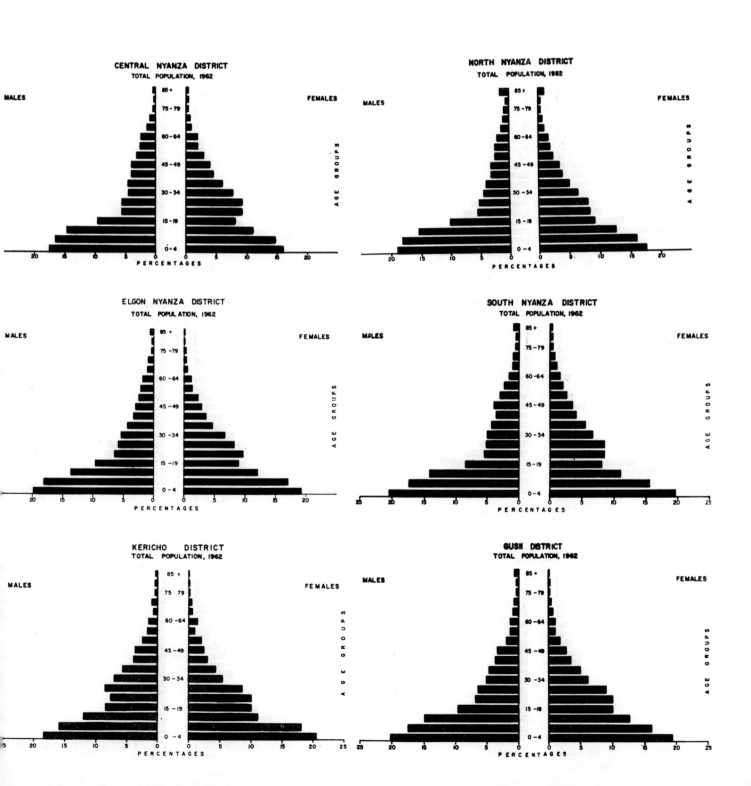

Figure 7.8   *Figure 7.9*

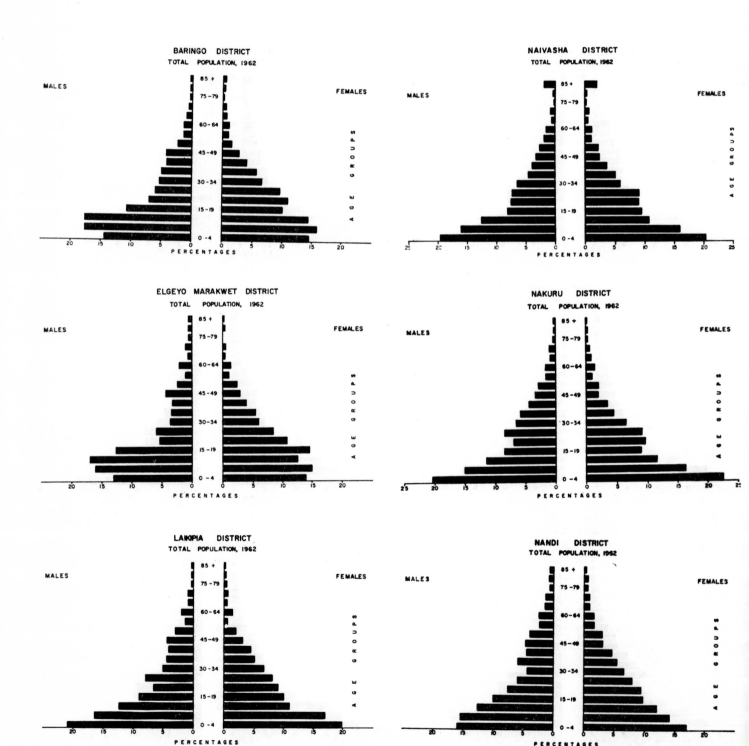

Figure 7.10

Figure 7.11

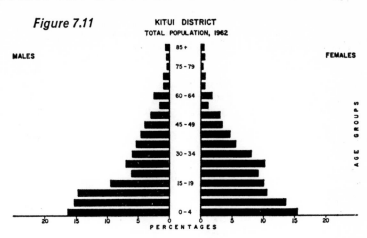

KITUI DISTRICT
TOTAL POPULATION, 1962

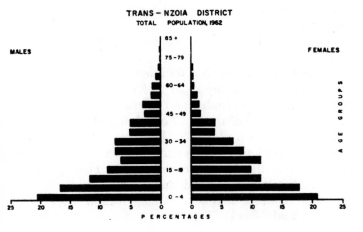

TRANS – NZOIA DISTRICT
TOTAL POPULATION, 1962

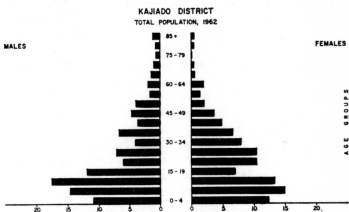

KAJIADO DISTRICT
TOTAL POPULATION, 1962

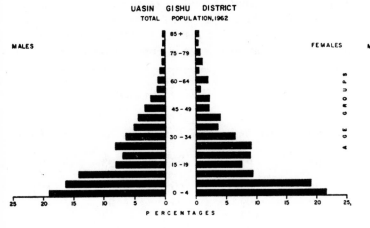

UASIN GISHU DISTRICT
TOTAL POPULATION, 1962

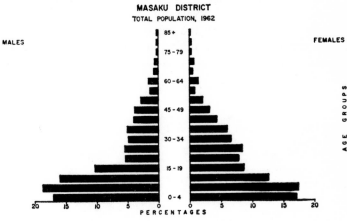

MASAKU DISTRICT
TOTAL POPULATION, 1962

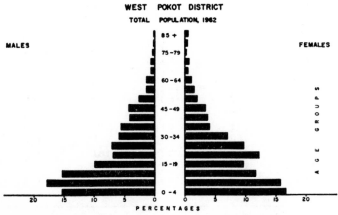

WEST POKOT DISTRICT
TOTAL POPULATION, 1962

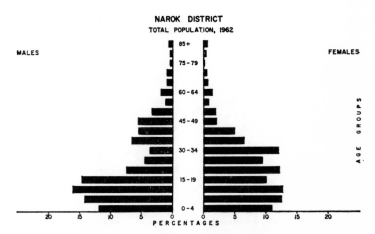

NAROK DISTRICT
TOTAL POPULATION, 1962

Table 7.11 NAIROBI CITY (AFRICAN): 1962 CENSUS TOTAL POPULATION

Age	Sex Ratio	Age	Sex Ratio
0–4	104	50–54	589
5–9	102	55–59	712
10–14	120	60–64	473
15–19	120	65–69	406
20–24	147	70–74	313
25–29	244	75–79	197
30–34	354	80–84	219
35–39	417	85–89	157
40–44	501	90+	344
45–49	579		

Table 7.12 MOMBASA DISTRICT (AFRICAN): 1962 CENSUS

Age TOTAL POPULATION	Sex Ratio	Age TOTAL POPULATION	Sex Ratio
0–4	104	50–54	220
5–9	103	55–59	236
10–14	152	60–64	174
15–19	121	65–69	184
20–24	118	70–74	188
25–29	167	75–79	236
30–34	224	80–84	190
35–39	258	85–89	200
40–44	241	90+	140
45–49	289		

reflected in the patterns for the districts of Nyanza, Central, Southern and to a lesser extent Coast Province (Tables 7.13-7.45). In Nyanza province administrative units such as Central, North and South Nyanza districts showed the male deficiency between the ages of 19 and 54. But there were marked differences from district to district. Central and North Nyanza deficiencies occurred between 15 and 54 years. In Elgon Nyanza it was between 15 and 49 years and in Kisii the effect was most pronounced between 15 and 39 years. In South Nyanza the age-sex ratio showed male deficiency between 20 and 44 years. But even in the less affected districts of Elgon, Kisii and South Nyanza, women invariably outnumbered men between the ages of 19 and 44. This imbalance in some cases is not clearly shown by the age-sex pyramids.

The Central Province districts of Embu, Fort Hall, Kiambu, Meru and Nyeri all showed the effect of migration. Considering the age-sex ratio as a critical guide the deficiency of males in most districts ranges between the ages of 15 and about 55. But even in this respect it will be noted that there are important differences between the districts (Tables 7.18, 7.19, 7.20, 7.21, and 7.22).

While Fort Hall and Nyeri's male population are more affected by the loss, the losses in Kiambu and the more remote districts of Embu and Meru were not as pronounced as in the districts of Fort Hall and Nyeri.

In the Southern Province, indications of differential rates of migration from the rural districts are supported by analysis of the African age-sex ratios. These show the contrast between the Kitui and Machakos districts on the one hand and the remaining Masai districts of Kajiado and Narok (Tables 7.23, 7.24, 7.25). In the Kitui district the low sex ratios between the ages of 15 and 44 suggest that the effect of the movement in the area is felt earlier. This is in marked contrast to the conditions in Machakos district where the deficiency in the male population is most intense between the ages 20

Age	Table 7.13 CENTRAL NYANZA Sex Ratio	Table 7.14 ELGON NYANZA Sex Ratio	Table 7.15 KISII Sex Ratio	Table 7.16 NORTH NYANZA Sex Ratio	Table 7.17 SOUTH NYANZA Sex Ratio	Table 7.18 EMBU Sex Ratio	Table 7.19 FORT HALL Sex Ratio	Table 7.20 KIAMBU Sex Ratio	Table 7.21 MERU Sex Ratio
TOTAL POPULATION	88	92	97	89	95	87	87	93	101
0–4	98	95	101	96	99	97	96	97	103
5–9	100	98	105	101	106	99	95	98	106
10–14	117	103	114	108	124	113	107	107	109
15–19	101	100	93	97	102	94	100	110	99
20–24	50	62	65	60	64	53	60	79	76
25–29	46	64	69	57	59	59	56	80	77
30–34	48	74	80	60	71	62	70	78	70
35–39	65	87	90	70	77	72	74	82	99
40–44	76	80	103	71	83	83	67	82	104
45–49	87	98	118	86	110	92	64	82	114
50–54	95	103	107	90	116	92	71	80	111
55–59	120	140	131	115	120	95	123	88	143
60–64	121	131	128	120	104	98	68	98	124
65–69	138	162	135	120	124	86	56	71	142
70–74	131	160	171	149	119	111	93	83	150
75–79	170	126	226	210	163	128	80	98	178
80–84	174	183	158	180	140	105	262	161	129
85–89	164	241	272	284	251	115	191	80	108
90+	188	235	271	121	223	222	109	154	115

to 44. Both are therefore affected by migration from the rural areas.

In the Masai districts of Narok and Kajiado the deficiency in the male population appears to be more important between the ages of 20 and 34 years. In the case of Narok district the figures are even lower than for some of the migration sources of Central and Nyanza Provinces (Tables 7.25 and 7.26). Other factors may be at work in stimulating movement of men which the low sex ratio suggests. But the conclusion is that even these districts are affected by the outflow of population.

The distortion in the rural sex balance due to movement of population is continued in the Coast Province (Tables 7.27–7.30). Here there is clear evidence in Kilifi-Malindi district which showed male deficiency between the ages of 15 and 44 years. It will be seen later that among the Coast districts Kilifi-Malindi was one of the most important sources of population supplying the majority of people who migrate up-country. In the

districts of Kwale and Lamu, it would appear that the outward migration begins much earlier than in Tana River and Taita. In Kwale district, women outnumber men largely between the ages 15 and 34 years. But it will be noted that there is a high masculinity ratio particularly between the ages 35 and 39 years. It is possible that this distortion could be due to the flow of population to the plantation areas. Lamu district shows a deficiency in males between the ages of 15 and 34. In Tana River, migration seems to start much later than in the other Coast districts. This is indicated by the extremely low proportion of men between the ages 20 and 24. It will be shown that in terms of numbers this district is one of the most important Coast sources of migratory population.

Within the Rift Valley Province the sex ratio shows a distinct male deficiency falling largely between the ages 20 and 39 years (Tables 7.31–7.34). This is the case in Baringo, Nandi and Elgeyo-Marakwet. But in the West Pokot district the effect is felt from the age of 15. It is therefore, possible to conclude that the former African districts show the effect of outward movement of males but this is largely limited to the period between 20 and 39 years. These districts seem to show the same trend as the Masai districts of Kajiado and Narok. We have already observed that the male deficiency indicated may not be entirely due to outward migration of men from these areas.

So far we have been considering the distortion in the age-sex ratios of the urban areas and the rural sources of the urban population. The age-sex ratios of the urban areas and the rural districts have been examined to show more clearly migration and its effects on the population at different ages. There is a third area where the effect of regional shift of population can be clearly studied. This area covers the settled districts of the former 'White Highlands'. Included here are the rural districts such as Kericho in Nyanza, Trans-Nzoia, Uasin Gishu, Laikipia, Nakuru and Naivasha in the Rift Valley Province, Thika and Nanyuki in the Central Province, and the Coast district of Taita which includes the plantation areas of Voi and Taveta (Table 7.35).

A closer examination of these rural districts shows a distortation of the expected rural pattern. In the age-sex pyramids there is an incipient bulge falling between the

Table 7.22 NYERI	Table 7.23 KITUI	Table 7.24 MACHAKOS	Table 7.25 KAJIADO	Table 7.26 NAROK
Sex Ratio	Sex Ratio	Sex Ratio	Sex Ratio	Sex Ratio
91	92	96	100	91
102	97	96	88	98
95	103	103	97	103
112	127	121	132	116
98	87	114	169	132
63	62	65	57	56
65	63	63	69	44
63	69	69	52	28
66	81	82	99	94
80	92	88	76	104
96	110	116	126	261
85	92	123	170	162
109	125	146	123	134
87	129	118	91	124
114	129	145	237	122
108	135	90	198	169
153	156	119	283	167
965	82	86	143	100
870	118	84	214	128
124	118	—	231	67

ages of 15 and 35 years. In this respect the districts closely resemble the urban areas whose patterns have already been explained as reflecting the effect of inward migration. The imbalance between the sexes is more clearly shown below.

Here again there is a clear distinction between the Kericho and Taita districts and the other districts. In Kericho district the African age-sex ratio show a deficiency in males limited to the ages 15 to 19 and 20 to 24 years. There is high masculinity ratio from 25 years onwards (Table 7.35). However, the most significant feature is the high masculinity ratio rising from 110 to 170 between the ages of 25 and 50 years. This is a major departure from the remaining districts of Nyanza Province where the ratios were between 50 and 90. The following sex ratio for the age range 25 to 29 years clearly show the difference between Kericho and the remaining districts of Nyanza (Table 7.37). The same pattern is suggested by the difference between Taita and the other Coast

districts (Table 7.36). An attempt has already been made to explain the high masculinity ratio of Kwale between the ages of 35 and 39 years.

The cases presented by Kericho and Taita districts can be largely explained as indicating the effect of movement of predominantly male population from outside the district into these areas. Analysis of the economic structure of these districts drew attention to the important plantation farming of sisal and sugar. This relates their demographic patterns to those of other large scale farming areas of Kenya.

We may now turn to consider in detail the nature of the distortion in the sex structure of the second group of districts. These are the districts which formerly constituted part of the 'White Highlands of Kenya'. An outstanding feature of the sex ratio of these districts is the high masculinity ratio of the population in general. But even among these districts there are significant differences (Tables 7.39–7.45).

Table 7.27 Table 7.28 Table 7.29 Table 7.30 Table 7.31 Table 7.32 Table 7.33 Table 7.34 Table 7.35 Table 7.36

Age	KALIFI-MALINDI Sex Ratio	KWALE Sex Ratio	LAMU Sex Ratio	TANA RIVER Sex Ratio	BARINGO Sex Ratio	NANDI Sex Ratio	WEST POKOT Sex Ratio	ELGEYO-MARAKWET Sex Ratio	KERICHO Sex Ratio	TAITA Sex Ratio
TOTAL POPULATION	93	96	114	96	104	100	90	116	113	113
0– 4	94	98	114	88	101	93	82	107	102	100
5– 9	110	98	134	101	116	109	102	124	100	97
10–14	127	128	135	129	127	105	118	153	123	127
15–19	78	76	72	108	109	104	92	101	93	114
20–24	63	66	43	39	66	80	50	58	87	99
25–29	69	72	90	69	66	75	67	81	112	100
30–34	79	88	73	89	86	66	76	72	146	128
35–39	92	110	149	122	95	108	124	73	150	114
40–44	86	98	181	97	110	95	103	100	144	158
45–49	108	118	262	145	162	154	118	182	171	161
50–54	119	115	200	127	173	124	125	122	131	138
55–59	108	157	259	123	174	139	89	130	180	106
60–64	106	125	244	143	138	145	118	190	117	119
65–69	127	138	284	181	149	171	127	225	145	125
70–74	147	181	95	216	125	142	86	216	173	165
75–79	184	176	625	179	163	104	142	804	270	111
80–84	140	103	69	99	123	96	63	192	233	80
85–89	286	140	222	22	70	567	23	59	285	39
90 +	169	157	62	20	96	816	39	333	159	—

Table 7.37 NYANZA PROVINCE: AGE-SEX RATIO
25-29 AGE GROUP 1962 CENSUS

DISTRICT	Sex Ratio		Sex Ratio
Kericho	112	North Nyanza	57
Central Nyanza	46	Kisii	69
Elgon Nyanza	64	South Nyanza	59

Table 7.38 COAST DISTRICTS

	Sex Ratio		Sex Ratio
Taita	100	Lamu	90
Kilifi-Malindi	69	Tana River	69
Kwale	72		

The most striking of these are the patterns represented by the former Thika District and Nyeri District. In these areas the African age-sex ratio between the ages of 15 and 45 are well over the 100 mark. Thika district emerged as a predominantly masculine district particularly between the ages of 10 and 80. Nanyuki district figures also show the same pattern. For the critical ages of 25 to 49 the age-sex ratio in the districts varied between 119 and 250. The two districts clearly showed a considerable flow of the male population to the areas concerned. In the important district of Nakuru a similar pattern could be seen. Here the dominance of the males in the population was shown by a sex ratio of well over 100. Extremely high ratios were characteristic of the ages between 25 and 60 (Table 7.41).

Nakuru district pattern is undoubtedly affected by the presence of the growing highland township and the provincial capital of the Rift Valley. We have already shown that the Municipality alone had a sex ratio of 150

for the African population. These figures show that movement into the district was not primarily directed to the urban area. However, even in this as in most Rift Valley districts the inward migration has a small outward component. In the case of Nakuru this appears to fall between the ages of 20 and 24 years. There is a distinct male deficiency in the population which suggests that the districts also contribute to the national migration particularly of males.

In the remaining Rift Valley districts, it appears that although there is evidence of an inflow of males, this is not sufficiently heavy as to obliterate the distinctive loss of males from the district between the ages of 15 and 45 years.

Laikipia district showed above average ratio between the ages of 25 and 29. But in general the sex ratio for the remaining age ranges between 15 and 45 is generally less than 100. Naivasha district indicated a ratio of 114 between the ages 30 and 34 years. But for the remaining

	Table 7.39	Table 7.40	Table 7.41	Table 7.42	Table 7.43	Table 7.44	Table 7.45
						UASIN GISHU	
	THIKA	NANYUKI	NAKURU	LAIKIPIA	NAIVASHA		TRANS-NZOIA
Age	Sex Ratio	Sex Ratio	Sex Ratio	Sex Ratio	Sex Ratio	Sex Ratio	Sex Ratio
TOTAL POPULATION	121	146	112	104	103	120	104
0- 4	94	95	102	108	100	106	103
5- 9	104	107	104	99	104	104	97
10-14	118	135	122	115	122	180	106
15-19	110	172	107	93	90	127	92
20-24	102	168	82	74	88	22	60
25-29	119	157	104	102	82	107	89
30-34	130	163	114	77	114	121	112
35-39	159	165	151	92	91	167	141
40-44	190	263	147	96	116	134	135
45-49	202	230	190	152	144	190	198
50-54	209	252	148	172	122	134	236
55-59	217	625	179	276	249	213	246
60-64	191	176	132	161	151	82	311
65-69	187	257	103	207	128	215	213
70-74	156	169	129	136	141	59	145
75-79	174	267	146	67	133	136	167
80-84	91	53	86	165	126	36	198
85-89	113	100	22	470	97	203	—
90 +	180	600	221	84	100	127	37

Table 7.46 Persons born outside Enumeration Province

CENSUS AREAS	Total	%
Nairobi Extra-Provincial District	155,558	25·73
Central Province	67,629	11·18
Coast Province	77,626	12·84
Nyanza Province	27,900	4·61
Rift Valley Province	263,333	43·55
Southern Province	12,624	2·09
Total	604,700	100·00

Table 7.47 Birthplace of Inter-provincial Migrants

PROVINCE	Total	%
Nairobi (E.P.D.)	8,901	1·47
Central Province	215,356	35·61
Coast Province	5,741	0·95
Nyanza Province	211,482	34·97
Rift Valley Province	41,887	6·93
Southern Province	106,502	17·61
Northern Province	14,831	2·45
Total	604,700	

critical adult age groups of 15 to 39 the ratio is well under 95. There is thus a significant outflow which is not masked by the inward migration into the district.

Further west, Uasin Gishu district showed a very similar trend to the district of Nakuru. On the whole this is a highly masculine district except for the age group 20 to 24 years. We may conclude that the district is largely affected by an inflow of a predominantly male population. But on the contrary, there is also evidence of its contribution to the national movement between the ages of 20 and 24.

In the more distant district of Trans-Nzoia, there was a definite deficiency of men between the ages of 15 and 29. In this age bracket the sex ratio was between 60 and 90. But the inflow of men was more apparent at about 30 years. There is a steep rise in the masculinity of the population well beyond the age of 60 years (Table 7.45).

4. THE VOLUME AND DIRECTION OF MOVEMENT

In an attempt to assess the magnitude and direction of population movement in Kenya we should turn to consider a summary of birthplace information for the African population as recorded for the Census areas in 1962 (Tables 7.46 and 7.47). These figures give a clear indication of the significance of the incoming population for the six census areas. The first is a major contrast between the Rift Valley, Nairobi Extra-Provincial District, the Coast Province and the remaining provinces. The largest figures of external birthplaces were for the Rift Valley Province which accounted for 43·55 per cent of the total for the six census areas and Nairobi Extra-Provincial with 25·73 per cent of the total. (Table 7.46)

The Coast Province had 12·84 per cent and the Central Province had 11·18 per cent of the total. The Nyanza and Southern Provinces had 4·61 and 2·09 per cent respectively. We see here emerging, a basic contrast that has already been noted between the former 'White Highlands' farming areas and the associated urban centres and the predominantly African rural provinces of Nyanza and Southern Nyanza. A further analysis will show that the Central Province is more appropriately classified with the second group of provinces although in 1962 it showed a larger proportion of the inward moving population than the other provinces.

Before considering the destinations and sources in detail we may make two observations from these sets of figures. First there is the general spread of sources which presents a more balanced picture in contrast to the concentration at the receiving end of Nairobi Extra-Provincial District, and the Rift Valley.

If we consider the six census areas for which the figures of incoming population are available an interesting pattern emerges. This shows three areas which appeared on the basis of these figures to be gaining population at the expense of other areas. These were, the Rift Valley, Nairobi Extra-Provincial District and the Coast Province. The Rift Valley had 221,446 persons over and above those that the Province contributed to the pool. Nairobi Extra-Provincial District had 146,682 more persons and the Coast Province 71,885 persons more. Nyanza Province received 183,582 less, Central Province 147,727 less than their contribution to the national stream. The size of the population involved and the clear division between the provinces call for a more detailed analysis of the destination and sources of the moving population.

i. *The Rift Valley migration stream* (Figure 7.12)

The Rift Valley has emerged as the most important destination of the migrating population in Kenya. It accounted for approximately 44 per cent of a total population of 604,700 distributed between the various destinations throughout the country. A detailed analysis of this stream is of vital importance to the understanding of the nature of migration and factors that stimulate the migratory movements.

The provincial sources of the Rift Valley stream were dominated by the nearby Central Province which contributed 48·24 per cent of the total and Nyanza 43·58 per cent. The remainder came from the Southern (4·05 per cent), Northern Province (3·48 per cent), Coast (0·26 per cent) and Nairobi Extra-Provincial District (0·36 per cent).

From the Central Province, analysis of birthplace records showed that in 1962 majority were from Kiambu with 35·62 per cent of the Central Province source. Fort Hall had 33·22 per cent and Nyeri 28·08 per cent. The remainder was contributed largely by Embu, Meru, Nanyuki and Thika.

Figure 7.12   **MIGRATORY MOVEMENTS OF POPULATION/123**

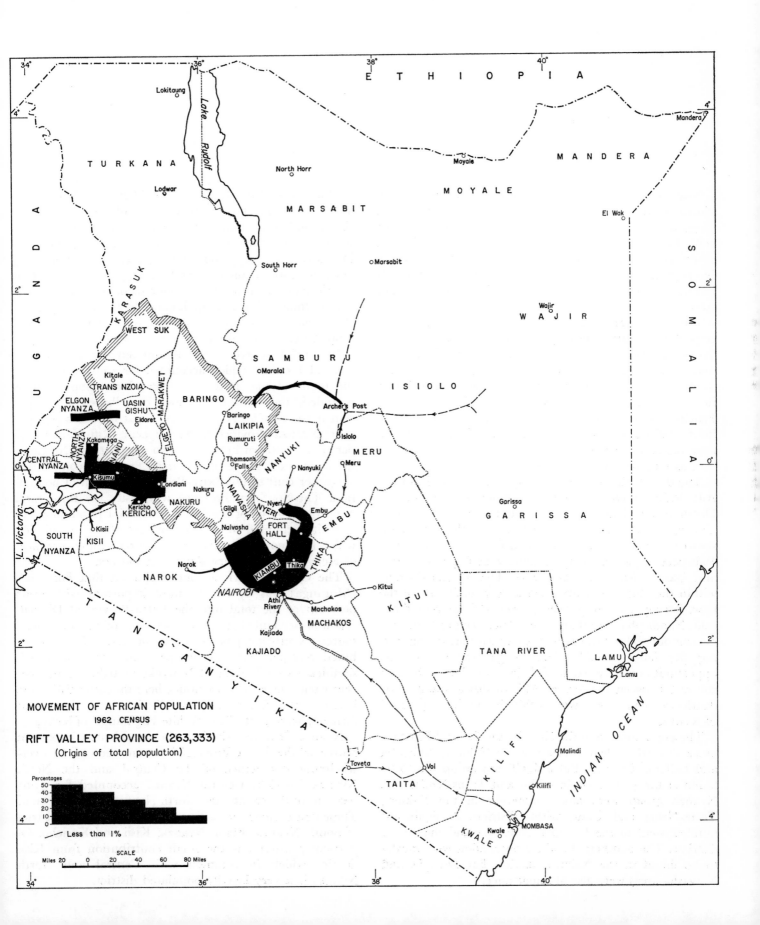

MOVEMENT OF AFRICAN POPULATION
1962 CENSUS

RIFT VALLEY PROVINCE (263,333)
(Origins of total population)

Percentages
50
40
30
20
10
0

Less than 1%

SCALE
Miles 20   0   20   40   60   80 Miles

The Nyanza source was largely dominated by the North Nyanza movement. North Nyanza had contributed 33·37 per cent of the provincial total, Kericho 24·13 per cent, Elgon Nyanza 21·00 per cent and Central Nyanza 16·03 per cent. The Rift Valley had therefore drawn its population primarily from the districts of the adjacent and well populated provinces to the east and west.

From the Southern Province, came the third most important stream. Over 40 per cent of the Southern Province population came from the districts of Machakos and Kitui. But Machakos was the second most important source after Narok which at that time was not included in the present Rift Valley Province. The Northern Province sources showed the importance of the neighbouring districts of Lodwar-Turkana and Samburu. These movements underline the importance of short range as well as long distance migrations.

The distribution of the incoming population within the Rift Valley underline the importance of the Nakuru District. It had about 44 per cent of the total for Rift Valley. The allocation of the remainder of the population showed the importance of Laikipia (12·3 per cent), Naivasha (13·3 per cent), Trans-Nzoia (14·8 per cent) and Uasin Gishu (11·7 per cent). The African districts within the Rift Valley attracted a very small part of the flow. Baringo had 1·0 per cent, Elgeyo-Marakwet 0·6 per cent, Nandi 1·6 per cent and West Pokot 0·6 per cent. This distribution follows the expected pattern that the migrating population would select to go where economic opportunities were greatest. It brings out the emphasised contrast between the former African districts and those districts which formerly were within the 'White Highlands' of Kenya.

The population from the Nairobi and Central Province areas showed a clear preference for Nakuru, Naivasha and Laikipia Districts. But a significant group was to be found as far west as Uasin Gishu and Trans-Nzoia. The Nyanza group were more numerous in the Nakuru, Trans-Nzoia and Uasin Gishu districts. A significant number went to the Laikipia, Naivasha and the Nandi districts. The Southern Province population were mostly to be found in the Nakuru district. But Laikipia and Naivasha areas were also of importance.

ii. *The Nairobi Extra-Provincial District stream* (Figure 7.13) We have already noted that in terms of volume, this was the second most important stream accounting for 25·73 per cent out of the total pool. Out of a total population into this area of 155,588 some 130,628 persons or 83·95 per cent were for the City of Nairobi (Figure 7.14). This figure actually represented about 83·60 per cent of the City's total African population. For Nairobi Extra-Provincial District the figure was 79·01 per cent of the total African population.

Provincial sources were dominated by the nearby Central Province which accounted for 42·64 per cent of the total volume. If the Extra-Provincial population is excluded, the Central Province contributed 44·90 per cent to the total for Nairobi City, Coast Province 1·48 per cent, Nyanza Province 35·28 per cent, Rift Valley 1·38 per cent, Southern Province 16·70 per cent and Northern Province 3·08 per cent. Nyanza Province contributed 31·30 per cent to the Extra-Provincial stream of population. The Southern Province was easily the third most important source of the Extra-Provincial population. In 1962 it accounted for 22·32 per cent of the population which had moved into the area. The remaining provinces of Kenya were not very significant sources.

The Central Province sources showed that Fort Hall (Muranga) was by far the most important with 41·07 per cent of the total into the Extra-Provincial District. Kiambu accounted for 28·02 per cent of the Provincial source, Nyeri 20·69 per cent. Embu and Meru contributed 7·74 per cent and 1·75 per cent respectively. It is significant that Thika and Nanyuki contributed 0·27 per cent each. Once more we notice here the same distinction between the former African districts and those that formerly were part of the 'White Highlands' of Kenya.

Nyanza Province which as the second most important source of the Extra Provincial stream showed an overwhelming dominance of the Central and the North Nyanza Districts. Central Nyanza accounted for 45·05 per cent of the stream and North Nyanza 42·46 per cent. These figures show very little contribution from the district of South Nyanza, Elgon Nyanza, Kisii and Kericho. Of particular interest is the small contribution from Kisii district which in common with Central and North Nyanza is a very heavily populated district.

Figure 7.13

MIGRATORY MOVEMENTS OF POPULATION/125

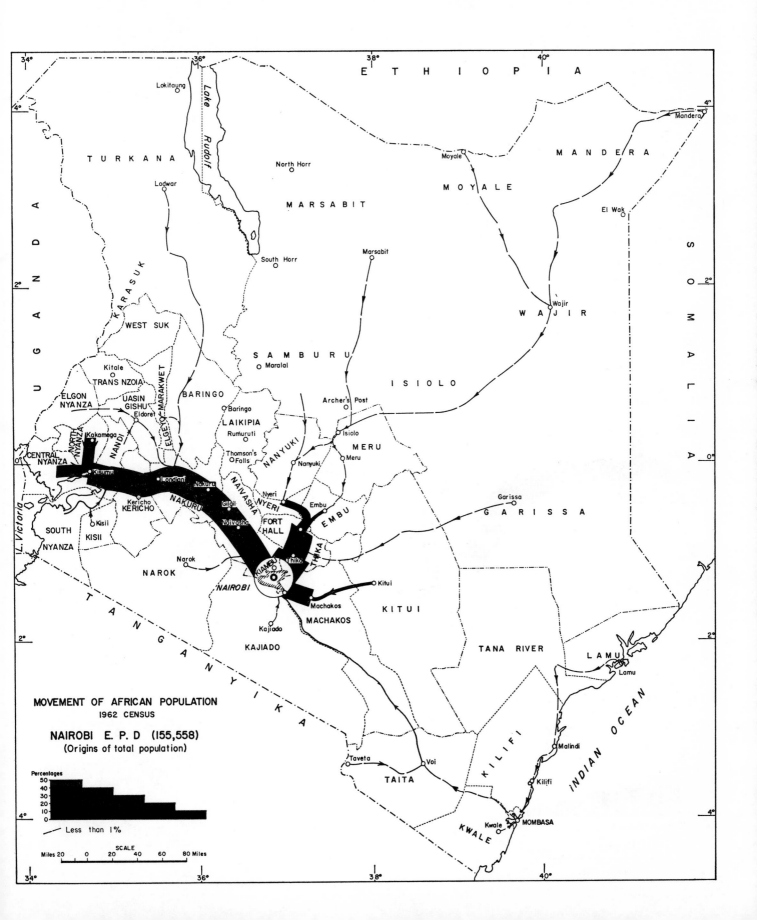

MOVEMENT OF AFRICAN POPULATION
1962 CENSUS

NAIROBI E. P. D (155,558)
(Origins of total population)

Figure 7.14

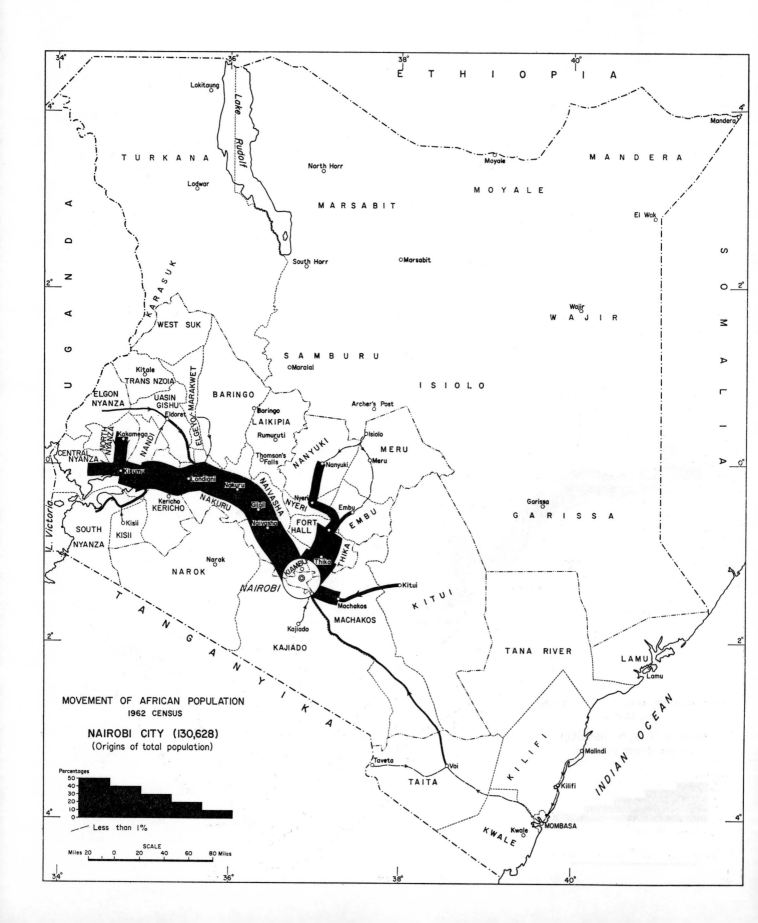

MOVEMENT OF AFRICAN POPULATION
1962 CENSUS

NAIROBI CITY (130,628)
(Origins of total population)

Percentages
50
40
30
20
10
0

— Less than 1%

Miles 20   0   20   40   60   80 Miles
SCALE

The Southern Province source which ranked third in importance of Extra-Provincial population sources showed an overwhelming dominance of the nearby Machakos District. Machakos accounted for 83·89 per cent of the Provincial source and Kitui 13·63 per cent. Only a small part of this population came from other sources.

The most important sources in the Rift Valley were the districts of Naivasha with 47·97 per cent, Nakuru 16·03 per cent and Nandi with 15·43 per cent. The remaining districts of Baringo, Elgeyo-Marakwet, Laikipia, Trans-Nzoia and Uasin Gishu contributed a very small share.

From the Coast Province sources 52·32 per cent were from Taita District, 27·96 per cent from Mombasa and 12·74 per cent from Kilifi-Malindi. The remaining district sources were relatively unimportant. Northern Province which is the remaining source showed concentration of people from the district of Isiolo. This district alone accounted for 57·77 per cent of the total provincial source.

Sources of Nairobi's population confirm the importance of the main population regions of Lake Victoria Basin and the area east of the Rift Valley. This area east of the rift includes the former African districts of Kikuyu, Embu and Meru peoples. But whereas in the City area the majority of the African population were from Central Province, Nyanza and Southern in order of importance, in the Peri-Urban area, most people came from the Southern and Central Provinces. A very small proportion of the Nyanza population was to be found in the Peri-Urban area. Nyanza's preference was therefore clearly for the City.

iii. *The Coast Province stream* (Figure 7.15)

The Coast Province is the third most important destination of the in-coming population. Record of birthplace information in 1962 showed that the stream accounted for 77,626 persons. The bulk of this stream is directed towards Mombasa District. A further analysis shows that out of a total of 77,626 into the Coast Province, 36,917 were in Mombasa District from outside leaving 30,609 to be distributed between the remaining districts of the Coast Province. Mombasa District therefore accounted for 47·55 per cent of the total Coast stream.

Sources of the Coast Population stream show that 49·37 per cent was contributed by the Southern Province. Of the remainder, Nyanza Province contributed 33·79 per cent, Central Province 11·44 per cent, the Rift Valley 3·52 per cent, Nairobi Extra-Provincial District 1·39 per cent and the Northern Province 0·46 per cent. As in the case of the Rift Valley and Nairobi areas the nearby province here played a dominant role.

Among the Southern Province source, Machakos was clearly the most important. It accounted for nearly 70 per cent of the Southern Province population. The remaining districts of the province were relatively insignificant in their share of the movement of population.

A similar concentration was noted among the Nyanza population where 51·16 per cent of the persons came from the districts of Central Nyanza and 23·35 per cent from North Nyanza. It will be noted that the remaining districts of Nyanza showed very little response to this destination. South Nyanza accounted for 6·20 per cent, Elgon Nyanza 1·81 per cent, Kisii 1·60 per cent and Kericho 0·63 per cent of the total provincial source. The small contribution of Kericho is significant in explaining the causes of population mobility. There was less concentration from the Central Province sources. The total population involved was small but was better distributed throughout the districts. Embu District made the highest contribution with 34·47 per cent, Kiambu had 19·33 per cent, Fort Hall 18·49 per cent and Nyeri 12·64 per cent. These were the most important origins of the Coast stream from Central Province.

Rift Valley emerged with a much smaller contribution. Most of the Rift Valley population came from Nandi District. The predominance of Nandi District in this stream needs further investigation. The observed importance of the Nandi may have an economic or social origin. But more information is needed to make a valid conclusion. However, the small contribution may represent Nandi's contribution to the Services, domestic employment and recent settlement in the Coast Province. The remaining sources of the Coast population were not significant. It had already been noted that 47·6 per cent of the total Coast stream had Mombasa district as its destination. The next most important destinations were Kwale District with 32·0 per cent and Taita District which had

Figure 7.15

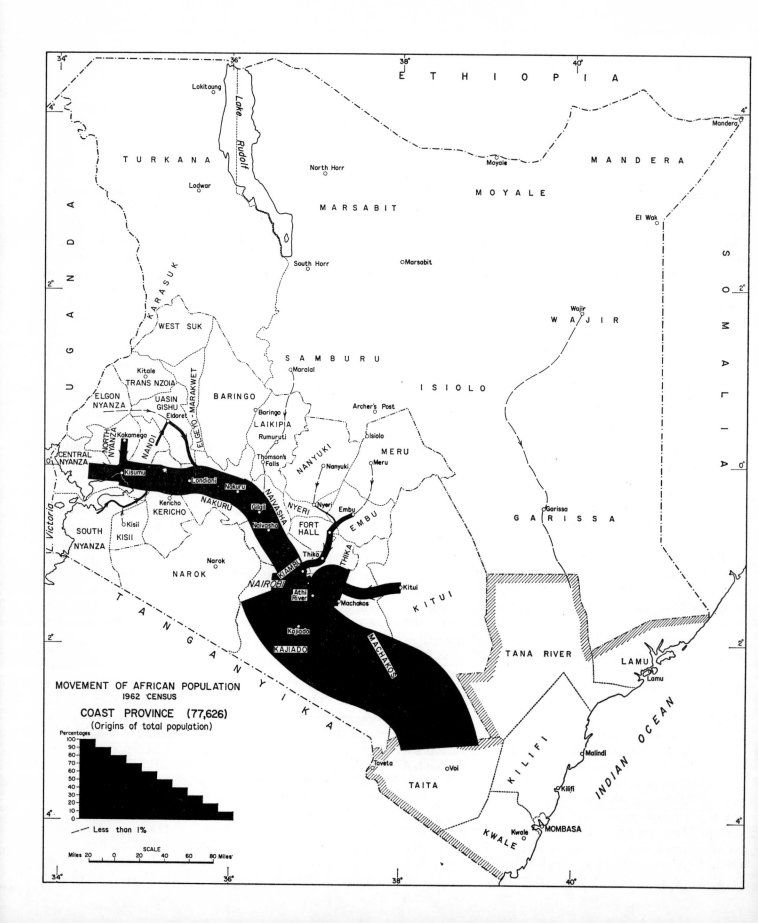

MOVEMENT OF AFRICAN POPULATION
1962 CENSUS

COAST PROVINCE (77,626)
(Origins of total population)

Percentages
100
90
80
70
60
50
40
30
20
10
0

– – – Less than 1%

SCALE
Miles 20   0   20   40   60   80 Miles

Figure 7.16

MIGRATORY MOVEMENTS OF POPULATION/129

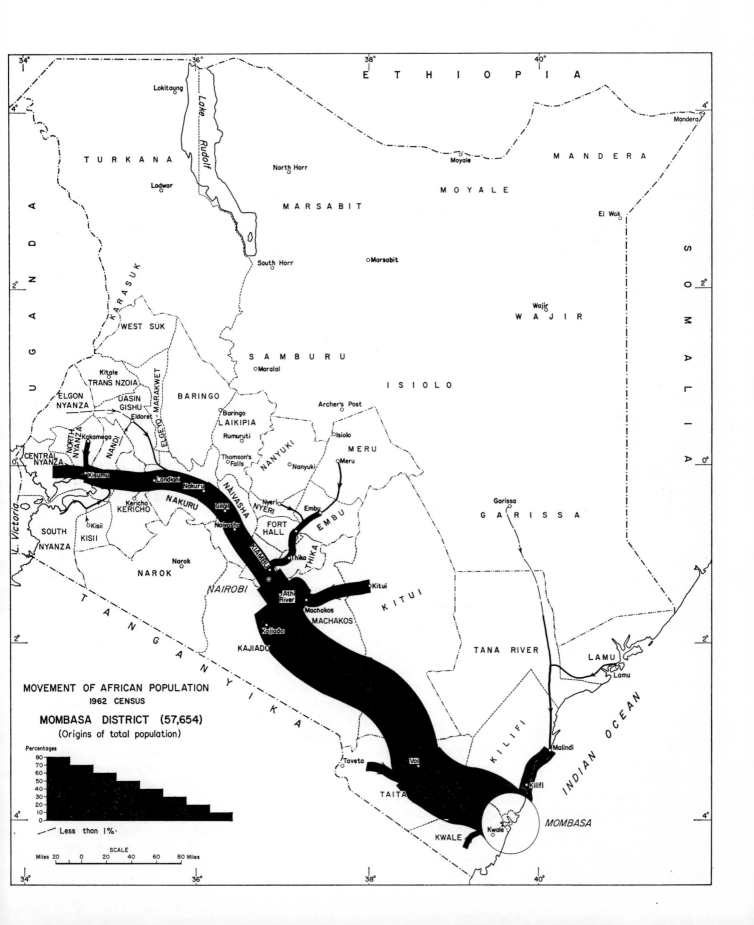

MOVEMENT OF AFRICAN POPULATION
1962 CENSUS

MOMBASA DISTRICT (57,654)
(Origins of total population)

18·2 per cent of the total. The importance of Kwale and Taita in the migration suggest a close association between the stream of migration and the large scale plantation farming which had been developed and which were described earlier. Kwale alone accounted for 24,905 persons as compared to 14,113 for Taita and 1,115 for Kilifi-Malindi districts.

People from Nairobi area and Central Province showed a preference for Mombasa, Taita District and Kwale. The Nyanza group also showed a preference for the same area. The Rift Valley group was largely concentrated in the Kwale District. Among the Southern Province people, Kwale, Mombasa and Taita Districts were the most important.

In treating the Coastal stream we have merely considered population coming from outside the Coast. A large portion of the local Coast population flowing into Mombasa has therefore been excluded. A comparison of this volume with the contributions of the rest of the country provides a useful picture of the national importance of Mombasa District.

The total population moving into Mombasa District from the areas around and from up-country sources was 57,654 (Figure 7.16). The most important provincial source was the Coast itself with 35·97 per cent of the total. Nyanza Province came second with 24·96 per cent and the Southern Province 24·23 per cent. Central Province accounted for 12·25 per cent of this total population.

The remaining sources in the Rift Valley and the Northern Province made a modest contribution to the total flow. Nairobi Extra-Provincial District contributed 1·40 per cent, Rift Valley 0·82 per cent and the Northern Province 0·37 per cent.

The majority of the Coast source came from Kilifi-Malindi District with 14·90 per cent of the total, and Taita with 11·24 per cent. Kwale District to the south of Mombasa contributed 6·55 per cent of the total. It is worth noting here the small contribution of the northern and poorer districts of Tana River (0·91 per cent), and Lamu (1·23 per cent). Taking the Coast sources alone majority of the people came from the districts of Kilifi-Malindi (41·41 per cent), Taita (31·23 per cent) and Kwale (18·20 per cent).

In the Nyanza Province stream Central Nyanza contributed 15·58 per cent of the total for Mombasa. The next source in North Nyanza accounted for only 5·56 per cent of the total for Mombasa stream. The least affected districts were South Nyanza, Kericho and Kisii. A summary of Nyanza sources showed concentration in the two districts of Central Nyanza (62·41 per cent) and Northern Nyanza (22·29 per cent). The Southern Province source showed in this case the importance of Kitui District which contributed 16·25 per cent of the total for Mombasa. Kitui's contribution was just over twice as much as the Machakos figures. Machakos source accounted for 7·23 per cent of the total Mombasa stream. Narok and Kajiado made very small contributions. About 67 per cent of the Southern Province population came from Kitui and only 29·80 per cent from Machakos. This preference is in contrast to the pattern for Nairobi.

The only other important source of Mombasa's population is Nairobi and Central Province area. This source though relatively small accounted for 13·66 per cent of the total for Mombasa and majority came from Embu, Kiambu, Fort Hall, Nairobi City and Meru. In common with Nairobi, Mombasa's influence taps the main areas of population concentration. But its influence is affected by the demand for Nairobi which filters most of the up-country population destined for area.

iv. *The Central Province stream* (Figure 7.17)
The Central Province is similar to Nyanza and the Southern Provinces in that the total population received from the rest of the country was far less than the contribution of the province to all other destinations. It received 67,629 persons from the rest of the country but appeared to have lost well over 140,000 persons.

Provincial sources confirmed that the most important contributors to the Central Province stream were the Southern Rift Valley and Nyanza Provinces, the nearby Southern Province contributed a total of 21,856 persons or 32·31 per cent of the total. Rift Valley was the next most important source with 29·64 per cent and Nyanza third with 27·08 per cent. Of the remaining sources, the Northern Province accounted for 6·12 per cent, Nairobi Extra-Provincial District 3·44 per cent and the Coast Province 1·41 per cent. Except for the Rift Valley, the

Figure 7.17   **MIGRATORY MOVEMENTS OF POPULATION/131**

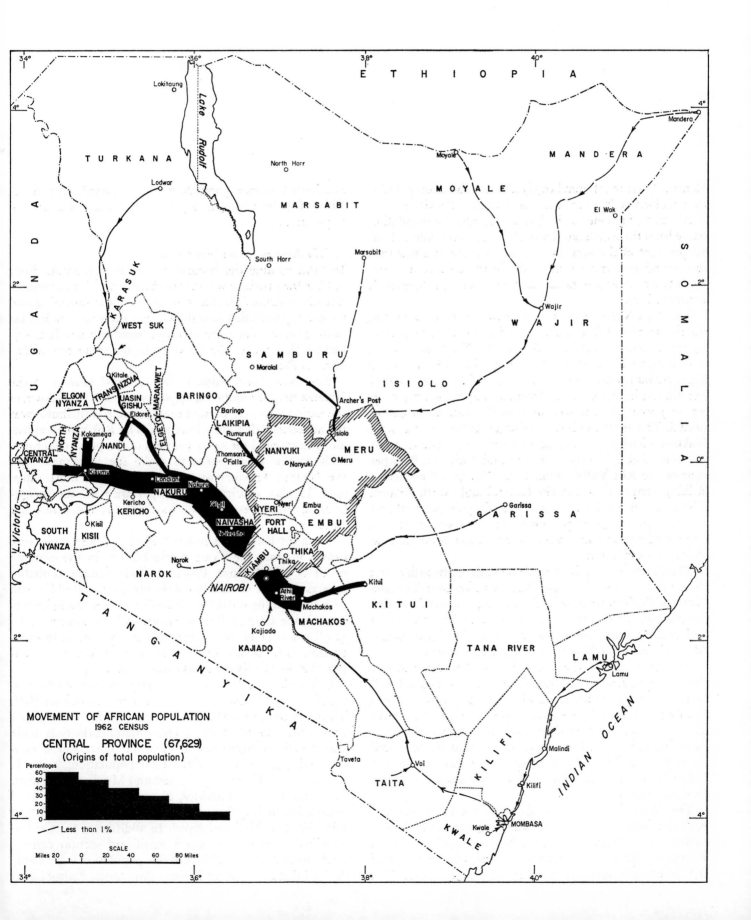

MOVEMENT OF AFRICAN POPULATION
1962 CENSUS

CENTRAL PROVINCE (67,629)
(Origins of total population)

Percentages
60
50
40
30
20
10
0

—— Less than 1%

SCALE
Miles 20   0   20   40   60   80 Miles

Central Province stream largely affected the main population regions of Nyanza and the Southern Provinces.

About 75 per cent of the Southern Province population came from the Machakos District. Kitui contributed about 18 per cent of the total from that province and was thus the second most important district in the area. Apart from these two sources the remaining sources made rather small contributions.

The Rift Valley source was drawn from a variety of district sources. But there appeared to be a concentration in the Nakuru, Nandi, Laikipia and Naivasha sources with only small numbers from Trans-Nzoia, Baringo and Elgeyo-Marakwet. The prominence of the Rift Valley population in the Central Province may reflect migrants whose parents had moved over to the Rift at an earlier period. This may also be true of other destinations as well. Nakuru District contributed 18·77 per cent, Nandi 13·81 per cent, Laikipia 11·35 per cent and Naivasha 8·89 per cent of the Rift Valley total. From Nyanza, there was a striking concentration in the Central and North Nyanza Districts. Central Nyanza contributed 43·26 per cent and North Nyanza 43·29 per cent. The remaining sources compared unfavourably with the above sources of Central Province population.

The Northern Province made a small contribution and most of these were from Samburu and Lodwar-Turkana districts. Each contributed just over 30 per cent of the total population. The least contribution came from the Coast and mainly from the poorer northern district of Kilifi-Malindi and from Mombasa and Taita districts.

Analysis of destinations brought out the importance of the farming districts of Thika, Kiambu and Nanyuki. It will be noted that these are areas with large scale and modern farming activities. These are also the districts which have developed a significant degree of processing and manufacturing industries. It has been shown that Kiambu and in particular Thika have some of the most important industries in Kenya. Nanyuki as a destination is mostly a farming country.

The Nyanza stream showed preference for Thika and Kiambu whereas the Rift Valley movement showed preference for Kiambu, Nyeri, Nanyuki and Fort Hall. Except for the concentration in Kiambu the remainder of the important districts had about equal shares. The

Southern Province population were primarily moving to Thika District which is adjacent to this major source of population.

v. *The Nyanza stream* (Figure 7.18)

In total volume the Nyanza stream of population from outside the province was far less than those of the provinces already examined. But a comparison of the incoming and outgoing population had shown that the province lost far more people than were received from outside. It is this feature that places the Province in the same role as the Central Province.

The total contribution of the national sources to the Nyanza stream numbered 27,900 persons. A breakdown of the national sources showed that the main contributor was the adjacent Rift Valley Province. The Rift Valley source alone accounted for 44·04 per cent of the provincial total. This source would seem to make the movement into the Nyanza Province at the time largely a short range one. It also confirms the importance of the neighbouring province which we have already noted in other cases.

From the Rift Valley source majority of the people were drawn in from the Trans-Nzoia District in the extreme north of the Nyanza Province. This feature probably reflects the close connection of the northern part of Nyanza with the farming district of Trans-Nzoia. Second in importance is the Central Province source which accounted for 32·96 per cent of the Nyanza stream. But even in comparison with the flow to the major destinations of population this flow to Nyanza was rather small.

Of the Central Province source 41·31 per cent came from the districts of Kiambu and 16·95 per cent from Fort Hall. The third most important source was Nyeri with 13·38 per cent of the total population. The remaining districts made very small contributions to the total flow. Embu contributed 9·42 per cent of the total population, Nanyuki 7·80 per cent, Thika 1·63 per cent and Meru 1·05 per cent. From the Central Province, Nyanza therefore attracted population mainly from the heavily populated districts of Kiambu, Fort Hall and Nyeri. In addition to the Central Province source there was a significant section coming from the Nairobi area. Part of this population is probably derived from the strong Nyanza flow to the Nairobi area

Figure 7.18

MIGRATORY MOVEMENTS OF POPULATION/133

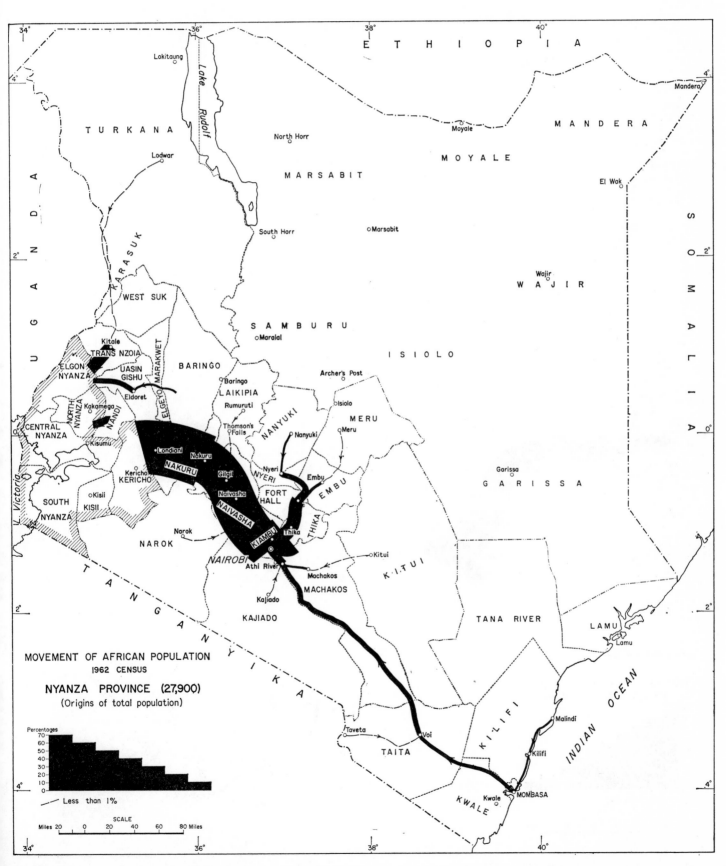

MOVEMENT OF AFRICAN POPULATION
1962 CENSUS

NYANZA PROVINCE (27,900)
(Origins of total population)

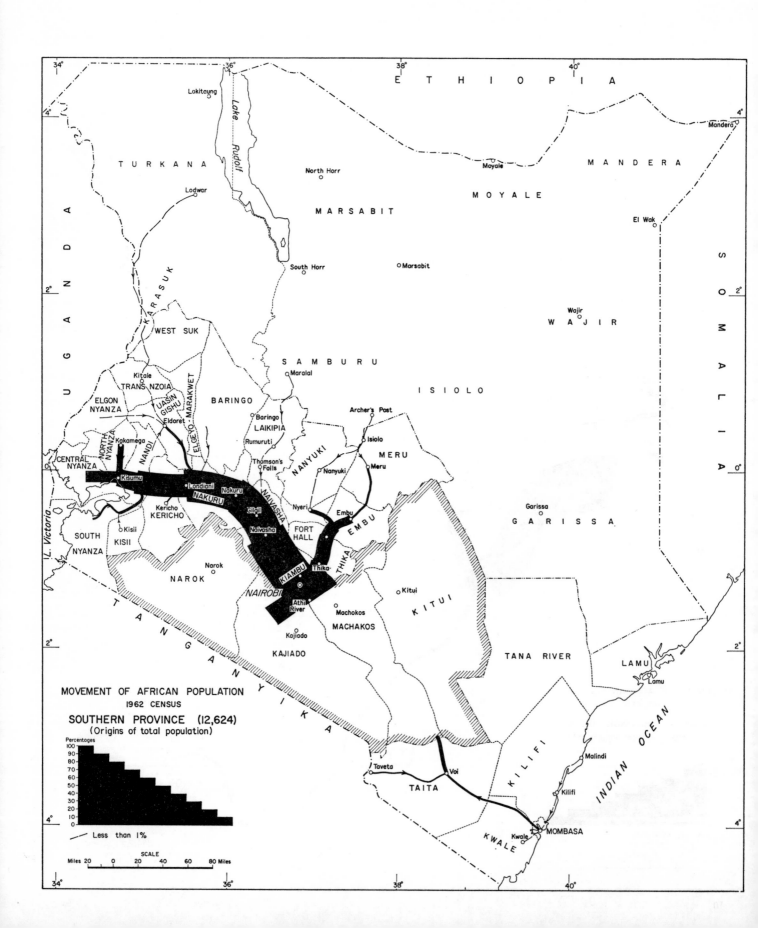

MOVEMENT OF AFRICAN POPULATION
1962 CENSUS
SOUTHERN PROVINCE (12,624)
(Origins of total population)

Percentages
100
90
80
70
60
50
40
30
20
10
0

___ Less than 1%

SCALE
Miles 20   0   20   40   60   80 Miles

and may not reflect the attraction of the Province to Nairobi population as such.

There were very few people from the Coast Province which accounted for only 5·86 per cent of the total population. Of these some 44·92 per cent were born in Mombasa. The second most important source of population was Kilifi-Malindi with 36·00 per cent of the Coast total. However, the Coast as a whole made a very modest contribution. It accounted for 3·25 per cent as against 0·81 per cent for the Northern Province.

The destination within the Nyanza area clearly showed the importance of the tea area of Kericho. Kericho District accounted for 31·28 per cent of the total stream. It is reasonable to assume that this lead by Kericho represented largely the demand for labour in the thriving tea industry and the development of the economy in general. However, earlier we noted that the consolidated holdings of the Kericho District were also becoming an important source of employment for the Nyanza population. Well over a half came from Nairobi area and Central Province and about a quarter from the Rift Valley.

Elgon Nyanza was the second important destination. By far the greater part of the population to this district was made up of the Rift Valley group and sources in the Nairobi area and Central Province. The importance of the Rift Valley source is probably due to its position in relation to the province in question. The contribution to Elgon Nyanza was 25·26 per cent of the total.

Central Nyanza was the third most important destination with 18·16 per cent of the total Nyanza stream. Majority of these were from the Nairobi area and the Central Province as well as the Rift Valley. The importance of Central Nyanza district may well be understood in relation to the role of Kisumu. But it is an indication of the predominant character of the population involved that the Central Nyanza District with Kisumu Township did not occupy a higher place. The lowest figures were recorded for North Nyanza (11·37 per cent), South Nyanza (7·98 per cent) and Kisii (5·95 per cent).

vi. *The Southern Province stream* (Figure 7.19)
The general poverty of the Southern Province at the time of the 1962 Census is reflected in the very small volume of migration that the province attracted from outside.

Despite its enormous size, it accounted for only 12,624 persons. It seems here that with its large areas of semi-arid and arid country it had not built up an economic base to attract a larger population. The majority of the migrant population recorded came from the main population regions of Central Provinces, Nyanza and from the adjacent Rift Valley Provinces.

The Central Province contribution accounted for 30·67 per cent and most of these came from Kiambu, Embu, Nyeri, Fort Hall, Nanyuki and Meru. Thika contributed a very small share. Out of the above total Kiambu, the leading contributor accounted for 31·50 per cent of the provincial total. Embu gave 23·52 per cent and Nyeri 16·50 per cent.

Nyanza Province, the next most important source accounted for 27·32 per cent of the total population. From this source just over 50 per cent was the Central Nyanza contribution to the stream. North Nyanza contributed 28·26 per cent of the total population. The adjacent Rift Valley Province provided 28·65 per cent of the total population mostly from Naivasha and Nakuru. The remaining districts of Kenya made very small contributions to the flow. From the Coast Province, 40 per cent had their origins in Taita and Mombasa districts. By far the greater part of the incoming population went to Machakos district. This district alone had some 48·44 per cent of the total. The concentration in Machakos reflects the greater opportunities in that district. Some parts of Machakos had large scale modern farming.

5. SELECTIVE CHARACTER OF POPULATION MOBILITY AND ITS EFFECTS ON THE MAJOR ETHNIC GROUPS

So far reference has been made to the evidence of population movements in the provinces, districts, and urban populations. It is also possible to show that factors responsible for stimulating mobility of population operate with differing intensity between different parts of the country and within different section of the population. Knowledge of the selective nature of migration is of importance in assessing the problems that arise and those that face the economic and social planners in the various parts of the country and at various ages in the population.

Emigration rates worked out on the basis of 1962 Census and for the various ethnic elements shown below confirm the selective impact of the population movements in Kenya. There is evidence of wide differences between the various ethnic groups. The figures given below are derived from subtracting the total for the home district from the national total and expressing the resulting figure as a percentage (Table 7.48).

A survey of the figures for the total emigration rates show that the ethnic groups most affected include the Kikuyu and Tharaka in the Central Province, the Luhya, Luo, Itesio and Kuria in the Nyanza Province and the Kamba in the Southern Province. Considerable movement is also shown by the Nandi, Pokot, Sabaot and the Kipsigis in the Rift Valley Province and by the Pokomo Riverine group, the Swahili-Shirazi, the Bajuni, Taita and Mijikenda in the Coast Province. The groups least affected by the movements included the Mbere and Meru of the Central Province, the Kisii of Nyanza Province, the Masai in the Southern Province, the Elgeyo and Tugen of the Rift Valley Province. Very low emigration rates were recorded for the Somali and Galla population of the Northern Province.

But the emigration rates analysed above conceal important age and sex differences in the movement. A comparative analysis on a district basis had already revealed considerable differences and that the Kenya movement is a predominantly male affair. In the Central Province the male emigration rates were far in excess of the females among the Kikuyu, Embu and Mbere. In the Nyanza Province the highest differences were among the Luhya, Luo and Kuria. A similar wide difference between the sexes was noted for the Kamba of the Southern Province. In the Rift Valley where the differences were not as wide, the Pokot and the Tugen were the most outstanding. A predominantly male movement was also recorded for the Taita, the Pokomo Riverine and the Mijikenda groups at the Coast Province.

However, for a clearer picture of the selective impact of the population movements on the population of Kenya, we may now turn to consider the age-sex pyramids for the various ethnic groups in detail. Analysis of these diagrams show clearly the widespread effects of population movements and their age range implications to the various communities among the African population. In this analysis the causes of the migration would be clearer

Table 7.48 EMIGRATION RATES OF THE PRINCIPAL ETHNIC GROUPS BY PROVINCES 1962

	Total %	Males %	Females %
Central Province			
Kikuyu	40·0	42·3	37·8
Tharaka	15·9	16·6	15·3
Embu	6·6	9·1	5·1
Mbere	3·4	5·5	1·6
Meru	1·9	3·0	0·8
Nyanza Province			
Luhya	17·6	21·7	14·3
Luo	14·0	16·8	11·2
Iteso	13·3	14·6	12·1
Kuria	8·1	11·7	4·6
Kisii	4·9	6·6	3·3
Southern Province			
Kamba	12·4	15·6	9·3
Masai	9·3	10·7	8·0
Rift Valley Province			
Nandi	37·2	38·0	36·3
Pokot	30·4	32·8	28·1
Sabaot	19·4	19·7	19·2
Kipsigis	16·5	17·6	15·4
Elgeyo	9·8	10·3	9·2
Tugen	5·9	7·5	4·3
Marakwet	2·8	3·8	1·8
Northern Province			
Somali-Galla	3·6	3·7	3·5
Samburu	3·4	4·3	2·6
Coast Province			
Pokomo-Riverine	33·0	35·0	31·0
Swahili-Shirazi	21·4	21·4	21·4
Bajuni	19·8	20·9	18·7
Taita	14·3	18·3	10·7
Mijikenda	11·2	13·0	9·3

Figure 7.20

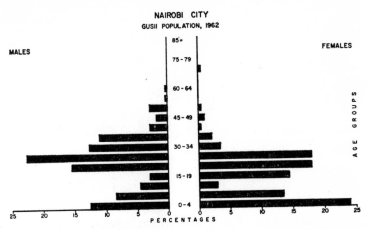

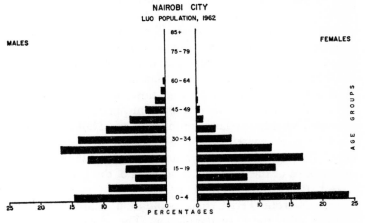

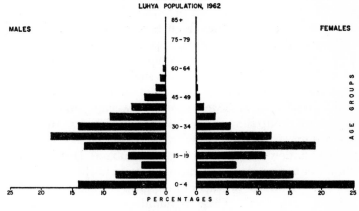

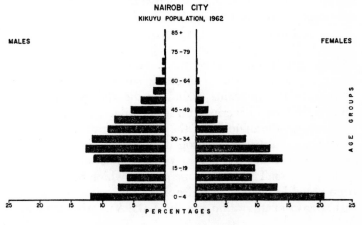

if the main destinations and the sources are considered in detail.

i. *Age-sex pyramids of the main urban destinations*

The characteristic features of the age-sex pyramids for the total African population in the Nairobi and Mombasa areas have been described. The distinctive feature noted in these areas is a distortion of the pyramid showing evidence of an influx of persons between the ages of 15 and 54 years. These figures though they reveal the youthful character of the population in these areas do not show the contributions of the various ethnic elements to the flow of population as shown below (Figures 7.20–7.29).

The pyramids for the City area show the overwhelming influence of the influx of young people in their more productive years. The standard pattern here is a broad child base followed by relatively few persons between the ages of 5 and 15 and a distinctive bulge generally between the ages of 15 and 54 years (Figures 7.20–7.22).

Within this general pattern there are subtle differences between the various ethnic groups, but age-sex pyramids for the Kikuyu group differ slightly from that of the remaining groups such as the Kamba, Luo, Luhya and others who make up the City's heterogeneous population (Figure 7.20 and 7.21). Whereas the influx of Kikuyu population shows the dominance of the ages of 15 to 54 years. The Kamba age-sex pyramid was very similar to that of the Kikuyu. But there are very few people beyond 60 years of age. Among the Taita there were very few persons beyond the age of 40. The marked absence of persons beyond this age was also a noticeable feature of the long distance movement from Nyanza and the Coast. However, among the Kikuyu there were a significant number of people beyond the age of 49.

The female migration rate which is lower than that of the males appears primarily to affect the ages of 15 and 35. But among the Mbere the women were mostly ages 15 to 30 years (Figure 7.22). The population movement is thus not merely selective between the sexes but also operates differently within the same population and sex group.

Among the Kikuyu in Nairobi, there were more women beyond 35 years of age. Among the Nyanza group few women were migrating beyond the age of 44. Similarly the

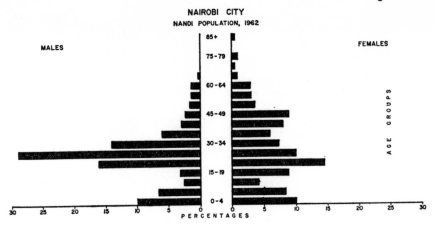

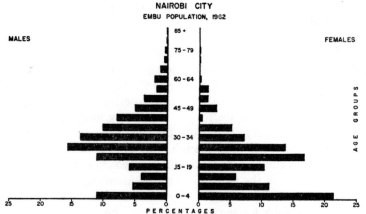

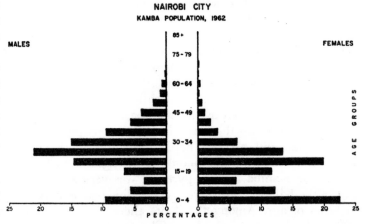

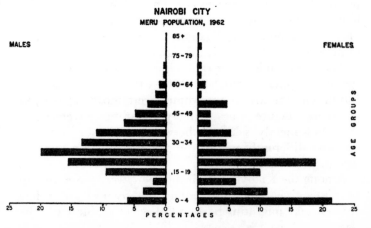

Coast group also had very few women beyond that age. In this respect the Nandi female pattern is unique. The Nandi are not among the foremost migrants and yet their age-sex pyramid showed a significant proportion of the women in the ages above 34 years. The same feature is noted among the Kipsigis population of the City of Nairobi. Although a fuller explanation would require more research, it is possible that this pattern reflects the historic differences in the employment pattern among the men and women. A large number of the Nandi females have been associated with the domestic services in the City. The age dominance among the men showed the importance of the 25–29 whereas most of the City women were between the ages of 20–24.

The Nairobi Peri-Urban population shared similar features with the City population. There was the same tendency for most of the population to fall between the ages of 15 and 54. But even here the differences between the sexes are quite distinct (Figures 7.23 and 7.24).

Most of the Kikuyu women appeared to be aged 19 to 40 years. The most dominant group was between the ages 25 and 29. The Kamba group was slightly younger and so were the majority of the Luhya women. The Luo women in the Peri-Urban area were mostly between 25 and 29 but the Nandi group showed the dominance of the 15–19 year age group.

The national importance of Mombasa District in population movements is clearly expressed in the following age-sex pyramids of the ethnic groups most affected (Figure 7.25–7.27). These pyramids suggest two main features. There is first the distinctive feature presented by the major up-country population such as the Kikuyu, Tharaka, Embu, Meru (Figure 7.25) and the Luhya, Luo, Kamba, Gusii (Kisii) (Figure 7.26) the Nandi, Kipsigis, Mbere and Kuria (Figure 7.27). Secondly, there is the group representing the main ethnic sources of the Coast. These are the migrants including the Bajuni, Swahili-Shirazi, Pokomo Riverine and Mijikenda. The last group accounts for the majority of the Coast migrants.

The up-country population drawn from the principal ethnic sources shown is dominated by the population aged 15 to 49 years. This is the same pattern which has already been noted in the case of Nairobi. The principal groups in this stream of migration are the Lake Victoria elements

Figure 7.22

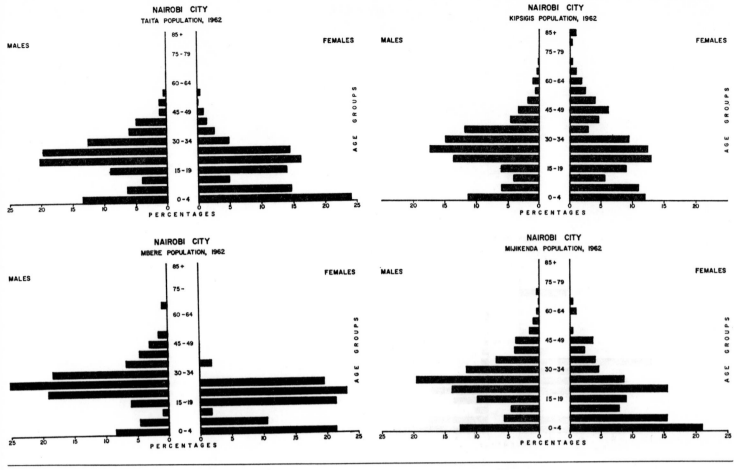

NAIROBI CITY
TAITA POPULATION, 1962

NAIROBI CITY
KIPSIGIS POPULATION, 1962

NAIROBI CITY
MBERE POPULATION, 1962

NAIROBI CITY
MIJIKENDA POPULATION, 1962

Figure 7.23

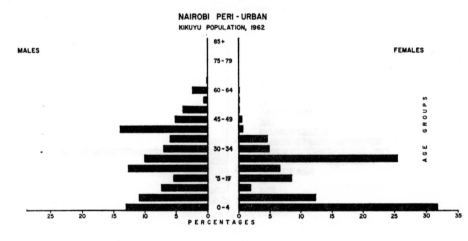

NAIROBI PERI - URBAN
KIKUYU POPULATION, 1962

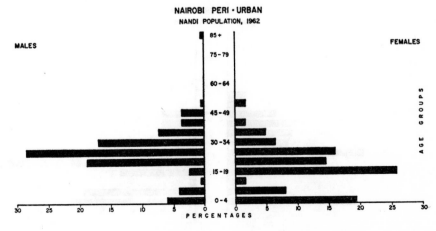

NAIROBI PERI - URBAN
NANDI POPULATION, 1962

Figure 7.24

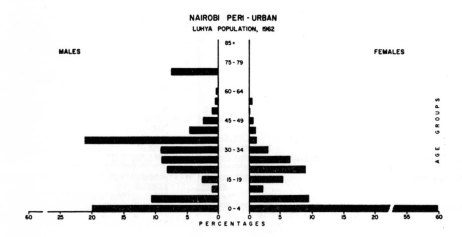

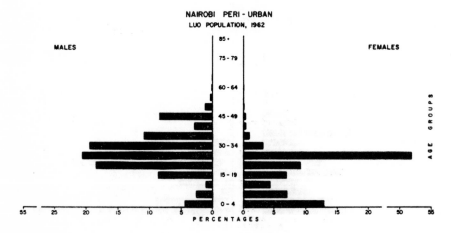

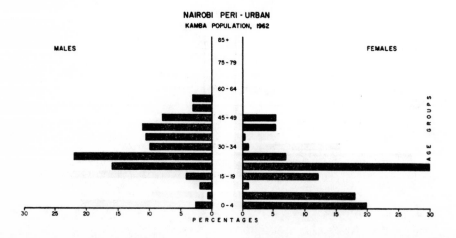

Figure 7.25

Figure 7.26

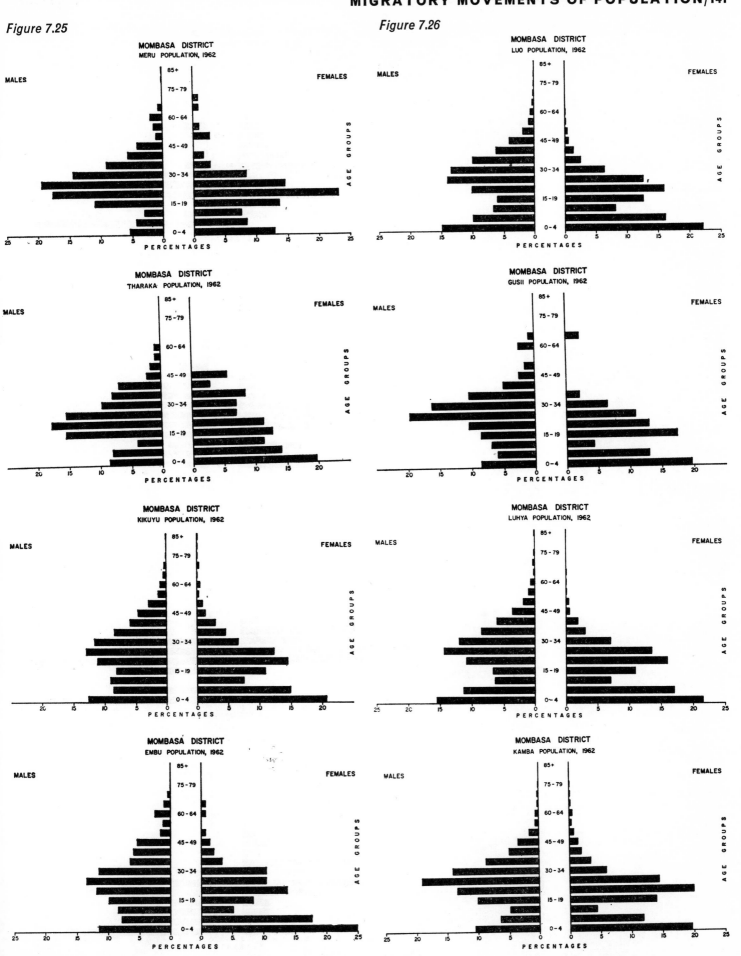

Figure 7.27

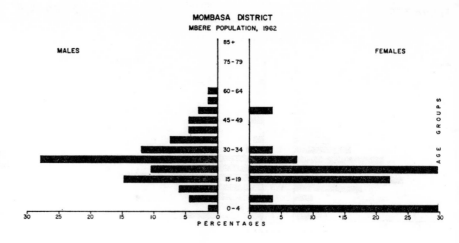

MOMBASA DISTRICT
MBERE POPULATION, 1962

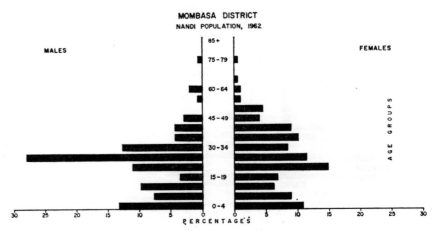

MOMBASA DISTRICT
NANDI POPULATION, 1962

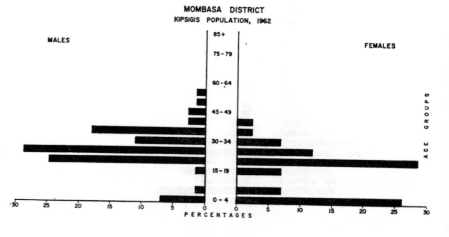

MOMBASA DISTRICT
KIPSIGIS POPULATION, 1962

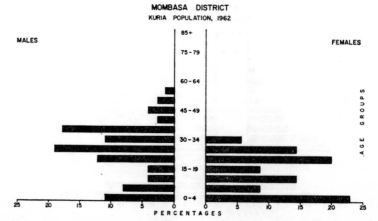

MOMBASA DISTRICT
KURIA POPULATION, 1962

Figure 7.28

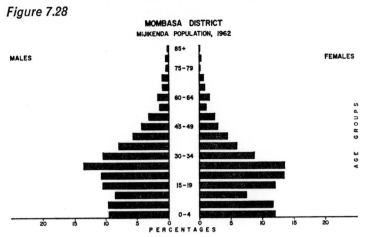

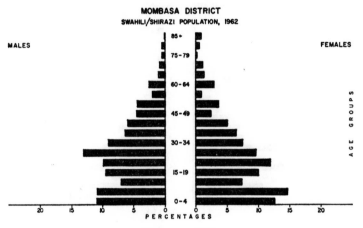

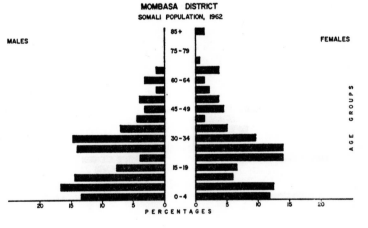

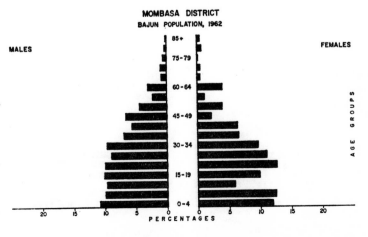

such as the Luo and the Luhya groups (Figure 7.26). The Eastern Province group is dominated by the Kamba. These are the population elements whose composition have such a profound effect on the structure of Mombasa's population. However, it will be noted that among them there are subtle differences. In the case of the Nandi, (Figure 7.27), the proportion of women in the age group above 35 is far higher than in most groups. The Mbere group is largely a male community with very few children and women. These last elements of the Mbere population were largely between the ages of 15 and 30 years.

Among the Coast migrants there are definitely more children in the population samples (Figure 7.28). The Swahili-Shirazi and the Mijikenda groups suggest population approaching some stability. However, the influence of migration between 15 and 54 years is still clear. In these groups there appear to be far more older people in the population between the ages 40 to 60 years. Even among the more distant Bajuni population, the proportion of children in the population is quite high. The Somali population is clearly a migrant group which has more in common with the up-country patterns considered earlier. The Pokomo-Riverine group, the Taita, and Taveta, all show the impact of the movement into Mombasa.

ii. *Age-Sex pyramids of the Rift Valley* (Figures 7.30–7.50)
The rural areas of Kenya are affected by two types of movements of unequal intensity. There is the inward movement for which the provincial units have been used as a basis. In this first category of movement we are involved primarily with the problem of inter-Provincial exchange of population. Analysis of the 1962 birthplace statistics has already established the inward flow of population into the Rift Valley Province as the largest in volume. In this national movement the inflow of population far exceeds the outflow. However, in addition to this important inter-provincial exchange of population, there is evidence of inter-district exchanges of population which throw light on the causes of population movement. In this sense, it is necessary first to consider the selective impact of the movements on the ethnic groups normally resident in the Rift Valley Province. Here again the distinction between the former 'White Highland' districts and the predominantly African districts emerges.

Figure 7.29

Figure 7.30

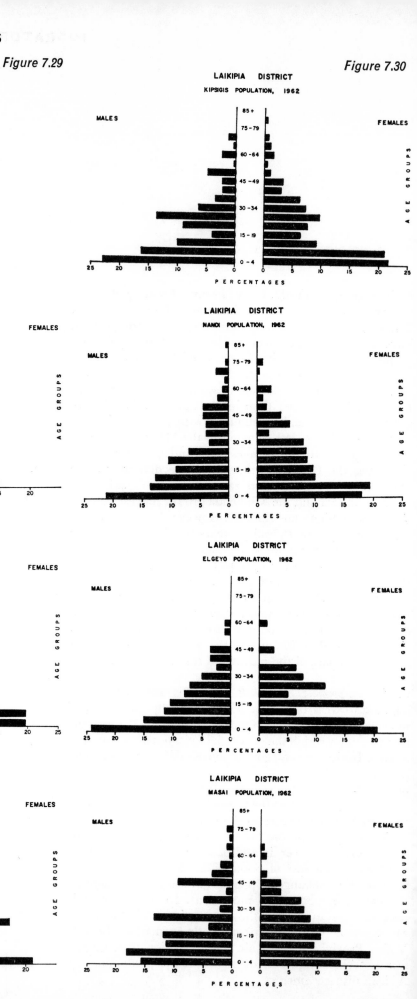

MOMBASA DISTRICT
POKOMO/RIVERINE POPULATION, 1962

MALES · FEMALES · AGE GROUPS

MOMBASA DISTRICT
TAVETA POPULATION, 1962

MALES · FEMALES · AGE GROUPS

MOMBASA DISTRICT
TAITA POPULATION, 1962

MALES · FEMALES · AGE GROUPS

Figure 7.31

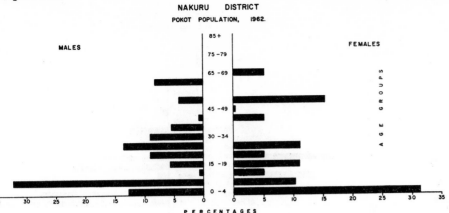

NAKURU   DISTRICT
POKOT POPULATION, 1962.

MALES   FEMALES

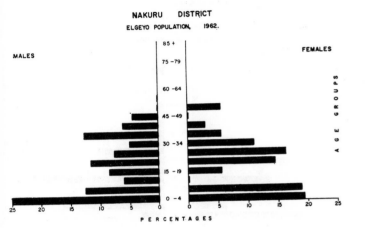

NAKURU   DISTRICT
ELGEYO POPULATION, 1962.

MALES   FEMALES

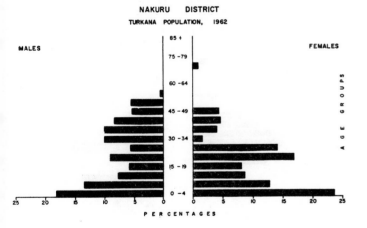

NAKURU   DISTRICT
TURKANA POPULATION, 1962

MALES   FEMALES

In the Laikipia district the age-sex pyramids show a distinctive movement of the Kipsigis element into the district (Figure 7.30). But there is hardly any evidence of a recent significant inflow of the Nandi population. The Nandi pyramid in fact suggest a deficiency of men especially between the ages 30 and 34. Further there is evidence of Masai movement into the district which draws in the male population between the ages of 15 to 34. There appears to be another bulge in the male population between the ages 40 and 50. On the female side the movement seems to affect mostly the ages between 10 and 39 years.

Nakuru district provides the most striking example of selective migration (Figure 7.31). The effect on the ethnic groups is nationwide. But in the Rift Valley itself the movement appears to have affected the Pokot, Elgeyo, Turkana, Tugen, Kipsigis, Nandi and the Masai. The Pokot migration is a short distance movement involving the male population between the ages 15 to 39 years. But the age range among the women shows the dominance of the 15–19 year age group and those between 25 and 29 years.

The Elgeyo movement is more clearly defined with the men showing the dominance of the 15–30 year age group and those between 35 and 39 years. The age emphasis among the women is primarily between 15 and 44 years. Among the Turkana the male population moving into Nakuru district is largely aged 15 to 25 and 25 to 50 years. The women are mainly concentrated between 15 and 29 years. However, there is a marked increase in the proportion of males between the ages of 25 and 50. The female inward migration appears to affect largely the age range 15 to 29. Most of the females were aged 20 to 24 years. The dominant age bracket for the males was between 20 and 24 years.

An interesting pattern is presented by the Tugen population in the district (Figure 7.32). Here we see a definite bulge in the male population between the ages 10 and 34. This is a comparatively youthful movement. It is matched on the female side by the preponderance of the ages 10 to 49 years. In the case of the Kipsigis population of Nakuru the male movement has attracted the adults between the ages of 20 and 54 years. The women were mostly found between the ages of 15 and 49 years. There is similar

Figure 7.32

Figure 7.33

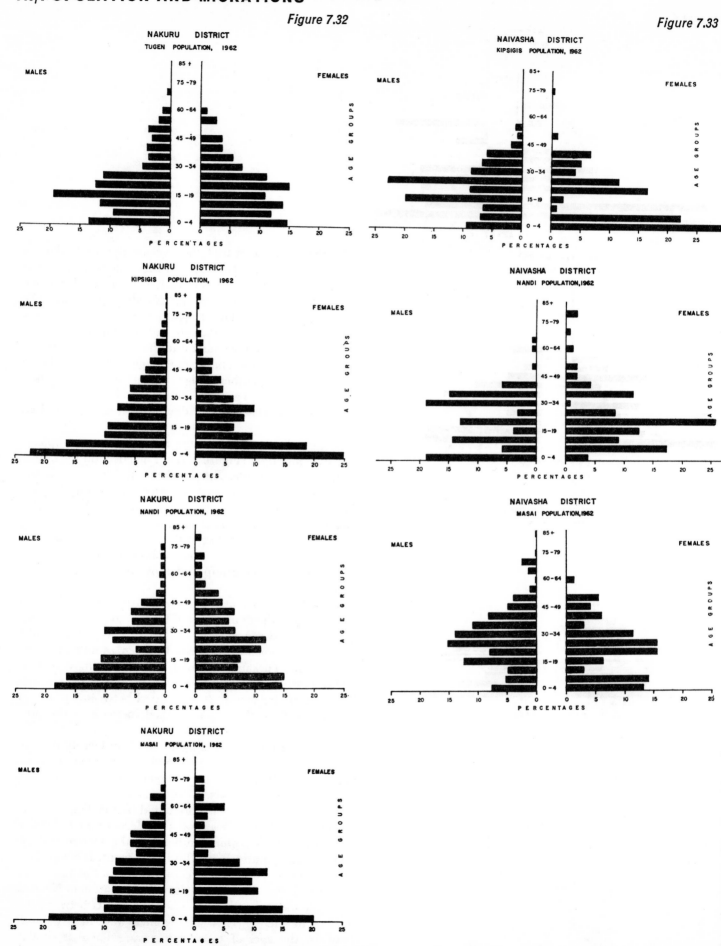

Figure 7.34

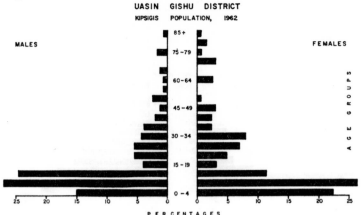

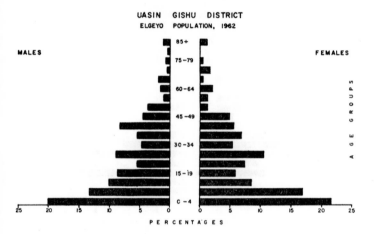

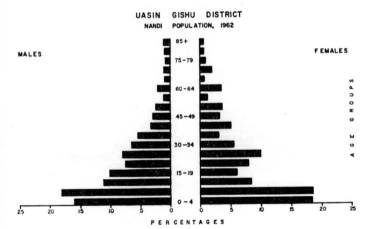

evidence of movement of the Nandi population with the men being grouped between the ages 20 and 49 years and the women falling between the years 15 to 54 (Figure 7.32).

The Masai group were found both in the Rift Valley and in the Southern Province. The movement into the Nakuru District which the age-sex pyramid suggests may be partly due to the extra-provincial sources or from the Masai resident in other Rift Valley districts. The men appeared to be aged between 20 and 24 and 35 to 50 years but the women were mainly aged 15 to 34 years.

In general it could be said that movement into Naivasha district seems to have attracted the same ethnic groups as Nakuru. The important Nandi group here shows an inflow of male youths and adults. The former were mostly aged 10 to 14 but the adult groups showed concentration at two different points. There were males aged 20 to 24 and 30 to 40. The females were largely between 15 and 29 and also from 35 to 44 years of age (Figure 7.33). The Kipsigis group showed a similar trend with the males being selected between the ages 15 to 24 and also from 25 to 40 years. The females appear to have been largely from the older groups with most of them falling between 20 and 29 years and from 34 to 45 years. The Masai males show a preference between the ages of 15 to 20 and between 20 and 50 years whilst the females were mostly aged 15 to 34 years and from 35 to 54 years.

In the Uasin Gishu District (Figure 7.34) the inward movement of the indigenous population of the Rift Valley Province seems to have largely affected the Elgeyo population. Here a double peak is characteristic of the male population between the ages of 20 and 49 years and female population between 15 and 49 years. The Kipsigis population in the district also showed an inflow and appeared to be largely overburdened by children. The majority of the males and females were aged 15 to 39 years.

In the Trans-Nzoia district there is a definite evidence of movement involving the Iteso, Nandi, Kipsigis, Masai, Turkana and even the Sabaot population (Figures 7.35 and 7.36). The Nandi movement appears to conform to the standard migratory pattern affecting mainly the age groups 15 to 40 years among the males and females. In the case of the Kipsigis a similar pattern is suggested, but most males were within the age range 25–34 years. Among the women the immigrating population generally appeared to

Figure 7.35   *Figure 7.36*

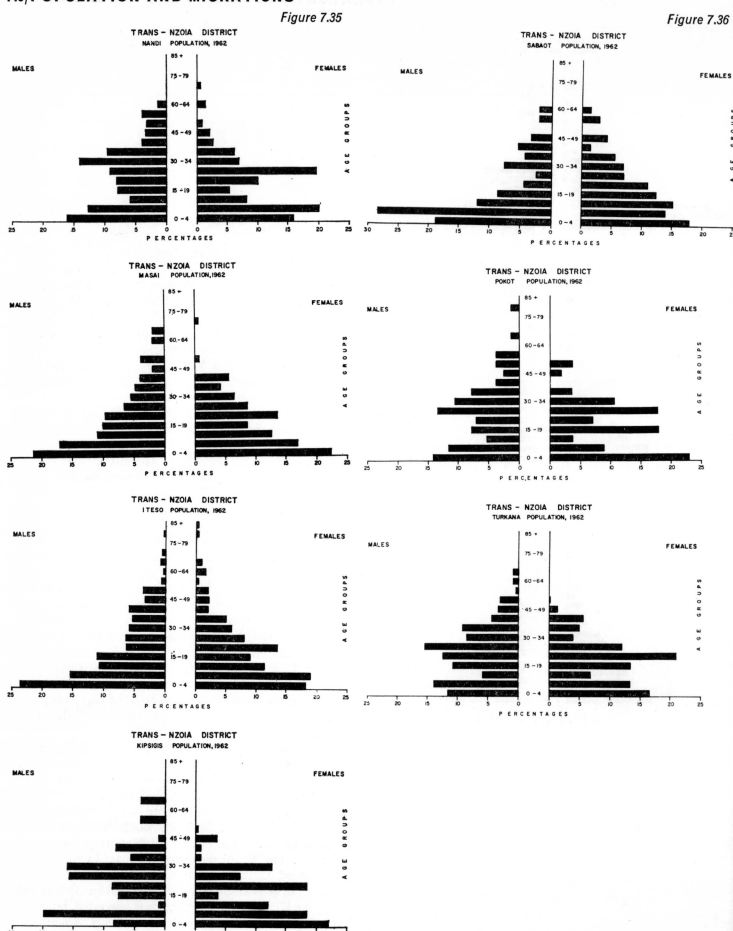

Figure 7.37

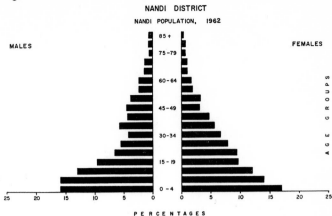

be aged 15 to 34 years but the most important age bracket was 20 to 24 years. Evidence of movement among the Masai was clearer in the female population between the ages of 15 and 44.

Perhaps more striking are the short range movements of the Pokot, the Turkana population. They could be regarded as the normal pattern of migration largely falling between the ages 15 to 45 years. The Pokot pyramid shows the male population to be dominated by the 25 to 29 year age group whereas that of the women shows the 15 to 19 year and the 25 to 34 year age groups as most important.

The Turkana population clearly shows the movement into the district between the ages 15 and 54 for the men. The female population is dominated by the age range 15 to 49 years. The most important age group among the men is 25 to 29 and for the women 20 to 24 years.

In contrast to the movements outlined above the former African districts appear to function within the Rift Valley province as sources of population for the inter-district movement as well as for the national migrations. In the Nandi district, the age-sex pyramid of the Nandi shows a drain of the male population between 15 and 35 years (Figure 7.37). A similar feature appears among the Suk and the Tugen populations of Baringo district where the deficiency occurs between the ages 20 and 34 years (Figure 7.38 and 7.39).

In West Pokot, the Pokot movement appears as a deficiency in the male pyramid between the ages 15 and 44. There was however slight movement of the Sabaot into West Pokot (Figure 7.40). But the Turkana pattern suggests some movement into the district. The shortage of the male population is far more pronounced in Marakwet and the Elgeyo population of Elgeyo-Marakwet district (Figure 7.41). Movement of the Rift Valley ethnic groups is therefore primarily short range in character between the various districts within the Rift Valley. But the deficiency noted in the home districts of some groups is most certainly a reflection of the extra-provincial flow or transfers of population.

However, the evidence of population mobility which affects the Rift Valley element is just part of the national movement. The influence of this movement on the various ethnic groups of Kenya is strikingly shown in the former settled districts. From the provincial point of view, it

Figure 7.38

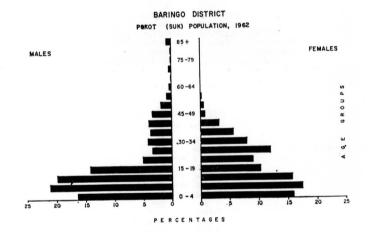

Figure 7.39

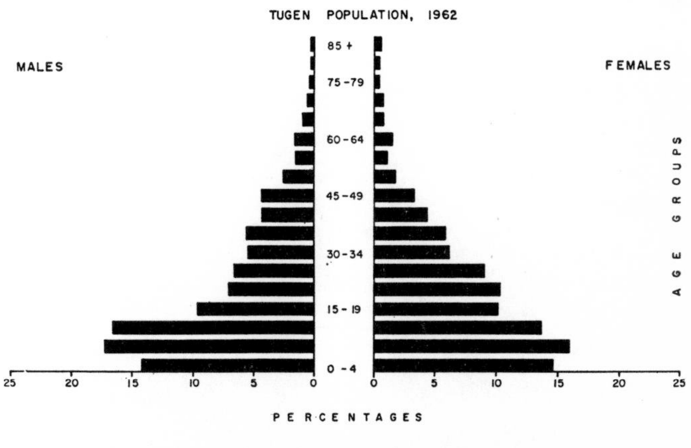

Figure 7.40

Figure 7.41

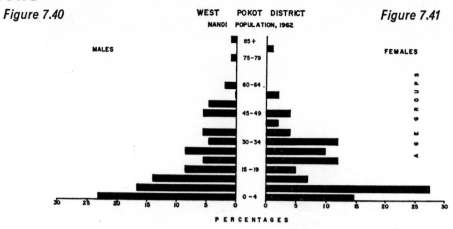

WEST POKOT DISTRICT
NANDI POPULATION, 1962

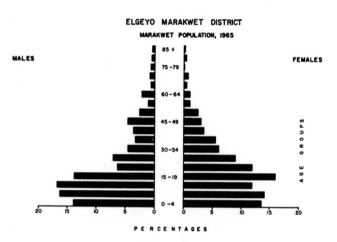

ELGEYO MARAKWET DISTRICT
MARAKWET POPULATION, 1965

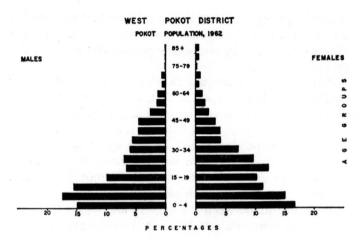

WEST POKOT DISTRICT
POKOT POPULATION, 1962

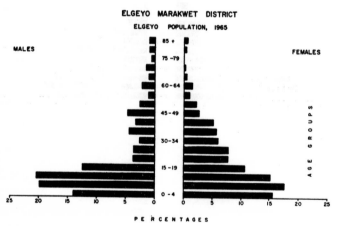

ELGEYO MARAKWET DISTRICT
ELGEYO POPULATION, 1965

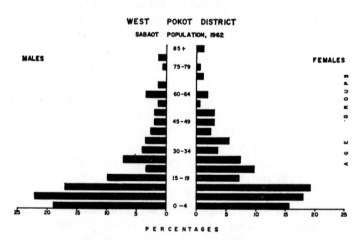

WEST POKOT DISTRICT
SABAOT POPULATION, 1962

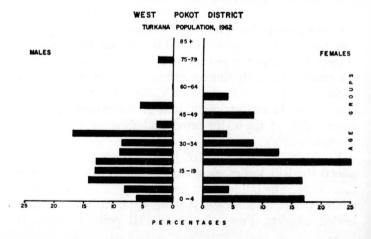

WEST POKOT DISTRICT
TURKANA POPULATION, 1962

Figure 7.42

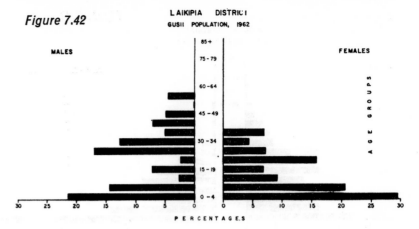

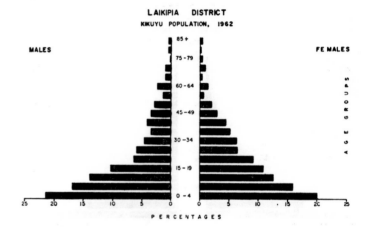

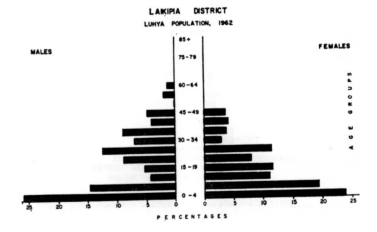

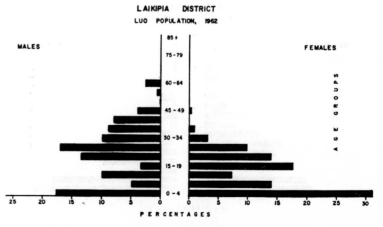

would appear that the Kikuyu element should be regarded as an important movement into the Rift Valley. But examination of the Laikipia district shows the Kikuyu element here as a well established population showing a slight deficiency of the male population between the ages 20 and 39. (Figure 7.43)

The Kikuyu element might be regarded as an older movement which differs from the more recent migrant pattern of the Luhya population. The Luhya group is a typical pattern dominated by an inflow of males between 15 and 49 years. There is a corresponding flow of females between the ages 15 and 29. Apart from the Luhya the district appears to have attracted the Gusii (Kisii) and the Luo (Figure 7.42). The Gusii pyramid shows the importance of the age group 14–24 among the males. There is a secondary affect showing the prominence of the 20 to 49 year age bracket in the population. Among the Gusii women the predominance of the age group 20 to 24 should be noted. As in most cases of the younger migrants, the young children form the largest proportion among the sexes. Luo movement appears to have attracted the males largely between the ages of 15 to 49 whilst the female age range falls between 10 and 39 years. The most important age group among the males is 25 to 29 years whereas the women tend to be much younger and generally between 15 and 19 years of age.

Nakuru district has emerged as one of the most important destinations for the national migration. The movement into this district is national in importance. Here the ethnic groups most intensely affected are the Kikuyu, Luo, Luhya, Kamba, Gusii, Iteso and Taita (Figure 7.43–7.44). The Kikuyu pyramid here again shows a striking difference with the remaining ethnic groups from outside the Rift Valley. It is a population that appears to have been living in the district for some time. However, it is possible that the bulge between 20 and 34 years is caused by inward migration (Figure 7.43).

The remaining age-sex pyramids show the standard pattern of recent movements involving the 15 to 54 years age bracket among the Luo males and 15 to 44 among the females. The most important male group is aged 25 to 29 years whereas among the women this is confined to between 20 and 24 years. There is a similar range among the Luhya who already form one of the most important

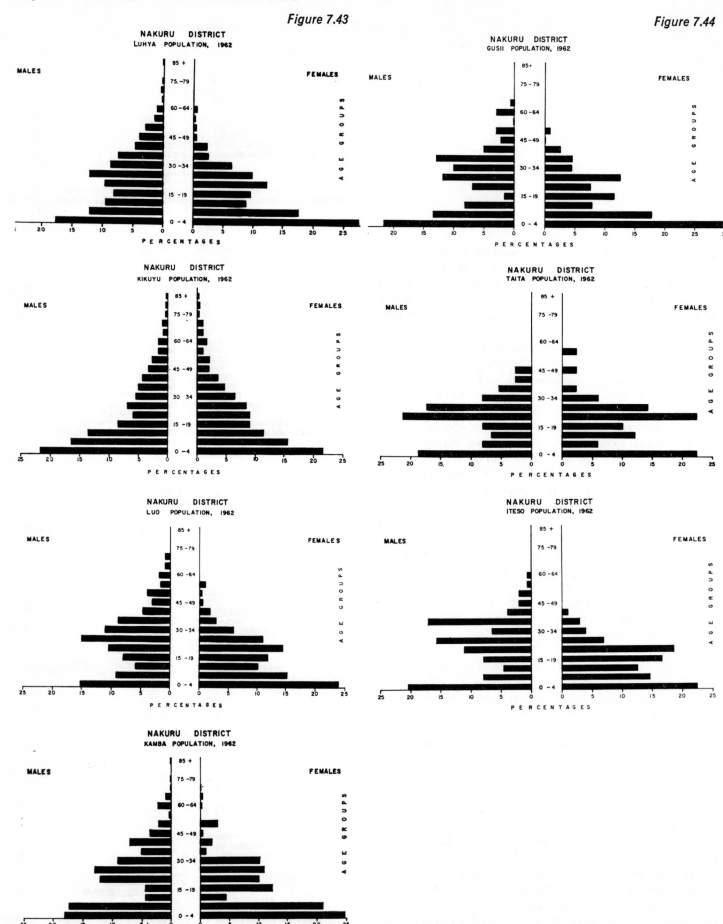

Figure 7.43

Figure 7.44

Figure 7.45

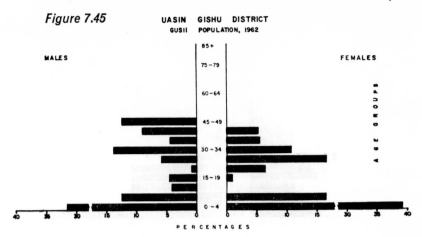

UASIN GISHU DISTRICT
GUSII POPULATION, 1962

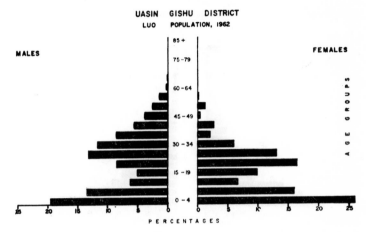

UASIN GISHU DISTRICT
LUO POPULATION, 1962

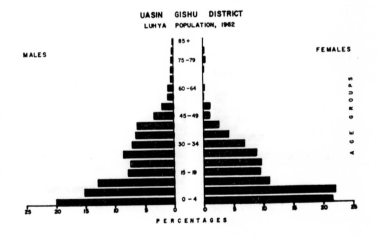

UASIN GISHU DISTRICT
LUHYA POPULATION, 1962

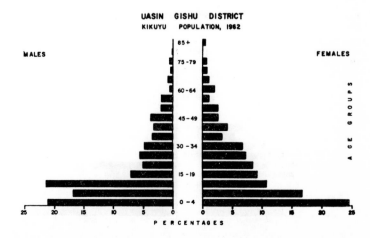

UASIN GISHU DISTRICT
KIKUYU POPULATION, 1962

elements in the national population mobility. Here the age-sex pyramid shows that the movement into Nakuru district is dominated by the male group in the 15–54 age bracket and for the females 15 to 44 years (Figure 7.43). Among the Kamba population the age-sex pyramid shows a distortion generally between 15 and 49 years for the males. But the female movement largely affects the younger people between 15 and 34 years of age. This is the standard pattern of rural to urban and rural to rural movements in response to economic situations (Figure 7.43).

In the remaining groups the Gusii movement into Nakuru draws between the ages 20 and 54 (Figure 7.44). But among the females the age range seem to fall between 10 and 44 years. The most important age bracket for the men is 35 to 39 and the women 25 to 29 years. Iteso movement of males appears generally to affect the ages 15 to 40. But there were very few women beyond the age of 34 (Figure 7.44). The age-sex pyramid for the ethnic group showed the dominance of the 10 to 24 year bracket. The most important was the 20 to 24 year age group. This again is essentially a youthful population characterised by a broad base of young dependants and concentration of population between 15 years and 39 years.

The influx of a youthful population of both sexes which is a feature of the above ethnic groups is repeated by the Taita age-sex pyramid of Nakuru district (Figure 7.44). The Taita males are moving largely between the ages 15 and 49 years. By far the most important group is composed of young men between the ages of 20 and 24 years. The females are more numerous between 14 and 34 years.

In the Uasin Gishu district the Kikuyu age-sex pyramid conforms to the pattern we have observed for the other districts in the Rift Valley. This lends support to the view that the Kikuyu population is either dominated by the long established farm labour or is selective of a more balanced population sample (Figure 7.45).

A typical migrant pattern is reflected in the age-sex pyramid for the Luo population (Figure 7.45). We have already noted a similar pattern in the urban areas. Here the Uasin Gishu movement appears to attract the males between the usual ages of 15 and 54 and the females between 15 and 44 years of age. This youthful population has a broad base of children between the ages 0–9 years.

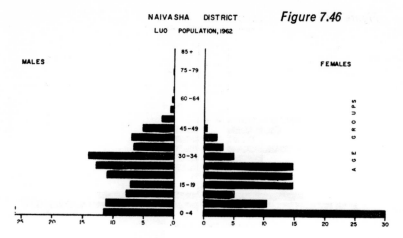

NAIVASHA DISTRICT   *Figure 7.46*

LUO POPULATION, 1962

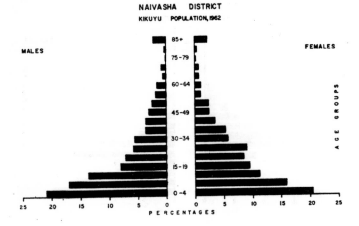

NAIVASHA DISTRICT

KIKUYU POPULATION, 1962

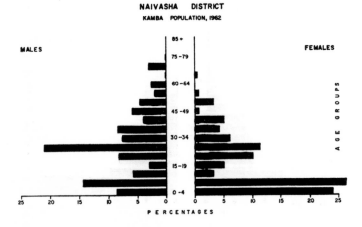

NAIVASHA DISTRICT

KAMBA POPULATION, 1962

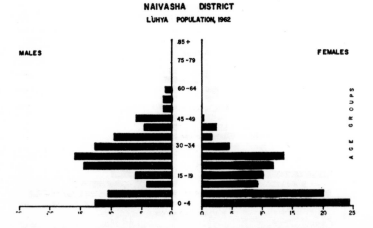

NAIVASHA DISTRICT

LUHYA POPULATION, 1962

The very young ones from 0 to 4 years dominate the population samples.

Less striking is the Luhya pyramid (Figure 7.45). This sample is of interest in that it reflects the effect of proximity of the district to the Luhya source districts. The pyramid is not intensely distorted by an influx of the 15 to 44 age group. But there is definite evidence of an inflow between the ages 15 to 40 years for both sexes. There are more older male people over 50 years.

Gusii migration is limited to men between the ages 25 to 49. Most of the females are aged 20 to 44 years (Figure 7.45). The age-sex pyramid does not show males over 9 years and women over 44 years.

In the Naivasha district, the history of the Kikuyu population again emerges clearly in the age-sex pyramids (Figure 7.46). The distortion between the ages of 15 and 45 years which characterises the ethnic groups most affected by recent influx of people of working age is absent. In fact there is virtually no difference between the age-sex pyramid for the ethnic group as shown by Naivasha and what are regarded as the home based districts of the Kikuyu people. Here is another example of an age-sex structure which stands in sharp contrast to those of groups such as Kamba, Luhya and the Luo which constitute the principal recent movements into the district. Since Naivasha is located next to the source districts of Kikuyu population this movement is a short range transfer of population.

The Kamba migration here appears to have attracted primarily those between the ages of 15 and 59 years. Among the females, the population movement is more important between 10 and 44 years and the age-sex pyramids shows clearly the importance of young children age 0–9 years (Figure 7.46).

The Luhya pattern is a clearly defined migrant pattern. Among the males it appears that the movement has again involved the able bodied persons between the ages 15 to 44 years (Figure 7.46). The women are in general younger and there seem to be more younger children in the female sample. The age range for the female movement is between 10 years and 39 years with the age bracket of 25 to 29 as the most important. It is interesting in this as in most migrant samples that there are virtually no women above the age of 50.

Figure 7.47

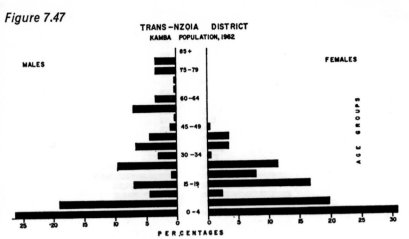

TRANS–NZOIA DISTRICT
KAMBA POPULATION, 1962

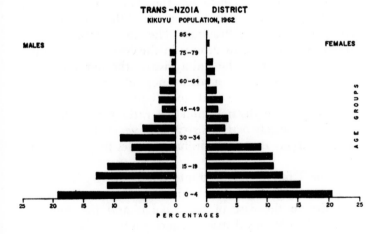

TRANS–NZOIA DISTRICT
LUO POPULATION, 1962

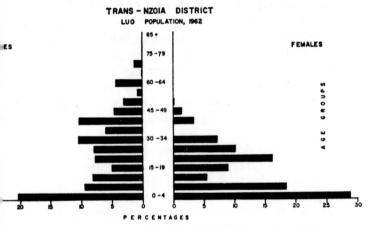

TRANS–NZOIA DISTRICT
KIKUYU POPULATION, 1962

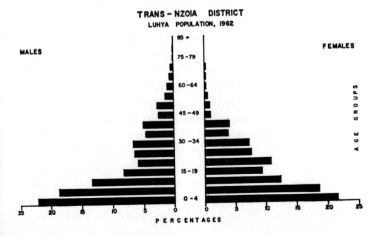

TRANS–NZOIA DISTRICT
LUHYA POPULATION, 1962

The Naivasha Luo population (Figure 7.46) closely resembles the age pattern of the Luhya. But there appears to be a concentration of the migration between 15 and 54 years. Most of the males were within the 30 to 34 years age range. But the female movement appears to have attracted the 15 to 34 year age group. The Luo therefore appear to bring with them much younger women to places of work.

In the extreme north-west of the former 'White Highlands' the Trans-Nzoia district appears to rely on immigration of the Kikuyu, Kamba, Luo and Luhya element. The example presented here may have been affected by certain inaccuracies in reporting and smallness of sample (Figure 7.47). However, it is possible to note the distinctive effect of an inflow of Kikuyu population. This appears to have affected the males between the ages of 10 and 35 years.

In the Kamba movement, while the general pattern seems to suggest a number of movements the most important age group among the migrants appear to be the 25 to 29 age bracket. The females were mostly aged 15 to 29. A further heaping of male and female population between the ages of 30 and 49 should also be noted.

Inward migration is also the main explanation of the pattern of the Luo ethnic group, in the pyramid movement appears to have affected the age range 15 to 44 years among the males. Two age groups from 36 to 34 and from 40 and 44 are particularly prominent in the samples. Among the females the movement had largely drawn people aged 15 to 34 years. But the most important age bracket among the adults is the 20 to 24 year group.

The Luhya pattern is distinctly different from that of the other ethnic groups. The effect of influx of both males and females between the ages of 20 and 39 is here masked by a probable influence of a long resident stable population and out migration. The stability of the Luhya population is further suggested by the presence of more older people both men and women above the age of 50 years and suggests a similar situation to that of the Kikuyu in Naivasha and Nakuru districts. (Figure 7.47)

Movement of ethnic elements from outside the Rift Valley Province into the former African districts is of a very limited nature. Analysis of the age-sex pyramid shows some movement of the Luhya people into Nandi district mostly of younger males between the ages 15 and 34

Figure 7.48

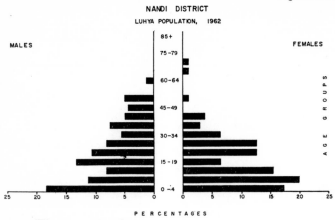

NANDI DISTRICT
LUHYA POPULATION, 1962

Figure 7.49

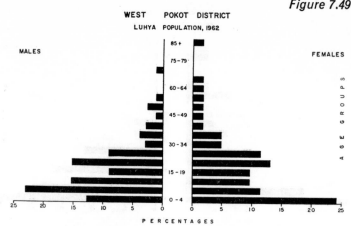

WEST POKOT DISTRICT
LUHYA POPULATION, 1962

years (Figure 7.48). There is a similar movement of Luhya people into the nearby West Pokot district (Figure 7.49). A similar minor movement of the Kamba people is suggested in the Baringo district (Figure 7.50).

iii. *Age-Sex pyramids of the Coast Province* (Figures 7.51–7.59) In the earlier summary on population mobility the Coast Province emerged as the third most important destination. It was also noted that the Coast stream of migration is overshadowed by the effect of the port of Mombasa and Mombasa district. Analysis of the impact of Mombasa district has shown that the selective effect is national.

Movement into the province and within the province is only partly urban. The population movements in the rural areas of the Coast form an important chapter in the total national migration. The evidence for this mobility appears among the various ethnic groups of the province and also among the ethnic elements that are attracted to the Coast Province from other parts of the country. Examination of the age-sex pyramids of the Coast ethnic groups show the importance of the Pokomo-Riverine, the Swahili-Shirazi, the Bajuni, Taita and the Mijikenda in the migrations. These ethnic groups are not merely involved in the inter-district mobility but are also affected by the national pull of certain areas outside the Coast Province.

In general the most important Coast ethnic groups show little evidence of movement within the Coast Province. The age-sex pyramid for Mijikenda, the largest of the ethnic groups actually shows a deficiency of the adult male population in the home districts of the group at the Coast. This deficiency reflects more its contribution to the national stream of migration from the districts of Kwale and Kilifi-Malindi (Figure 7.51). In Kwale and Kilifi-Malindi districts the males between the critical ages of 20 and 29 generally comprise less than 8 per cent of the population where the female proportion is 10 per cent or more. Movement within the Coast Province is confined to Mombasa District and to Tana River, Lamu and Taita districts.

In Tana River district movement of the Mijikenda population appeared to have attracted males between the ages of 20 and 39 and females between the ages of 15 and 44 years. Males were most dominant in the 25 to 29 age bracket and the female adults were most numerous

between 20 and 24 years of age. Lamu district has a predominantly Arab population. But the age-sex pyramid of the Mijikenda suggests movement into this district of males largely aged 20 to 49 years. The population sample clearly showed a very small percentage of children. This then is primarily a movement of adult population. The females showed the dominance of the 20 to 44 year age bracket. But majority of the females were aged 25 to 29 years.

In the interior district of Taita, the Mijikenda is one of the main sources of labour. The movement appears to have affected the males aged 15 to 29 years and 29 to 49 years. Among the females the pyramids show the 15 to 29 year group and the age bracket of 29 to 44 years as the most important in the sample (Figure 7.52).

The age-sex pyramids for the Taita underlines the importance of this ethnic element as the second largest group in the Coast Province. The Taita population are among the prominent groups in the Mombasa stream of migrations. Within the Taita district the pyramid of the ethnic group shows a deficiency of males especially between the ages 20 and 39 (Figure 7.52). This is in contrast to the district total sex ratio which showed a deficiency largely between 20 and 24 years. The difference here is largely due to the influx of males from outside the district.

Some Taita have moved into Kwale district. The population here shows features which we have associated with stability in the case of the Kikuyu and the Luhya in certain Rift Valley districts. There is a broad base of child population and a significant proportion of older people above the age of 50 years (Figure 7.52).

In the case of the Pokomo-Riverine group the loss of male population between the ages of 20 and 24 years is suggested. Unlike the men, the Pokomo-Riverine females seem to be staying behind especially between the ages of 20 and 34 years (Figure 7.53). However, in the Kilifi-Malindi district, the Pokomo-Riverine population form a small but significant group of migrants. The most important age bracket seems to be 20 and 34 years for the males and 15 to 24 for the females. But the presence of an important group of males aged 40 to 44 should be noted. The Pokomo-Riverine migration is primarily an adult movement with few children below the ages of 14 years. Apart

Figure 7.50

Figure 7.51

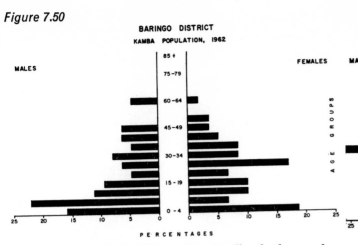

BARINGO DISTRICT
KAMBA POPULATION, 1962

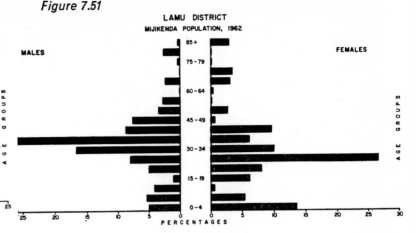

LAMU DISTRICT
MIJIKENDA POPULATION, 1962

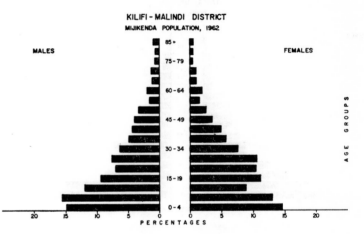

KILIFI - MALINDI DISTRICT
MIJIKENDA POPULATION, 1962

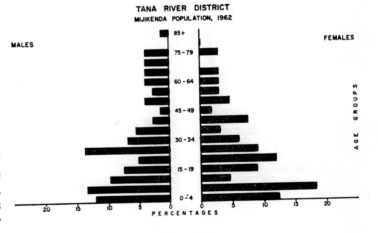

TANA RIVER DISTRICT
MIJIKENDA POPULATION, 1962

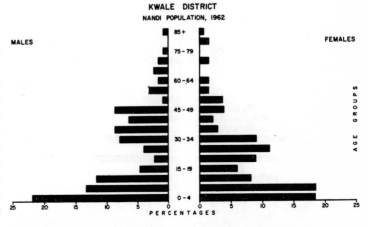

KWALE DISTRICT
NANDI POPULATION, 1962

from the inter-district migrations outlined above, there are other movements which involve the smaller Coast ethnic elements. Among these are the Boni-Sanye, the Swahili-Shirazi, and the Bajuni population to Lamu. There is a significant movement of Pokomo-Riverine population to the same district.

The Coast Province has in the past largely drawn its labour force from the important up-country ethnic elements such as the Kamba, Luo, Kikuyu and the Luhya. But in addition the age-sex pyramids show movement of the pastoral communities largely into the north-eastern areas of the Province. This latter movement is small compared to the volume of the up-country flow on which much of the economy of the Province has depended. Although the migrating population is youthful in character, there are significant differences between the districts which the age-sex pyramids of the area show.

In Kilifi-Malindi district the most important elements were the Kamba, Luo, Luhya and Kikuyu (Figure 7.54). The Kamba movement from their districts adjacent to the Coast appears to have affected the adult male population between the ages 20 and 49. Most of the adult males were within the 35 and 39 age bracket. Among the females, migration has tended to affect the population between the ages 10 to 34 years. In this the dominant adult age bracket was 25 to 29 years. The general features of the Kamba pyramid show a changing population. It suggests an earlier migration which though still dominated by an influx of young people between the ages of 15 to 35 is changing towards a more stable pattern. There were far more people above the age of 50 in the case of both sexes than is common among the other migrants. A further significant feature of the population is the presence of a large number of dependent children aged 0 to 9 years (Figure 7.54).

The Luo age-sex pyramid for Kilifi-Malindi district shows a number of striking features. There is no doubt about the importance of an influx of adults between the ages 20 and 44. The male migration is clearly concentrated between the ages 20 and 44 years with the 30 to 34 years as the most important age bracket. However, it should be noted that even in this population sample, there is a significant group of older people increasing from above 40 which probably suggests an earlier movement. The

Figure 7.52

Figure 7.53

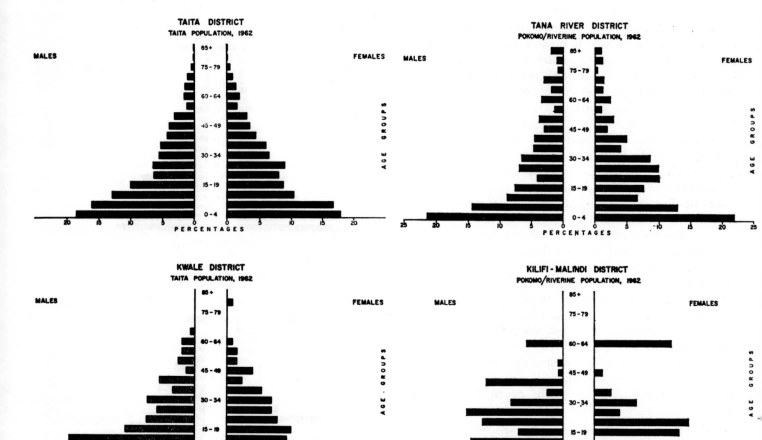

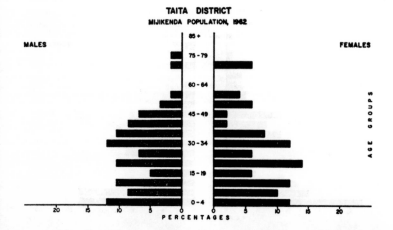

Figure 7.54

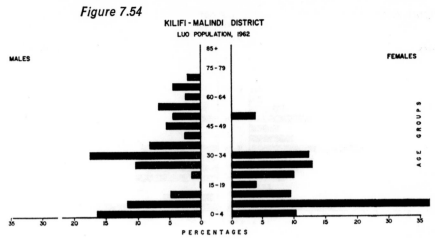

KILIFI - MALINDI DISTRICT
LUO POPULATION, 1962

MALES   FEMALES

AGE GROUPS

PERCENTAGES

female migration is more effective in the age group 15 to 34 years. But the most important age bracket is again here between 25 and 29 years. There were virtually no women beyond the age of 34 years (Figure 7.54). The Luhya age-sex pyramid though broadly similar has some important differences. The males affected appear to fall between 20 and 29 years and there are indications of an earlier movement in the population sample. The most important age group here was between 20 and 24 years (Figure 7.54). The age-sex pyramid for the Kikuyu suggests movement of adult males largely between 15 and 45 years. But there is evidence to suggest the importance of ages between 30 and 34 and the 40 to 44 year age bracket (Figure 7.54).

Kwale district is perhaps one of the most important rural destinations of up-country migrating population. The Kamba ethnic age-sex pyramid suggests a well established population with evidence of outward movement of males between the ages 20 and 44 (Figure 7.55).

But the principal elements in contemporary migration were mainly represented by Kamba, Luo, Kikuyu, Nandi and the Luhya population. Luo movement here appears to have selected the adult males between the ages 15 and 54. The most dominant male population was aged 30 to 34 years. Among the females we see a similar trend with most of them being aged 15 to 34 years. The population includes a broad base of dependent children especially females between the ages 0 to 9 years. There were virtually no women above the age of 39. This is a characteristic which tends to recur in most Luo migrant populations (Figure 7.55).

Although the Kikuyu ethnic element was one of the smallest migrant group in Kwale District in 1962, the age-sex pyramid showed the dominance of the 20 to 34 year age bracket and 35 to 59 years among the male population. The most numerous group among the adult population was the 25 to 29 age group. Among the females migration generally involved a younger population between 10 and 39 years of age. However there is evidence here that among the adult those between 30 and 34 years were most important (Figure 7.55).

Movement of the Nandi population into the district affected mostly the adult males aged 20 to 44 and females within the age range 15 to 39 (Figure 7.56). Here again the 25 to 29 year age group was the dominant element in

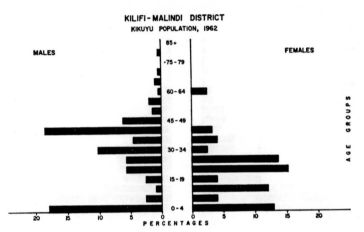

KILIFI - MALINDI DISTRICT
KIKUYU POPULATION, 1962

MALES   FEMALES

AGE GROUPS

PERCENTAGES

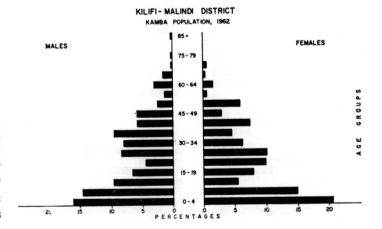

KILIFI - MALINDI DISTRICT
KAMBA POPULATION, 1962

MALES   FEMALES

AGE GROUPS

PERCENTAGES

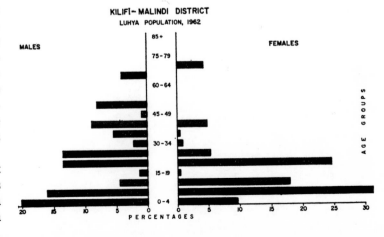

KILIFI - MALINDI DISTRICT
LUHYA POPULATION, 1962

MALES   FEMALES

AGE GROUPS

PERCENTAGES

Figure 7.55

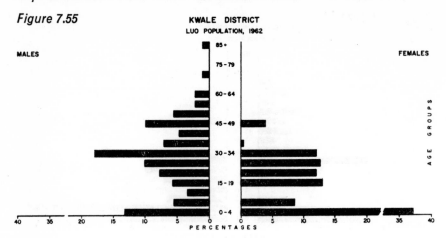

KWALE DISTRICT
LUO POPULATION, 1962

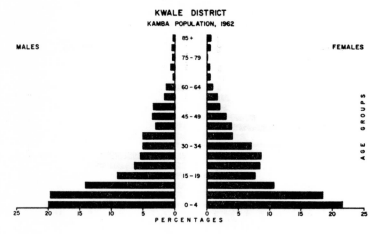

KWALE DISTRICT
KAMBA POPULATION, 1962

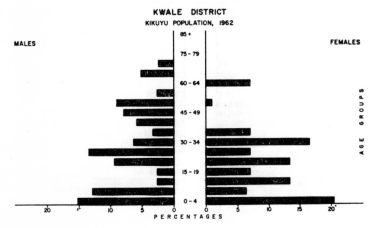

KWALE DISTRICT
KIKUYU POPULATION, 1962

the adult population. A further feature of interest in the Nandi population is the preponderance of young people aged 0 to 14 years.

Among the Luhya the age-sex pyramid shows the importance of movement among males aged 20 to 44 years. But the most numerous element in the population appears to have been confined to those aged 55 to 59 years. Among the females the pattern shows the dominance of the age range 15 to 29 years. The population was further characterised by a large proportion of dependent female children (Figure 7.56).

Taita district owes its importance to broadly similar plantation activities which underlie migrations into Kwale district. The principal ethnic groups affected again include the Kamba, Luhya, Luo and Kikuyu (Figure 7.57). Movement of the Kamba element is clearly concentrated among the section of population aged 15 to 54 years. The labour force is predominantly provided by the Kamba aged 30 to 34 years. Among the females the movement has tapped the 10 to 44 years age bracket. But the dominant element is mainly aged 20 to 24 years. There is in addition a broad base of dependent children (Figure 7.57).

The Luhya group provides another excellent example of the influx of younger people aged mostly 10 to 39 years. But even here we notice the selection of the age range 25 to 29 as the most important among the males. There is a secondary preponderance of the 40 to 44 age range. Among the Luhya women a similar tendency to formation of a double peak is to be noted. There is first clearly the dominance of the two age brackets from 15 to 19 years and between 25 and 29 years (Figure 7.57). The Luo are noticeable as recent migrants in the dominance of those in the age range from 15 to 59 years among the male population with an emphasis on those between 20 and 34 years of age. There is a secondary bulge in the population pyramid between 40 and 54. There are virtually no women above the age of 54 years. In common with Luhya case, this population has a large base of dependent children (Figure 7.57).

Closely resembling the Luo pattern is the Kikuyu age-sex pyramid which shows the movement of this ethnic group into Taita district and similarly affects the adult males between the ages 15 and 49 and the female adults aged 15 to 39 years. In both cases the dominant element

Figure 7.56

Figure 7.57

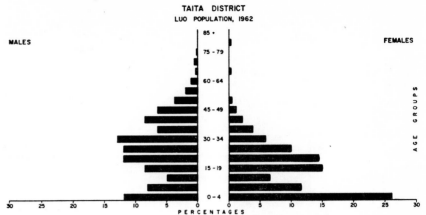

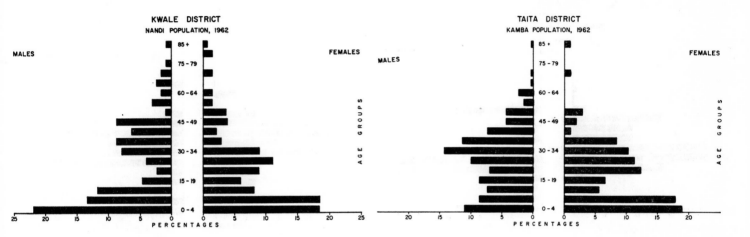

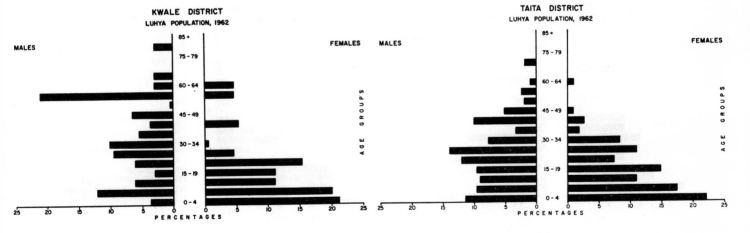

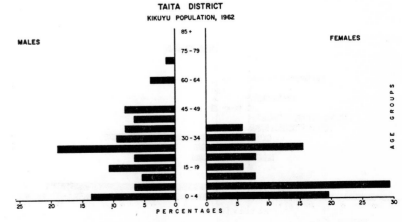

Figure 7.58

Figure 7

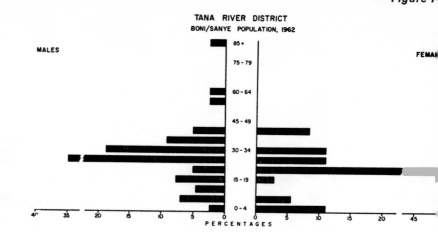

TANA RIVER DISTRICT
BONI/SANYE POPULATION, 1962

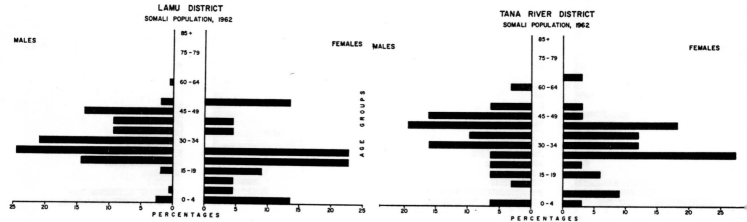

LAMU DISTRICT
SOMALI POPULATION, 1962

TANA RIVER DISTRICT
SOMALI POPULATION, 1962

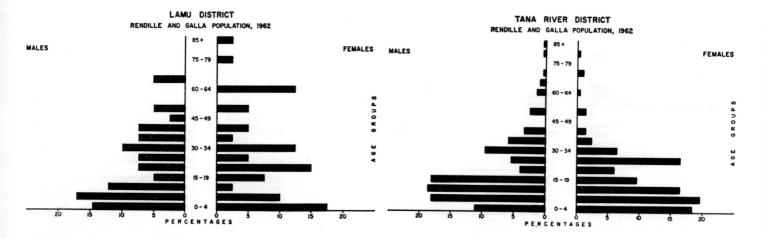

LAMU DISTRICT
RENDILLE AND GALLA POPULATION, 1962

TANA RIVER DISTRICT
RENDILLE AND GALLA POPULATION, 1962

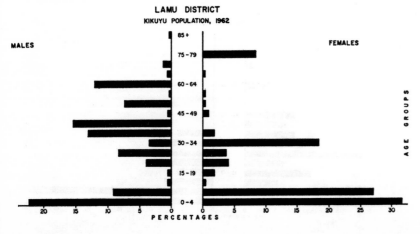

LAMU DISTRICT
KIKUYU POPULATION, 1962

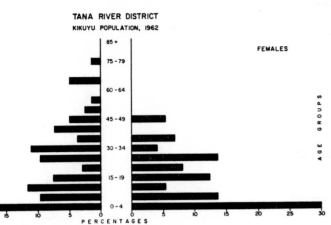

TANA RIVER DISTRICT
KIKUYU POPULATION, 1962

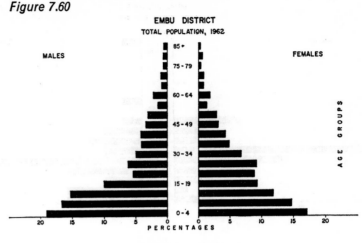

EMBU DISTRICT
TOTAL POPULATION, 1962

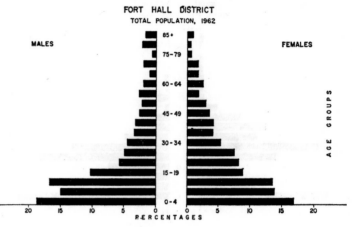

FORT HALL DISTRICT
TOTAL POPULATION, 1962

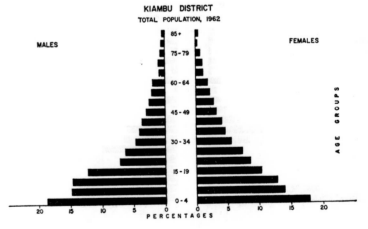

KIAMBU DISTRICT
TOTAL POPULATION, 1962

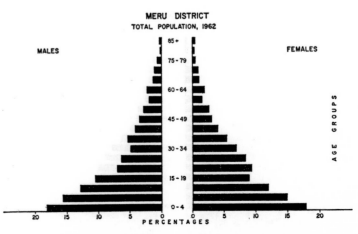

MERU DISTRICT
TOTAL POPULATION, 1962

in the population is found within the 25 and 29 age bracket. It should be noted that there were no Kikuyu women above the age of 39 years. The youthful population is here again associated with a broad base of dependent children (Figure 7.57).

In the remaining parts of the Coast Province the inflow of population from outside the province is very small in volume. Apart from the more widespread movement of the Kikuyu ethnic group, movement into Tana River and Lamu districts mainly affects the neighbouring nomadic population of the adjacent drylands of the north and north-east (Figure 7.58). There is for example the movement of Boni-Sanye group largely confined to the adult population of males aged 20 to 40 years and females aged 15 to 34 years. In this ethnic group the 25 to 29 age bracket is the dominant element in the population. The age-sex pyramids of the Rendille-Galla group and the Somali population into Tana River District is also primarily indicative of the immigration of persons aged 20 and 44 years of age (Figure 7.58). Among the Somali there were very young people aged 0–14 years. A similar pattern of movement among the nomadic population is reflected in the age-sex pyramid of the ethnic group in the Lamu district (Figure 7.59).

The distances of the Coast rural areas from the major sources of population appear to have eliminated most elements which appear in the national migration elsewhere.

iv. *Age-sex pyramids of the Central Province* (Figures 7.60–7.70) It has been noted that the dominant feature of the African age-sex pyramids in the former African districts of the Province is a marked deficiency in the male population particularly between ages 15 and 50 (Figure 7.60). Further examination show that this distinctive characteristic is a reflection of the selective impact of the population mobility on the dominant ethnic groups in these areas. The pyramids for these ethnic groups in their base districts such as Meru, Embu, Fort Hall (Muranga), Nyeri and Kiambu all show a broad base of dependants between the ages 0 to 10 years. For a clearer understanding of the nature of the movements it is necessary to consider the former African districts excluding Kiambu apart from the rest and to trace further the movements into the Central

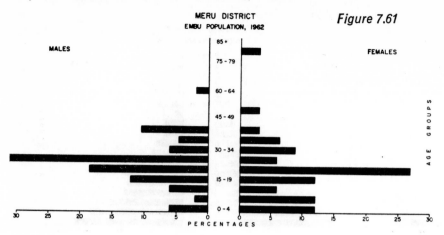

MERU DISTRICT
EMBU POPULATION, 1962

Figure 7.61

MALES   FEMALES

AGE GROUPS

PERCENTAGES

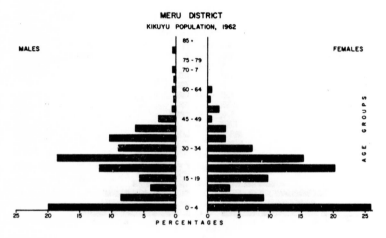

MERU DISTRICT
KIKUYU POPULATION, 1962

MALES   FEMALES

AGE GROUPS

PERCENTAGES

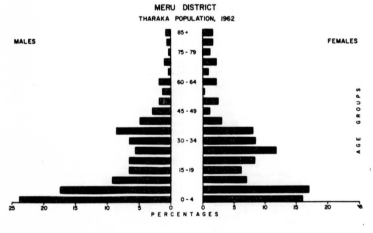

MERU DISTRICT
THARAKA POPULATION, 1962

MALES   FEMALES

AGE GROUPS

PERCENTAGES

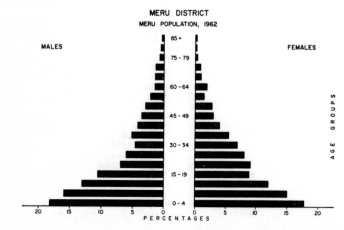

MERU DISTRICT
MERU POPULATION, 1962

MALES   FEMALES

AGE GROUPS

PERCENTAGES

Province of elements from outside. Here the presence of the Kikuyu in the former settled areas will be viewed as evidence of more recent movements.

In the Central Province as a whole, the districts of Fort Hall (Muranǵa) and Nyeri are quite distinct from the others. These are deficit districts where there was little development to attract population either from within the Central Province or from the other national sources. But there is an important movement of population from the remoter districts of Meru and Embu to the Kiambu districts which forms part of the pull of Nairobi. There is also an inflow on a small scale from the Kikuyu lands in reverse direction.

The Meru district age-sex pyramids revealed a significant movement involving some Embu and Kikuyu. The movement of the Embu into Meru district appear to have affected the adult population between the ages of 15 and 44 years (Figure 7.61). Movement of the adult males is more effective within the 25 to 29 age range. Although the female pattern in the district generally conforms to that of the males, the recurring dominance of 20 to 24 year group which appears to be an established feature of such migration is again evident. The Embu population in Meru district whether rural or urban is essentially a youthful population. But there are very few children aged 0 to 9 years and very few people over the age of 44 years.

The Kikuyu pattern is that of a typical migrating group very similar to the patterns of urban migrations into Nairobi and Mombasa. Here is a population characterised by the inflow of adults aged 15 to 49 years. The males are mostly affected between the ages 15 and 49. Within this broad age grouping, the 25 to 29 year age bracket is most outstanding. Among the females there is a similar balance showing concentration between the ages of 15 to 44 years. Among the females, it will be noted that the majority are younger and fall between 20 and 24 years of age. This then is a youthful movement accompanied by the younger dependants between the ages 0 to 1 years. According to 1962 Census, the Kikuyu were the third largest group from outside Meru district. The vast majority of these were in Nthima location.

The Tharaka pyramid presents some problem. It would appear that this pyramid reflects the movement of the Tharaka that affects primarily the 15 years and 49 age

Figure 7.62

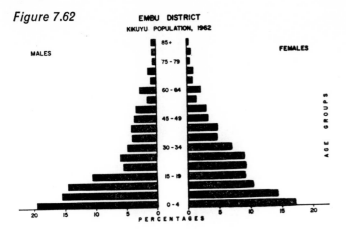

EMBU DISTRICT
KIKUYU POPULATION, 1962

MALES — FEMALES

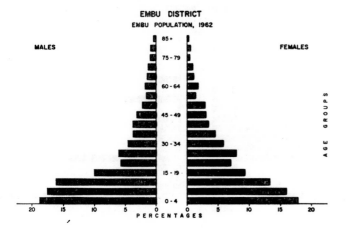

EMBU DISTRICT
EMBU POPULATION, 1962

MALES — FEMALES

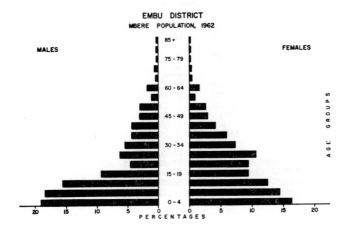

EMBU DISTRICT
MBERE POPULATION, 1962

MALES — FEMALES

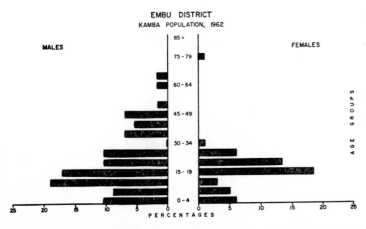

EMBU DISTRICT
KAMBA POPULATION, 1962

MALES — FEMALES

group among the males and the females. The age-sex pyramid for the group suggests that there has been a movement of additional Tharaka population into the area from the surrounding districts affecting the males between 15 and 49 years and the females between 15 and 44 years.

In Embu district the Embu ethnic pyramid confirms this group as a typical source population with a marked deficiency between the ages 15 and 44 years (Figure 7.62). A similar pattern is reflected in the Mbere age-sex pyramid of the district. The Mbere are migrating largely between 20 and 39 years. There is a district deficiency of the male population between these ages similar to that of the Kikuyu group.

In terms of total numbers, the old Embu district had more Kikuyu than Embu people. The age-sex pyramid of the Kikuyu ethnic group merely reflects the fact that this was one of the base districts for the Kikuyu. There is a marked indication of outward movement which largely affects the male population between the ages 20 and 44 years. Between these ages the women appear to outnumber men in the population.

But for a clearer demonstration of the Central Province movement we must first examine the patterns presented by the ethnic groups originating from outside the Province for the districts of Meru, Embu, Nyeri and Fort Hall (Muranǵa) and then consider the more complex movements into the former settled districts of Nanyuki and Thika. In this respect Kiambu district is closer to the former White Highland districts already mentioned.

Movement into Meru, shows the Kamba as the main element. The age-sex pyramid of the Kamba ethnic group in Meru is a typical migrant pattern involving mainly adults between the ages 15 and 49 years in the case of both sexes. The male movement shows the concentration particularly on those aged 25 to 29 years. They were the most numerous age bracket in the male population and their age-sex pyramid is in sharp contrast to that of the Kikuyu (Figure 7.63). Among the females the effect seems to have been most intense among the 20–29 year age group. The base of dependants shows the characteristic preponderance of the females aged 0–9 years.

The Kamba also appear among the migrants in Embu district (Figure 7.62). According to 1962 Census, they were the fourth most numerous group. The age-sex pyra-

Figure 7.64

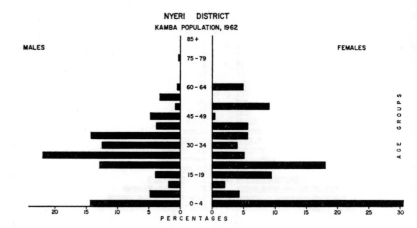

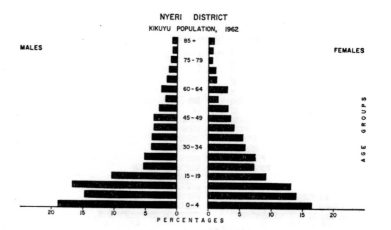

Figure 7.63

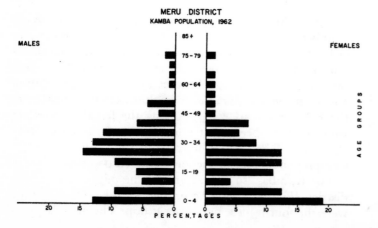

Figure 7.65

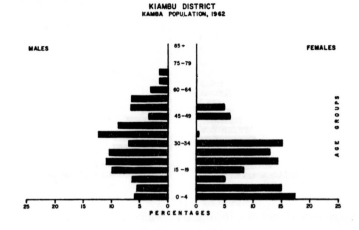

KIAMBU DISTRICT
KAMBA POPULATION, 1962

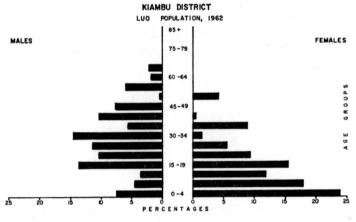

KIAMBU DISTRICT
LUO POPULATION, 1962

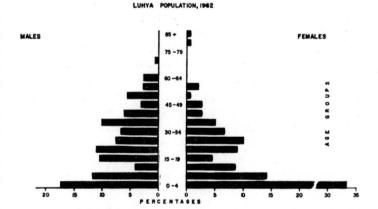

KIAMBU DISTRICT
LUHYA POPULATION, 1962

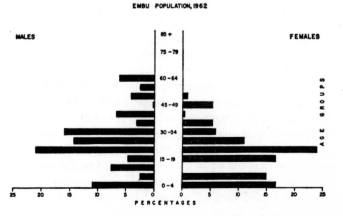

KIAMBU DISTRICT
EMBU POPULATION, 1962

mid shows that the group consisted primarily of recent migration into the district affecting male persons aged 10 to 49 and females aged 10 to 34 years. The female population showed concentration between the ages 10 and 34 years. The male population showed concentration between the ages 10 to 29 years and from 30 to 49 years. The most numerous groups in the male population were between 10 and 19 years old.

The youthful nature of Kamba male population is matched by a similarly young female movement. The most dominant age group was between 10 and 19 years of age. In the cases of most migrating groups, it has been noted that the dominant group in the population sample tends to fall between 20 and 24 years. The fact that a young Kamba population was moving into the Embu district is also reflected in the very small proportion of dependants aged 0 to 9 years.

Whilst the Nyeri Kamba pyramids shows some differences it makes clear that there the movement involves primarily the adult population in their working years. There is a clear concentration of the male population between the ages 15 to 49 years with the usual age bracket of 25 to 29 as the dominant group (Figure 7.64). The female sample showed a similar concentration between 15 and 44 years. But the most affected age bracket was 20 to 24 years. There were in addition rather older women above 34 years of age. The Kamba population was associated with a broad base of very young children in which the female group was clearly most dominant. Among the females those aged 0 to 4 years were most numerous. Thus the Kamba age-sex pyramid shows a pattern that suggests a different role from that of the Kikuyu with its marked male deficiency between 15 and 44 years (Figure 7.64).

Although the Kiambu district is one of the main sources of migrating population, it differs from the other source districts of the province in the character of economic activities. This is reflected in the dominance of mobile ethnic elements such as the Kamba, Luo, Luhya and the Embu. In this sense the trend in Kiambu is much closer to that of the former settled districts which will be described later (Figure 7.65).

The Kamba movement appears to have concentrated on the adults aged 15 to 44 years among the males. But

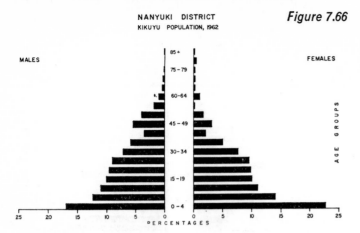

NANYUKI DISTRICT
KIKUYU POPULATION, 1962

Figure 7.66

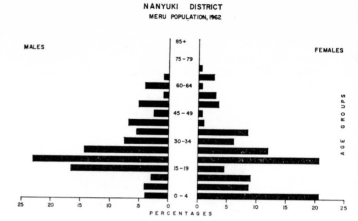

NANYUKI DISTRICT
MERU POPULATION, 1962

there is evidence of a secondary concentration between the ages 45 and 60 years. There is a striking increase of older people between the ages 15 and 60 years. This is a changing population which is becoming more established though still dominated by an influx of young people (Figure 7.65). Among the females the age-preference is between 10 and 39 years. There were very few Kamba women over 40 years in the Kiambu district. The most important age group among the females was between 30 and 34 years. The total sample shows the imbalance of population between the sexes. Female children between 0 to 9 years were more numerous in proportion to the total population of females (Figure 7.65).

According to 1962 Census the Luo ethnic group was the third largest after Kikuyu, Luhya and Kamba in the Kiambu district. Out of a total population of 402,886 for the district, the Luo were 1,925. This is the result of migration into the district of a relatively young population consisting of males between 15 and 49 years. The male population showed dominance of four distinct age brackets. In the younger age group the most dominant age brackets were 15 to 19 years and 30 to 34. The next distinct concentration was the 40 to 44 year age group. In the middle age category the 55 to 59 age group was most important. The small proportion of young male persons aged 0 to 9 years should be noted. This is in sharp contrast to the dominance of the female children aged 0 to 4 years. They formed about 25 per cent of the female sample of population (Figure 7.65). The Luhya ethnic group was according to 1962 Census the second most numerous group after the Kikuyu in the Kiambu District. The age-sex pyramid showed this to be a migrant population dominated by the male population between the ages 15 to 34 and 34 to 49. Beyond this there was an important group between 49 and 64. Migration among the female group was concentrated between the ages 15 to 49 years. In the case of the male movement, there is evidence of the dominance of the 20 to 24 age bracket among the younger migrations and the 35 to 39 year group among the older population.

The female population shows the striking effect of movement on the adult population aged 15 to 49. The most important group is the 25 to 29 age bracket. On the whole the Luhya population could be regarded as a youthful population with a broad base of young dependants. It will be noticed that there is a clear dominance of the female dependants between 0 to 9 years in the female sample. This age group forms between 10 to 33 per cent of the total female population. Among the males the 0 to 9 year olds form between 10 to 18 per cent of the total population.

We may conclude that although Kiambu district is one of the main sources of population movement, there is an important stream of movement which tends to attract population from a much wider field. This more widespread effect of the district on the mobile population is an indication of the nature of economic development in the district, especially industries and large scale farming.

In respect of population mobility the remaining districts of the old Central Province form a district category. Development of Nanyuki and Thika district as farming districts has brought these areas much closer to similarly settled districts of the Rift Valley Province.

In the Nanyuki district the pyramid of the Kikuyu from the contiguous districts suggests that this ethnic group has been resident in the area for a much longer period. The distortion reflected between the ages 40 to 59 probably suggests an earlier movement (Figure 7.66). The Meru in Nanyuki district are predominantly a recent movement attracting the age group 15 to 49 years among the males. Among the females the concentration is largely confined between 15 and 39 years. The most affected group is between 20 and 24 years among the males. But for the females the most dominant group is between 20 and 24 years. Whilst the male children were less than 5 per cent of the total population, the females were about 9 to 20 per cent of the total population.

In Thika District it would appear that the age-sex pattern of the Kikuyu group reflect their long established presence in the area. However, there is a distinct influx of both male and female population particularly between the ages 25 and 29 years. Further, there is a broad base of dependants aged 0 to 9 years which is not a characteristic feature of other migrating groups (Figure 7.67).

The Embu age-sex pyramid in the Thika District resembles the pattern for the same ethnic group in the Kiambu district. This is clearly the effect of recent movement into the district. The males are largely bunched between the ages 15 and 44. But the female sample shows the dominance of the age group 15 to 49 years. The most dominant group among the male Embu population was 20 to 44 years (Figure 7.67). In the case of the females, there is the importance of the age group 15 to 49 years. The most important group was the 20 to 24 years. There were more female children age 0 to 9 years in proportion to the total population.

The importance of Nanyuki and other former 'White Highlands' districts may be seen in the range of ethnic groups attracted from outside the province. The most important groups in the movement into Nanyuki district were the Kamba, Turkana, Nandi and Luo (Figure 7.68).

According to 1962 Census, the Kamba were the fifth most numerous group in the Nanyuki district. This group consisted of a typical youthful population aged 15 to 49 years. Among the males those aged 30 to 34 years were the most numerous. There were very few above 49 years of age in the group. The Kamba females were on the average much younger in age. The age-sex pyramid here shows an influx of females aged 15 to 44 years. But the most dominant age bracket was from 15 to 19 years. This is in marked contrast to the standard pattern among the important migrating elements such as the Luo, Kikuyu and Luhya for which the 20 to 24 years was the most common (Figure 7.68).

There is a further feature of interest in this age-sex pyramid. The proportion of male children in the male sample was far lower than the corresponding age level for the females. Here the female children aged 0 to 9 years formed between 20 and 25 per cent of the population sample.

Apart from the migrating Kamba, Nanyuki district population showed a significant group of Turkana (Figure 7.68). The Turkana was the fourth most numerous ethnic group after the Kikuyu, Nderobo and Meru. The age-sex pyramid of the group possibly reflects two movements. The most recent is the effect of the influx of young persons aged 15 to 39 years among the males and 15 to 34 among the females. It is possible to consider the distortion of the male and female pyramids between 40 and 55 years and that of the females between 40 and 54 years as reflecting residual effect on an earlier movement. This is a feature which recurs in a number of the mobile ethnic groups in the farming districts. The dominant age bracket among the Turkana males is 25 to 29 years

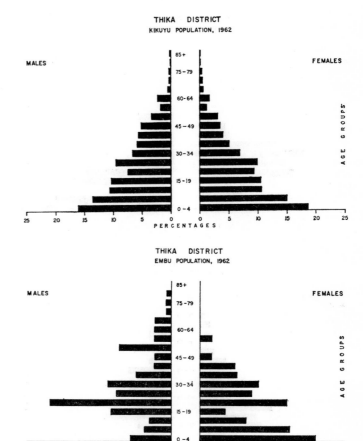

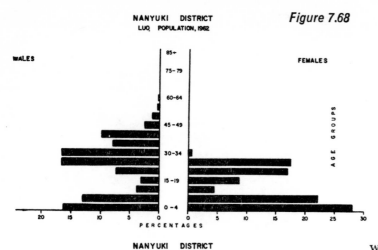

Figure 7.68

NANYUKI DISTRICT
LUO POPULATION, 1962

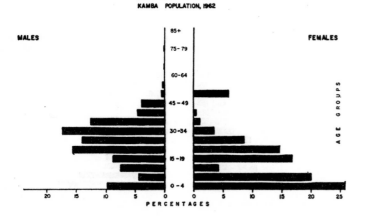

NANYUKI DISTRICT
KAMBA POPULATION, 1962

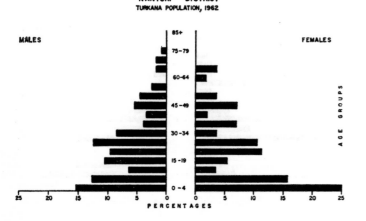

NANYUKI DISTRICT
TURKANA POPULATION, 1962

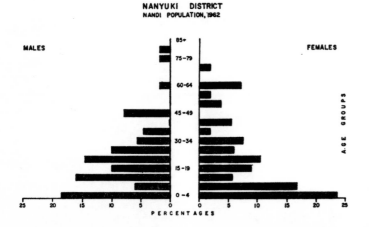

NANYUKI DISTRICT
NANDI POPULATION, 1962

whereas the female dominant group is generally aged 20 to 24 years. The Turkana are migrating with the young children between the ages of 0 and 9 years. Here as well there is the imbalance between the male and female children in the population. The latter formed between 15 to 25 per cent of the total female population (Figure 7.68).

Nandi movement into Nanyuki district is shown by the age-sex pyramid in which the migrating males and females are aged 10 to 39 (Figure 7.68). Although there were older people over 39 years, the movements of young people between these ages clearly dominate the structure of the population. There appears to be emphasis on young males aged 10 to 14 and those between 20 and 24 years. Among the females, the most popular group is the 20 to 24 age bracket. The young Nandi were clearly moving with children aged 0 to 9 years. In the case of this ethnic group the very young ones aged 0 to 4 years were about evenly balanced.

The most clearly defined migrant pattern is that of the Luo ethnic group. Though not numerous they formed a distinct group between the ages 20 and 44 years among the males. The most dominant male age groups were 25 to 29 and 30 to 34 years (Figure 7.68). The Luo age-sex pyramid showed a much younger female population. The movement as in other areas, appears to have attracted men and their women folk. The latter were concentrated mainly between 15 and 29 years of age. The most important group was aged 25 to 29 years and there were no women over the age of 34 years. The Luo sample had a base of young dependants aged 0 to 9 years with the female children clearly dominant in the female sample. They formed between 20 and 25 per cent of the total female population whereas the males were mainly between 10 and 15 per cent of the total male sample.

Movement into Thika District from outside the Central Province is dominated by the Kamba, Luo and Luhya ethnic groups. The Kamba age-sex pyramid is very similar to the pattern of the Kikuyu which forms the most numerous element in the population (Figure 7.69). According to 1962 Census, there were 26,342 Kamba people in the district which ranked them as the second most numerous element after the Kikuyu. The age-sex pyramid of this sample represents a long estab-

Figure 7.69

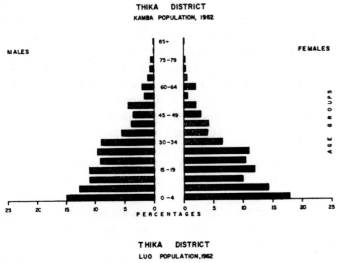

THIKA DISTRICT
KAMBA POPULATION, 1962

MALES   FEMALES

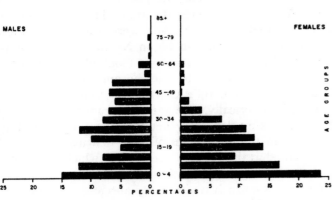

THIKA DISTRICT
LUO POPULATION, 1962

MALES   FEMALES

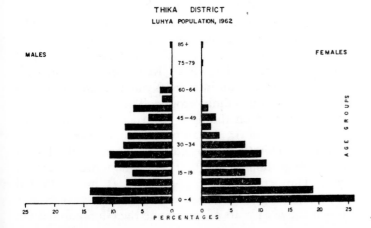

THIKA DISTRICT
LUHYA POPULATION, 1962

MALES   FEMALES

lished population with a far larger proportion of older people than is the case among the mobile elements. But even in the case of the Kamba population it is possible to differentiate the effect of an inflow between the ages 20 and 39 years. The Kamba population is thus on its way to being one of the basic elements of the district's population.

The long distance movement among the Luo appears to have attracted mainly males aged 20 to 54 years. The Luo population of Thika was on the average much older than in certain areas into which they have moved. There were far more male people over the age of 40 years in the district. The female group appeared to be much younger. Here they were mainly aged 10 to 39 years. The most numerous group was aged 15 to 19 years. This youthful population had associated with it a base of young dependants between the ages 0 to 9 years in which females were most outstanding.

There was a similar pattern among the Luhya ethnic group. The Luhya were a very small group in Thika as compared to the Luo element. Here their age-sex pyramid showed preference for persons aged 15 to 49 for the males and 15 to 39 among the females. In the case of the males it would appear that the effect was most intense among those aged 25 to 29 years whereas the female dominant group was aged 20 to 24 years. The Luhya were migrating with young dependants aged 0 to 9 years showing the usual dominance of the female element (Figure 7.69).

The analysis of movement in the Central Province thus underlines the importance of former areas of European farming and the pull of the Southern districts of Kikuyuland. The development in these areas is both local and national and is clearly reflected in the age-sex pyramids examined. It is these movements that accounted for a significant inflow of population into the Province. However, it is necessary to stress that the age-sex pyramids reflect other complex influences on the history of the population. Their effect in indicating the nature of movement is just one of the factors of importance.

v. *Age-sex pyramids of the Nyanza Province*

The Nyanza age-sex pyramids reflect the effect of both the movements of Nyanza ethnic groups and also of those elements that have been moving in from outside the

Figure 7.70

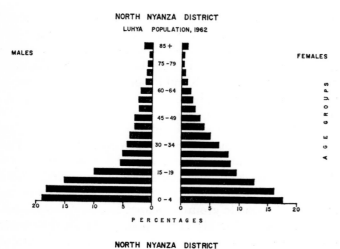

NORTH NYANZA DISTRICT
LUHYA POPULATION, 1962

MALES   FEMALES

AGE GROUPS

PERCENTAGES

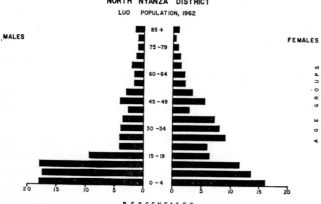

NORTH NYANZA DISTRICT
LUO POPULATION, 1962

MALES   FEMALES

AGE GROUPS

PERCENTAGES

Province (Figures 7.70–7.81). A distinctive effect of outward movement in North Nyanza is shown in the population pyramid as a marked deficiency of males, Luhya as well as the Luo. North Nyanza at the time of the Census included locations with a substantial permanent Luo population. Apart from this outward flow there does not seem to be a significant effect of inward migration. This was one of the poorer districts with heavy population concentration and in which there was little to attract other Nyanza ethnic groups (Figure 7.70).

Deficiency of the Nyanza male population is again the main feature that emerges from the Luhya age-sex pyramid of Elgon Nyanza district. A similar trend may be observed among the Sabaot population who form the third most important ethnic group in the district (Figure 7.71). This deficiency is particularly marked between the ages 20 and 29 years. The effect of outward movement is again more intense among the Iteso. The Iteso who are closely related to the Sabaot were the second most numerous ethnic group in Elgon Nyanza at the time of the 1962 Census. Iteso movement out of the district is more marked between the ages 20 and 29 years.

According to the 1962 Census, the Luo ethnic group was third numerically. The age-sex pyramid of the group shows a striking deficiency between the ages 20 and 39 years. As in the other cases of male deficiency this is to be regarded as the effect of the outflow which forms part of the national stream of migration.

Central Nyanza is traditionally an emigration district. This is clearly shown in the population pyramid of the Luo and the Baluhya, the two most dominant ethnic groups in the area at the time of the 1962 Census. The shortage is more marked between the ages 20 and 44 years just at a time when most of the males are away at work (Figure 7.72). The Gusii (Kisii) age-sex pyramid is another example of an internal Nyanza migration which affects the various ethnic groups. The effect appears to be more marked on the ages 10 to 44 years. But in the male sample the 15 to 19 year age bracket is most important. This Gusii movement is more youthful than similar migration among other ethnic groups (Figure 7.72). The female Gusii population is most affected between the ages 15 to 34 years. There were very few women above 34 years of age among the Gusii population.

Figure 7.71

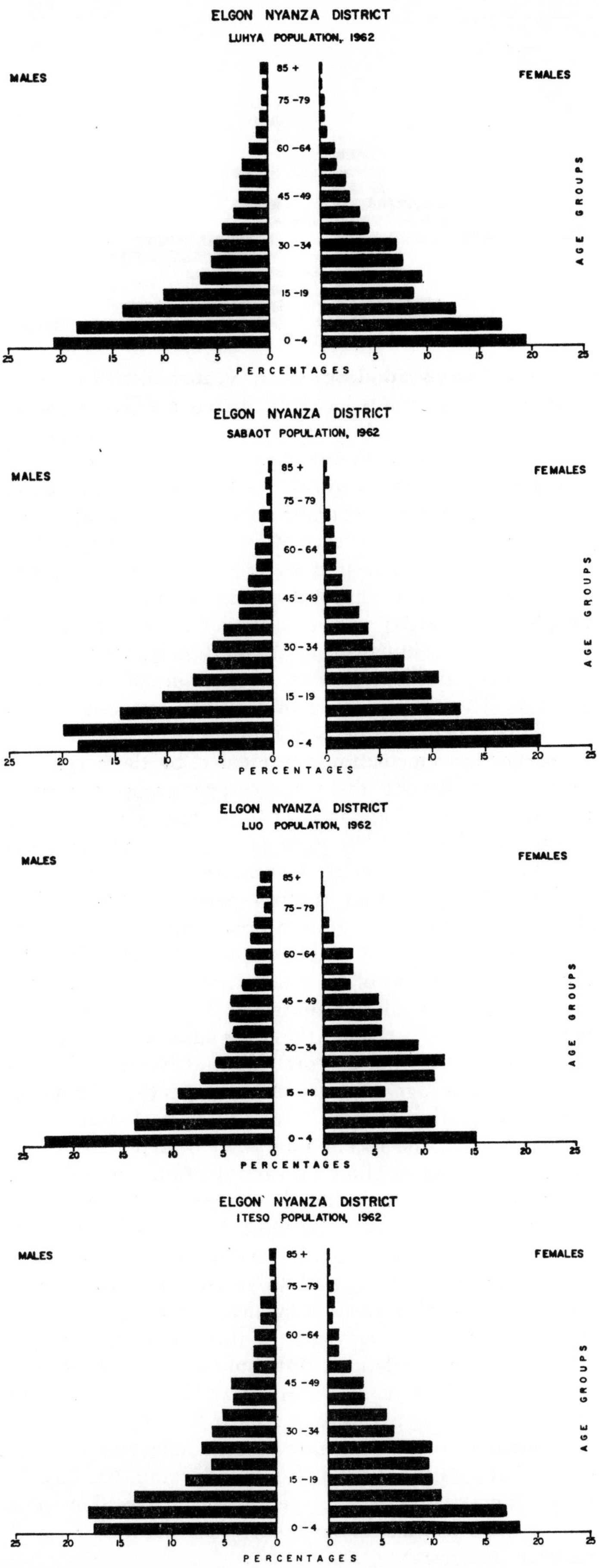
ELGON NYANZA DISTRICT
LUHYA POPULATION, 1962
ELGON NYANZA DISTRICT
SABAOT POPULATION, 1962
ELGON NYANZA DISTRICT
LUO POPULATION, 1962
ELGON NYANZA DISTRICT
ITESO POPULATION, 1962
MALES
FEMALES
85 +
75 - 79
60 - 64
45 - 49
30 - 34
15 - 19
0 - 4
AGE GROUPS
PERCENTAGES
25
20
15
10
5
0

Figure 7.72

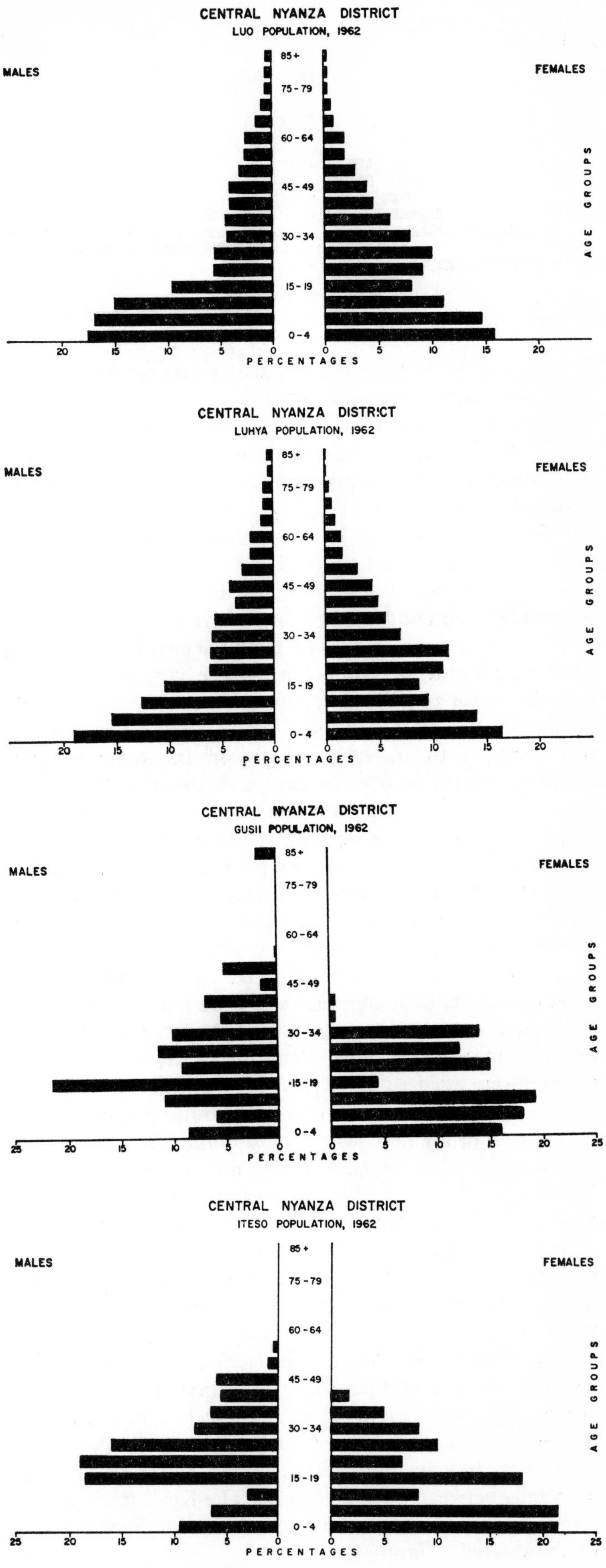
CENTRAL NYANZA DISTRICT
LUO POPULATION, 1962
CENTRAL NYANZA DISTRICT
LUHYA POPULATION, 1962
CENTRAL NYANZA DISTRICT
GUSII POPULATION, 1962
CENTRAL NYANZA DISTRICT
ITESO POPULATION, 1962
MALES
FEMALES
85 +
75 - 79
60 - 64
45 - 49
30 - 34
15 - 19
0 - 4
AGE GROUPS
PERCENTAGES
25
20
15
10
5
0

Figure 7.73

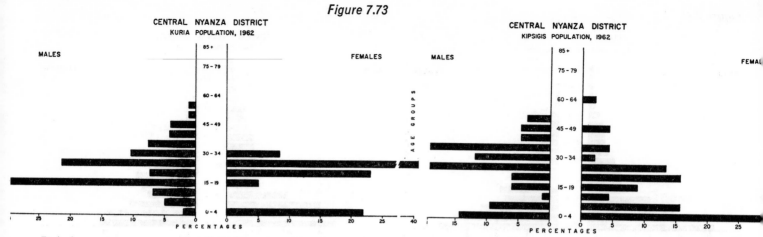

CENTRAL NYANZA DISTRICT
KURIA POPULATION, 1962

MALES   FEMALES

CENTRAL NYANZA DISTRICT
KIPSIGIS POPULATION, 1962

MALES   FEMAL

AGE GROUPS

85 +
75 - 79
60 - 64
45 - 49
30 - 34
15 - 19
0 - 4

PERCENTAGES

It is important to note the imbalance among the dependent population aged 0 to 9 years.

The Iteso age-sex pyramid is a clearer case of migration into Central Nyanza district (Figure 7.72). The Iteso population is here dominated by an influx of adults between 15 and 49 years of age. Among the males the movement appears to have attracted mostly younger persons aged 15 to 29 years. The dominant age bracket was between 20 and 24 years. Iteso male adults far outnumber the children aged 0 to 9 years.

The female migration has largely selected persons aged between 10 and 44 years. There were very few women over the age of 39 years. In contrast to the situation among the males, the most dominant group among the women was aged 15 to 19 years. Whilst in the male sample children aged 0 to 9 years ranged between 5 to 10 per cent of the total male population in the case of the females the proportion was as high as 21 per cent.

The Central Nyanza age-sex pyramid for the Kipsigis show that there is a significant migration of this ethnic group into the district (Figure 7.74). Here again the pyramid for the adult population shows a distortion by an inflow of persons generally aged 15 to 39 years. The most dominant male age brackets were between 25 to 29 years and 35 to 39 years of age. Although there were a number of women older than 39 years, most of the women were aged 15 to 34 years. The Kipsigis population in Central Nyanza is essentially a youthful population. In the case of the females the most dominant age-sex was between 20 and 24 years. A further migration into Central Nyanza is reflected in the Kuria age-sex pyramid (Figure 7.73). This movement largely affects males aged 15 to 49 and females aged 15 to 34. As in many other migrant patterns the female dependants are far more dominant in the sample whereas the males form a very small proportion.

The contribution of South Nyanza district to the national stream of migration is suggested by the Luo age-sex pyramid (Figure 7.74). There is a deficiency of the male population between 20 and 44 years. A similar deficiency appears in the case of the Kuria population especially between 25 and 29 years. The Kuria is a resident population and is located in the extreme southern portion of the district (Figure 7.74).

The Luhya pyramid for South Nyanza district suggests that the ethnic group has contributed a cross-section of the population including young people as well as adults and elderly persons (Figure 7.74). Certainly this is not a population of recent origin. It consists of a broad base of dependent children and fewer people of advancing years. The age-sex pyramid is that of an established population of long standing. The pattern suggests an earlier movement. It is known that substantial number of Luhya people have moved into the district in search of land since the establishment of modern administration.

Gusii population suggests a number of interesting features. There is evidence of movement of both males and females between the ages 10 to 39 years, and possibly an earlier movement now represented by those aged 40 to 70 years. Among the younger age group the male population affected are aged 15 to 39 years. The dominant age bracket here is from 30 to 34 years among the males and 20 to 24 years among the females.

Gusii (Kisii) District pattern presented here differs slightly from the main source areas which have contributed to the bulk of the mobile population. Here although there are indications of male deficiency between the ages of 15 and 34 the effect of outward flow of population is not comparable to that in the areas such as Central and North Nyanza as well as Fort Hall and Nyeri in Central Province. The age-sex pyramid suggests that the Gusii are not migrating in such large numbers (Figure 7.75). In the district, the recent migration is well reflected in the age-sex structure of the Luo and the Luhya population. Here again male migration has largely attracted those aged 15 to 49 years and the most dominant age bracket is 25 to 29 years. Among the females the age range most affected lies between 15 and 39 years. The female range conforms to earlier cases in which the most dominant group is aged 20 to 24 years. In this population sample there is a more balanced distribution of the male and female dependants aged 0 to 9 years (Figure 7.75). From the Luhya age-sex pyramid, it is clear that the population is dominated by rather young persons reflecting a recent movement into the district. Luhya migration has largely involved males and females aged 15 to 39 years. The most affected age bracket in both cases lies between 20 and 24 years (Figure 7.75).

Figure 7.74

Figure 7.75

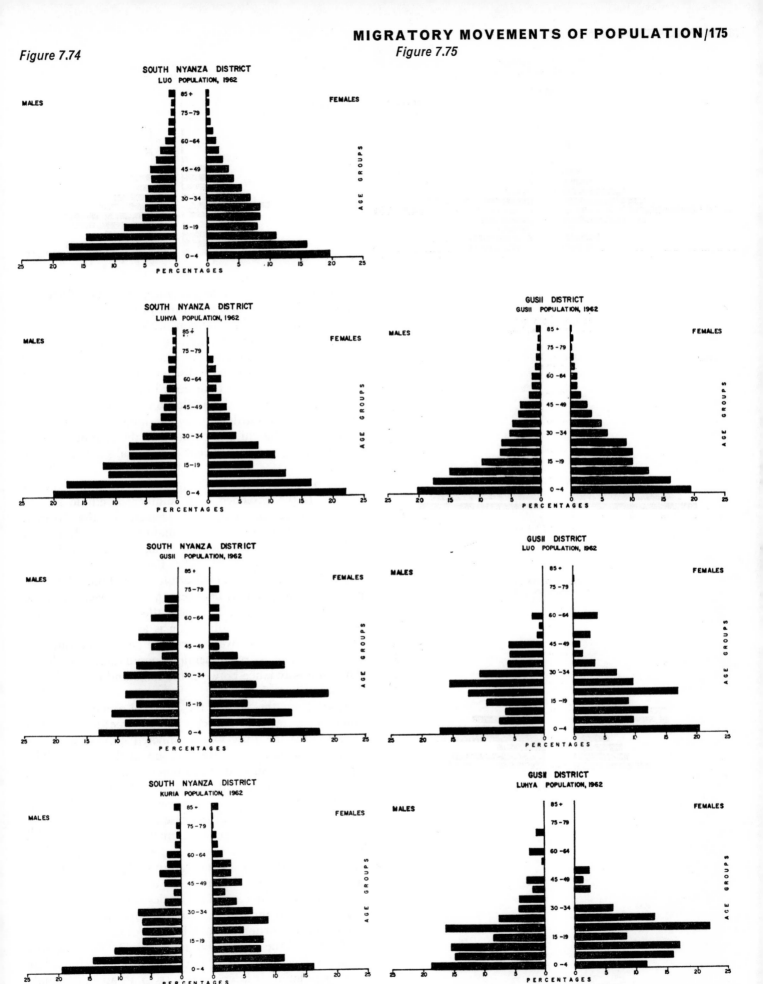

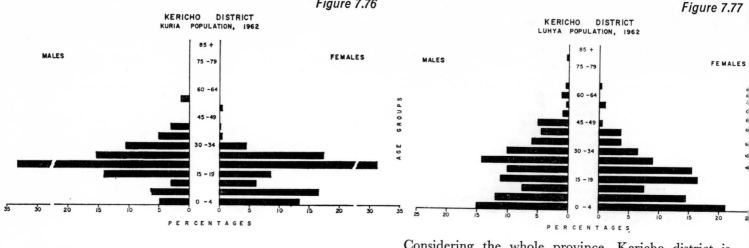

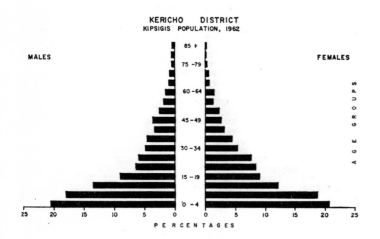

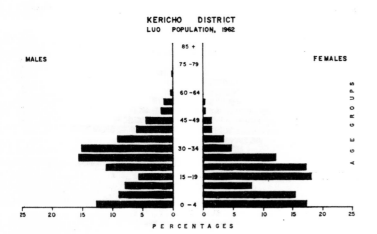

Considering the whole province, Kericho district is unique in its population structure. In this respect Kericho district has more in common with the former settled districts of the Kenya Highlands (Figure 7.76). The Kipsigis age-sex pyramid is similar to those of other ethnic groups in their base districts. The most important features here include a deficiency in the male population between 20 and 34 years. But on the whole this is a population overburdened by a large proportion of dependants. The child population in the case of each sex is between 15 and 20 per cent of the total sample (Figure 7.76).

But the most striking feature of Kericho population pattern is the presence of a number of ethnic groups dominated by the migration element of the Nyanza population. It is clear that the main sources of Kericho's labour force are the Kuria, Luo, Gusii and Luhya (Figures 7.76 and 7.77). The Kuria movement from South Nyanza has attracted adult population. The male population largely falls between 15 and 44 years and the females 15 to 34 years. The most affected age bracket for the male and female population is aged 20 to 24 years. In both cases, there were very few persons beyond the age of 44. The Kuria dependent population of children shows the imbalance between the male and female in the population sample.

Apart from the Kuria, the Luo are among the most numerous element in Kericho labour force; according to 1962 Census the Luo, who numbered 33,144, were the second most numerous ethnic group in the district. The age-sex pyramid show that this population was dominated by the male adult population aged 15 to 49 years and a female population about the same age range. The most affected age group was in the case of the male population 25 to 29 years and in the case of female population 20 to 24. This is a pattern which has been observed among the Luo and other migrating ethnic groups. Again the female children were more dominant in the female population sample than in the case of the males (Figure 7.76).

The last two important ethnic groups that supply an important proportion of the labour force in the area were the Gusii and the Luhya (Figure 7.77). The Gusii age-sex pyramid is very similar to that of the migrant Luo. The male population is largely aged 15 to 49 and the female

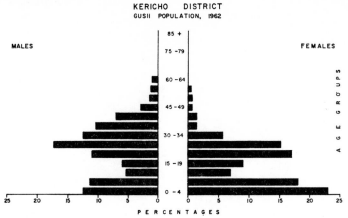

KERICHO DISTRICT
GUSII POPULATION, 1962

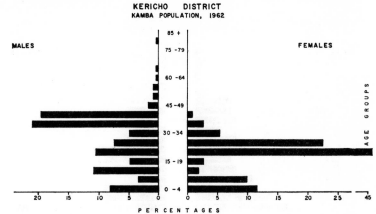

KERICHO DISTRICT
KAMBA POPULATION, 1962

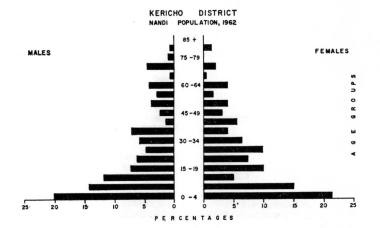

KERICHO DISTRICT
NANDI POPULATION, 1962

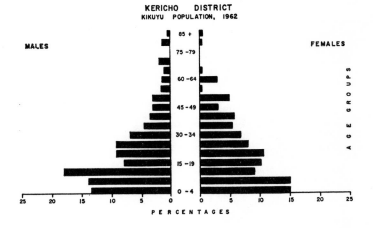

KERICHO DISTRICT
KIKUYU POPULATION, 1962

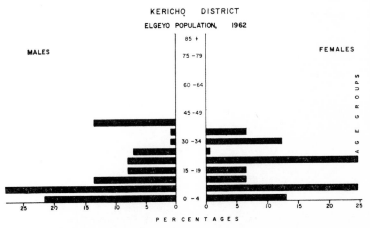

KERICHO DISTRICT
ELGEYO POPULATION, 1962

population is concentrated between 10 and 34. The dominant element in the male population is the 25 to 29 age bracket and for the females 20 to 24 years. The Luhya group shows a higher proportion of older people but generally resembles that of the Luo. The migration has attracted male persons aged 15 to 49. As in the case with the Luo sample the most dominant group is aged 25 to 29 years. The females are in general much younger. The most dominant age group among the females is the 15 to 19 years (Figure 7.77).

As a major farming area, Kericho had its share of mobile population. The best examples are here shown by the age-sex structure of the Kamba and the Kikuyu (Figure 7.78). Both the Kikuyu and the Nandi age-sex structure show populations of long standing in the area. There is evidence of age distortions between 15 and 39 years. In the case of the Nandi, there is evidence of some outward movement. Even the Elgeyo age-sex pattern appears to be influenced by outward migration. The deficiency between 15 and 29 years has considerably modified the age-sex structure.

It will be seen that in North Nyanza, the stimulus to migration is reflected in the presence of the Kamba, Nandi and Kikuyu (Figure 7.79). The nearby Nandi population shows a more stable structure than those for the Kamba and the Kikuyu. The Nandi group suggests a population long in residence in the district. There is a clear evidence of inward flow of the Kamba and the Kikuyu into the district.

The Kamba population of North Nyanza consisted of male adults mainly between 29 and 44 years and females aged 20 to 34 years. The youthful character of the population is reflected in the broad base of dependent children aged 0 to 9 years. It would appear that there has been some movement into Elgon Nyanza by the Nandi and the Kikuyu elements of the population (Figure 7.80). But this age-sex structure also suggests population of long standing. There is further evidence that these elements are also affected by a measure of outward flow of population.

In Central Nyanza, extra-provincial population consisted mainly of the Kamba, Nandi and the Kikuyu. Their individual age-sex structure reflected in Figure 7.81 also shows considerable variation. All are dominated by

Figure 7.79   *Figure 7.80*

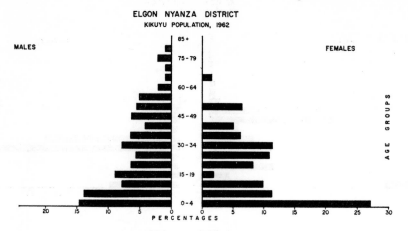

ELGON NYANZA DISTRICT
KIKUYU POPULATION, 1962

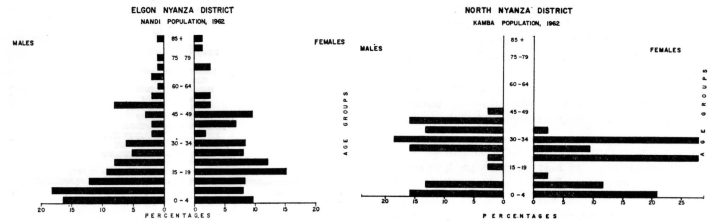

ELGON NYANZA DISTRICT
NANDI POPULATION, 1962

NORTH NYANZA DISTRICT
KAMBA POPULATION, 1962

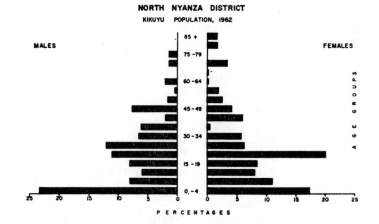

NORTH NYANZA DISTRICT
KIKUYU POPULATION, 1962

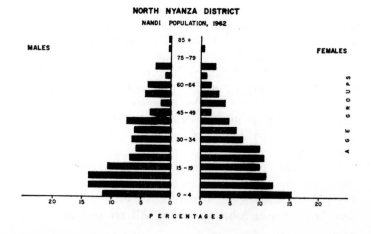

NORTH NYANZA DISTRICT
NANDI POPULATION, 1962

Figure 7.81

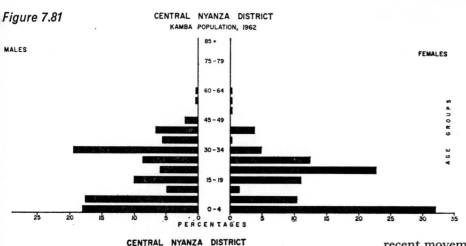

CENTRAL NYANZA DISTRICT
KAMBA POPULATION, 1962

MALES

FEMALES

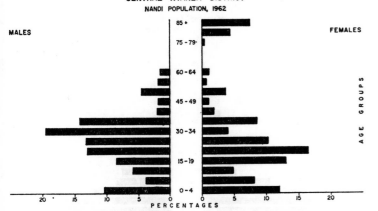

CENTRAL NYANZA DISTRICT
NANDI POPULATION, 1962

MALES

FEMALES

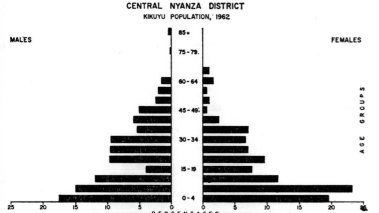

CENTRAL NYANZA DISTRICT
KIKUYU POPULATION, 1962

MALES

FEMALES

recent movement of persons in early adolescence and late maturity.

vi. *Age-sex Pyramids of the Southern Province*
(Figures 7.82–7.85)
A distinctive feature of the population mobility affecting the Southern Province is the wide gap between the incoming volume and the outgoing numbers. It has already been noted that whereas the numbers which had moved in totalled 12,624, the Province has contributed considerably to the national outgoing population.

Analysis of the age-sex pyramids of the Province show the contrast between the sparsely populated Masai districts of Narok and Kajiado and the Kamba district of Machakos and Kitui. It has already been noted that the district pyramids of total population all show the selective effect of population movements which is confirmed by the male deficiency roughly between the ages of 20 and 39 years.

Consideration of the effect on the ethnic elements in the Province indicated that the district deficiencies for Kajiado and Narok were due to outward movement of the Masai element. In Kajiado district, it would appear that the Masai movement though more intense for the age groups 20 to 24, 40 to 44 is on the whole spread between 20 and 44 years (Figure 7.83). In contrast to the above situation the Narok movement is concentrated on the age group 20 to 34 years (Figure 7.82).

In the other two districts of the Province, the large volume of outward migration is reflected in the age-sex pyramids of the Kamba ethnic group. There is a marked male deficiency which extends from the age of 15 years to as late as 44 years in Kitui district. This outflow of male population is more marked in the Machakos district. Here a clear disparity is shown in the population among the various age groups falling between 20 and 44 years of age (Figure 7.84). It is the contribution of these two ethnic groups that accounted for the large outflow of population from the Province. It has been indicated that this outflow is primarily to the Nairobi area, Rift Valley and the Coast Province.

The small inward migration into the Southern Province is reflected in the restricted impact that the development

Figure 7.82

Figure 7.84

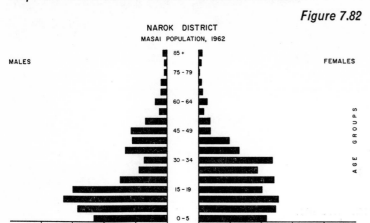

NAROK DISTRICT
MASAI POPULATION, 1962

MALES

FEMALES

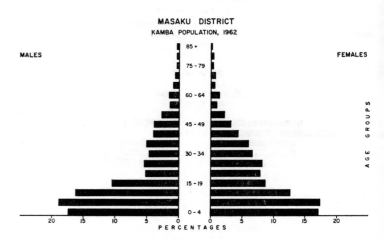

MASAKU DISTRICT
KAMBA POPULATION, 1962

MALES

FEMALES

Figure 7.83

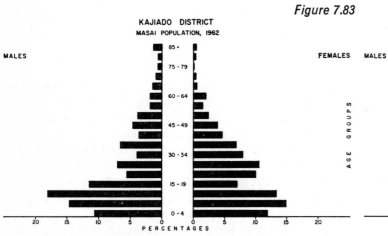

KAJIADO DISTRICT
MASAI POPULATION, 1962

MALES

FEMALES

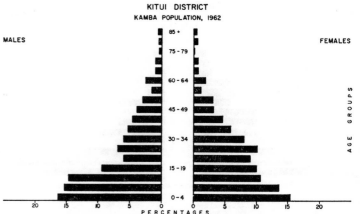

KITUI DISTRICT
KAMBA POPULATION, 1962

MALES

FEMALES

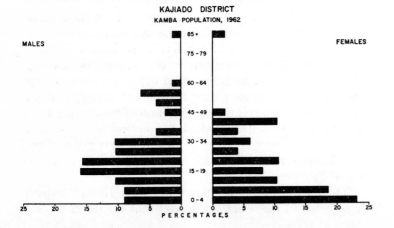

KAJIADO DISTRICT
KAMBA POPULATION, 1962

MALES

FEMALES

Figure 7.85

of the area has had on the varied ethnic groups of the country. The Kikuyu and the Kipsigis were the most numerous ethnic groups from outside the Province. In terms of district distribution, the two Masai districts of Narok and Kajiado attracted very little attention apart from a few elements of Kikuyu, Luhya and Luo (Figure 7.85). The large group of Nandi and Kipsigis recorded at the time of the 1962 Census probably represented long established population from the nearby Nyanza and Rift Valley Province.

Analysis of the age-sex pyramids show that movement into the Southern Province was largely confined to Machakos district. A significant number of the Kikuyu and Tharaka populations appear to have moved into Kitui district. But the main goal of migration from the other national sources was Machakos district.

The most numerous ethnic group from outside the Province was the Kikuyu element. According to 1962 Census there were 3,345 Kikuyu in Machakos district. The age-sex pyramid for the ethnic group showed evidence of migration affecting mostly males between 20 and 44 years of age. There were 2,078 males as against 1,267 females. An interesting feature of the Kikuyu pyramid is the presence of a significant number of people aged 50 and over. The most affected age groups among the males are 20 to 29 years. There were few males aged 15 to 19 years in Kikuyu movement. But the female migration seems to concentrate on the age range 20 to 24 years. As in the case of males there was a significant element of elderly population above 50 years.

A typical migration pattern is reflected in the age-sex pyramid of the Luo ethnic group. The Luo were the second most numerous element from outside Machakos district. According to 1962 Census there were 1,664 Luo in Machakos district. The age-sex pyramid shows that this is a selective movement mainly affecting the active population. In the case of the males the movement involved persons aged 20 to 54 years. The most affected age bracket was 30 to 34 years. The female population is primarily between the age of 19 and 34 years. There were very few women between the ages of 35 to 54 and none above 54 years. The movement to Machakos district thus conforms to similar long distance migrations to other centres of economic activities including the urban and the farming areas.

The importance of Machakos district as a goal for long distance migration from Nyanza is reflected in the pattern of the Luhya age-sex pyramid. The Luhya who in 1962 numbered 943 in the district were the third largest ethnic element from outside the Province. Migration of the Luhya population as in the case of the Luo is primarily confined to the active section of the population aged 20 to 49 years in the case of males and between 20 and 34 years in the case of women. There were no Luhya women in the population over the age of 44 years.

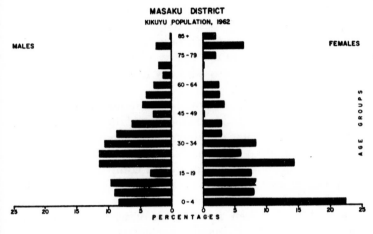

MASAKU DISTRICT
KIKUYU POPULATION, 1962

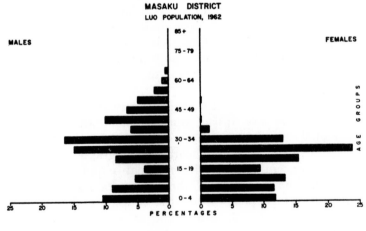

MASAKU DISTRICT
LUO POPULATION, 1962

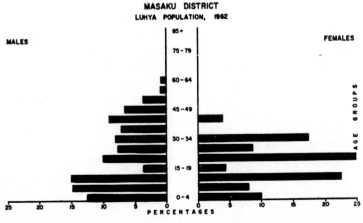

MASAKU DISTRICT
LUHYA POPULATION, 1962

8 A Summary of the Major Types of Migrations; Their Causes and Implications in Kenya

This study has been concerned with the examination of the movements of population. In the earlier chapters, it was necessary to describe the nature of the land resources and their development as a basis for a clearer understanding of the factors underlying population movements. However, it has been equally important to show evidence of population movements.

In this concluding chapter it is important to draw attention to some of the difficulties which limit the implications of the study. A scientific study of migrations of population calls for more refined methods of recording vital statistics of migration data. These sources have not been available. Further it is necessary to draw attention to the restricted information which it was possible to include in the second national census. Further statistics on local movements of population within districts were not available. Thus in the absence of statistical basis for a more refined treatment of population movements, we must accept that many of the social and economic implications would not receive the careful attention which they deserve.

But birth place statistics from which it is possible to work out a residence index give no indication as to the time at which the migration occurred. The movement could have taken place at any time between the birth and the time of enumeration. Some of the reported outgoing migrations or incoming migrations may be survivors of groups who departed or arrived at their destinations many years before the Census date. The age-sex data has been used to trace the nature and effect of migration of various districts and provinces. But they also provide a picture that leads to an understanding of the impact of the movements and their probable causes.

Despite these limitations the importance of migration as a subject and the need for its scientific study as a basic social change in developing Kenya cannot be ignored. To understand the distributive effects of our rapid social and economic changes requires a close study of population mobility backed by adequate data. National migrations within the boundaries of the state could be a symptom of deep regional and social problems. Because of its influence in a wide variety of social, economic and political problems of the nation, this is a relevant field of research which cannot be neglected by social scientists.

The first major conclusion in considering the problem of population movement is the need for improvement in the recording of the basic data. This study forms the beginning of a series of periodic analyses which will be necessary for us to gain a clearer picture of the nature of the problem and means whereby it can be influenced at various policy levels.

A study of national population mobility presupposes the importance of stable boundaries. Unfortunately, as it was shown in earlier chapters, the internal boundaries of Kenya have been notoriously unstable. Thus except for the fixed location of urban area, a comparative study of population movements between the provinces and districts and within these boundaries may be increasingly more difficult. Even at the time of writing there were moves for still further boundary changes. The problem of boundary instability however is not peculiar to the study of population. It is a major limitation in a number of important areas of social research. With these preliminary remarks on the research problems we now turn to summarise the main features of the dynamism of Kenya's population.

Earlier it was stated that movements of population in Kenya have two broad aspects. There are the international migrations which have received superficial treatment in various research monographs. But this study concentrates on the national population movements. The definition of these types of movements is that they take place within the country and with reference to provincial, district and urban and other such boundaries.

The movement which has been analysed is a study at a point of time and a reflection of decades of social and economic policies in the country. The first main feature of the movement is its small volume in comparison with the population of Kenya as a whole. Looked at on a national plane, migration of population as reflected in the statistics of birth places had affected a very small portion of the country's eight million population. But it will be noted that the small volume of the movement does not give an adequate impression of the differential effect on various aspects of the life of the community. Its impact is more pronounced in the limited number of urban settlements.

1. RURAL TO RURAL MIGRATIONS

The first obvious type of movement affecting the population of Kenya may be defined as rural to rural movement. This rural to rural migration is a reflection of the basic distinction between the former African areas and what came to be known administratively as the 'White Highlands' of Kenya. But it will be shown that there are other similar movements not covered in the study.

Into this area population has moved from nearly all parts of Kenya, though in varying numbers. The widespread distribution of Kikuyu, Luo, Luhya and Kamba elements which are shown in the age-sex pyramids of the districts of the former 'White Highlands' is a clear example of the importance of the development of the highland area on the population of the country.

The nature of this type of movement is to be clearly seen in the old Rift Valley districts and in a few of the old Central Province districts such as Thika, Kiambu and Nanyuki. In these movements it is possible to distinguish two main components. The national component seems to have attracted population from well beyond the province. Thus in this type we find the Luo, Kamba, Luhya and Kikuyu in the Rift Valley districts formerly defined as 'Scheduled Areas'. In the Central Province the national component is mainly represented by the presence of Nyanza, Rift Valley and Coast elements in the migration stream.

However, within each province there is a distinct pull affecting the elements normally resident in the province. There is thus a substantial migration within the Rift Valley involving an exchange of population between the former African districts and those of the former Scheduled Districts. We have noted the presence of the Pokot, Elgeyo, Turkana and Tugen in the Nakuru district, and the prevalence of elements from Nandi and other Rift Valley districts population in Trans-Nzoia and Uasin Gishu. In the Central Province, the age-sex pyramids clearly show the importance of the Kikuyu element in Thika and Nanyuki Districts. A considerable proportion of the extra-provincial foreign population might represent infiltration from the areas bordering these migration destinations.

But movement of population has not been wholly directed to farming areas of the former 'White Highlands' districts. The study shows an important movement into the farming areas of the old Nyanza Province such as Kericho and the islands of plantation farming in the Coast districts of Kwale, Kilifi-Malindi and Taita. It is important at this stage to say that such a widespread effect in a relatively undeveloped economy could only have been made possible by direct stimulation of population mobility. This will be referred to in the section on causes of the movements.

The clearest evidence of a large volume of rural to rural mobility is the dominance of the Rift Valley Province. Analysis of birthplace showed the wide gap between the 263,333 inmigrating stream and 41,887 out-migrating group. Similarly, it could be said that a large part of the Central Province incoming stream of 67,629 persons was primarily a movement to the farming areas of Thika, Kiambu and Nanyuki.

2. RURAL TO URBAN MOVEMENTS

In the survey, the rural–urban movements of population form one of the most important aspects of population changes. According to 1962 Census some 7·8 per cent of Kenya's total population was living in the urban areas of the country. It has already been shown that between 1948 and 1962 the urban population rose steeply from 285,445 to 670,945 a growth rate of 135 per cent or an average compound rate of growth of 6·3 per cent every year over the intercensal period of fourteen years.[1] Between 1947 and 1957, the City of Nairobi nearly doubled its size.[2] The importance of migration in the growth of towns in Kenya is reflected in the fact that between 1948 and 1962, the urban Africans increased by 174 per cent. Rural-urban movements are concentrated in the fast expanding urban centres of Nairobi and Mombasa. A considerable proportion of immigrating population into the Rift Valley is accounted for by the main urban centres such as Nakuru, Eldoret, Kitale and Naivasha.

There is a fundamental difference in the nature of movements to the urban areas. The towns are far more national in their impact than the development of the rural

[1]Bloomberg N. & Abrams C. *Report of United Nations Mission to Kenya on Housing,* Government Printer, Nairobi p. 4, 1965
[2]Smith T. E. & Blacker J. G. C. *Population Characteristics of the Commonwealth Countries of Tropical Africa* p. 21, 1963

Table 8.1 PER CAPITA INCOME 1962:
(MONETARY ONLY)

		£
(a)	Nairobi E.P.D.	252·55
	Rift Valley	22·58
	Coast Province	38·78
(b)	Central Province	12·15
	Nyanza Province	5·94
	Southern Province	5·41

SOURCE: Economics and Statistical Division, Ministry of Finance and Economic Planning

areas of the Rift Valley Province and certain districts of the Central Province and the Coast. Aided by transport facilities, the towns have an impact that penetrates far into the rural life of most parts of the Republic. The role of towns in the movements of population is best understood through the analysis of the effects of migrations. With the rapid growth of certain towns in the country the rural-urban movement is a growing problem rather than a diminishing one. The problem is concentrated in a north-west to south-east axis extending from the Lake basin to Mombasa at the coast.

But rural-urban movement shows even more clearly the contrast between the pull in the immediate vicinity and the long distance national movement. The City of Nairobi shows clearly its overwhelming impact on the dense population that occupy the former Central Province districts of Kiambu, Fort Hall (Muranga), Nyeri, Embu and Meru. Similarly, Mombasa's impact locally is seen in the surrounding districts of Kwale, Kilifi-Malindi and even the more remote coast districts of Taita, Tana River and Lamu. But the bulk of the migrating population to Mombasa is still composed of the up-country stream from the Lake Basin, Central Province and the districts of Machakos and Kitui.

3. CAUSES OF POPULATION MOVEMENTS

The study of population mobility in Kenya is in its infancy and the statistics available and results of researches that have been carried out in this field permit certain tentative observations. There is no doubt that the causes which lead to these well defined movements are to be found in the complex inter-relationships of natural and man-made influences. As a general rule we may consider three aspects of these movements. There are the influences which push people away from their home bases, the attractions of the areas to which they go and the means through which these movements take place. These are questions of environmental pressures, the expectations of the destination of the movements and the technological influences of transport and communication. Geographically these form part of the larger problem of the nature and development of the country's natural and human resources. There has always been some form of mobility of population in response to environmental adjustment.

But we must begin with the obvious causes of movements which are in themselves of recent origin.

The primary cause of current shifts of population is the environmental disequilibrium which began with the development of European settlement in the highland areas of Kenya. Before this change the gap between the economies of various regions of Kenya was small. The subsistence economy, whether with a pastoral or agricultural bias, was an insufficient basis for the large scale movements which are now part of our social and economic life.

The evolution of the 'White Highlands' economy in the rural areas of Kenya had an impact somewhat similar to the development of mineral resources in central and southern Africa. The island of European settlement and economy intensified the gap between the area and the rest of rural Kenya and thus set the pace for the changing, though continuing, mobility of population between these areas. The overwhelming importance of the Rift Valley is the clearest proof of effect of the development of the Highland resources. Even subsequent interest in the development of African rural areas has not been sufficiently intensive to affect the trend appreciably. The cumulative effect of the high rate of capital investment aided by transport facilities of road and rail are crucial factors in the flow of population to and from these areas.

The effect of divergent policies in the economic development of the former European and African areas are reflected in the per capita income of the Provinces (Table 8.1).

The Nairobi area, the Rift Valley and the Coast Province with the Port of Mombasa are areas which have attracted a high rate of capital investment and therefore offer better prospects for earning a higher income. The levels of per capita income in these areas are in sharp contrast to the former predominantly African areas of Central, Nyanza and Southern Provinces. But such overall figures mask the areal differences in the level of expenditure which account for the enormous importance of the former scheduled lands in the economy of the country and hence in the general shift of population. The figures in Table 8.2 give some idea of the wide differences even within the rural areas of the former scheduled lands

Table 8.2 CAPITAL EXPENDITURE IN FARMS NET OF SALES, 1959/60 AND 1960/61

	Non-residential Buildings		Residential Buildings		Mechanical Equipment		Other Permanent Improvements		Total £'000	
	1959/60	1960/61	1959/60	1960/61	1959/60	1960/61	1959/60	1960/61	1959/60	1960/61
Laikipia	18	14	38	23	83	62	93	74	231	173
Naivasha	34	22	54	39	186	117	111	92	385	269
Nakuru	54	36	90	62	325	248	218	187	686	533
Trans-Nzoia	28	21	47	24	166	134	108	80	349	259
Uasin Gishu	52	29	55	40	226	248	191	188	524	505
Lumbwa/Songhor	20	40	36	56	61	67	109	106	226	269
Kibos/Chemelil	22	11	22	25	67	68	81	92	192	196
Sotik	26	12	36	6	32	40	115	94	209	153
Kericho/Nandi	104	91	196	156	119	156	529	555	948	959
Nairobi	130	48	93	76	94	69	186	186	503	379
Mount Kenya	17	8	35	31	91	67	119	72	262	178
Thika	68	41	87	59	140	121	283	308	578	530
Machakos	30	2	12	13	42	21	80	66	165	103
Voi	9	—	19	65	27	25	149	94	214	183
Coast	27	31	11	27	28	64	48	68	114	191
Total	638	406	830	703	1,698	1,509	2,422	2,263	5,587	4,881

SOURCE: *Agricultural Census 1961 Scheduled Areas and Coastal Strip* Table 32, p. 118. Economics and Statistics Division

and other islands of modern plantation farming in the Lake Victoria Basin and along the Coast.

Industrial development in Kenya has concentrated mainly in the larger urban centres with Nairobi and Mombasa far ahead of the smaller towns.

So far we have merely considered those influences which exert a pull on the rural population. In the early stages there was pressure and inducement for rural labour to work on the farms. But having established a stream a momentum was built up which continued to draw rural labour into such paid employment.

A careful examination of the main sources of the mobile population shows that they coincide with certain major concentrations of population. The source in the Lake Victoria basin was primarily made up of the population from the main centres of heavy concentration in North, Central, South Nyanza and Kisii districts. East of the Rift the national stream of migration is supplied mainly by the source region extending from Mount Kenya foothills south-west to Nairobi area. This is one of the most important population regions of East Africa. Close to the east of the Mount Kenya-Nairobi axis of population, the hills of Ukambani in the district of Machakos and Kitui emerge as one of the primary sources of migrating population.

The association of source regions of the migrating population with the major concentrations of population located so far apart suggest that natural factors are important in the mobility of population. These are areas where due to advantages of the natural environment population tended to concentrate. In these same areas, population has increased to the extent that the available land cannot maintain an adequate standard of living or even support improved living conditions.

A study of the population and land use in the Western areas of Kenya showed that in 1948 well over 60 per cent of the land had been devoted to the growing of crops. In the more densely peopled parts of North Nyanza, fragmentation had reached an advanced stage. Over the lower parts of Central and South Nyanza, the land was too poor to support the heavy population concentration. Mention of population concentration and fragmentation suggests that evidence of an agrarian crisis should be one of the characteristics of the major source areas of population. This is certainly the case in parts of the old Nyanza, Central and Southern Provinces.

In areas where the 1961 survey was carried on a holding basis these show significant differences which strongly support the agrarian crisis as a factor in our population movement.[3] In the area of survey by holdings the average size showed a variation from 18·52 acres in the less closely settled Elgon Nyanza to 3·61 acres in the more heavily populated districts of Fort Hall (Muranga).[4] But the indication of areas of acute land problems is best seen in the more detailed figures by district and divisions given in Table 8.3.[5]

In Kiambu the average acreage of parcels in the holdings were well below the district acreage in Kiambaa and Kikuyu divisions. In Nyeri district divisional average acreage of parcels was far lower than the average for Kiambu district. The district average of 4·27 acres compared unfavourably with 5·15 for Kiambu. Lowest figures and therefore the most extreme fragmentation was a feature of Fort Hall District which had an average acreage of 3·61. Divisional acreage varied from 2·95 acres for Kangema to 4·67 acres for Kigumo. It will be

[3] *Kenya African Agricultural Sample Census 1960/61* Part I pp. 17–21. Economics and Statistics Division
[4] *Kenya African Agricultural Sample Census 1960/61* Table 12 p. 18
[5] *Kenya African Agricultural Sample Census 1960/61* Part II Table 241 pp. 138–9

Table 8.3 NUMBER, AREA AND FRAGMENTATION OF HOLDINGS IN AREAS SURVEYED ON HOLDING BASIS

DIVISION/ DISTRICT/ PROVINCE	HOLDINGS			FRAGMENTATION		
	Number '000	'000 Acres	Average Acreage	No. of Parcels '000	Average Parcels '000	Average Acreage of Parcels
Gatundu	13·3	74·9	5·64	13·3	1·00	5·64
Githunguri	10·4	64·0	6·17	10·4	1·00	6·17
Limuru	3·8	23·1	6·10	3·8	1·00	6·10
Kiambaa	4·1	13·5	3·31	4·1	1·00	3·31
Kikuyu	7·4	24·9	3·37	7·4	1·00	3·37
Kiambu	38·9	200·3	5·15	38·9	1·00	5·15
Mathira	11·7	45·8	3·91	11·7	1·00	3·91
North Tetu	10·5	39·4	3·77	10·5	1·00	3·77
Othaya	7·6	38·0	5·01	7·6	1·00	5·01
South Tetu	8·0	38·2	4·76	8·0	1·00	4·76
Nyeri	37·8	161·3	4·27	37·8	1·00	4·27
Kiharu	12·3	37·0	3·02	12·3	1·00	3·02
Kandara	13·5	53·7	3·99	13·5	1·00	3·99
Kangema	6·1	18·1	2·95	6·1	1·00	2·95
Kigumo	5·8	26·9	4·67	5·8	1·00	4·67
Fort Hall	37·6	135·8	3·61	37·6	1·00	3·61
Gichugu	9·4	77·1	8·21	9·4	1·00	8·21
Ndia	13·2	83·1	6·31	13·2	1·00	6·31
Embu	22·6	160·2	7·10	22·6	1·00	7·10
CENTRAL PROVINCE	136·8	657·6	4·81	136·8	1·00	4·8
Manga	12·3	89·3	7·25	12·3	1·00	7·25
Kuja	8·4	74·4	8·87	9·1	1·08	8·21
Lambwe	5·9	38·2	6·43	15·7	2·64	2·44
Kendu	22·2	85·2	3·84	63·8	2·58	1·33
Migori	13·1	403·9	30·75	13·1	1·00	30·75
SOUTH NYANZA	61·9	690·9	11·16	114·0	1·84	6·06
Nyando	27·2	167·0	6·15	116·6	4·29	1·43
Nyahera	14·3	32·9	2·30	36·0	2·52	0·91
Maseno	19·2	162·9	8·47	47·7	2·48	3·42
Bondo	19·7	214·2	10·90	41·8	2·12	5·13
Boro	11·7	135·4	11·58	42·1	3·60	3·22
Ukwala	15·3	75·3	4·91	20·3	1·32	3·71
CENTRAL NYANZA	107·4	787·7	7·34	304·5	2·84	2·59
Vihiga	33·8	116·1	3·43	36·5	1·08	3·18
Ikolomani	41·4	167·8	4·05	45·6	1·10	3·68
Mumias	18·6	211·9	11·38	22·4	1·20	9·45
Lurambi	11·8	208·6	17·61	14·0	1·18	14·92
North Nyanza	105·7	704·3	6·66	118·5	1·12	5·94
Eastern	11·4	173·7	15·30	11·7	1·03	14·86
Central	12·0	261·0	21·79	12·4	1·04	21·04
Western	14·6	269·0	18·38	14·6	1·00	18·38
Elgon Nyanza	38·0	703·7	18·52	38·7	1·02	18·18
Upper Belgut	8·8	88·5	10·07	9·7	1·10	9·14
Lower Belgut	1·9	58·8	30·18	2·0	1·02	29·59
Bomet	8·6	85·1	9·90	8·6	1·00	9·90
Itembe	12·5	114·0	9·11	12·5	1·00	9·11
Buret	8·3	76·5	9·21	8·5	1·02	9·04
Kericho	40·2	422·9	10·52	41·2	1·03	10·23
NYANZA PROVINCE	353·2	3,309·5	9·37	616·9	1·75	5·36
Central	3·4	47·9	14·08	3·4	1·00	14·08
Northern	5·6	115·7	20·69	5·6	1·00	20·69
Southern	6·4	88·2	13·85	6·5	1·02	13·60
Eastern	4·4	72·7	16·39	4·6	1·03	15·93
Nandi	19·8	324·4	16·38	20·0	1·01	16·22
ALL AREAS	509·8	4,291·5	8·42	773·7	1·52	5·55

SOURCE: Kenya African Agricultural Sample Census 1960/61 Part III, Table 241, p. 138-9

Table 8.4 MODE OF OPERATION OF HOLDINGS
IN AREAS COVERED BY FARM SURVEYS

Not by holder

District/Province	Number '000	% of Total	Area '000 Acres
Kiambu	17·00	44	72·1
Nyeri	13·2	35	50·8
Fort Hall	12·8	34	36·8
Embu	7·3	33	50·9
Central Province	50·3	37	210·6
South Nyanza	5·6	9	70·2
Central Nyanza	22·0	20	98·2
North Nyanza	18·2	17	76·4
Elgon Nyanza	*Figures not available*		
Kericho	2·7	7	12·8
Nyanza	48·5	15	257·6
Nandi	1·2	6	21·5
ALL AREAS	100·0	21	489·7

SOURCE: *Kenya African Agricultural Sample Census* 1960/61
Vol. I, Table 18 p. 22

noted that the situation in the three main Kikuyu districts was quite different from Embu where not only the district average but the divisional average acreage were much higher.

Extreme fragmentation in the former Nyanza Province is clearly indicated in the district average acreage for the parcels and in the divisional averages for Central Nyanza. Here it will be noted that the district average was as low as 2·59 acres. However, the divisional average acreage for the parcels of land ranged from 0·91 acres in the heavily populated Nyahera Division to 5·13 acres in Bondo. Analysis of the intensity of fragmentation showed that 62 per cent of the holdings in the district were fragmented. A total of 45,000 holdings or 42 per cent of the total holdings were fragmented into parcels varying from three to nine and over.[6]

In North Nyanza, divisional averages were low for the more closely settled areas of Vihiga and Ikolomani. But Lurambi division showed parcel average acreage of about three times the sizes in the former two divisions. In districts such as Elgon, Kericho and Nandi which contributed little to the stream of migration the average acreage of parcels were well over ten acres.

Thus in Nyanza the dominance of elements from Central, North and South Nyanza could be related closely to the social and economic conditions in the land. North and Central Nyanza, which contributed the bulk of the migration streams, were according to 1948 land use analysis dominated by a well defined area covering the wetter parts in which the average acreage of cropland available per person was well below one acre.[7] In the drier lake shore areas of Central and South Nyanza, the proportion of land devoted to cropland was much lower. Except for Uyoma location in Central Nyanza, most areas showed that less than half of the land surface was devoted to cropland. This low acreage for cropland is an indication of the climatic difficulties of the area and the general poverty of the soils, most of which is lateritic. The carrying capacity of the land in Nyanza is thus a crucial element in the migration. But pressure of population as a factor in mobility of population is not limited to Nyanza. The problem of man-land ratio is clearly an important factor in the rural situation of Kikuyuland where there has been a long tradition of outflow of population to the

farms. Certainly the figures on fragmentation must take into consideration the fact that many people have moved out of these areas.

The limited coverage of the Kenya African Agricultural Sample Census also showed considerable degree of absentee holders in the heavily populated districts of Central Province and Nyanza Province. The figures in Table 8.4 bring out the significance of this problem in Kiambu, Nyeri, Fort Hall, Embu, Central Nyanza and North Nyanza. Districts which contributed little to the stream of migration, such as Kericho and Nandi, had few absentee holders.

The problem of population pressure on the land is closely related to the nature of population increase. Data is not available in adequate coverage to show the regional distribution of such vital statistics as natality, mortality and fertility. But a recent study by Ansley J. Coale based on estimates of such vital statistics showed that Nyanza Province is located in a ridge of high fertility extending from the Red Sea in Sudan to Central Africa.

In this region total fertility varied from 6·50 to well over 8·00. Nyanza area in particular was among the highest with fertility rates of 8·00 to 8·49. More accurate data would probably show the Kikuyu-Embu and Meru area to the east of Nairobi as an area of high fertility.[8] The situation in Nyanza does suggest that a high rate of population increase is a basic factor in the migration especially from the major source areas outlined. However,

[6]International Bank for Reconstruction and Development Report 'Experience in Central Nyanza' p. 10

[7]Ominde S. H. 'Land and Population in the Western Districts of Nyanza Province, Kenya (Unpublished Ph.D Thesis, London University) 1963

[8]Coale A. J. 'Estimates of fertility and mortality in tropical Africa' Proceedings of the First African Population Conference, Ibadan 1967

it will be necessary to secure more reliable data before an accurate picture of the relationship between the regional distribution of areas of high fertility and the major source areas of migrating population can be established.

The foregoing analysis of causes of population movements have concentrated primarily on environmental, economic and demographic factors. In modern Kenya it is becoming more and more evident that it is not solely economic but rather socio-economic situations in the rural areas of the country that underlie the streams of migration. This is not the place to enlarge on the impact of education in population mobility. However, the recent focus on the problem of primary school leavers provides a useful background to the understanding of the age selection of the migrations in Kenya. Thousands of youths are leaving schools at the end of primary education or earlier with no prospects of employment.

4. PROVINCIAL PATTERNS OF SELECTIVE MOVEMENTS

To the social and economic planner, perhaps the most significant feature of the national mobility of population is its selective nature. The problem of who leaves the rural areas and at what age is one of the basic problems of planning for the rural and urban development.

Population movement in Kenya is highly selective of age and sex. It is confirmed by the age-sex ratio and age-sex pyramids that rural Kenya is affected by movement of persons generally between the ages of 15 and about 39 years of age. This is a movement of varying intensity as shown by the district sex ratio and sex pyramids by five year age groups. The impact of age and sex selection is most striking in the main source districts of rural Kenya. It has been shown that these are the districts which are located in the major population centres of the Lake Victoria Basin, the highland area, east of the rift, the hills of Machakos and Taita and finally the populated strip along the coast. At the receiving end, the selective impact of migration is clearly demonstrated in the age-sex ratio and age-sex pyramids of the urban areas as well as rural districts which depend on labour migration.

Perhaps the most significant conclusion in this study is

the overwhelming masculine character of the migrating population in Kenya. Whereas the City of Nairobi showed an African sex ratio of 149 males to 100 females, in the Peri-Urban area we have seen that the proportion was 181 African men to 100 women. A similarly high ratio of men to women is a feature of all the remaining centres of the Republic. According to 1962 the ratio varied from 125 men to 100 women in the case of Lamu to 213 men to 100 women for Athi River. In this respect the Kenya towns present a major contrast to many towns in North and West Africa where women are in the majority.

This high masculinity of the migration is not confined to urban areas. The proportion of men to 100 women in the main receiving districts of the Central Province of Nanyuki and Thika was 125 to 127 respectively. It is significant that the same pattern is repeated in the former Nyanza district of Kericho and in the former 'White Highlands' districts of the Rift Valley Province.

But mobility of population in Kenya is not merely selective of the sexes. A closer examination of the district age-sex ratio by five year age groups shows clearly that it is concentrated on the male population in their pre-productive years. In Nyanza Province the predominantly masculine movement out of the district affects the age group from 15 to about 55 years except in Elgon Nyanza which showed an age range for the outflow of males between 15 and 49 years. South Nyanza showed a later movement between 20 and 39 years. The age-sex ratio here shows the age range more clearly than the sex pyramids. Even Kericho district shows an outward movement of males between 15 and 25 years.

In the Central Province selective migrations appeared to start about the same time. But the male deficiency in terms of sex ratio for Embu, Kiambu and Nyeri showed a much higher age limit. In Embu, the deficiency is as late as 69. In Fort Hall males are away between 15 and 54 and again there appeared to be marked deficiency between 60 and 79 years. Kiambu male migration starts at about 20 years and the deficiency is noted up to 79 years. Nyeri pattern is broadly similar to Fort Hall. Deficiency in late years suggests that this pattern has existed for some decades.

The sex ratio for the Southern Province shows the

concentration of the outward movement between 20 and 44 years. In the Coast Province migration of males starts at about 15 years but it has been shown that it generally ends much earlier. The upper age limit here for men seems to be 34 years except for Kilifi-Malindi in which it continued up to 44 years. In the Rift Valley the lower age limit seems to be 20 years and the upper age limit for men is between 34 and 39 years.

But our conclusion on the selective nature of migrations on the basis of sex ratio masks the increasing flow of women and children into our expanding urban areas.[9] Blacker (1965) has shown that the masculinity of the urban African population was less pronounced in 1962 than in 1948. In 1948 the urban African population had a sex ratio of 295 males per 100 females and the adults formed 64 per cent of the total. But in 1962 there was a ratio of 163 males per 100 females in the towns and the adult population had decreased to 44 per cent of the total African population.

It has been shown that on the whole the migration into the urban areas and other farming districts tends to attract women between the ages of 15 to 34 years. In some cases the lower age limit is about 10 or 14 years. In most cases the dominant age group is 20 to 24 years among the females. However, it is also important to note the considerable differences that exist between the various ethnic groups.

Mobility of population in Kenya is clearly varied in its impact on the various ethnic groups in the country. It may be argued that the dominance of certain ethnic elements in the movement is primarily due to the location of their home districts in relation to the main source regions. This certainly is an important factor. However, it does not follow that the drive to migrate from the more densely peopled or poorer areas can be taken for granted. In the old Nyanza Province, the Gusii people live in a region with one of the highest densities of population. But both the males and females showed low emigration rates.

In the old Central Province selective emigration is dominated by the Kikuyu and Tharaka ethnic elements. Emigration rates for the Embu, Mbere and Meru were very low. Meru with large areas of land showed the lowest emigration rate. Nyanza Province showed the dominance of the Luo, Iteso and Luhya ethnic elements

in the migration stream. The Gusii had the lowest emigration rate in the Province. The Southern Province stream was predominantly a Kamba ethnic movement.

Calculated emigration rates for the Rift Valley Province underline the importance of the Nandi, Pokot, Sabaot, Kipsigis and Elgeyo. Very low migration rates were recorded for the Tugen and Marakwet. In the Northern Province both the Somali and Galla gave very low emigration rates. Even the Samburu were not moving in appreciable numbers. The Coast Province showed rather high migration rates especially among the Pokomo Riverine, Swahili-Shirazi and Bajuni ethnic elements.

Transport facilities play an important role in stimulation of mobility of population. The low rates of emigration among the Galla-Somali and the more remotely situated Rift Valley ethnic elements are partly due to the isolation of the areas or to poor accessibility.

5. CONSEQUENCES OF INTERNAL MOVEMENTS OF POPULATION IN KENYA

Some of the important aspects of population which results from migration have already been touched upon in describing the evidence for population movements and the nature of these movements throughout Kenya. However, for purposes of a concluding summary on consequences we need to consider the demographic, social and economic implications.

Briefly, movements of population in causing a shift of population between various parts of the country have altered numbers in these areas. Changing numbers are an important geographical element whether at the supplying end or at the receiving end. Perhaps the most important problem here which needs examination is the effect of migration in the congested parts of the country, the pressure in the limited urban areas, and the effect of movement into areas which were formerly sparsely peopled. In these aspects population mobility is of vital importance in the human geography of the country.

We have already touched on the striking evidence of movement in terms of age-sex ratio and age-sex pyramids. Because of its selective nature we now have a clear view of the character of the residual population in the rural

[9]Bloomberg N. & Abrams C. *Report of United Nations Mission to Kenya on Housing* p. 4 para. 13, p. 60 U.N.O. 1965

areas and the changing balance of population in the major destinations of the national movement. The distortions in the age-sex ratio and age-sex pyramids have important implications to planning which will be examined further. Unsatisfactory coverage of statistics does not allow generalisation over the effects of migrations on fertility and mortality either in the rural or in the urban areas.

In social terms we need to consider the effect of mobility in the chances of the groups moving to adjust themselves. Kenya is culturally a heterogeneous society. Movements of large numbers of people at certain ages to certain parts of the country has vital social implications which have yet to be analysed. We shall refer to this in the treatment of the urban areas.

Further, selection of persons through education and their movement away from their home area is most likely a weakening factor to the supplying areas. The question is whether at their destination social integration has taken place to permit their maximum contribution.

Housing is one of man's basic requirements. The movement of large numbers of persons naturally creates a housing crisis and a worsening of social conditions. This problem is particularly relevant to our developing urban areas. Finally, we must examine to what extent the economic motives of migrations are realized. Very often movement of population may have an adverse effect on the actual expectation of the persons migrating.

i. Consequences of Internal Migrations in Rural Areas

We have already noted that in terms of the total population of Kenya, the volume of migrating population is small. But the dominance of the main population centres of the former Nyanza, Central and Southern Provinces requires special emphasis. As sources of the migrating population, movements of people from the overcrowded parts of Nyanza is a welcome relief. The economic consequences of migration away from the rural areas of former North Nyanza, Central parts of South Nyanza and Kisii arise from the relationship of population numbers to available land. Similarly it may be said that the movement of the Kamba people from the crowded parts of Machakos and Kitui has had a welcome consequence in these areas.

Perhaps the most striking consequence of population movement in Kenya is the widespread nature of Kikuyu migration throughout most districts of Kenya. The Kikuyu districts of Kiambu, Fort Hall, Nyeri have especially benefited from the redistribution of population to which they have contributed a large share. In this process of movement the poorer areas of Kenya have not benefited. Thus the economic stagnation in the semi-arid and arid lands of Kenya can be partially explained by their failure to attract the type of population which has been involved in the national migration.

The rural farming areas of the Rift Valley have definitely increased their population as a result of migrations on a national scale. In fact during the initial phase of the economic revolution of the area, the sparse settlement by the pastoral communities was an insufficient basis for the modern type of economy which the European settlers began to establish. For a long time recruitment agencies were organised in the major centres of population. During the Second World War there was conscription to make up for the shortage of labour in the area. The departure of European farmers since 1960 has partially reversed the trend of employment in these areas.

In supplying districts of Central Province, it is migration of population that largely accounts for the striking predominance of women in the population of Nyeri, Fort Hall (Muranga), Kiambu, Embu and Meru. Thika and Nanyuki which attracted the male migration have already been shown to have a high masculinity ratio. In the Coast Province, Kilifi-Malindi, Kwale, Lamu and Taita were slightly less affected. But even in these districts the 1962 Census showed a slight tendency to male deficiency.

In the Western areas of Kenya the major supplying districts such as Central Nyanza, North Nyanza were similarly affected. Even Elgon Nyanza and South Nyanza also showed male deficiency. The heavily populated district of Kisii was the least affected. But even here there was evidence of an outflow of males. Kericho district which is an important goal of migration showed a high masculinity ratio. It can therefore be shown that there is a definite demographic pattern in the supplying and receiving rural areas of Kenya which arises directly from population migration.

Drawing their population from an ethnically diverse country, the main farming districts have a heterogeneous population as yet not integrated into a closely knit community. The migrating person is thus socially a maladjusted person and represents a potential source of return migration. We have already drawn attention to this as a possible source of some of the extra-provincial births. But the problem of an ethnically diverse population which is not fully integrated is more striking in the close environment of the urban centres than in the rural areas.

It has been mentioned earlier that migration creates pressure on housing. Poor housing conditions in the rural areas are directly related to migration. The absent farm labourer rarely has sufficient funds to keep the temporary house at home in repair. At the receiving end the housing of the rural farm labourer has long been known to be of a very low standard. The stereotyped labour lines, mostly of grass roofs and mud walls, represent an effort to cope with the cost of housing under different conditions from those of the urban areas. In the more prosperous farming areas such as Kericho, more permanent structures can be seen in the tea plantations.

Perhaps the most important consequence of migration is the successful development of modern farming which has played such a vital role in the economy of Kenya. The development in the 'White Highlands' and outlying islands of modern farming in Nyanza, Central, Southern and Coast Provinces has been made possible not only by application of capital, but also by an assured employment goal for labour from the main population regions of Kenya. In moving to these areas rural populations have broadened the range of occupations to include employment in some of the tertiary activities. The development of the rural economy outlined above therefore represents the more positive aspects of rural population mobility. But even if we confine our scrutiny to the source areas of population it is possible to say that problems of overcrowding, fragmentation and general rural poverty would have been much worse without the outlet through migrations away from the rural areas.

Movement of population has an important bearing on the problems of under-employment and unemployment. There are no exact statistics available on a national basis. However, it is now known that the Primary School leavers form a large proportion of the stream of movement away from the rural areas. This flow of population from the rural areas is already far in excess of available job opportunities.

Agriculture and forestry have been the main fields of employment. But recent changes in farm ownership have resulted in a considerable reduction of wage employment. The transfer of large European owned farms to settlement schemes has been partly responsible for this fall. Between 1960 and 1965 wage earners in agriculture and forestry fell from 272,000 to 210,000. Although resettlement employment has created new jobs the balance has not been sufficient to offset the loss. Rural unemployment is unevenly distributed and is most prevalent particularly in those areas which heavily depended on hired labour on European farms.[10]

ii. *Consequences of Internal Migrations in Urban Areas*
Population of Kenya is increasing rapidly and urbanisation, though only affecting a small fraction of this population, is raising many critical problems. The natural rate of population growth is not only high in the country as a whole but it is also high in the urban areas. In the larger City of Nairobi, it is reckoned that population rate of increase is between three and five times faster than that of the total population in the country.[11] It is not the size of the urban population but the rate of increase of the population that poses difficult problems. These difficulties arose partly from the demographic situations in these urban areas and the resources available.

We have already noted the sharp contrast between the age-sex structures of the urban and rural areas. The decisive influence on these age-sex structures is migration. The rapid and recent character of migration to the urban areas of Kenya is reflected in a universal surplus of men or high masculinity ratios. The reported recent increase in the migration of females into the urban areas has not yet seriously upset the masculine dominance in these areas.

A further consequence of the type of migration observed in Kenya is that these urban settlements are largely

[10]Ndegwa P. and Norbye O. D. K. 'Rural Development: The Strategy of Kenya's Development Plan 1966/70' Education, Employment and Rural Development, 1966
[11]*Report of the Workshop on Urbanisation in Africa* p. 18 Economic Commission for Africa, Addis Ababa 1962

populated by people of working age. But at the same time the current large base of dependent children between the ages of 0 and 10 in the urban areas is a feature of great importance to the social and economic planner. The demographic characteristics have a bearing on such problems as employment, education, housing, public health and industrial location. In general, progress in public health does suggest that mortality in the urban areas might be low. But due to overcrowding in certain areas of Kenya's urban centres, infant mortality is still much higher than it should be.

To the youthfulness and masculinity of the urban population in Kenya must be added the ethnic diversity. This diversity is a reflection of the origins of the rural population. The urban population of Kenya is drawn from the four main ethnic groupings that were described earlier in this volume. Until quite recently the urban areas of Kenya were predominantly alien, the African population being found largely in the unplanned peripheral areas. Indeed some of the towns of Kenya are still striking for the foreign composition of their population.

The rapidity of growth of the urban African population has already been mentioned. Considered against the background of wide ethnic differences the urban areas consist of diverse ethnic elements which have not integrated into a homogeneous community. Thus socially the newcomer has to adjust himself to urban worlds rather than the simple rural patterns of his origin. There is a whole area of research here of great importance in planning the future development of our urban society. In most cases, the cry of 'tribalism' is most prominent in the urban areas of the country.

It has been noted that the urban age-sex pyramids are distorted by the influx of young people roughly between the ages of 15 and 49. A large proportion of these people consists of primary school leavers. A growing problem has emerged in these urban areas of fewer job opportunities being pursued by an increasing influx of unskilled labourers and domestic servants. The situation has been made worse by the decline in the employment opportunities especially in the building and construction industry, and domestic service which are largely concentrated in the urban areas (Table 8.5).

Earlier it was mentioned that much of the recent movement of population into the urban centres of Kenya has been of women and children, the child population being largely between 0–9 years. There is thus a pressure for educational facilities at the lower end of the Primary School system which has created immense difficulties for planning. To meet this influx it is necessary for urban authorities to make allowance especially in the centres of more rapid growth.

An acute housing problem, overcrowding and increase in crimes are some of the major problems arising from the influx of population from the rural to the urban areas. In Kenya, the problem has been aggravated by the increased tempo of migration following the raised expectation of the post-war period. As early as 1923 Nairobi Council was compelled to build dormitories for Africans to get rid of the insanitary settlements which had sprung up. The long established deterioration in urban condition of Africans was well recognised by the East African Royal Commission 1953–1955. The Report noted that the Mombasa riots of 1939 were primarily caused by poor housing. In Nairobi, the serious deterioration in the housing situation by 1948 is clearly recorded in the following paragraph from the Municipal African Affairs unpublished report: 'It was disheartening to see legitimately employed Africans sleeping under the verandahs in River Road, in noisome and dangerous shacks in the swamp, in buses parked by the roadside and fourteen to the room in Pumwani, two to a bed and the rest on the floor.'[12]

The race since the war between the increase in the population and the provision of accommodation is clearly indicated by the experience of Nairobi City. By 1947 when the City had an estimated African population of 77,032, it was reckoned that the difference between figures of population and capacity of housing available was 26,000.

In 1949 a total of 10,000 people needed housing but only 450 were housed in that year. By 1951 it was estimated that 10,000 bed spaces were needed. To meet this, some two schemes to house 2,000 were begun but no new housing was completed during that year. In 1953 when 20,000 houses were needed in Nairobi, Mombasa Municipality needed housing for 27,000 people.[13]

[12]*East African Royal Commission Report* 1953–55 Cmnd 9475 p. 207 para. 26 H.M.S.O., London 1955

[13]*East African Royal Commission Report* 1953–55 p. 211 para. 40

Table 8.5

INDUSTRY GROUP	Compound annual average rate of change 1956–65
Private Sector	− 0·4
Agriculture and forestry	− 1·2
Manufacturing and repairs	+ 1·6
Mining and quarrying	−14·0
Building and construction	−12·2
Electric light, power and water	+ 0·9
Commerce	+ 4·9
Transport & Communications	+ 3·3
Other services (including domestic)	+ 1·5
Public Sector	+ 1·0
Kenya Government	− 1·8
East African Railways and Harbours	− 3·5
East African Posts and Telecommunications	− 1·0
East African Common Services Organisation	+ 1·0
Other Public sector (local and foreign, government and defence, civilians only)	+11·1
Total wage and salaried employment	− 0·5

SOURCE: Ray R. S. 'Rates of change in Reported Wage and Salaried Employment in Kenya 1956–65' Education, Employment and Rural Development 1966, p. 195.

Table 8.6

NO. OF ROOMS	Total Persons		NAIROBI Persons		MOMBASA Persons		OTHER PERSONS Persons	
	2+ %	3+ %	2+ %	3+ %	2+ %	3+ %	2+ %	3+ %
1	78	54	78	57	72	49	72	51
2	61	35	60	34	63	35	61	36
3	47	22	49	20	52	22	46	20
4	38	16	33	10	45	16	43	16
TOTAL	71	49	74	52	68	43	69	48

SOURCE: *United Nations Mission to Kenya on Housing* 1965 p. 15

From 1952 up to about 1960, it has not been possible to assess the total demand for housing in Nairobi due to the distortion of the Emergency conditions. By the end of 1958 the City of Nairobi's waiting list showed that there were 7,399 Africans officially in need of housing. But this list did not include the Kikuyu, Embu, and Meru demand for housing.[14] At the end of 1959 City records showed that 7,412 had applied for housing.[15]

By 1960, the situation had rapidly worsened as a result of pre-independence political developments. The effect of the Kenya Government's decision to lift Emergency in January was to aggravate the situation. The concern of Nairobi City Council is clearly expressed in the following paragraph:

'Despite warnings voiced by this Council no special plans were made to deal with the flood of Kikuyu, Embu and Meru people which entered the City chiefly in search of employment after many years of restriction to their reserves. The number variously estimated between 15,000 and 50,000 grossly exceeded the practicable absorption rate into housing particularly into employment where vacancies were fewer as the year progressed. The immediate problem was one of overcrowding in the African Estates of the City and in the consequential increase in water demands and pressure on the health services.'[16]

Added to the problem described above, the City faced increasing difficulties arising from the growth of unauthorised hawking and street trading as well as an increase in crime figures. The problem of street trading is being faced through the establishment of permanent stalls in the City. But the growing volume of demand for housing has continued with little relief. In 1964, Nairobi City Council still had 12,020 on the waiting list,[17] and by 1965 this list had increased to 15,000.

The national implication of the increasing urban housing requirements must in reality depend on the expansion of the urban population. It has been suggested that between 1962 and 1970 the growth of Nairobi will

[14]*Annual Report of the Social Services and Housing Department* 1958 City Council of Nairobi
[15]*Annual Report of the Social Services and Housing Department* 1959 City Council of Nairobi
[16]*Annual Report of the Social Services and Housing Department* 1960 City Council of Nairobi
[17]*Annual Report of the Social Services and Housing Department* 1964 City Council of Nairobi

be slower because of racial adjustment following the departure of some Europeans. The housing requirements will thus be governed largely by the strength of migration and the demographic characteristics of the urban African population. It has been estimated that Nairobi would require 3,400 additional units per year from 1962 to 1970 an increase of 3·9 per cent per annum as compared to a population increase of 4·9 per cent.[18]

Mombasa showed a higher rate of growth of the African population between 1948 and 1962. It has been estimated that the Municipality will require 1,900 units per year between 1962 and 1970. This would represent an annual rate of growth of 4·6 per cent in new housing units as against a population increase of 5·2 per cent per annum.[19]

Mounting influx of rural population into urban areas is reflected in the overcrowding in limited accomodation available or in the setting up of substandard settlements in the vicinity of the towns. The Royal Commission (1953–1955) received evidence that in Nairobi 3,000 men, women and children were occupying accommodation in one estate designed to house 1,200 people.[20] A later report on Mombasa revealed a similar serious overcrowding of the urban African population. The Mombasa Social Survey in 1958 reported that 18·5 per cent of all the Africans of Mombasa Island were living in overcrowded conditions.[21]

Table 8·6 shows the nature of overcrowding in African urban households in Kenya. Overcrowding is serious in the one to two roomed accommodation in all the urban areas of Kenya. Nairobi had the highest percentage of overcrowding in the one roomed accommodation.

Detailed information on overcrowding for individual urban centres is not available and social surveys to reveal the serious consequences are not readily available. There is thus the need for a critical study of the problem of overcrowding in relation to the pattern of migration considered in this volume. The urban planners are faced with the double problem of mounting demand and a backlog of accommodation requirements which had led to the continuing problem of overcrowding and its attendant social maladjustments.

In concluding the subject of the consequences of migration, it is important to draw attention to the local migration within a district for which statistics were not available. There are already in Kenya important local shifts of population which have come about as a result of the application of the government policy on resettlements. It is possible to conclude that the liquidation of the former 'White Highlands' of Kenya will result in important reorganisation of population. Such changes are already taking place in the affected areas of the Rift Valley, Western, Nyanza and Central Provinces.

[18]U.N.O. report 1965 p. 14 paras 74 and 75

[19]U.N.O. report 1965 p. 15 paras 75 and 76

[20]H.M.S.O. 1955 *East African Royal Commission Report* 1953–55 p. 210 para 38

[21]*Mombasa Master Plan* Mombasa Municipal Council 1962 p. 29

Conclusion

When analysis of the relationship between the resource development and its impact on the population of Kenya has been completed it is necessary to return to consider the contribution of such a geographical study to the practical issues which face Kenya. This is the realm of applied geography where we are specifically concerned with the application of research and analysis to the practical purposes of planning development. Before plunging into planning implications of this study it is necessary to be clear of what we mean by the term planning in the context of Kenya's development problems. These problems call for many different forms of planning whether social, economic or physical (land use). In more developed countries planning in the wider regional context has been defined as involving proposals for the 'distribution of population and industry, the location of main transport routes, the distribution of rural services and the location of large non-agricultural uses in open country to a greater degree of detail than would be comprehended in a national plan.'[1]

Planning as thus defined is essentially physical planning and differs from the more comprehensive approach of the definition incorporated in the Kenya Development Plan of 1966–70. This concept of planning embraces not only the physical, social and economic but financial aspects as well. In terms of this study the challenge of planning takes two forms. There is clearly the problem of rural urban balance of development to absorb the increasing volume of annual additions to the labour force as well as those who have lost jobs in the course of contracting employment opportunities.

As a problem of population movement it is essentially a problem of rural development, which forms the source of the swelling volume of the migrating population. But for proposals to be effective it is necessary to distinguish the nature or scope of planning.

Planning in Kenya is, in the main, of short term duration. Short term planning of five year duration is in contrast to the long term planning of fifteen years or more. There are good reasons in the absence of adequate statistics why our planning should in the meantime be of short duration. But it is possible to see in this study that some of the problems raised require forecasting into the more distant future.

Attention has been drawn to the rural focus of development problem in Kenya. The economic aspect has been effectively summarised by Ndegwa and Norbye (1966).

> It is therefore evident that the non-agricultural sector of the economy will not be able to absorb most of the increase in the labour force until the time when non-agricultural sectors have so expanded as to represent a far larger proportion of total employment than they do at present. The planners in Kenya must therefore work under the constraint that income and employment must be created in the agricultural sector of the economy if the benefits of development are to reach the majority of the people directly.[2]

One of the most valuable contributions of this study has been to demonstrate the importance of accurate demographic statistics as a basis for explaining planning problems. Even in this study, analysis of trends has been hampered by the inadequate nature of the statistics and lack of comparable data for earlier years.

The geographer needs these statistics from the national and periodic censuses in order to prepare basic maps and plans on which effective planning could be based. In this area there is the urgent need for closest co-operation between the Planning Ministry, field Administration and the University research organs in the stabilisation of boundaries, in the collection of statistics and in the analysis of data. As planning process must depend on national censuses, it follows that this form of co-operation must be a continuing process beginning with the initial preparation for the census, analysis and publication of results. Whether in the field of social, economic, physical or financial planning, the flight of population from the rural areas of the country must now be regarded as basic information in any development plan. It has been established with the inadequate information that this rural flight is selective of the economically active age group between 15 and 44 years of age. The problems it presents to the planner vary according to whether the destination is the traditional large scale rural farming areas or whether it is one of the major urban centres.

In the rural areas we have already noted the tendency

[1] Keeble L. *Principles and Practice of Town and Country Planning* p. 18 Third Edition Estate Gazette, London 1964

[2] Ndegwa P. & Norbye O. D. K. 'Rural Development: The Strategy of Kenya's Development Plan 1966–1970' Education, Employment and Rural Development, Kericho, 1966 p. 88

to falling employment opportunities following on the change of management of the farms. Nationally there may well be an increase in the employment opportunities with the break up of former large landed estates of Europeans. But since some of these areas drew their labour force from the major population regions of Kenya, it follows that there may well be an important measure of unemployment. There is need to replan the future of these farming areas in the light of the established flow of labour force that their development created.

But movements of rural population into such areas do not merely pose employment problems. Serious social problems associated with the quality and demographic characteristics of the moving population continue to engage government attention. Amenities such as rural housing, education and health cannot stagnate at their colonial level. We need to consider these rural problems in the framework of long term plans. Probable trends in agricultural employment and rural migration to non-agricultural sectors of employment must be foreseen.

Perhaps more important, social programmes to improve the effectiveness of the rural labour force are necessary. We have noted that problems are created by the influx of unskilled labour force into rural areas of agricultural employment. With changes in types of employment avenues in the rural areas, it is necessary to plan a parallel educational programme for the retraining of this potential labour force. Development plans will have to be devised to reduce drastically this flow from the rural areas with a view to strengthening the ability of the source areas to maintain and expand rural social services.

The most pressing problems arising from the mobility of population in Kenya are to be found in a few of our rapidly growing urban centres. Planning problems as seen in these areas are largely social, economic and physical. The study has touched on the urgent problem of providing housing in adequate numbers to the rapidly expanding population of the urban centres. But even in this area we are handicapped by the patchy nature of statistics on migration and absence of an adequate programme of vital registration. The housing implications of migration are but just one aspect of the multiple social problems which affect education, health and other amenities. It is specially in these respects that the urban areas are superior to the rural areas. Lack of these facilities are among the major causes of movement away from the rural areas of the country.

Because the towns of Kenya can only provide a limited number of additional jobs, the exodus from the rural areas to urban areas merely leads to a worsening of the social conditions in the urban areas. Growing unemployment, development of slums, and overcrowding in schools and hospital facilities are among the practical issues that have to be faced by urban authorities.

In the field of further industrial development the economic challenge posed by migration calls for an industrial location policy that does not merely depend on the advantage of the existing infrastructure. Karmiloff (1965), when he examined the problem of Regional Development and Industrial Location in East Africa made the following comments:

> The general conclusion that emerges is that scarcity of capital precludes East African Governments from pursuing an effective policy of regional development by means of transfers and loans to subsidize preferentially those regions which are most in need of development and to which industry should be induced to go.[3]

The main source regions in Kenya of migrating population are problem areas from a development point of view. These are among the areas where successful rural employment programmes could have the desired effect of reversing the exodus from rural to urban areas. But it is precisely the problem of directing development to these areas that is implied in the above paragraph.

The main planner must be brought into decisions affecting industrial location. These decisions need to be backed up by intensive studies of ways in which informed decentralisation in location of industries could be secure without sacrificing internal economies of scale or external economies arising from concentration of industries and consistent with maximisation of employment. He will need to be guided in deciding on the location of industrial estates, by their contribution to the known problem of rural exodus of population as well as to their importance to the growth of economy as a whole.

Existing townships were developed in response to a specific economic policy. This policy has been changed in important respects since independence. The growth of new urban settlements must now become a part of the overall planned national development while existing towns may also need planned enlargement. We may have to examine this possible implication of using the industrial estates as a means of developing new settlements in the framework of larger regional plans.

[3]Karmiloff C. *Regional Development and Industrial Location in East Africa: Problems of Economic Development in East Africa*, African Contemporary Monographs No. 2. E.A. Institute Press 1965

NOTES FOR APPENDIXES I & II ON OPPOSITE PAGE

[1]Between 1948 and 1962 boundary changes affected the locations of West Nyokal (57) Kasigunga (40) Kaksingiri (43) and East Konyango (44). Out of these the new settlement unit of Lambwe Valley was created. Adjustments have been made in the area of locations affected.

[2]Location areas shown here were computed from a manuscript map compiled by the author from the Survey of Kenya 1 : 50,000 sheets. Additional information on boundaries was obtained from District Offices.

[3]In all cases, they excluded parts of the locations which appear on official maps as Forest Reserves.

[4]For clarity, the index numbers of locations are bracketed in the text. (See chapter on geographical distribution of population)

District	Index	Location	1948 CENSUS			1962 CENSUS		
			Area[1]	Total Population	Density per sq. mile	Area[2]	Total Population	Density per sq. mile
Elgon and North Nyanza	2	Elgon	68	7,853	115	68	22,344	329
	3	Malakisi	122	24,222	199	122	39,267	322
	4	Kimilili	244	54,637	244	244	94,990	389
	5	South Bukusu	335	44,651	133	335	73,013	218
	6	Itesio	217	33,626	155	217	47,121	217
	7	Buhayo	168	27,604	164	168	36,530	217
	8	Wanga	219	51,508	233	219	73,213	334
	9	Bunyala	67	10,325	154	67	18,644	278
	10	Kabras	196	31,212	159	196	55,848	285
	11	Isukha	100	35,688	357	100	57,608	576
	12	Butsotso	91	15,261	168	91	24,799	273
	13	Marama	93	31,083	334	93	45,087	485
	15	Buholo	37	11,375	307	37	15,034	406
	17	Marach	219	25,597	272	94	34,827	370
	21	Kisa	48	25,109	523	48	35,764	745
	22	Bunyore	55	45,382	825	55	68,598	1,247
	23	Maragoli	76	71,271	976	76	99,368	1,361
	24	Idakho	55	28,578	520	55	40,446	735
	25	Teriki	39	29,743	763	39	43,262	1,109
	26	Nyang'ori	26	18,169	699	26	25,503	981
Central Nyanza	14	South Ugenya	22	8,368	380	22	12,047	564
	16	North Ugenya	116	33,930	293	116	52,985	457
	18	Samia	199	42,521	214	199	60,222	303
	19	Alego	205	55,859	272	205	75,821	370
	20	Gem	146	54,961	376	146	76,554	524
	27	Kajulu	15	7,970	531	15	8,996	600
	28	Kisumu	83	34,860	420	83	49,595	598
	29	Seme	123	33,829	275	123	48,067	391
	30	Asembo	55	19,153	348	55	26,344	479
	31	Sakwa	166	20,831	125	166	28,034	169
	32	Yimbo	70	7,145	102	70	10,208	146
	34	Uyoma	85	17,822	210	85	24,348	286
	35	West Kano	108	36,783	341	108	52,967	490
	36	West Kano	177	36,601	207	177	52,220	295
	37	Nyakach	141	36,793	261	141	51,476	365
South Nyanza and Kisii	38/49	Kabondo-Kasipul (East and West)	200	43,613	218	200	68,611	344
	39	Karachuonyo	166	46,111	278	166	69,568	419
	40	Kasigunga[1]	99	3,386	34	62	5,166	83
	45	Kanyada	61	15,022	246	61	24,848	407
	41	Rusinga Island	17	4,540	267	17	5,409	318
	42	Mfang'ano Island	25	3,702	148	25	4,404	176
	43	Kaksingiri[1]	112	2,739	23	94	3,572	38
	44	East Konyango[1]	230	24,137	105	173	35,402	205
	46	Gem	60	11,460	191	60	16,891	282
	47	North Nyokal	54	14,119	261	54	20,510	380
	48	Wanjare	58	17,540	302	58	27,850	480
	50	Kitutu	188	65,579	349	188	162,363	864
	51	North Mugirango	143	44,914	314	143	115,494	808
	52	Nyaribari	116	42,670	368	116	73,332	632
	53	Bassi	94	21,732	231	94	47,464	505
	54	Majoge	86	25,976	302	86	55,978	651
	55	South Mugirango	73	19,131	262	73	36,672	502
	56	East Nyokal	177	33,821	191	177	52,500	297
	57	West Nyokal[1]	120	10,990	92	105	16,032	153
	58	Gwasi	84	10,466	125	84	10,712	128
	59	West Konyango	233	22,167	91	254	43,516	171
		[Amalgamated with Mohuni (61) in 1962]						
	60	Kanyamkago	123	12,061	98	123	25,148	204
	61	Mohuru	21	2,872	137	Amalgamated with West Konyango (59)		
	62	Suna	231	16,612	72	231	36,505	158
	63	Butende	74	7,847	106	74	9,823	133
	64	Bukuria	143	19,783	138	143	28,997	203
	65	Lambwe Valley[1]	—	—	—	127	4,021	32

District	Index	Location	Area[1]	Total Population	Density per sq. mile	District	Index	Location	Area[1]	Total Population	Density per sq. mile
Kiambu	1	Karai	15	16,094	1,073	Embu	54	Kiine	49	18,753	383
	2	Ndeiya	15	12,429	828		55	Mwerua	66	20,221	306
	3	Limuru	8	18,349	2,294		56	Mutira	50	20,796	416
	4	Ngecha	15	10,591	1,513		57	Inoi	30	23,699	789
	5	Muguga	8	15,814	1,976		58	Kabaare	77	21,012	273
	6	Dagoretti	19	34,753	1,829		59	Baragwe	28	18,755	670
	7	Kabete	11	20,413	1,856		60	Ngariama	100	20,226	202
	8	Kiambaa	27	31,391	1,163		61	Thiba/Mwea	224	20,201	90
	9	Ndumberia	10	19,786	1,979		62	Mavuria	299	15,713	53
	10	Githunguri	47	41,108	875		63	Gaturi	57	26,385	463
	11	Gatamaiyu	35	13,344	381		64	Ngandori	40	25,406	635
	12	Lari	10	21,750	2,175		65	Kagaari	61	22,270	365
	13	Kiganjo	40	19,950	499		66	Nthawa	163	9,272	57
	14	Komothai	18	15,557	864		67	Evurore	135	13,277	98
	15	Gatundu	32	31,916	997		68	Kyeri	35	16,329	467
	16	Chania	30	17,811	594						
	17	Ndarugu	36	14,553	404	Meru	69	Magumoni	90	15,954	177
							70	Karingani	73	20,402	279
Fort Hall	18	Ward 16	35	10,912	312		71	Muthambe	42	12,724	307
	19	1	35	25,085	738		72	Mwimbe	99	31,030	357
	20	4	35	29,673	848		73	Igoje	55	16,481	300
	21	5	28	24,465	874		74	Nkuene	110	40,779	371
	22	3	26	13,929	536		75	South Tharaka	197	16,794	85
	23	3	49	13,998	286		76	Lower Abothuguthi	78	14,031	180
	24	9	22	7,407	337		77	Upper Abothuguthi	53	30,520	576
	25	8	45	29,132	647		78	Ntima	19	24,210	1,274
	26	18	18	15,880	882		79	Nyaki	81	21,531	266
	27	6	28	23,982	857		80	Mikinduri	146	25,926	178
	28	7	28	17,949	641		81	North Tharaka	375	12,423	33
	29	11	21	14,699	700		82	Akachiu	86	18,027	210
	30	10	24	19,117	797		83	Maua	83	26,284	317
	31	12	22	17,517	796		84	Ithima	100	39,231	392
	32	19	34	15,767	464		85	Njia	35	23,395	668
	33	14	33	21,971	666		86	Mathura	46	16,744	364
	34	13	18	11,158	620		87	Akithii	32	15,151	473
	35	15	39	12,172	312		88	Kianjai	58	25,738	444
	36	20	28	5,785	207		89	Kiirua	64	10,408	163
	37	17	20	9,798	490		90	Kibirichia	56	7,682	137
							91	North Grazing Area	645	1,017	16
Nyeri	38	Lower Muhito	9	3,147	350						
	39	Gikondi	14	9,814	701						
	40	Chinga	20	8,928	446						
	41	Othaya	30	19,300	643						
	42	Muhitu	18	15,769	876						
	43	Gethi	21	12,072	575						
	44	Konyu	23	17,381	756						
	45	Kirimukuyu	21	18,764	894						
	46	Aguthi	31	23,248	750						
	47	Mahiga	15	12,269	817						
	48	Thegenge	33	23,885	724						
	49	Tetu	16	19,786	1,979						
	50	Muhoya	12	13,698	1,141						
	51	Ruguru	21	16,085	766						
	52	Magutu	13	14,235	1,086						
	53	Iriani	19	13,197	695						

[1]Location areas shown here are computed from a manuscript map compiled by the author from the Survey of Kenya, 1 : 50,000 sheets. Additional information on boundaries was obtained from District Offices.

[2]In all cases, parts of the districts which fall within the Forest Reserves were not included in the calculation of population density per square mile. The figures are therefore more useful in assessing the relationship between total population and area available for its support.

[3]For clarity the index numbers of locations are bracketed in the text.

REFERENCES

CHAPTER I

Fearn H. *An African Economy* Oxford University Press, London 1961

Ingham K. 'Uganda's Old Eastern Province: the Transfer to East African Protectorate in 1902' *Uganda Journal* pp. 41–7 Vol. 21 No. 1 1957

Johnston H. *Uganda Protectorate* Vol. I Hutchinson, London 1902

——————— *Uganda Protectorate.* Vol. II. Hutchinson, London 1902

Kenya *Report of the Northern Frontier District Commission* Cmnd. 1900 London 1962

——————— *Colonial Annual Report* 1927 'Colony and Protectorate of Kenya' pp. 4–15

——————— *Kenya Constitutional Conference* 1962 Cmnd. 1700

——————— *Report of the Regional Boundaries Commission* 1962 Cmnd. 1899 H.M.S.O. London

——————— *N.F.D. Miscellaneous Report* 1915–23 (unpublished)

——————— *Proclamation Rules and Regulations* Vol. III, VIII and XII. Proclamation No. 158, 1929.

Matson A. T. 'Uganda's Old Eastern Provinces and East Africa's Federal Capital' *Uganda Journal* pp. 43–53 Vol. 22 No. 1 March 1958

McDermott P. L. *British East Africa* Chapman and Hall, London 1893

Oliver R. & Matthew G. (Editors) *History of East Africa* Vol. I Clarendon Press, Oxford, 1963.

Ward F. & Milligan J. W. *Handbook of East Africa* 1912

Uganda *Atlas of Uganda: Uganda Lands and Surveys* First Edition 1962

CHAPTER II

Buxton P. A. *The Natural History of Tsetse Flies* Lewis, London 1955

Dixey F. *The East African Rift System* Colonial Geology and Mineral Resources Supplement Series: Bulletin Supplement No. 1. London, H.M.S.O. 1956

East African Meteorological Department *Collected Climatological Statistics for East African Stations* Nairobi 1950

——————— Summaries of rainfall for the years 1904–1955

East Africa *Report of the Royal Commission* 1953–1955 Cmnd. 9475 H.M.S.O., London 1955

Edwards D. C. *Horn of Africa (including Kenya): Vegetation Map* Government Printer, Nairobi 1945

——————— 'A Vegetation Map of Kenya' *Journal of Ecology* pp. 377–385 Vol. 128 1940

Edwards D. C. 'Climatic types of vegetation in Kenya' *East African Agricultural Journal* pp. 248–254 Vol. 5 1939–40

——————— 'The Grasslands of Kenya' *The Empire Journal of Experimental Agriculture* pp. 153–60 Vol. 3 No. 10

Edwards D. C. & Bogdan A. V. *Important Grassland Plants of Kenya* Pitman, London 1951

Glover J. &c 'Provisional maps of the reliability of annual rainfall in East Africa' *Quarterly Journal of the Royal Meteorological Society* pp. 602–9 Vol. 80 1954

Griffiths A. L. 'Dry Woodlands of Africa South of the Sahara' *Unasylva* Vol. 15 No. 1 F.A.O. 1961

Griffiths J. F. *An initial investigation of the annual rainfall in East Africa:* East African Meteorological Department 1958

——————— 'Climatic zones of East Africa' *East African Agricultural Journal* pp. 179–85 Vol. 23 No. 3 1958

Kenya *Atlas of Kenya* Survey of Kenya, Nairobi 1963

Kenworthy J. M. & Glover J. 'The main rains in Kenya' *East African Agricultural Journal* pp. 267–72 Vol. 23 No. 4

Lewis E. A. 'Land use and tsetse control' *East African Agricultural Journal* pp. 160–8 Vol. 18 No. 4 1953

——————— *Second Progress Report of tsetse fly and trypanosomiasis survey and control in Kenya* Office of Agriculture and Natural Resources Nairobi 1947

Manning H. L. *Limits of expected monthly rainfall* Empire Cotton Growing Corporation Research Memoir No. 9, 1951

——————— *The Statistical Assessment of rainfall probability and its application in Uganda's agriculture* Empire Cotton Growing Corporation Research Memoir No. 23, 1956

Moomaw J. C. *A Study of Plant Ecology of the Coast Region of Kenya Colony, British East Africa* Nairobi 1960

Morris D. R. S. 'Studies in the epidemiology of sleeping sickness in East Africa' *Transactions of the Royal Society of Tropical Medicine and Hygiene* Vol. 54 No. 1 pp. 71–86

Pulfrey W. *The Geology and Mineral Resources of Kenya* (revised) Bulletin No. 2 Government Printer, Nairobi 1960

——————— *The Shape of the Sub-Miocene Bevel in Kenya:* Geological Survey of Kenya, Bulletin No. 3, Government Printer 1960

Russell E. W. (Editor) *The Natural Resources of East Africa* East African Literature Bureau, Nairobi 1961

Sansom H. W. *The Climate of East Africa* East African Meteorological Department Memoir Vol. III, No. 2, Nairobi 1954

Trapnell G. C. & Griffiths J. F. 'The Rainfall Altitude Relation and its ecological significance in Kenya' *East African Agricultural Journal* pp. 207–54 Vol. 25 1960

CHAPTER III

Blacker J. G. C. *Population Growth and Urbanisation in Kenya* United Nations Mission to Kenya on Housing Appendix A. 1965

Bloomberg L. N. & Abrams C. *Report of United Nations Mission to Kenya on Housing*, Government Printer, Nairobi 1965

Brown L. H. *A National Cash Crop Policy for Kenya* Parts I & II, Government Printer, Nairobi 1963

Colonial Office *Land and Population in East Africa* Colonial No. 290 H.M.S.O. London 1952

East African High Commission *Lake Victoria Fisheries Service: Annual Report* 1954/55, Government Printer, Nairobi 1955

Economist Intelligence Unit *The Economy of East Africa: A Study of Trends* 1955

Enlow C. R. *Some Observations on Agriculture in Kenya* 1958, Government Printer, Nairobi 1961

Fearn H. 'The Gold Mining Era in Kenya Colony' *The Journal of Tropical Geography* pp. 43–59 Vol. II, 1958

Gibb Sir A. & Partners (Africa) *Kenya Nile Water Resources Survey* Metcalf and Cooper, London 1956

International Bank for Reconstruction & Development *The Economic Development of Kenya*, Government Printer, Nairobi 1962

Kenya *Report of inquiry into the General economy of Farming in the Highlands* (Commissioner L.G. Troup), Government Printer, Nairobi 1953

————— *Kenya African Agricultural Sample Census* 1960/61 Part I. Economics and Statistics Division, Government Printer, Nairobi 1962

————— *Kenya Agricultural Census 1962; Scheduled Areas and the Coastal Strip: A Statistical Analysis* Economics and Statistics Division, Ministry of Finance and Economic Planning 1963

————— *African Land Development in Kenya 1946–55*

————— *Development Plan 1964–1970* Ministry of Economic Planning and Development, Government Printer, Nairobi 1964

————— *Development Plan 1966–1970 (revised)* Ministry of Economic Planning and Development, Government Printer, Nairobi 1966

————— *Economic Survey 1965* Statistics Division, Ministry of Economic Planning and Development, Government Printer, Nairobi 1965

————— *Economic Survey 1966* Statistics Division, Ministry of Economic Planning and Development, Government Printer, Nairobi 1966

————— *Kenya Census of Industrial Production*, Government Printer 1963

————— *Industry in Kenya 1964–1965*, Nairobi 1965

————— *Statistical Abstract 1963* Economic and Statistics Division, Ministry of Finance and Economic Planning, Government Printer, Nairobi 1963

————— *Statistical Abstract 1964* Ministry of Finance and Economic Planning, Government Printer, Nairobi 1964

Lowe (McConnell) R. H. *Observations on the Biology of Tilapia (Pisces-Cichlidae) in Lake Victoria, East Africa* Supplementary Publication No. 1. Uganda Argus, Kampala 1956

Mitchell P. *The Agrarian Problem in Kenya* Government Printer, Nairobi 1947

Morgan W. T. W. 'The "White Highlands of Kenya".' *Geographical Journal* pp. 140–55 Vol. 129 Part 2 1963

O'Connor A. M. *An Economic Geography of East Africa* Bell and Sons 1966

————— *Railways and Development in Uganda* East African Studies No. 18, East African Institute of Social Research, Kampala 1965

Pereira H. C. 'The Development of Tea Estates in Tall Rain Forest' *East African Agricultural and Forestry Journal* Vol. 27 Special Issue, March 1962

Pulfrey W. 'The Geology and Mineral Resources of Kenya' *Bulletin of the Imperial Institute* pp. 277–99 Vol. 45 No. 3 1947

South Nyanza District Agricultural Gazette 1955

Swynnerton R. J. M. Booth J. E. P. & Moon J. F. *The Agricultural Problems and Potential of the African Lands of Kenya*, Department of Agriculture, Technical Memorandum, February 1953 (unpublished)

Swynnerton R. J. M. *A Plan to Intensify the Development of African Agriculture in Kenya*, Government Printer, Nairobi 1954

Van Dongen I. S. *The British East African Transport Complex*, University of Chicago Research Papers No. 38 Chicago 1954

————— 'Mombasa in the Land and Sea Exchanges of East Africa' *Erdkunde* Band XVII 1961 pp. 16–37

Wagner G. *The Bantu of North Kavirondo* Vol. II. Oxford University Press, London 1956

CHAPTER IV–V

Barbour K. M. Prothero R. M. &c *Essays on African Population* Routledge and Kegan Paul, London 1961

East African Railways & Harbours *Rail-served Industrial Areas of East Africa* East African Railways and Harbours, Nairobi 1961

Kenya *Statistical Abstract* 1963

————— *Kenya Census of Manufacturing 1961*, Government Printer, Nairobi 1963

————— *Report of the Regional Boundaries Commission* Cmnd. 1899 H.M.S.O. London 1962

Mombasa Municipal Council *Mombasa Master Plan* 1962

Othieno-Ochieng N. A. *The Port of Mombasa: A Summary Review of Port Facilities* (unpublished report) 1965

Petersen W. *Population* Macmillan, New York 1961

Pollock N. C. 'Industrial Development in East Africa' *Economic Geography* p. 344 Vol. 36 No. 4 October 1960

Survey of Kenya *Aerial Contract* 63/2 *KE*/27 1 :12,000 October 1962

Walmsley R. W. *Nairobi: The Geography of a New City* East African Literature Bureau, Nairobi 1957

White L. W. T. *Nairobi Master Plan* 1948 H.M.S.O. London 1948

CHAPTER VI

Butt Audrey 'The Nilotes of the Sudan and Uganda' *Ethnographic Survey of Africa: East Central Africa* Part IV. International African Institute, London 1952

Colonial Office *Land and Population in East Africa* 1952

Crazzolara J. P. *Lwoo Migrations* Vol. I. Instituto Missioni Africani Verona 1950

——————— *Lwoo* Vol. II. *Traditions* Editrice Nigrizia, Verona 1951

——————— *The Lwoo* Vol. III. *Clans*. Editrice Nigrizia, Verona 1954

Dundas C. K. 'The Wanga and other tribes of the Elgon District, British East Africa' *Journal of the Royal Anthropological Institute* pp. 19–75 Vol. 43

Etherington D. M. 'Projected Changes in Urban and Rural population in Kenya and the implications for Development Policy' *East African Economic Review* pp. 1–19 New Series Vol. I No. 2 1965

Evans-Pritchard E. E. 'Luo Tribes and Clans' *Rhodes-Livingstone Journal* No. 7 1936

Fair F. J. D. 'A Regional Approach to the Economic Development of Kenya' *South African Geographical Journal* pp. 55–77 Vol. 45 1963

Fallers C. L. *Bantu Bureaucracy* Heffer, Cambridge 1961

——————— 'The Eastern Lacustrine Bantu (Ganda, Soga)' *Ethnographic Survey of Africa* East and Central Africa Part II 1960

Fearn H. 'Population as a factor in Land Usage in Nyanza Province of Kenya Colony' *East African Agricultural Journal* pp. 198–200 Vol. 20 No. 3 1958

——————— Cotton Production in the Nyanza Province of Kenya Colony 1908–1954. *Empire Cotton Growing Review* pp. 1–14 Vol. 33 No. 2 1956

Fortes H. &c *African Political Systems* Oxford University Press, London 1940

Glover J. &c 'Provisional maps of the reliability of annual rainfall in East Africa *Quarterly Journal of the Royal Meteorological Society* pp. 602–9 Vol. 80 1954

Goldthorpe J. E. *Outlines of East African Society* Makerere University College, Kampala 1958

Greenberg J. H. *Studies in African Linguistic Classification* Compass Publishing Co., New Haven 1955

Gulliver P. & P. H. 'The Central Nilo-Hamites' *Ethnographic Survey of Africa* Part VII International African Institute, London 1953

Hauser P. M. & Duncan O. D. (Ed.) *The Study of Population* pp. 383–99 Chicago 1959

Humphrey N. *The Liguru and the Land*, Government Printer, Nairobi 1947

Huntingford G. W. B. *The Eastern tribes of the Bantu Kavirondo Peoples of Kenya*, No. 14. Nairobi, Ndia Kuu Press 1944

——————— 'The Northern Nilo-Hamites' *Ethnographic Survey of Africa* Part IV. International African Institute, London 1953

——————— 'The Southern Nilo-Hamites' *Ethnographic Survey of Africa* Part VIII. International African Institute, London 1953

Kenya *Report of the Native Land Tenure in Kikuyu Province* 1929

——————— *Report of the Committee to carry out an Economic Survey of South Nyanza and Kericho District*, Government Printer, Nairobi 1957

——————— *Report of the Northern Frontier District Commission* Cmnd. 1900 H.M.S.O. London 1962

Kirk D. & Northman Dorothy 'Population Policies: The World Scene' Proceedings of First African Population Conference, Ibadan 1966

Lambert H. 'The Systems of Land Tenure in the Kikuyu Land Unit' Part I. Communications from The School of African Studies, New Series University of Cape Town No. 22 1949

Lewis I. M. 'Somali Conquest of the Horn of Africa' *Journal of African History* pp. 215–30 Vol. I No. 2

Lury D. A. *Population Data in East Africa* Discussion Paper No. 18, Institute for Development Studies, University College, Nairobi 1966

Martin C. J. 'The East African Population Census 1948' *Population Studies* pp. 303–20 Vol. 3 1948

Mayer P. *Gusii Brideswealth, Law and Custom* Rhodes-Livingstone Paper No. 18. Oxford University Press, Cape Town 1950

Morgan W. T. W. *Kenya 1:1 M. Population Distribution Map* 1962 Department of Geography, University College, Nairobi 1963

——————— *Density of Population Map* 1962 Department of Geography, University College, Nairobi 1964

Ogot B. A. 'Movements of Peoples in East Africa' *East Africa* Editions Présence Africaine, Paris 1964

Ominde S. H. *Land and Population in the Western Districts of Nyanza Province, Kenya*. (Unpublished Ph.D. Thesis, London University) 1963

——————— *The Ethnic Map of the Republic of Kenya* Occasional Memoir No. 1. Department of Geography, University College, Nairobi 1965

Otis D. D. 'Measurement of Population Distribution' *Population Studies* pp. 27–45 Vol. 2 1957/58

Owen W. E. 'The Bantu of Kavirondo' *Journal of East Africa and Uganda Natural History Society* pp. 67–77 No. 45/46 1932

Prins A. H. J. *The Coastal Tribes of the North-Eastern Bantu Ethnographic Survey of Africa,* Part II. London, International African Institute 1952

Seligman C. G. *Races of Africa* Third Edition. Oxford University Press, London 1957

Thompson J. *Through Masailand* Low, London 1887

Trewartha G. T. 'A Case for Population Geography' *Annals of the Association of American Geographers* pp. 71–97 Vol. 43 No. 2 June 1953

Wagner G. *The Bantu of North Kavirondo* Vol. I. Oxford University Press, London 1949

————— *The Bantu of North Kavirondo* Vol. II. Oxford University Press, London 1956

Wrigley C. C. 'Kenya: The Patterns of Economic Life 1902–1945' *History of East Africa* Vol. II Clarendon Press, Oxford 1965

CHAPTER VII

Barbour K. M. 'Rural–Rural Migrations in Africa: A Geographical Introduction' *Cahiers de l'Institut de Science Economique Appliquée* pp. 47–68 October 1965

Beaujeu-Garnie J. *Geography of Population* Longmans, London 1966

Chorley R. J. & Haggett P. *Frontiers in Geographical Teaching* Methuen, London 1965

Hyrenius H. *New Technique for Studying Demographic-Economic-Social Inter-relations* Demographic Institute, Report 3, University of Goteborg, Sweden 1965

Kenya *Kenya Population Census 1962* Tables Vol. 1. Directorate of Economic Planning Ministry of Finance and Economic Planning 1964

————— *Kenya Population Census 1962* Tables Vol. II. Statistics Division, Ministry of Economic Planning and Development, Government Printer, Nairobi 1965

Ministry of Economic Planning and Development *Birth Place. Analysis by Tribe, Sex and Five Year Age Groups (African) 1962 Census*

Morril R. L. *Migration and the spread and growth of Urban Settlement* Lund Studies in Geography, Series B. Human Geography, No. 26, Department of Geography, Lund, Gleerup 1965

Ominde S. H. 'Population Movements to the Main Urban Areas of Kenya' *Cahiers D'Etudes Africaines* pp. 593–617 Vol. V No. 20 1965

Ominde S. H. 'Some Aspects of Population movements in Kenya' Proceedings of the First African Population Conference, Ibadan 1966 (to be published)

Smith L. T. *Fundamentals of Population Study* Lippincot, New York 1960

Spengler J. J. & Duncan O. D. *Population, Theory and Policy* The Free Press, Illinois 1956

Spengler, J. J. & Duncan O. D. *Demographic Analysis: Selected Readings* The Free Press, Illinois 1956

Tanganyika *African Census Report 1957* Government Printer, Dar es Salaam 1963

Uganda *Uganda Population Census 1959* Government Printer, Kampala 1961

CHAPTER VIII

Bloomberg N. & Abrams C. *Report of United Nations Mission to Kenya on Housing* Government Printer, Nairobi 1965

City Council of Nairobi *Annual Report of the Social Services and Housing Department* 1958

————— *Annual Report of the Social Services and Housing Department* 1959

————— *Annual Report of the Social Services and Housing Department* 1960

————— *Annual Report of the Social Services and Housing Department* 1964

Coale A. J. 'Estimates of fertility and mortality in tropical Africa' Proceedings of the First African Population Conference, Ibadan 1967 (to be published)

International Bank for Reconstruction and Development *Experience in Central Nyanza* (unpublished) 1965

Karmiloff C. *Regional Development and Industrial Location in East Africa: Problems of Economic Development in East Africa,* African Contemporary Monographs No. 2, Nairobi, East Africa Institute Press 1965

Keeble L. *Principles and Practice of Town and Country Planning.* Estates Gazette, London 1964

Kenya *African Agricultural Census 1960/1961* pp. 17–21

————— *African Agricultural Sample Census 1960/1961,* Part II pp. 138–139

Ndegwa P. & Norbye D. K. 'Rural Development: The Strategy of Kenya's Development Plan 1966/1970' Education, Employment and Rural Development, University College, Nairobi 1966

Ray R. S. 'Rates of change in Reported Wage and Salaried Employment in Kenya 1956–65' Education, Employment and Rural Development, University College, Nairobi 1966

Smith T. E. & Blacker J. G. *Population Characteristics of the Commonwealth Countries of Tropical Africa* University of London, Athlone Press 1963

United Nations Organisation *Report of the Workshop of Urbanisation in Africa* Economic Commission for Africa, Addis Ababa 1962

1000002650

WILKES COLLEGE LIBRARY

1000002650

WILKES COLLEGE LIBRARY